FROM THE DEPTHS

From the Depths

The Discovery of Poverty in the United States

BY ROBERT H. BREMNER

NEW YORK UNIVERSITY PRESS

SIXTH PRINTING 1972

ISBN 8147-0054-3 Cloth
ISBN 8147-0055-1 Paper

Library of Congress catalogue card number: 56-7622
Printed in the United States of America

To

G. L. B.

S. E. B.

C. M. B.

ACKNOWLEDGMENTS

IN A STUDY of this kind the author's principal debt is to the sources consulted in the preparation of the work. Even heavier documentation than I have employed would be required to indicate the full extent of my obligation for inspiration and information to earlier writers and researchers.

Of the many persons who have aided me in assembling the materials for the book I should like to express my particular gratitude to Mr. J. G. Phelps Stokes, of New York, who gave me access to his fine collection of papers relating to social-justice movements of the Progressive era, and to the officers of the Community Service Society of New York, who allowed me to utilize the historical records of the Society. The librarians of the New York School of Social Work, the New York Public Library, the Library of Congress, and the Newberry Library have been unfailingly cooperative; none, however, have been more consistently helpful than the staff members of the Ohio State University Library.

The investigation was supported in part by funds granted to the Ohio State University by the Research Foundation for aid in fundamental research. I received further and very welcome assistance from University officials during a portion of one academic year in which I was relieved of teaching responsibilities and assigned to research duty.

During the several years the study has been in progress I have often been heartened by the interest taken in it by my wife, Catherine Marting Bremner. I have also benefited from the encouragement and constructive criticism offered by Professors Foster Rhea Dulles, Paul A. Varg, and Harry Coles. Mr. Wilson Follett of the New

York University Press gave the manuscript a close and sympathetic reading and suggested stylistic changes that I have been most happy to incorporate in the final revision. To Mrs. Helen Varg, who cheerfully typed and retyped various drafts of the manuscript, and to Dr. Morton Borden, who helped me in countless ways in the last stages of the work, I offer my sincere thanks.

CONTENTS

PART THREE

Social Striving, *c.* 1897–1925

LIST OF ILLUSTRATIONS

Following page 64

INTRODUCTION

In contrast to the peoples of less fortunate lands, who have accepted poverty as inevitable, Americans have tended to regard it as an abnormal condition. Our belief that want is unnatural and unnecessary originated in a hopeful view of human nature. It has been strengthened by our faith in the unlimited resources of the New World and, especially in more recent years, by pride in the productive achievements of the American economic system. This optimistic outlook has not always served us well in dealing with the misery that has in fact, and despite all our advantages, existed in our midst. We have sometimes acted as though we expected distress to cure itself, or have assumed that economic ills could be treated by spiritual disciplines. Confidence in the eradicability of poverty has nevertheless been a dynamic force for reform in the United States. Because of our assumption that want is man-made, not God-made, we have never lacked earnest critics to call us to account for both our individual and our social failings. In every generation they have reminded us that poverty is shameful, not only to those who suffer from it, but also to the society that allows it to exist.

This book is a study of America's awakening to poverty as a social problem. It is not a history of economic distress in the United States, but an attempt to explain the factors that made Americans conscious of and sympathetic to the misfortunes of their fellows. My objectives are to trace the growth of factual information about social conditions, to characterize and account for changing attitudes toward poverty, to describe the ways in which writers and artists have handled the subject of poverty in their work, and to present the experiences and influences that led to the enactment of legislation affecting housing, child labor, women in industry, and industrial accidents. Broadly stated, the purpose of the book is to show how philanthropic movements have added to our awareness and understanding of the poverty problem.

Although I have not fixed precise dates for the beginning or the end of the study, the period treated in most detail extends from the middle decades of the nineteenth century to the 1920's. It was in these years that the poverty problem as we now understand it arose in the United States. It was in this period also that the attitude toward the problem that still prevails took shape. A broader definition of poverty than had previously obtained in the United States came into general use, and opinion regarding its cause and cure underwent significant alteration. By the close of the period insufficiency and insecurity had come to be regarded as even more disturbing issues than dependency; the industrial causes of misery were recognized as more important than the moral; and social rather than individual reform was being urged as the appropriate remedy for want. Partly because of these developments, partly because of fundamental changes in the nation's economic and social structure, the earlier philanthropic interest in the poor had evolved into concern with the condition of labor and the standard of living of the population as a whole.

The chief point made in the book is that the humanitarian reform movements that swept the United States in the first two decades of the twentieth century proceeded in large measure from the new view of poverty. I have tried to demonstrate the importance of organized philanthropy in the formulation of the new view, and have emphasized the leading roles played by charity agents and settlement residents in the fight for reform. The major contribution of social work to social reform, as I see it, was to promote a factual, undogmatic approach to economic issues.

In the course of the study I have been impressed by the parallel development of factualism in the social sciences and realism in the arts. So far as the book has a thesis it is that we owe our progress in humanitarian reform and our best achievements in literature and art to those individuals, regardless of field of endeavor, who have been eager to discover, reveal, and be guided by the truths of actual life.

The heroes and heroines of the book are the "do gooders"—the responsible Americans in every generation who have heard and heeded the cry from the depths. These men and women have helped the poor, but they have helped the rest of us even more; for by seeking to aid and to understand the people at the bottom of the social pile they have made our society more wholesome, our culture more humane, and our spiritual life richer. They have taught us to respect and to be more considerate of one another. Because of their labors we are in a better position to continue the fight against poverty wherever it exists; and because of the gains they made we are, or ought to be, more confident than ever of eventual victory.

Since human need is a continuing fact, which each age discovers, or thinks it discovers afresh, this book ends where the contemporary problem of poverty begins. It deals only with the era in which poverty made its initial impact on the conscience of the American people. The adoption during the depression years of some of the preventive measures proposed in the earlier period is barely touched upon because it constitutes a different problem from the one here discussed. So, too, does the story of the beginning made in more recent years toward attacking poverty on an international front.

The task of assisting vast numbers of people in other areas of the world to overcome want is a much more difficult assignment than any that Americans have yet attempted. Compared to the work that remains to be done on this still-unsolved and almost-untouched problem the achievements we have scored against poverty in our own country seem small. It is my belief, however, that an account of our first conscious efforts to cope with the poverty problem at home has relevance to the present issue; and it is my hope that readers of this book will derive from it further appreciation of the need, and the opportunity, and the hope for organized efforts to eliminate and prevent misery in the larger community in which we now live.

Part One

AMERICA AWAKENS TO POVERTY c. 1830-97

CHAPTER I

The Problem Emerges

> Society must act on the highest principles, or its punishment incessantly comes within itself. The neglect of the poor, and tempted, and criminal, is fearfully repaid.
>
> CHARLES LORING BRACE, *The Dangerous Classes of New York and Twenty Years' Work Among Them.*

LARGE numbers of Americans first awoke to the social problem of poverty at a time when the nation was pouring forth unprecedented quantities of wealth and promising even richer harvests for the future. During the first two centuries of the country's development most Americans took it for granted that the majority of men would always be poor. Poverty was the state from which thousands of emigrants fled when they embarked, in hope or despair, on the difficult journey to the New World; in the form of hardship, privation, and suffering it was the lot, not only of the first settlers on the alien coast, but of generations of pioneers on successive inland frontiers. An increase in wealth, with a consequent improvement in general living standards, was the condition precedent to an aroused interest in poverty, for only in an era of material advance could want seem incongruous; and only in the nineteenth century when, decade by decade, the output of farm, factory, and mine climbed to higher and higher totals, did Americans begin to question the age-old assumption that poverty was the normal condition of the masses.

Unfortunately, the very economic processes that promised ultimately to free mankind from want had the immediate effect of aggravating, rather than alleviating, the distress of the working class. Mechanization and the factory system, by minimizing the value of traditional crafts and skills, reduced the bargaining power of the individual workman almost to the vanishing point; what little he had left was lost in contests with other men—and women and children, too—for jobs which one was as competent to fill as another. The prize in these races nearly always went to the cheapest. Despite the fiction of freedom of contract, all the advantages in the arrangement of terms of employment lay with the hirer. Employers, impelled not only by desire for profit but also by the necessity for meeting the competition of rivals, drove sharp bargains with their hands; they altered pay and hours as they saw fit and dismissed help whenever and for whatever reason they chose. These hard facts were made yet harsher by the prevailing theory of political economy which held that the welfare of individual laborers was a matter of small consequence either to employers or to the state.

Under the circumstances, especially in the hard times that followed the panics of 1819 and 1837, numbers of Americans sank into depths of degradation and dependency previously unknown in this country. At mid-century there was ample evidence that a poverty problem, novel in kind and alarming in size, was emerging in the United States. Many other issues clamored for attention, and then, as later, most Americans found admiration of wealth a more profitable occupation than contemplation of misery. Nevertheless a sizable body of men and women agreed that there was no valid excuse, moral or economic, for the presence of want in the midst of plenty; they condemned the bending of human lives to the will of the machine as inhumane and unwise; and they expressed regret and concern at the signs of growing estrangement between social classes.

It was in the slums of the larger cities that Americans discovered the new poverty that was invading the nation in the wake of industrialization, urban growth, and immigration. Here were new worlds of wretchedness characterized by ways of life foreign to American experience and menacing to conventional standards of decency. "It is often said that 'one half of the world does not know how the other half lives,'" observed the pioneer sanitary reformer, Dr. John H. Griscom, in the 1840's. Almost half a century before the publication of Jacob Riis's *How the Other Half Lives*, and in language strikingly similar to that Riis was to employ, Griscom described "the mournful and disgusting condition" in which thousands of the "laboring population" of New York passed their lives.[1]

In Boston, at almost the same time, William Ellery Channing was denouncing the practice of "letting cellars and rooms which cannot be ventilated, which want the benefits of light, free air, and pure water, and the means of removing filth!" The inhabitants of these rooms were constantly exposed to "putrid, damp, and noisome vapors" which, in Channing's opinion, worked sure destruction upon their characters and bodies. They had less access to the blessings of nature than the birds and the beasts, he said; and they were denied "those cheering influences of the elements" that even savages enjoyed.[2]

When Griscom and Channing wrote, as for many years thereafter, the most notorious slum in the nation was the Five Points district of New York City. A popular novelist of the period compared the Five Points to a great basin made of brick and mortar collecting "all the nauseous drainage of the higher thoroughfare."[3] That energetic sight-seer, Charles Dickens, visited the Five Points by night during his first tour of the United States. In *American Notes* (1842) he depicted the "leperous houses" of the district; they appeared to have been made prematurely old by debauchery, he thought, and their broken and patched windows seemed "to scowl dimly, like eyes that have been hurt in drunken frays." Investigating the attic of one battered structure (under the guard of two policemen), Dickens watched fascinated as half-awakened creatures crawled from their corners "as if the judgment hour were at hand and every obscene grave were giving up its dead."[4]

The initial reaction of the fortunate classes to slum dwellers was one of repugnance rather than compassion. Dickens could not resist asking whether the scavenging hogs owned by the inhabitants of the Five Points did not occasionally wonder why their masters walked upright and talked instead of grunting. Robert M. Hartley, founder of the New York Association for Improving the Condition of the Poor, denied that the "debased poor" were deserving of sympathy. "They love to clan together in some out-of-the way place," he reported, "are content to live in filth and disorder with a bare subsistence, provided they can drink, and smoke, and gossip, and enjoy their balls, and wakes, and frolics, without molestation."[5] Another observer, a clergyman, stated that residents of cellar lodginghouses were devoid of moral feeling and sense of shame. "They are not as decent as brutes," he said, referring to the unfortunate inhabitants of a tenement which he described as "impregnated with a stench that would poison cattle."[6] Josiah Strong, zealous advocate of home and foreign missions, characterized slum life as "a commingled mass of venomous filth and seething sin, of lust and drunkenness, of pauperism and crime of every sort."[7] As late as 1894 a report of the United States Commissioner of Labor defined slums as "dirty back streets, especially such as are inhabited by a squalid and criminal population."[8]

In the planless, rapidly growing cities extremes of fortune and misfortune often dwelt side by side. Poverty might be dismissed as a personal matter but the slums could not be brushed aside so easily. Regions of "squalid want and wicked woe" lay little more than a stone's throw from busy commercial streets and comfortable residential districts. Periodically, murderous and destructive riots beginning in the turbulent slums terrorized entire cities for days at a time. During the middle third of the century brawling regularly marked the observance of the Sabbath, the celebration of holidays, and the conduct of elections in the congested wards where the poor lived. It was not entirely without reason or in a spirit of pure snobbery that Charles Loring Brace, organizer of the Children's Aid Society, referred to the inhabitants of these blighted areas as "the dangerous classes."

Where casual observers saw the slum as the refuge of the already criminal and degenerate, philanthropists such as Brace and Hartley emphasized the importance of the slum environment in producing undesirable citizens. Brace was frankly fearful of "that vast and ignorant multitude, who, in prosperous times, just keep their heads above water . . . and who look with envy and greed at the signs of wealth all around them."[9] For this very reason he counseled against indifference toward the poor. Hartley argued that bad housing was a prime factor in weakening the ability of laborers to support themselves, an almost insuperable obstacle to the economic, moral, or religious elevation of the poor, and, consequently, a major cause of the high taxes about which the well-to-do grumbled.[10] Horace Greeley's *New York Tribune* summed up the reformers' case against the slums in 1864:

> In those places garbage steams its poison in the sun; there thieves and prostitutes congregate and are made; there are besotted creatures who roll up blind masses of votes for the rulers who are a curse to us; there are the deaths that swell our mortality reports; from there

come our enormous taxes in good part; there disease lurks, and there is the daily food of pestilence awaiting its coming.[11]

Like many of his contemporaries, Greeley believed that the most serious menace held out by the slums was the constantly increasing threat to public health. "Public" being a vague term, the reformers sometimes expressed the idea in language better calculated to appeal to the self-interest of the prosperous classes. "It is a well-established fact that diseases are not confined to the localities where they originate, but widely diffuse their poisonous miasma," advised a sanitary report issued in 1853. "Hence, though the poor may fall in greater numbers because of their nearer proximity to the causes of disease, yet the rich, who inhabit the splendid squares and spacious streets . . . often become the victims of the same disorders which afflict their poorer brethren."[12]

By the 1860's the connection between insanitary conditions in crowded tenements and recurring epidemics of typhoid, cholera, smallpox, and other diseases was fairly well recognized. Nevertheless, for many years thereafter both charity agents and public-health officials reported frequent instances of dangerous and offensive violations of the most elementary principles of hygiene. In 1884 an inspector employed by the Association for Improving the Condition of the Poor noted that in a house typical of hundreds of others the plumbing was "as much an inlet for sewer gas as an outlet for waste water." Close by the one hydrant serving all the occupants of a five-story tenement the inspector found the only toilet accommodations available to the tenants of the building: a row of privies whose floors were "slippery with urine" and whose seats, "foul with abominable matter," were arranged in long, undivided ranges.[13] As long as such plague spots were tolerated, Greeley's prediction that the slums would someday exact a frightful revenge upon society was realized, not once, but repeatedly, in city after city across the nation.

The simplest and most frequently advanced explanation for the manifold problems created by the slums was immigration. In the earlier part of the century, at least in those sections where labor was in short supply, the newcomers were welcomed enthusiastically. The *Chicago American* rejoiced in 1835 because

the floodgates of enterprise seem to be let loose upon us and the multitudes are crowding on to this young land, as if the pestilence were

> behind, eager to find a better home, where they can build their fortunes and their hopes, and enjoy the plenty which our fat fields yield to the hand of industry. . . .[14]

From an early date the seaboard cities regarded the matter in an entirely different light. In 1819, in its *Second Annual Report*, the New York Society for the Prevention of Pauperism listed immigration as the principal cause of pauperism. The Society bemoaned the likelihood that for years to come "winds and waves will still bring needy thousands to our seaports" and warned that New York was "liable to be devoured by swarms of people."

Samuel F. B. Morse, author of two widely circulated books whose contents are clearly suggested by their titles, *Foreign Conspiracy Against the Liberties of the United States* (1834) and *Imminent Dangers to the Free Institutions of the United States Through Foreign Immigration* (1835), was an unsuccessful candidate for mayor of New York in 1835. Two years later, however, the Whigs and Native Americans secured the election of their candidate to the office. In his first message to the council the new mayor complained that the hordes of foreigners were driving native workmen into exile, "where they must war again with the savages of the wilderness." He continued his attack on the immigrants with these observations:

> It is apprehended they will bring disease among us; and if they have it not with them on arrival, they may generate a plague by collecting in crowds within small tenements and foul hovels. What is to become of them is a question of serious import. Our whole Alms House Department is so full that no more can be received there without manifest hazard to the health of every inmate. Petitions signed by hundreds, asking for work, are presented in vain; private associations for relief are almost wholly without funds. Thousands must therefore wander to and fro on the face of the earth, filling every part of our once happy land with squalid poverty and profligacy.[15]

Similar expressions of opinion became more common as the depression of 1837 wore on; and they became even more familiar after the great influx of Irish and German emigrants in the late 1840's and early 1850's. Behind immigration nativists professed to see a sinister design on the part of Old World tyrannies to destroy the United States by inundating it in a flood of paupers and criminals.[16]

Certain European cities did, in fact, rid themselves of such paupers as could be induced to emigrate by paying their passage to America. Thus, in 1839, in the midst of the depression, a miserable company of immigrants, many still wearing the uniform of the Edinburgh almshouse, arrived in New York; their transportation had been arranged by the overseers of the poor of Edinburgh.[17]

The necessity of caring for these and other immigrants who were unable to support themselves imposed a considerable burden on American taxpayers and philanthropists. In some cities uncontrolled immigration had the effect of doubling, or more than doubling, the cost of poor relief; not infrequently the foreign-born outnumbered native-born Americans three to one on the rolls of private charities.[18] The harshness which nineteenth-century students thought appropriate to the administration of charity and relief stemmed in no small part from the settled conviction that numerous applicants for aid had brought disaster upon themselves, and inconvenience to the community, by their ill-advised and uninvited removal to the United States.

In the heat of their resentment against the European practice of shipping destitute persons to this country, Americans tended to overlook other and more important reasons why recent immigrants were so often compelled to ask for relief or charity. Most of them were poor to begin with, and some exhausted what meager resources they possessed in getting to America. Many were lured from home by false pictures of ease and abundance painted by high-pressure agents of shipping companies. The voyage was so difficult and steerage conditions so bad that not a few of the immigrants (one out of every six in some years) died on the way, sometimes leaving widows or orphans to make their way unaided by husbands or fathers. Those who survived arrived undernourished and in poor health; they were met by sharpers who preyed on their ignorance and bewilderment. When they found work they were paid so little that they could scarce build up reserves to tide them over sickness or unemployment. A recent student comments: "If the economic pattern of the time had involved a fair return for the great contribution of the immigrant, the number of foreign-born paupers would have been negligible."[19]

In the latter half of the century population movements, like everything else, were conducted on a grander scale than ever before.

Of the approximately twenty million persons who migrated to the United States in the nineteenth century, all but about four million, or roughly four out of five, came after 1860. Now the tendency to blame immigration for whatever was disreputable in American life became almost irresistible. Not only pauperism and crime, but hard times, political corruption, intemperance, and pestilence were laid at the door of the newcomers. A new prejudice against the allegedly inferior races of southern and eastern Europe reinforced the earlier Protestant bias against Catholic immigrants. Nativists in the 1850's, resenting the foreign-born voters' activity in politics, had sought not only to restrict the admission of foreigners but to limit the political rights of those already in the country. Later and more reputable reformers deplored the misuse of the suffrage by the "ignorant and vicious poor," especially the immigrants in the slums, who gave their fealty to saloonkeeping bosses in exchange for petty kindnesses and pauperizing gifts of money, food, and fuel. Thomas Bailey Aldrich called his poem "Unguarded Gates" (1892) a "protest against America becoming the cesspool of Europe," and declared that Kipling's description of the government of New York—"a despotism of the alien, by the alien, for the alien, tempered with occasional insurrections of decent folk"—applied to every American city.[20]

As the century drew to a close there was suspicion at nearly all levels of society that the immigrants, if not actually bent on the destruction of American institutions, were nevertheless quite capable, either through illiteracy or political immaturity, of subverting the foundations of the republic. Conservatives, never very confident of the ability of their fellow citizens to withstand the temptations of foreign radicalism, protested that each ship bearing degraded and undesirable persons to American ports carried an invisible cargo of anarchism, communism, and other dangerous doctrines. Meanwhile, spokesmen for labor declared that industry's systematic policy of flooding the labor market with aliens was the major cause of unemployment and low wages. The most moderate view, and the most valid, was that uncontrolled immigration greatly complicated the poverty problem in the United States by yearly increasing the numbers of the very poor.[21]

The immigration question kept the problem and, to a certain extent, the plight of the desperately poor before the nation. As already suggested, some observers attributed the hardships encountered by American labor in its struggle for decent standards of work and wages to the competition of "pauper labor" recruited overseas.[22] But the furor over immigration also tended to obscure fundamental economic questions in a fog of religious and national prejudices. It provided such a convenient rationale of all the nation's ills that other industrial issues received less attention than they deserved. John R. Commons, writing in the mid-nineties, commented that the only labor problem that seemed to excite much interest among clergymen and church members was working on the Sabbath.[23]

From time to time an occasional student such as Orestes Brownson, deeply stirred by the crosscurrents of political democracy and industrial servitude, described the relations between capital and labor as a class struggle.[24] For the most part, however, through all the vicissitudes of the nineteenth century, most American writers clung to the belief that paternalism offered the proper solution to industrial problems. If only employers could be induced to deal kindly with employees, they reasoned, workmen would respond by rendering faithful and loyal service. Then labor strife would disappear; there would be no sweating, no unions, no strikes, and no black lists. Capital, as befitting its superior position, would act as the guardian of the interests of labor. Subordinate, but not exploited, labor would become the stanch support of capital.

That something like this relationship prevailed in certain establishments is beyond question. But there were many more instances in which neither capital nor labor was content to play the role assigned it by benevolent outsiders. One factory manager boasted: "I regard my workpeople just as I regard my machinery. So long as they can do my work for what I choose to pay them, I keep them, getting out of them all I can."[25] Some employers, however, regarded their machinery with more tenderness than their workpeople—at least the high toll of industrial accidents seemed to indicate an extravagance in regard to human costs in otherwise economically managed enterprises. A sympathetically portrayed businessman in a novel published in the 1880's summed up the whole problem when he remarked of certain industrialists, "They want to become rich in five years and how can they do that except by oppression?"[26]

Whether justly or not, many workers were dissatisfied with both the conditions and the rewards of their labor. Whenever they were strong enough to do so they delivered their protest at the polls, through trade-unions, and by acts of violence. Strikes for the ten-hour day were plentiful in the boom years before the depression of 1837; fifty years later they were being waged for the eight-hour day. During the seventies, eighties, and nineties workingmen expressed their discontent with existing conditions in a series of strikes that outdid in number and virulence any yet known in American history. It is almost impossible for a later generation to conceive of the chaotic upheavals that periodically rocked whole communities at a time when industrial relations consisted of intimidation on one side and terrorism on the other, when spying was countered by sabotage, and when a "labor dispute" meant an armed skirmish between embattled strikers and entrenched employers.

As a rule public opinion condemned strikes; for the anarchy of labor was deemed more reprehensible than the despotism of capital. Many observers unhesitatingly put the blame for industrial strife on "socialistic agitators and communistic tramps." Nevertheless, these bitter conflicts brought to light shocking examples of exploitation, and their total effect was to compel thoughtful men and women to give more serious study to labor problems. The novelist and essayist Charles Dudley Warner believed unionism "an extraordinary tyranny," but he was willing to admit its usefulness in focusing public attention upon "certain hideous wrongs, to which the world is likely to continue selfishly indifferent unless rudely shaken out of its sense of security."[27]

Incessant industrial warfare convinced a number of students that something must be done to compel employers to treat their workers better. Remedial action, including the enactment of factory laws, seemed imperative both on humanitarian grounds and to remove a major cause of social tensions. Cardinal Gibbons chided employers for paying less heed to the welfare of the driver of the horsecar than to the well-being of the car horse.[28] Josephine Shaw Lowell, a nationally known leader in scientific philanthropy, early announced her conviction that fair wages rather than doles of charity were the answer to industrial unrest.[29] W. S. Rainsford, pastor of a leading institutional church in New York City, declared that a visit to Pittsburgh at the time of the Homestead strike had removed all doubt from his mind as to the need for unions. The lesson of Homestead, he said, was that workingmen must cooperate with one another if they were to secure the simplest of human rights.[30]

Such expressions of opinion were deplored by conservatives, who denied that employers had neglected their responsibilities to employees, and maintained that any outside interference with industrial labor policies, whether by workers' organizations or by legislation, was an invasion of the prerogatives of management. Furthermore, they argued, there was no cause for complaint since everyone agreed that the average workingman in 1890 was better off in every way—except possibly in morality and respect for authority—than his grandfather in 1830. Throughout the century the conservative prescription for labor's discontent was not higher wages but harder work and stricter economy. Employers' spokesmen criticized the movement for a shorter workday on the grounds that ten hours instead of twelve, or eight instead of ten, would result only in increased idleness and dissipation. During the depression of 1819 distressed families were urged to take advantage of the savings offered by a recipe for a cheap and wholesome dish composed of rice and mutton suet.[31] Philanthropists offered similar advice in later emergencies; toward the end of the century a New England insurance executive invented a cookstove called the Aladdin Oven, and drew up principles of food preparation which he estimated would save working-class families five cents a day per person—sufficient, he thought, to enable laborers to subsist adequately on prevailing wages.[32]

Household economy was a singular panacea to press upon the working poor at a time when the idle rich were indulging themselves in riotous extravagance. The real weakness of the conservative argument, however, was that it failed to reckon with the tendency of men to compare themselves with their contemporaries rather than with their ancestors.[33] As Josiah Strong pointed out, if material conditions had altered greatly in two generations, men had changed even more. They had more wants and more confidence in their ability to satisfy them, more education and more self-respect.[34] The unrest which was so characteristic of the closing decades of the nineteenth century had its origin in the fact that a great many of the working people were unwilling to live out their days in the social steerage.

Few experiences were more unsettling to the average American's peace of mind than the depressions which, although always unexpected, recurred with almost monotonous regularity at intervals of from fifteen to twenty years after 1819. Long before the end of the century the nation had become familiar with soup lines, demonstrations by the unemployed, demands for the relief of debtors–rich as well as poor–lamentations over past errors, and dire predictions for the future. "Let every individual calculate for himself what he, personally, has lost, what chances have been sacrificed by him, what he might have done, and what he might have been, if the prosperity of the country had not been arrested," mused a writer in 1840.[35] We cannot gauge the precise extent to which these calamitous events shook the common man's confidence in hard work and thrift as an unfailing recipe for security. There is no doubt, however, that loss of jobs, farms, and savings as a result of cyclic panics and price fluctuations led to widespread disillusionment and bitterness. Even men and women who were not directly affected by bank or business failures had reason to fear that their means of livelihood might be snatched from them by remote and impersonal forces. Thus early, threads of anxiety were being woven into the traditionally optimistic fabric of American character.

In normal times Americans were accustomed to think of unemployment as exclusively the problem of the inefficient and indolent. Conservatives stuck to this view even in depression years. They recommended that relief be dealt out sparingly lest the recipients be tempted into permanent dependency. Respectable folk looked upon "tramps," a numerous but ill-defined group, as pariahs deserving only "the toe of a boot by day and a cold stone floor by night."[36] Under the impact of hard times, however, it was easier to grasp the distinction between voluntary and enforced idleness. From the 1840's onward, although in insignificant numbers until after the depression of 1893, some students were willing to admit that "nonemployment" was a constant problem, affecting the competent no less than the incompetent, the industrious as well as the slothful.[37] In the late thirties and forties Greeley's sympathies went out to the respectable mechanics "whose cry was, not for the bread and fuel of charity, but for Work!"[38] Almost fifty years later a *Tribune* writer, Helen Campbell, commented that the real issue was quite different from pauperism: it was the tragic, undeserved embarrassment of persons who wanted no charity and needed no correction.[39]

Dearth of work had a psychological as well as economic significance in the United States because the entire American creed of individualism and self-help was based on the assumption that earnest seekers could always find honest employment. Unemployment was by no means a new phenomenon, but never before the closing decade of the nineteenth century had its shadow hung so heavily over so many men and women. The sons and daughters of farmers and village tradesmen who had migrated to the cities to obtain salaried positions in stores and offices were more vulnerable than their parents had been to business crises. The immigrants who had deserted ancestral villages in Europe to swell the ranks of the American industrial army had nothing but their weekly wages to serve as bulwarks against want. At the end of the century urban Americans, in a real but novel sense, were living in a state of dependency. Even though, as individuals, they experienced unemployment only briefly and at rare intervals, if at all, the nagging fear of it was almost chronic with them.

This does not mean that the average citizen despaired of the future. Far from it. Despite misgivings about his present situation he believed that there lay ahead, and almost within reach, a more wholesome and commodious plane of life for all men. The expectation of reaching the promised land of security and plenty in the foreseeable future gave Americans confidence and hope. If doubts sometimes overtook men of small or moderate means, the reason was not so much that the climb was steep as that their footing was unsure.

Americans were immensely proud that in their land the long-despised common man had raised himself to a new level of material well-being. Yet they had not rid themselves of the chilling presence that Edward Bellamy called "the specter of uncertainty." Perhaps it was because they had risen so high that the possibility of plunging downward seemed so frightful. The insecurity of their position led them, by almost imperceptible degrees, to question and ultimately to alter their attitudes toward poverty.

CHAPTER 2

Shifting Attitudes

I think the best way of doing good to the poor, is, not making them easy *in* poverty, but leading or driving them *out* of it.

BENJAMIN FRANKLIN, *On the Price of Corn, and Management of the Poor.*

Write a sermon on Blessed Poverty. Who have done all the good in the world? Poor men. "Poverty is a good hated by all men."

RALPH WALDO EMERSON, *Journals*, entry for May 12, 1832.

IN the latter half of the nineteenth century the American attitude toward poverty was a somewhat incongruous composite of two sharply contrasting points of view. Mindful of Christ's dictum, "The poor always ye have with you," traditional religion taught that poverty was a visitation upon men of God's incomprehensible but beneficent will. Although inescapable, poverty was a blessing in disguise, for it inspired the rich to acts of loving charity and led the poor into the paths of meekness, patience, and gratitude. In contradiction to these teachings American experience indicated that poverty was unnecessary. When there was work for all, no man who was willing to do his share need want. Indigence was simply the punishment meted out to the improvident by their own lack of industry and efficiency. Far from being a blessed state, poverty was the obvious consequence of sloth and sinfulness.

More or less unconsciously the nineteenth-century American combined these divergent views into a creed that ran approximately as follows: Poverty is unnecessary (for Americans), but the varying ability and virtue of men make its presence inevitable; this is a desirable state of affairs, since without the fear of want the masses would not work and there would be no incentive for the able to demonstrate their superiority; where it exists, poverty is usually a temporary problem and, both in its cause and cure, it is always an individual matter.

This creed both followed and departed from the traditional religious view. It accepted the inevitability of want and need but attributed their cause to man rather than to God. It recognized the value of differences in economic status, not so much as a spiritual discipline in generosity and humility, but as a goad to spur the ambitious to success and as a penalty for failure in the competitive struggle. It did not deny the obligation of the fortunate to aid the unfortunate, but it so emphasized the responsibility of each individual to look out for his own interests that it promoted a kind of social irresponsibility. Despite its hardheaded practicality, it left uncertain whether poverty was to be regarded as the soil from which Lincoln and Carnegie had sprung, or the breeding ground of the dangerous classes.

The individualistic interpretation of poverty, like its corollary the individualistic interpretation of wealth, was based on a revolutionary concept of man, society, and religion. It was not a new thing to exhort the masses to work; throughout the centuries toil had been their lot. By tradition, however, labor was an onerous duty attaching to the lowborn. It had never been highly regarded, well rewarded, or entirely free. The boast of Americans, the characteristic that made American life seem so vulgar to older civilizations, was that here, for almost the first time in history, labor was prized for its own sake. The promise of America was not affluence, but independence; not ease, but a chance to work for oneself, to be self-supporting, and to win esteem through hard and honest labor.

The gospel of self-help was well suited to the needs and circumstances of American life in the earlier part of the nineteenth century. Then, in a very real sense, a man's ability to take care of himself was a social asset, and inability to do so a liability. In sparsely settled, rapidly growing communities, where labor was scarce, there was substantial truth in the assumption that willingness to work brought material well-being, while failure implied some personal defect in the sufferer. The experience of countless immigrants and native-born

Americans alike substantiated the national confidence in the common man's ability to achieve the good life through his own exertions. As one writer expressed it, the founding fathers may have intended the United States to be an asylum for the distressed peoples of the Old World; but it was a workhouse that they had prepared, not a refuge for idlers.[1]

The era of self-help in economics coincided with a similarly oriented period in religion. In the first half of the nineteenth century salvation through personal regeneration was a dynamic and still relatively novel theological doctrine. Americans embraced the belief that the door to heaven was open to all who made themselves worthy to enter with the same enthusiasm that characterized their faith in free enterprise and manhood suffrage. The new religious currents infused a spirit of optimism into discussions of economic no less than of religious questions. Previously the weight of ecclesiastical authority had more often than not been cast on the side of passive acceptance of inequality of status; for, as already suggested, the churches taught that providence decreed the existence of poverty among men. The Universalists, the Unitarians, and the numerous revivalistic sects, however, proclaimed that neither earthly want nor eternal damnation was foreordained for the masses of men. On the contrary, they asserted, just as any man could purify himself of sin, so he could purge himself of the bad habits that led to indigence.

Emancipation from the authoritarian puritanical theology and acceptance of religious creeds that emphasized the dignity and perfectibility of man loosed a tumult of energy for the cause of moral and humanitarian reform. It is not surprising that when this energy was directed toward the problem of poverty the initial impulse was to attack those individual vices, such as intemperance and immorality, that were regarded as barriers both to salvation and to temporal prosperity. Nor is it surprising that enlightened philanthropists in the nineteenth century should have deemed almsgiving as of less benefit to the poor than guidance into the path of morality and self-discipline.[2]

The individualistic interpretation of poverty began as a hopeful and essentially radical doctrine. Well before the end of the century, however, it had been converted into a formidable bulwark of that strange brand of conservatism espoused by the dominant business classes. Like the other principles of *laissez-faire* economics, the individualistic interpretation was given a supposedly scientific basis by the teachings of Herbert Spencer and his American disciples, and also by the early application of Darwinian biology to social thought. If, as the Spencerians and Social Darwinists asserted, competition was the law of life, there was no remedy for poverty except individual self-help. The poor who remained poor must pay the price exacted by nature from all the unfit. Any interference in their behalf, whether undertaken by the state or by unwise philanthropists, was not only pointless but absolutely dangerous. Protecting the weak in the struggle for existence would only permit them to multiply and could lead to no other result than a disastrous weakening of the species; it would thwart nature's plan of automatic, evolutionary progress toward higher forms of social life.[3]

Although the pseudoscientific assignments advanced to justify inequality and to condone misery never went unchallenged, the theory that poverty was caused exclusively by personal frailty was not easily supplanted. Endowed with a new aura of authority, this theory retained a loyal following long after the disappearance of the peculiar circumstances that had once given it a certain practical validity, and despite the emergence of conditions that strongly indicated the need for different hypotheses. For many years the problems of tenement dwellers in large cities, or of unemployed workmen in the breadlines, continued to be discussed as though the people involved were ne'er-do-wells in a frontier community. Nevertheless, under the impact of social and industrial changes the inadequacies and fallacies of the individualistic explanation became more obvious, and its critics gradually became more numerous and outspoken.

Herman Melville, writing in 1854, scoffed at the slander of the poor by the prosperous. "Of all the preposterous assumptions of humanity over humanity," he wrote, "nothing exceeds most of the criticisms made on the habits of the poor by the well-housed, well-warmed, and well-fed." In Melville's opinion, poverty was no blessing, actual or potential, but "a misery and infamy, which is, ever has been, and ever will be, precisely the same in India, England, and America." He felt that the mental anguish of the native American poor was more intense than that of any similar class in the rest of the world. This was because in the rich new land a sense of shame was attached to poverty, producing repugnance toward charity at all social levels; and also because there was an appreciation, on the part of the American poor, of "the smarting distinction between their ideal of universal equality and their grindstone experience of the practical misery and infamy of poverty. . . ."[4]

At the same time as Andrew Carnegie and Horatio Alger were preaching that poverty in youth was the key to prosperity in age, other observers were recalling Theodore Parker's warning that the destruction of the poor was their poverty. The findings of British students were quoted to prove that bitter need was a lesson in improvidence rather than in thrift; and that if intemperance led to poverty it was equally true that being poor drove men to drink.[5] Ira Steward, labor reformer and early advocate of the eight-hour workday, contended that "Poverty crams cities and their tenement houses with people whose conduct and votes endanger the republic." In his opinion, the problems that disturbed and perplexed mankind were incapable of solution while the masses remained poor.[6]

Americans long took comfort in the belief that the boundless opportunities offered by a rich and relatively unpeopled continent afforded a sure cure for the economic ills of the discontented classes. Orestes Brownson's warning, voiced in 1840, that the wilderness had receded so far that the new lands were already beyond the reach of the mere laborer, went unheeded.[7] Much more typical was the assurance given the Boston Society for the Prevention of Pauperism in 1844: "Untilled fields are around us; unhewn forests before; and growing villages and cities are springing up upon every side."[8] For half a century "the West" was the medicine prescribed for all those who wished to better their condition. Joseph Kirkland's *Zury* (1888), although more consciously realistic than most pictures of frontier life, began in a characteristic vein:

> In the prairies, Nature has stored, and preserved thus far through the ages, more life-materials than she ever before amassed in the same space. It is all for man, but only for such men as can take it by courage and hold it by endurance. Many assailants are slain, many give up and fly, but he who is sufficiently brave, and strong, and faithful, and fortunate, to maintain the fight to the end, has ample reward.[9]

Even as Kirkland wrote, however, "the myth of the garden" was being exposed to critical scrutiny. A contributor to *The Forum* dealt realistically with the practical obstacles that made it extremely unlikely that the masses in Eastern cities could improve their lot on Western homesteads; and Henry Demarest Lloyd declared in 1884: "Our young men can no longer go west; they must go up or down."[10]

Meanwhile, other critics denied the truth of another tenet of American individualism: the opportunity available to all to rise from a lower to a higher social class. The youthful John R. Commons declared in 1894:

> Class lines have become more rigid, and the individual, if his lot be in the unpropertied class, is destined, as a rule, to remain there. His economic resources determine, by relentless pressure, what shall be his social environment.[11]

Josiah Strong also contended that wealth and poverty were becoming more and more matters of inheritance and less and less products of character.[12] William Dean Howells took an even darker view of the situation. "Here and there one will release himself from it," he wrote of poverty, "and doubtless numbers are alway[s] doing this, as in the days of slavery there were always fugitives; but for the great mass captivity remains."[13]

It was particularly difficult for nineteenth-century Americans to accept the fact that in a complex economy individuals were no longer such independent agents as they had seemed to be but a few decades earlier. By the 1890's, however, numerous students were pointing out that not clerk nor factory hand nor farmer was as free as formerly to determine, by his own efforts, whether his labor would be well or ill rewarded, or even whether there would be a place for him in the productive processes of the nation. An impersonal element had invaded economics with the result that personal virtue, or the lack of it, counted for little in determining whether men were rich or poor. On the contrary, it was increasingly apparent that individuals suffered as often from the misdeeds and miscalculations of others as from their own failings. In the year before the panic of 1893 President E. B. Andrews of Brown University wrote prophetically that the worst vice of modern industry was that it frequently visited curses on men through events which they had no part in originating. Under existing circumstances, said Andrews, "a great many men are poor without the slightest economic demerit. They are people who do the best they can, and always have done so. . . . Yet they are poor, often very poor, never free from fear of want."[14] Josephine

Shaw Lowell wrote of the people rendered jobless by the depression of 1893 that the causes of their distress were "as much beyond their power to avert as if they had been natural calamities of fire, flood, or storm."[15]

Hard times on the farm, where the heaviest work, the plainest living, and the most abundant harvest sometimes brought but scant profit to the cultivator of the soil gave many Americans firsthand experience with the impersonal causes of poverty. Hamlin Garland's stories in *Main-Travelled Roads* (1891) were peopled by men and women who, like Garland's own parents, had nothing to show for years of drudgery except lined faces and gnarled hands. In "Under the Lion's Paw" he told of a farmer who saw the fruit of his toil consumed in one year by a plague of grasshoppers and in another by the equally voracious greed of a land speculator. Despite their traditional reliance on self-help, the farmers were among the first occupational groups in the United States to renounce the individualistic interpretation. They saw and felt the effects of poverty-producing factors with which individuals were unable to deal, not only in natural disasters such as drought, but in railroad abuses, the sharp practices of middlemen and moneylenders, and in governmental currency and fiscal policies. They did not hesitate to demand relief for sufferers from the acts of God, regulation of private businesses that affected the public welfare, and other legislation that ran counter to the assumed natural laws of *laissez faire*.[16] The agrarian parties were the radical ones of the seventies, eighties, and nineties because they proposed social remedies for the impersonal forces that imposed hardship on a large proportion of the nation's people.[17]

According to the creed of self-help it was as reprehensible to obtain wealth without working for it as to be poor because of laziness. In practice, criticism of the idle rich was less frequently voiced than condemnation of the shiftless poor, but it was by no means lacking. In a novel entitled *The Wreckers* (1886), George T. Dowling asserted that the most dangerous elements in society were "the rich who do not know how to use their riches." Several years later the author of an article in *Scribner's Magazine* declared: "The opulent who are not rich by the results of their own industry . . . suffer atrophy of virile and moral powers, and, like paupers, live on the world's surplus without adding to it or giving any fair equivalent for their maintenance."[18]

Grover Cleveland's vetoes of pension bills and his messages urging reduction of tariff duties directed public attention, not only to the specific issues at hand, but also to the broader question of the extent to which some persons profited through circumstances unrelated to their own merit. In his Fourth Annual Message, delivered after his defeat in the election of 1888, Cleveland told the Congress "We discover that the fortunes realized by our manufacturers are no longer solely the reward of sturdy industry and enlightened foresight, but that they result from the discriminating favor of the government and are largely built upon undue exactions from the masses of our people." Later in the same message he cautioned that

> . . . the communism of combined wealth and capital, the outgrowth of overweening cupidity and selfishness, which insidiously undermines the justice and integrity of free institutions, is not less dangerous than the communism of oppressed poverty and toil, which, exasperated by injustice and discontent, attacks with wild disorder the citadel of rule.[19]

Subsequently numerous critics of the plutocratic drift cited both the lavish bestowal of Civil War pensions and the granting to favored industries of unwarrantedly high tariff protection as largely responsible for the rise of "the pauper spirit" in American life.[20] The tariff controversy remained a heated one for many years and, by provoking a more critical study of the sources of wealth, fostered the development of a more realistic approach to the problem of poverty. By the turn of the century tariff reformers had convinced some Americans that the rich, to an even greater extent than the poor, were guilty of seeking "something for nothing."

No single figure in the last two decades of the nineteenth century was more successful than Henry George in arousing public opinion to an awareness of the social origins of wealth and poverty. Yet there was nothing new in his assertion that land values were created by the growth and needs of the community rather than by efforts of the proprietor; that was precisely the principle which canny land speculators had taken for granted ever since colonial days. Several years before the publication of *Progress and Poverty* (1879) the theory of unearned increment had been expounded in homespun dialect by a character in Edward Eggleston's popular novel *The Hoosier Schoolmaster*:

> Jack, he's wuth lots and gobs of money, all made out of Congress land. Jack didn't get rich by hard work. Bless you, no! Not him. That a'n't his way. Hard work a'n't, you know. 'Twas that air six hundred dollars he got along of me, all salted down into Flat Crick bottoms at a dollar and a quarter a acre. . . .[21]

George's contribution was to redirect attention from the individual benefits to the social consequences of private profit in land. He argued that permitting landlords to pocket the socially created value of land actually meant allowing them to take from the public wealth that properly belonged to the community as a whole. As a result, he said, the few were unmeritedly enriched, the many unjustly burdened. Furthermore, he continued, existing laws gave the owners of land and natural resources not only the legal right to fix the terms under which these necessities might be utilized, but also the power to hold them out of productive use. George believed that as long as these extraordinary powers resided in private hands it was inevitable that many citizens should experience involuntary and undeserved privation in the form of unemployment, inadequate wages, and extortionate rents.

The fact that George was an unusually eloquent advocate of free competition helps to explain why his diagnosis of society's ills won wide popular approval. His attack on private profit in land was not essentially different from the earlier *laissez-faire* economists' criticism of monopolies and other vested rights. Like them, George assumed that if monopolistic restraints on industry and trade could be removed, competition between free and unhampered individuals would work an automatic improvement in social conditions. Perhaps George differed from the earlier advocates of *laissez faire* mainly in the complete confidence he placed in competition as a beneficent and direct instrument for the welfare of all levels of society.[22]

The novelty of Georgian economics lay in its optimistic outlook and humanitarian bias. In no sense was George's influence more significant than in the conviction he inspired in the rising generation that poverty was abnormal—contrary to, rather than dictated by, natural law. To George involuntary poverty seemed, not an ineradicable problem, but, on the contrary, one that could be solved by simple and relatively painless social action. Even those who rejected the specific remedies he proposed were encouraged by his example to take up the fight against want.

Not only George's own writings but the protracted argument they excited between his supporters and opponents kindled new interest in all issues affecting human welfare. His contention that, despite all the material progress of the century, the rich were growing richer and the poor poorer provoked several pioneer efforts to estimate the distribution of property in the United States and the relative shares of the national income going to capital and labor. Although crude by later statistical standards, and generally unreliable since there was at the time no public or private registry of profits, these ventures were far from useless. If nothing else they revealed the need for more factual information on which to posit economic generalizations. In themselves they were evidences of the emergence of an objective, analytical approach to problems that had hitherto been looked at from an almost exclusively subjective and moralistic point of view.[23]

George's adulation of competition was not shared by some of the other students of social institutions who were his contemporaries. Felix Adler confessed that the Single Tax remedy—"a single draught of Socialism with unstinted individualism thereafter"—never attracted him.[24] Henry Demarest Lloyd, Edward Bellamy, George D. Herron, and William Dean Howells each expressed repugnance, not only for sharp business practices, but also for the selfishness which they thought underlay competitive economics. "We are not good enough or wise enough to be trusted with this power of ruining ourselves in the attempt to ruin others," cried Lloyd in 1884. Like the old antislavery agitator, Theodore Parker, Lloyd and the other critics of competitive capitalism insisted that the purpose of life was to live, not to amass property.[25] They rejected competition because they thought it produced an atmosphere of insecurity in which conscience and kindness were subordinated to the naked instinct of economy. The central idea of Edward Bellamy's *Looking Backward* (1888) was the comparison of a kindly and efficient cooperative society with a blundering, helplessly cruel competitive way of life. Helen Campbell, a forerunner of the muckrakers, wrote a series of newspaper articles on New York sweatshops in 1886 in which she cited instances of well-intentioned employers who were forced, by the intense competition prevailing in the needle trades, to choose between giving up their scruples and getting out of business.[26] E. B. Andrews pursued the same theme when he alleged that under competition one could not obey conscience without becoming a martyr. "The best men in a trade do not fix its maxims," he asserted, "but the worst. . . . Out of this murderous competition there is survival not of the fittest but of the unfittest, the sharpest, the basest."[27]

The moral objection to competition arose in large part from a feeling that such savage strife as individualism implied was not only unseemly, but unnecessary. Said George D. Herron: "There is enough in this world for all to have and enjoy in abundance, if there were a system by which there could be an equitable distribution of that abundance upon the principle of the divine economy."[28] To men such as Herron, who thought that capitalism was unchristian, the so-called personal causes of poverty appeared insignificant in comparison with the larger problem of a fantastically inefficient system of economics. "What other result can we expect under our present organization than that great numbers of persons should be poor?" "Our economic order is not intended to serve any social purpose, but only to enrich individuals." Poverty was far from seeming an insoluble problem to the Christian Socialists, but they did not expect any significant improvement in conditions until society saw fit to adopt a system of production and distribution better suited to its physical and ethical needs.

Those who opposed competition on ethical grounds scorned what seemed to them the parvenu conception of society as a mere bundle of distinct and irresponsible individuals. Instead, they gave their allegiance to the much older ideal of society as an organism. Not only religion, but also the realities of contemporary industrial society made them think it was necessary to regard society as a unit. Josiah Strong used the analogy of an ocean liner to illustrate the unity of social interest. If the steerage goes to the bottom, he said, so does the cabin; if pestilence rages among third-class passengers, first-class travelers cannot afford to be indifferent. "Modern civilization is fast getting us all into one boat," wrote Strong, "and we are beginning to learn how much we are concerned with the concerns of others. . . ."[29]

The emphasis they so often placed upon the organic unity of society helps to explain why even the most vigorous critics of contemporary social conditions at the turn of the century refused to endorse violent methods of eliminating the evils they denounced. The idea of competing classes was no less repugnant to them than that of competing individuals; and they were convinced that drastic and revolutionary purges were useless to remedy the ills of society. If a house has fallen into ruin, said Washington Gladden, the sensible course may well be to tear it down and build another. But society is not an inanimate thing; it is a living organism, more like a tree than a house. And if a tree is pining we cannot cure its sickness by overturning it. "It may need pruning, and its life may need invigorating by the addition of fertilizers to the soil in which it grows: it cannot be pulled down and rebuilt."[30]

Recognition of the unwholesome results of individualism in economics was accompanied by a lessening emphasis upon individualism in religion. In the earlier years of the century an authoritarian theology had been rejected in favor of a more democratic creed of salvation through individual regeneration. That change, as we have seen, had produced a zeal for the elimination of the personal vices that made salvation impossible. By the eighties and nineties it was becoming apparent that environmental factors and external economic pressures made the task of individual moral improvement extremely difficult. Even good men, pious church members, and solid citizens were seen to be involved in the impersonal cruelties dealt out by corporate enterprise. Rich and poor alike appeared, to some observers, at least, to be enmeshed in an amoral system that too often rewarded cunning more than character and made men indifferent to their fellows. At the end of the century Washington Gladden was telling Yale divinity students that "one man can no more be a Christian alone than one man can sing an oratorio alone"—and entitling the collected volume of his addresses to them *Social Salvation*.[31] Gladden's view, which was by no means peculiar to him, was that society, even more than individuals, stood in need of regeneration.

Earnest reformers such as Theodore Parker and Stephen Colwell had demanded just such a reorientation of religious approach even before the Civil War, but it was not until the last two decades of the century that any considerable number of Protestant clergymen began to devote their attentions to the various problems growing out of rapid industrial and urban growth. The social gospel which then emerged had its roots in the religio-humanitarian movements of a half century earlier. It was in part a conscious effort to counteract the alienation of the working class from organized religion.[32] Examined from a slightly different angle, however, the social gospel may be interpreted as an attempt by conscientious pastors to shake their predominantly middle-class congregations out of complacent self-righteousness and make them realize their own responsibility for social injustice. There are more important moral questions than Sabbath breaking, card playing, and intemperance, urged the followers of the social gospel. The conditions under which men and women work and the circumstances in which they spend their lives are moral questions, too. Gladden warned that unless the churches became thoroughly aroused about these issues and used their influence to promote fundamental reform, they would cease to be religious bodies and degenerate into institutions for the preservation of meaningless rites and superstitions.

The Roman Catholic Church, adhering more closely than the Protestant sects to the traditional religious interpretation of poverty, was frankly critical of individualism whether in religion or economics. Catholicism took poverty for granted; it did not deny that some men were impoverished by lives of sin or habits of improvidence; but it also recognized that others were permitted to live in indigence by the mysterious dispensation of God. To Catholics, man was at best a weak vessel; his failings were an object of pity and an outlet for charity rather than a cause for scorn. Although holding to the idea that poverty was permanent and ineradicable—and perhaps because of this belief—Catholic doctrine was more tolerantly disposed toward the poor than was the case in some of the more individualistic Protestant denominations. Moreover, in view of the predominance of working-class families in many Catholic congregations, influential Catholic leaders such as Cardinal Gibbons recognized that the Church could not afford to take an implacably hostile attitude toward labor unions and collective bargaining.[33] The papal encyclical on the condition of the working class, *Rerum novarum* (1891), condemned socialism and defended private property; but it also upheld the principle of unionism, sanctioned moderate social legislation, and denounced the tendency of *laissez faire* to treat labor as a commodity to be bought cheaply and used hard.[34]

Clergy and laymen of all denominations were inspired by the example of the Salvation Army to take a more sympathetic interest in the people at the bottom of the social heap. A Boston settlement worker, Robert A. Woods, observed that "more than any other type of person in these days" members of General Booth's Army seemed "moved by a passion for the outcast and distressed."[35] The deeds of soldiers of the Army and of the bonneted lassies who moved "like sweet angels among the haunts of the lost" demonstrated to respectable folk that even the most desperate and vicious of the poor might be saved. No place was Godforsaken to the Army, no man or woman sunk so low as to be excluded from God's bounty.[36] In 1893 Josiah Strong wrote admiringly that "Probably during no hundred years in the history of the world have there been saved so many thieves, gamblers, drunkards, and prostitutes as during the past quarter of a century through the heroic faith and labors of the Salvation Army."[37] The Army's dramatic and apparently successful methods of dealing with the dangerous classes aroused new support for slum evangelization in the old-line churches. As will be shown in the next two chapters this work had not been wholly neglected before General Booth's organization came to the United States, but never before had the need and the opportunity been so effectively publicized.

No less significant than the impetus the Salvation Army's work gave to evangelical crusades was the interest it awakened in social reform. Charles R. Henderson, professor of sociology at the University of Chicago, saw in the Army's program a salutary reminder "that they who touch the soul must minister to the body, as Jesus did."[38] The publication in 1890 of General Booth's *In Darkest England* (ghost written by the journalist William T. Stead) did much to popularize the idea that the moral improvement of the poor was dependent upon the amelioration of their economic condition. This view, of course, was exactly the reverse of the individualistic assumption that if only the poor could be taught to lead moral lives their economic problems would disappear. The young economist Richard T. Ely hailed the book as "a trumpet blast calling men to action on behalf of the poorest and most degraded classes in modern society."[39] Booth himself was primarily concerned with the rescue of souls, but he insisted that as a first step "society, which by its habits, its customs, and its laws, has greased the slope down which these poor creatures slide to perdition," must be brought to mend its ways.[40]

At the close of the century political, economic, and religious influences were undermining popular allegiance to the individualistic interpretation of poverty. The idea that want was primarily the result of laziness, thriftlessness, and immorality was by no means moribund, but to a considerable body of Americans this view no longer seemed to square with the facts of real life. In its place there was emerging a more sympathetic attitude toward the poor which frequently descried persons in need as victims rather than as culprits.

CHAPTER 3

The Charitable Impulse

Give alms: the needy sink with pain;
The orphans mourn, the crushed complain.
Give freely: hoarded gold is curst,
A prey to robbers and to rust.
Christ, through his poor, a claim doth make,
Give gladly, for thy Saviour's sake.

ROBERT HARTLEY, *Eighth Annual Report* of the New York Association for Improving the Condition of the Poor, 1851.

Oh, pause in your pleasures, ye wealthy and grand, remember that hunger's abroad;
Oh, turn to the needy and stretch forth a hand, oh, now listen to sympathy's chord;
Its sweet holy strain encircles the soul, of the ragged, the fallen and low;
So pause in your pleasures, seek charity's goal, when poverty's tears ebb and flow.

EDWARD HARRIGAN, "Poverty's Tears Ebb and Flow."

THROUGHOUT the nineteenth century the charitable response of the American people was almost as generous as their pursuit of gain was selfish. The two streams of giving and getting converged, at the end of the century, in the gospel of wealth. This doctrine harmonized with the major tenets of individualism and, through the idea of stewardship, endowed individualism with moral sanctity. Earlier writers had taken the stand that the rich were God's agents in relieving the distress of the poor, but it was Andrew Carnegie who in word and deed gave the gospel of wealth its classic expression.[1] Believing that enormous differences in the economic conditions of men were normal and beneficent, Carnegie asserted that wealth was a sacred trust to be administered by the person possessing it for the welfare of the community. The aim of the millionaire, he declared, should be to die poor.

There was an engaging, childlike quality in Carnegie's belief that Robber Barons, in full career, would voluntarily convert themselves into Robin Hoods. It had the rosy aspect of a boy's daydream in which the hero, after almost impossible feats of strength and valor, seizes the pirate's gold and returns home to distribute it wisely and justly among his deserving but timorous townsmen—with this difference: Carnegie was a man and his dream had come true.

For all its undoubted romantic appeal the gospel of wealth added nothing to the understanding of poverty and suggested no solution to the problem other than the familiar one of self-help. The reason for these failures is obvious. Carnegie was not seeking to correct poverty but to justify wealth. His purpose was to demonstrate, as convincingly as the case permitted, that socially irresponsible methods of acquiring riches could be abundantly compensated for by liberality in bestowing charity.

In a sense Carnegie's creed typifies the approach to social problems that prevailed during most of the nineteenth century. The weakness of this approach lay in failure to recognize that the suffering society generously relieved with one hand was, in many instances, but the product of the ills that it casually sowed with the other. Consciousness of this fact came rather slowly, but its discovery was the distinctive contribution of the nineteenth century to social welfare. In large measure the discovery was the fruit of the labor of men and women who gave their lives, not just their fortunes, to philanthropy.

The private charities of the nineteenth century usually sought to provide the poor with moral instruction as well as material assistance. Frequently their purpose was to relieve the distress of a particular category of persons, such as the sick or widows with small children, or to meet some special need of the destitute classes. The establishment and maintenance of schools for poor boys and girls were favorite forms of charity in the first part of the century, and even after public-school systems had been inaugurated, philanthropic societies operated schools to train needy children in the manual and household arts. During the depression of 1819 a correspondent who signed himself "One of the People" offered a "Morsel of Advisement to the Rich." Stop extorting and oppressing the poor, he counseled; become "rich in good works," and "preserve your treasures from being moth-eaten."[2] In the eyes of many, however, the sorest need of the poor was their want of religious guidance and instruction. "Moral and Religious culture is the great blessing to be bestowed on the poor," said William Ellery Channing.[3] The "unchurched poor" were indeed in precarious straits in a day when the church was deemed a man's first resource, material as well as spiritual, in time of trouble.

It was to serve the families who were not connected with any religious group that the Unitarian clergyman, Joseph Tuckerman, began his ministry at large in Boston in the dark days following the depression of 1819. Until failing health caused his retirement in 1833 Tuckerman acted as pastor and friend to persons who, as he said, had been "living as a caste, cut off from those in more favored circumstances" and who, without his ministrations, would have been "doomed to find their pleasures and sympathy in their sufferings alone among themselves." Tuckerman was a Harvard classmate and lifelong friend of Channing, and it was Channing who was primarily responsible for his appointment as missionary to the poor.

As befitted a clergyman, Tuckerman was chiefly interested in the spiritual welfare of his charges but, as a result of visiting the poor in their homes, he became interested in a great many projects for improving their environment and opportunities. Housing, wages, education, delinquency, and relief all occupied his attention. From his "Poor's Purse," derived from contributions from wealthy supporters of his ministry, he gave charitable assistance to the needy, not fulsomely but with a Yankee firmness; where possible he made loans rather than outright gifts, sometimes exacting the pledge of a coat or other article as security for the debt. He studied British and continental works on poor relief, directed an investigation of the Massachusetts poor law system for the state legislature in 1832, and in 1834 brought about the establishment of an association to insure a measure of cooperation among the twenty-odd benevolent societies then operating in Boston. Tuckerman's contributions to the theory and practice of charity were rediscovered at the close of the century by advocates of scientific philanthropy who learned that this unassuming minister had anticipated by more than half a century the future course of social work in the United States.[4]

About the same time as Tuckerman was active in Boston, other religiously inspired individuals and groups were attempting to elevate the poor by printing and disseminating religious leaflets. In the late 1820's organizations such as the New York Mission and Tract Society were distributing moral literature on the docks and in the markets as well as in jails and almshouses. During the thirties the activities of the New York society were broadened to include missionary labors for the salvation of souls of the poor in neglected and degraded quarters of the city. Thereafter the Mission and Tract Society employed a small but increasing number of city missionaries (twelve in 1834, forty-five in 1866) who not only distributed tracts but also conducted religious services in the slums and city institutions, visited the poor in their homes, and sought to persuade them to attend church and to send their children to Sunday schools. In addition to their evangelical work the missionaries gave temporary economic assistance to poor families and attempted to find jobs for the unemployed.

Dr. John H. Griscom, whose study of *The Sanitary Condition of the Laboring Population of New York* (1845) was based in part on reports submitted by agents of the City Tract Society, believed that the missionaries knew more about the actual condition of the poor than any other persons. One of them informed him that the poor of New York were living "in circumstances as unfavorable to chastity and the common decencies of life as the Sandwich Islanders were previous to the introduction of Christianity among them by American missionaries."[5] "Thank God!" rejoiced a feminine novelist in the 1850's, "our people are coming to see that missionaries have a work to do at home."[6]

The Roman Catholic Church, with its long experience in the field of charity and its historic allegiance to the doctrine of good works, gave its support to eleemosynary enterprises in the United States at a comparatively early date. The Sisters of Charity of Saint Vincent de Paul, who came to this country in 1809, were particularly active in establishing hospitals and orphan homes; and the Little Sisters of the Poor, founded in 1840, assumed the task of caring for the aged poor. Members of the Society of Saint Vincent de Paul, a layman's group that spread to America around 1850, visited the sick and destitute of their parishes, inquired into and endeavored to meet the needs of these unfortunates, promoted the religious and elementary training of children, distributed moral and religious books, and undertook any other philanthropic works that their resources permitted.[7]

The most important single figure in American charity in the middle third of the nineteenth century was Robert M. Hartley, who served for more than thirty years as secretary of the New York Association for Improving the Condition of the Poor. Born in England in 1796, Hartley was brought to the United States in 1799. His father was a wool manufacturer, and as a boy Hartley himself worked in a woolen mill. It was during this youthful employment that he launched his first crusade: an effort to induce his fellow workers to substitute a debating society for gambling as their means of recreation. He settled in New York in the early 1820's, and, after a brief period as a salesman in a drygoods store, established himself as a merchant.

Organization of the A.I.C.P. in 1843 was not Hartley's initial venture in philanthropy but the culmination of nearly twenty years of work in behalf of the poor. Deeply religious, he had volunteered his services as a tract distributor shortly after his arrival in the city. Finding that widespread intemperance among the poor nullified his efforts to arouse their religious enthusiasm, Hartley became a leader of the City Temperance Society. The total-abstinence movement occupied most of his energies in the 1830's. Among his contributions to the cause was a pamphlet entitled "Way to Make the Poor Rich." He also visited distilleries, talked with owners and managers, and attempted to make them realize the evils of their ways.

These visits failed to accomplish their original objective, but they were nevertheless very enlightening to Hartley. In the course of them he came upon filthy sheds in which hundreds of cows were penned and fed upon distillery refuse. Horrified by the condition of the animals, and convinced that milk from them was unfit for human consumption, he traced sales of it to the homes of 25,000 tenement infants. Hartley's investigations led him to the conclusion that there was a direct connection between the use of still milk and the rise in infant mortality rates in New York in the preceding twenty-five years—an increase all the more alarming since in other cities the rate had declined during the same period. The erstwhile temperance reformer persevered in his crusade against distillery milk until in 1864 the state legislature prohibited its sale.[8]

Hartley's investigation of the milk problem, to an even greater extent than his earlier efforts on behalf of temperance and religious instruction, acquainted him with the daily environment of the poor. Familiarity with living conditions in the tenements helped him to recognize the helplessness of the individual tenement dweller to correct the situations that threatened the health and welfare of his family and himself. Like nearly all the other workers for human betterment in the nineteenth century, but earlier than most of them, Hartley came to believe that the material condition of the poor must be improved before their moral health could be restored.

The A.I.C.P. was a nonsectarian organization but, like the religious charities contemporary with it, it utilized the service of "friendly visitors" to call upon and assist the needy. At the time of its founding there were between thirty and forty charitable societies already functioning in New York City. A number of them had been organized to meet the extraordinary demands for help in the depression years of the late thirties and early forties. All of their resources had been sorely taxed by that emergency, and, in the opinion of some observers, their lax methods of dispensing aid had actually encouraged the growth of pauperism. Hartley's hope was that through the operation of the new organization the work of the existing agencies would automatically be coordinated. His plan, which was shortly copied in Brooklyn, Albany, and several other communities, divided the city for charitable purposes into districts coterminous with the political wards; these, in turn, were subdivided into sections. An advisory committee supervised the Association's work in each district, and a resident visitor carried on its activities in each section. The visitors were all volunteers and all men. Their work was to visit applicants for assistance living in their section, ascertain the facts of the case, and provide the deserving with the aid suited to their particular requirements. This might be either reference to the appropriate public or private agency or a grant of coal, food, or other necessities from A.I.C.P. funds. If the latter course were followed, the visitor was expected to give the needy family encouragement and counsel along the path to rehabilitation.[9]

The path, as Hartley saw it, was piety, total abstinence, frugality, and industry. In 1847 he issued Franklin's *Way to Wealth* for distribution to the poor by the friendly visitors. Finding the original "wanting in religious sentiment and feeling," Hartley took the liberty to revise it by "inserting a few appropriate texts." *The Economist*, also issued in 1847, gave instruction on the preparation of nutritious, inexpensive meals; and advised that 12½ cents a day spent on drink amounted to $45.62 a year—a sum ample to buy three tons of coal, one load of wood, two barrels of flour, 200 pounds of Indian meal, 200 pounds of pork, and eight bushels of potatoes. "Into a house thus supplied," Hartley said, "hunger and cold could not enter. And if to these articles is added what before [the laborer] has felt able to purchase, abundance and comfort would be the inmates of his dwelling."[10]

The primary function of the A.I.C.P. was to render service to individual families, but almost from the beginning it undertook what Hartley styled "incidental labors" for improving general social conditions, especially those relating to housing, health, and child welfare. In the second year of the Association's existence Hartley made a study of cellar tenements and issued a report branding the housing of the poor as morally debasing and, because of high rents, economically oppressive. In 1853 the Association made another and more comprehensive housing survey. This time Hartley published a thirty-two-page pamphlet describing the deplorable conditions brought to light by the survey.[11] His campaign for better housing led to the appointment of the first State Legislative Commission to investigate the tenement problem in the metropolis. Under Hartley's direction the Association essayed "a complete social, moral, and statistical census" of the congested area lying between Rivington and Fourteenth streets east of Avenue B.[12] It erected model tenements, built and operated a public bath and laundry, founded two dispensaries and a hospital for the treatment of crippled children; it was active in the campaign for compulsory school attendance laws and the appointment of truant officers; and it was tireless in its espousal of measures for promoting personal hygiene and public sanitation.[13]

Hartley sympathized with the distress imposed on the poor by the miserable environment the city offered them. He condemned the community's failure to provide even the elementary conditions of decent existence for thousands of its citizens. But he also criticized the poor for their refusal to leave the city. He thought they made their sad plight still worse by congregating in the slums, accepting idleness as their lot and charity as their due, and suffering their children to grow up—or die prematurely—in vicious surroundings. In *The Mistake* (1850) he addressed the poor:

> Many of you left your native country and came to this land of plenty, to escape from poverty and starvation. But if you lodge like driftwood where you land, exposed to disease in filthy courts and damp cellars, and eke out a precarious existence by alms, in what respect have you benefited?

Hartley was second to none in confidence that self-help and the West were sufficient to solve the major part of the nation's poverty problem. "Providence has bestowed upon us a vast extent of unoccupied territorial surface, with a fertile soil and genial climate," he thankfully observed. "If the hale and vigorous cannot earn their subsistence here, they should earn it elsewhere." In his opinion, the greatest kindness that could be shown the poor was "to cause them, if necessary by rigorous measures, to choose the interior for their home, where, by honest industry, they may recover self-respect and independence, and become blessings instead of burdens to the country."[14] His invariable counsel to the poor was

> Escape then from the city—for escape is your only recourse against the terrible ills of beggary; and the further you go, the better . . . a few dollars will take you hundreds of miles, where, with God's blessing on willing hearts and strong hands, you will find health, competence, and prosperity.[15]

Reduced to its essence, Hartley's advice to the poor amounted to little more than this: Go somewhere else.

Charles Loring Brace was another mid-century reformer who regarded the West as the ultimate solution to the social problems of crowded cities. Brace had studied for the ministry, and in the late 1840's he was working as a missionary to the prisoners on Blackwell's Island and "the squalid poor" of the Five Points of New York City. His introduction to the neglected children of the metropolis, whom he was later to call the most threatening members of "the dangerous classes," came in 1848 when he began to participate in a series of religious services for street boys. After several years Brace concluded that evangelical efforts, although meritorious, were not in themselves adequate to cope with a situation of extraordinary seriousness.

The problem that gradually unfolded before him was not just poor homes, but no homes at all for thousands of vagrant children. According to a police report in 1852 there were an estimated 10,000 abandoned, orphaned, or runaway children roaming the streets of New York. They slept in old boilers, boxes and privies, on barges and steps, and, especially, on steam gratings. Mrs. Elizabeth Oakes Smith wrote of their life in her novel *The Newsboy* (1854), expressing both pity for boys grown prematurely old and crafty, and admiration for their "sturdy individualism and unapproachable self-reliance."[16] To Brace, however, the homeless children seemed to bear to the respectable population of the city the same relation as wild Indians to Western settlers.

> They had no settled home [he wrote], and lived on the outskirts of society, their hand against every man's pocket, and every man looking upon them as natural enemies; their wits sharpened like those of a savage and their principles often no better.[17]

Consistent with the current spirit of individualism, Brace disliked the idea of institutional care for children. "The best of all Asylums for the outcast child," he asserted, "is the *farmer's home*."[18] One of the major purposes of the Children's Aid Society, which he organized in 1853, was to procure foster homes for New York's vagrant boys and girls in rural districts. Promoting emigration, however, was not the sole aim of the Society, but rather the final step in what Brace called the program of "moral disinfection." The first step was the assignment of a visitor or paid agent to a given neighborhood. It was his duty to learn all he could about the area, and to make himself acquainted with the children and their problems. The next move was to conduct informal religious exercises for boys of the neighborhood. In time, if circumstances warranted and resources were available, the Society established a free reading room, an industrial school (for children who were "too poor, too ragged, and undisciplined for the public schools"), and lodginghouses for newsboys and other homeless working children. Eventually, through vacation and convalescent homes, and a sick children's mission employing twelve doctors and four nurses to visit sick children in their homes, the original program was significantly broadened.[19]

The most promising cases discovered in the Society's varied activities were induced, where possible, to accept foster homes in the country. Applications for children poured into Brace's headquarters in response to circulars printed in newspapers in the hinterland. In its first twenty years of operation the Children's Aid Society transported an average of almost one thousand children a year to rural communities in New York, adjacent states, and the West. The emigrants moved in companies of from twenty to forty; when they arrived at a designated town they were welcomed by a committee of local citizens who supervised their placement in farmers' homes. As Brace acknowledged, the success of the emigration feature of "moral disinfection" was in part the result of the demand for cheap agricultural labor. The children received board and room, and the farmers obtained new hands to help with the planting, hoeing, and housework.[20]

The important task, as Brace saw it, was to get the vagrant children out of the city; he assumed that once the children were placed in an environment providing them with more wholesome influences and offering them better opportunities for individual advancement, the future would take care of itself. In practice, some of the children did not adjust readily to rural life and labor; irate Westerners sometimes complained that the Children's Aid Society was turning loose a horde of city hoodlums on the countryside and filling Western reformatories and jails with the scum of New York. In response to these objections the Society eventually discontinued the practice of sending older children to the country. Brace admitted that in some instances bad habits acquired on the city streets had become so deeply ingrained that even a radical change in environment could not eliminate them. He maintained, however, that in the vast majority of cases the transplanted children had become useful members of their adopted communities. Later investigators, upon checking the individual records of the emigrants, were inclined to agree that the net results of the removal policy were amazingly successful.[21]

Brace was a young man in his middle twenties when he helped to organize the Children's Aid Society; he remained executive officer of the Society for almost forty years. His own accounts of his work sometimes give the modern reader the impression that he was describing the capture of sparrows rather than the rescue of children. Yet he was probably more effective, and certainly more active, than any other figure of his generation in calling attention to the problem of neglected youth and in popularizing the idea of home as opposed to institutional care of orphans.[22] By his work and writings, which included descriptive articles on homeless children, essays on charity and reform, news items and editorials, Brace awakened large numbers of persons to the urgency of the problem of child vagrancy. Subsequent reformers who attacked the evils of child labor would be able to use the interest and concern Brace had aroused as a foundation for their efforts to take the children out of the factories, as he had sought to take them off the streets.

The Young Men's Christian Association, which was brought to America about the same time as the organization of the Children's Aid Society, addressed itself to a problem that was related to, but quite distinct from, the one with which Brace wrestled. Like the Children's Aid Society, the Y.M.C.A. worked with a group that was, in a sense, homeless, but its clientele was older and belonged to a higher economic level. The Y.M.C.A.'s concern was with uprooted youths who had reversed Brace's pattern and emigrated from the countryside to the city. Its functions were to provide a substitute for the friendly and familiar moral influences from which young men had been cut off by their removal to the cities, and to protect them against the dangers of irreligion, intemperance, and immorality.

The evangelical emphasis of some of the local Associations frequently involved them in a variety of general religious and welfare work. Their activities were so diversified that the historian of the Y.M.C.A. movement has noted that in its first decades the organization functioned as "a sort of cooperating agency for the advancement of any good work that any good man thought ought to be prosecuted." As late as 1874 relief ranked second only to the conversion of young men in the program of numerous local Associations. Most of them had a committee in charge of relief which supervised the distribution of money and clothing to poor families; not a few maintained soup kitchens during the depression of 1873; and some provided breakfasts and religious services on Sunday mornings to homeless men who had spent the night in police stations. Until other organizations had become strong enough to take over the work, the Associations in Washington and Chicago coordinated the relief and welfare facilities of their communities. In 1867 the Chicago "Y" reported that it was fast becoming "a society for the improvement of the condition of the poor, physical[ly] and morally," and that its

Relief Committee was seeking to impress upon all connected with its work that "our mission is not only to relieve the suffering but to improve the morals of those who are aided by us."[23] The Y.M.C.A. gradually limited its activities to work for young men and left the field of general philanthropy to other organizations. Service on the relief committees of the local Associations during the fifties and sixties nevertheless familiarized many serious young men with the conditions of the less fortunate and gave them at least a rudimentary training in charitable work.[24]

The Y.M.C.A.s also contributed to the development of the survey technique that was later to be widely used in social work. As a means of improving their program, and also as a basis for their appeals for funds, the Associations collected data on religious and moral influences in their cities. At first the surveys were limited to such matters as church membership, church attendance, and Sabbath observance, but by the 1860's they were being broadened to include information on tenements, saloons, brothels, sanitary facilities, recreational opportunities, and other factors affecting young men in urban communities. Conscientious secretaries upon assuming new positions made fresh studies of the localities which their Associations served. No doubt in order to prepare themselves for such assignments, students at the Y.M.C.A. college in Springfield, Massachusetts, formed a club to train themselves in gathering and interpreting survey data.[25] The Y.M.C.A. was therefore one of the pioneer agencies active in compiling factual information on urban social conditions; and it is worth noting that the surveys it sponsored were intended not to be of academic interest only, but to serve as a foundation for corrective action.

The Civil War affected the problem of poverty in multifarious ways. War and postwar political issues distracted attention temporarily from fundamental social questions and thereby postponed efforts at their solution. At the same time, however, the war destroyed slavery and thus removed from the arena of public debate the issue that had long overshadowed concern with poverty. To the North it brought a blood-born prosperity which temporarily eased economic tensions and gave nearly all classes a taste of greater material abundance than ever before. Yet it impoverished the South; and by accelerating the process of industrialization and encouraging both urbanization and immigration it transformed poverty from a local to a national problem. It accentuated the contrast between the conditions of the rich and poor and, in so doing, created an atmosphere of discontent and unrest. In particular, the war stimulated charities and greatly influenced their subsequent development.

During the war, members of the armed forces, their dependents, the freedmen, and other war sufferers were the recipients of charitable gifts of unprecedented magnitude. The United States Sanitary Commission and the United States Christian Commission, both federations of numerous voluntary associations, supplemented the work of government agencies in meeting the physical and spiritual needs of soldiers and sailors. The Sanitary Commission, which at one time had 500 agents in the field with Union troops, sent bandages, lint, clothing, and food to battlefields and encampments; it organized hospital units, established lodginghouses for men on furlough, provided receptions and meals to soldiers at railway stations, and maintained facilities to assist servicemen with claims for pay. The Christian Commission, closely allied to the Y.M.C.A., but also supported by numerous religious groups, furnished volunteer ministers to army camps, distributed Bibles, tracts, and books to the troops, and contributed stores of material relief similar to the goods provided by the Sanitary Commission.[26]

Dependents of fighting men received assistance on an even more generous scale. Volunteers' families were rewarded with gifts raised by community subscriptions, and in addition they often obtained aid from state and county funds. Bounties offered for enlistment were intended, in part, as a form of relief for the enlistees' families. The national government, states, and municipalities paid out an estimated $600,000,000 in bounty money during the war, and individuals raised an additional $100,000,000 for this purpose.

Contributions for the aid of combatants and their families by no means exhausted the charitable impulse. The National Freedmen's Relief Association and similar philanthropic groups endeavored to ease the immediate distress of the unsettled Negro population and also to inaugurate educational facilities to train them to become self-supporting. In somewhat similar fashion the American Union Commission provided destitute Union sympathizers in, or refugees from, the South with clothing, shelter, financial help, and aid in obtaining employment.

The exigencies of the war and the easy prosperity that accompanied it in the North accustomed numerous Americans to the habit of contributing generously to philanthropy. Furthermore, the war experience familiarized many persons who had hitherto looked upon charity as an individual or church obligation with the practice of making their gifts to the unfortunate indirectly, through the agency of secular welfare organizations. To a certain extent the war made Americans as a whole more cognizant of the impersonal causes of destitution operating in society, and war work acquainted some of them with the necessity of ministering to the physical wants of the suffering as well as to their spiritual needs. A Sanitary Commission official reported that medical attention was the chief need of the freedmen in a hastily improvised, overcrowded, and insanitary camp. "There are already teachers, missionaries, and chaplains enough in the field," he wrote; "without physicians there will soon be no scholars for the teacher to teach or souls for the missionary to save."[27]

As a direct consequence of generous bounty payments and public assistance to dependents of servicemen, local tax rates and assessments increased rapidly during the war period. This fact, plus well-merited suspicion of the honesty and ability of many public officials, confirmed the conviction of the propertied classes that "indiscriminate giving" was unwise and that public administration of relief was costly and inefficient. On the other hand, the war gave added luster to the principle of meeting emergency needs through voluntary associations, contributions, and service. The great war commissions not only seemed relatively effective but, perhaps more important, emotionally satisfying. They mobilized the charitable resources of the North, especially the militant energies of aroused womanhood.

The example of heroic self-sacrifice on the part of the young men who volunteered for the war kindled a desire for reciprocal service in the hearts of their sisters. Josephine Shaw, then a girl of nineteen, wrote in her diary on October 25, 1862:

> We, as a Nation, are learning splendid lessons of heroism and fortitude through it [the war] that nothing else could teach. All our young men who take their lives in their hands and go out and battle for the right grow noble and grand in the act, and when they come back (perhaps only half of those who went) I hope they will find that the women have grown with them in the agony. . . . Dear boys! How noble they are, and yet how can they help being noble? I have

> longed so to go myself that it seemed unbearable. . . . We can work though even if we can't enlist, and we do.[28]

For countless American women war-relief work was an emancipating experience. After the war a number of them were unwilling to retire serenely to the management of households. For some of them this was impossible, for their husbands, or the young men who might have married them, did not come back. Those war-bereft women carried forward into the new times the fervor for helpful service that had been awakened in the trial of the Union. They were the forerunners, and often in a literal sense the teachers, of that later generation of "dedicated old maids" of the Progressive era who also devoted their lives to assisting the unfortunate.

CHAPTER 4

The Rise of Social Work

> The great problem of all charity, public or private, is how to diminish suffering without increasing, by the very act, the number of paupers; how to grant aid, in case of need, without obliterating the principle of self-reliance and self-help.
>
> FREDERICK H. WINES, Secretary, Board of Public Charities of the State of Illinois, *Second Biennial Report*, 1872.

> But because we cannot do all we wish are we to do nothing? Even as things are, something can be accomplished. Is no life-boat to put out, and no life-belt to be thrown, because only a half dozen out of the perishing hundreds can be saved from the wreck?
>
> London Congregational Union, *The Bitter Cry of Outcast London.*

Public Relief and Scientific Philanthropy

PUBLIC poor relief was in bad repute in nineteenth-century America. Some observers, such as Josephine Shaw Lowell, attributed the disgraceful condition of almshouses at the close of the Civil War to the preoccupation of earlier reformers with the slavery issue. Even more directly, however, public indifference toward the helpless stemmed from the emphasis upon individual self-help which was the religion of the respectable in the vigorous young republic. The energies of the common man, so long smothered in older caste-ridden nations, were concentrated in America on demonstrating the worth and rewards of hard work in a free and fortunately endowed society. There was so much work to be done, so many opportunities for the competent to seize, that *noblesse oblige* was often deemed a relic of outworn aristocracies. The incompetent, no matter what the reason for their disability, seemed at best a burden on the community.

The aim of public relief in the nineteenth century was to prevent starvation and death from exposure as economically as possible. Sometimes, as in the case of the elderly sisters of whom Sarah Orne Jewett wrote in "The Town Poor," this meant that public authorities auctioned the destitute to the person who demanded the smallest sum for their care.[1] Under this practice, which a writer in 1860 called private enterprise in human stock, the low bidder sought to make a profit out of the transaction by skimping on the housing, fuel, food, and clothing furnished his charges.[2] Indenture was an even more economical method of dealing with the poor. In the early years of the century it was not uncommon to "bind out" idle or vagrant adults to labor for and under the supervision of respectable citizens.[3] Until about 1875 indenture continued to be a favorite means of providing for the custody and instruction of orphaned or otherwise destitute children.[4]

The ideal of economical administration was often defeated in practice because relief was managed by politicians who were apt to be kindhearted, inefficient, or corrupt—or all three. Public assistance to the poor in their homes in the form of donations of coal or payment of rent was so haphazardly administered that reformers agitated, often successfully, for its complete cessation.[5] But it was not only of maladministration that reformers complained: they were opposed to public outdoor (i.e., noninstitutional) relief in principle. Mrs. Lowell wrote in 1883 that the system of public support of paupers in their own homes was, if possible, less defensible than "openly advocated communism"; for "the principle underlying it is not that the proceeds of all men's labor is to be fairly divided among all, but that the idle, improvident, and even vicious man has the right to live in idleness and vice upon the proceeds of the labor of his industrious and virtuous fellow citizen."[6]

Mrs. Lowell and the other Americans who shared her views on public relief borrowed their ideas from the English poor-law reformers. They maintained that public assistance should be granted, not only sparingly, but grudgingly; it should be available only in institutions and dispensed only in ways that would discourage people from seeking it. Mrs. Lowell admitted the community's obligation to "save every one of its members from starvation, no matter how low or depraved such member may be," but she contended that

> the necessary relief should be surrounded by circumstances that shall not only repel everyone, not in extremity, from accepting it, but which shall also insure a distinct moral and physical improvement on the part of all those who are forced to have recourse to it—that is, discipline and education should be inseparably associated with any system of public relief.[7]

In the institutions which she envisaged the inmates would be required to work, exercise, and sleep "as much or as little as is good for them"; and be brought under the influence of "physical, moral, mental, and industrial training." When cured of the disease of pauperism by this strict discipline, they would be released to take their places as useful and independent citizens.[8]

No institutions of this type existed in the United States when Mrs. Lowell wrote. There were tax-supported almshouses, but these were better calculated to degrade than to reform their inhabitants; and commitment of a family to them had a tendency to transform temporary misfortune into permanent poverty. Throughout the better (or worse) part of the century public almshouses remained exile colonies of all categories of the homeless and helpless. They were social pesthouses in which an undifferentiated collection of discards including the aged, the blind, the insane, feeble-minded persons, epileptics, alcoholics, orphans, foundlings, and chronic paupers were crowded together, as the novelist Edward Eggleston observed, "like chickens in a coop."[9] Not infrequently hospitals and poorhouses were located side by side, or even placed in the same building.[10]

Before the Civil War control of almshouses, as of other provisions for public assistance, was in the hands of local officials. Township, county, and city officials administered indoor and outdoor relief without supervision from state authorities except as their activities might be scrutinized by grand juries or investigated by legislative commissions. During the 1860's, however, the more progressive states began to appoint permanent boards to inspect, report on, and suggest improvements in public charities, particularly reformatories, asylums, and almshouses.[11]

The reports of the state boards provided almost the first comprehensive and authoritative information on conditions in public institutions. Without exception they condemned the undifferentiated almshouse. In 1869 the newly appointed Ohio board called attention to the plight of the nearly one thousand children incarcerated in the county poorhouses:

> What is to be done with them? Think of their surroundings. The raving of the maniac, the frightful contortions of the epileptic, the driveling and senseless sputtering of the idiot, the garrulous temper of the decrepit, neglected old age, the peevishness of the infirm, the accumulated filth of all these; then add the moral degeneracy of [those who] from idleness or dissipation, seek a refuge from honest toil in the tithed industry of the country, and you have a faint outline of the surroundings of these little boys and girls. This is home to them. Here their first and most enduring impressions of life are formed.[12]

Frederick H. Wines of the Illinois board stated in 1872 that he and the other members had found conditions in the county almshouses which were almost too shocking to describe—"nakedness, filth, starvation, vice, and utter wretchedness, which a very slight exercise of common sense and of humanity might have entirely prevented." He called these institutions "living tombs."[13] Several years later William P. Letchworth reported equally deplorable conditions in New York poorhouses. Of a group of boys housed in the laundry of one of the institutions he wrote:

> They were intermingled with the inmates of the wash-house, around the cauldrons where the dirty clothes were being boiled. Here was an insane woman raving and uttering wild gibberings, a half-crazy man was sardonically grinning, and an overgrown idiotic boy of malicious disposition was teasing, I might say torturing, one of the little boys. There were several other adults of low types of humanity. The apartment . . . overhead was used for a sleeping room, and the floor was being scrubbed at the same time by one of the not overcareful inmates; it was worn, and the dirty water came through the cracks in continuous droppings upon the heads of the little ones, who did not seem to regard it as a serious annoyance. . . .

None of the children in this institution attended school.[14]

In several states the work of the official boards was supplemented by private associations. Wines of Illinois urged "the better class of citizens in each county" to form voluntary societies for the purpose of conducting a monthly investigation of jails and almshouses.[15]

Visiting committees for public hospitals had already been established in a few cities as an outgrowth of war-relief work; and in 1872 Louisa Lee Schuyler, whose philanthropic activities embraced service in the Children's Aid Society, the Sanitary Commission, and the Bellevue Hospital Visiting Committee, helped organize the New York State Charities Aid Association.[16] This society, and similar ones later founded in other states, promoted the organization of local visiting committees which made more frequent inspections of the almshouses than the state board could undertake, and kept the management of the institutions under constant and thorough surveillance.

Edward Eggleston's *The Hoosier Schoolmaster*, published in 1871, may well have aided in recruiting members for these local visiting committees. A miserably administered poorhouse in the backwoods of Indiana figured prominently in the story, and the author interrupted his narrative to assert that conditions were equally bad in almshouses in other parts of the country, including wealthy New York State. Eggleston assigned the blame for these conditions impartially to the dishonesty of county officials and the indifference of the prosperous churchgoing people of the community. The former corruptly allowed claims for repairs to the institution that were never made; the latter were so occupied in sending old clothes to the heathen of the South Sea Islands and the Five Points of wicked New York City that they were blind to the sorrow and poverty within their own reach.[17]

The combined efforts of the state boards and their volunteer adjuncts brought about some improvement in the almshouses, particularly in the removal of children and the mentally and physically disabled to specialized institutions. Nevertheless, undifferentiated almshouses were still in existence in parts of the country in the 1890's. As late as 1900 only one fourth of the states had passed laws providing for the removal of children from the poorhouses, and even in these states the laws were not fully enforced.[18]

While public aid to the poor was neglected, or even regarded with downright hostility, private charity flourished. Those who favored ending public relief outside almshouses and infirmaries argued that private benevolence was adequate to succor the needy who were not so completely dependent as to require institutional care. Pauperism and taxation were the twin bugbears of most nineteenth-century philanthropists. They wished to improve the poorhouses, but not to such an extent that people would cease dreading to be sent to them. They wanted to help the unemployed and the deserving poor, but not to be so kind about it that those groups would be tempted into permanent dependency. They yearned to feed the hungry and warm the cold—but they suspected that many persons who seemed to be famishing and freezing were actually impostors. They desired to do what was necessary to relieve suffering in an efficient, economical, and businesslike manner, and they wanted to do it by means of voluntary contributions and services rather than through tax-supported benevolence. It seemed to them—that is, to the well-to-do persons who had the leisure and resources to indulge in voluntary charitable work—that what the poor most needed was assistance in developing good character. In their scale of values, good character meant, first and foremost, ability to support oneself.

The charity organization movement, originating in 1869, in London, seemed such a practical method of obtaining the desired end of efficiency in dispensing aid to the poor that it was widely and rapidly copied in American cities. Like the various Associations for Improving the Condition of the Poor, which Hartley and others had established a generation earlier, the new Charity Organization Societies, or Associated Charities, as they were called in some cities, sought to foster a better administration of private charitable activities. The methods of the new movement, reflecting the changes wrought in business management in the intervening years, were somewhat different and, presumably, more scientific. The program of the charity organization societies was to coordinate the work of the numerous and occasionally competing philanthropic organizations already in existence, encourage the investigation of appeals for assistance, prevent duplication of effort by different groups, discover impostors, and suppress mendicancy. The goal of the movement was to husband the private charitable resources of the community so that money, instead of being dissipated on unworthy applicants, would be available to give adequate assistance to all worthy cases.[19]

Originally the charity organization societies were not relief agencies at all. They furnished no aid themselves, but were simply bureaus of information and investigation. Applicants for assistance who could pass the rigid examinations to which C.O.S. agents subjected them were certified as worthy and referred to one of the cooperating agencies for the relief of their needs. Thus, when prospective contributors to the New York C.O.S. asked Mrs. Lowell how much of their donation would go to the poor, she was able to answer proudly, "Not one cent."[20]

Circumstances eventually made it necessary for the charity organization societies to furnish relief from their own funds, but they continued to require candidates for assistance to prove their worthiness. In cases where a loan rather than an outright gift seemed appropriate, the New York C.O.S. referred applicants to its Provident Loan Society. This was, in effect, a pawnshop that charged half the legal rate of interest.[21] Where possible a work test was applied to alms seekers. In New York the Society maintained a woodyard: donors to the project received tickets which they, in turn, gave to men who asked them for aid; the bearers of the tickets took them to the woodyard, where they sawed or split wood for a designated number of hours, receiving, in exchange for their labor, bed, breakfast, and dinner. It is perhaps worth noting that among the members of the committee that supervised this enterprise was Clarençe S. Day, the author of *Life with Father*.[22]

Like the earlier movements in the direction of scientific philanthropy, the charity organization societies placed great emphasis upon the use of volunteers to visit, counsel, and instruct the poor; but where the A.I.C.P. had relied exclusively on men to do this work, the new organizations encouraged qualified women to engage in friendly visiting. By 1892 women far outnumbered men among the 4,000 volunteers enrolled in charity organization work in the United States.[23] Whether male or female, friendly visitors were expected to be combination detectives and moral influences. They were to ascertain the reason for the applicants' need and to help them overcome it. Their function was not to help the poor obtain charitable assistance, but by advice and example to stimulate them to become self-supporting. The premise of the friendly visitor's work was that some personal weakness of character, intellect, or body ordinarily redounded to the distress of the poor; only if those weaknesses were discovered and the sufferer induced to correct them could progress be made toward individual independence.

C.O.S. offices were repositories of the voluminous reports prepared by friendly visitors on the basis of their observation and interrogation of alms seekers. Each office contained a city-wide registry of names and addresses of individuals or families receiving assistance from the cooperating societies. One of the objectives was to compile a dossier on every person who had received or even asked for assistance. Officers of the organization strove to induce the police to be more stringent in campaigns against vagrants and beggars, and they lobbied in city halls and state legislatures against measures authorizing the free distribution of coal and other outdoor relief to the needy.

The charity organization movement and the scientific philanthropy it fostered were subjected to criticism from many sources. Boston's Irish-American poet, John Boyle O'Reilly, wrote scathingly of

> The organized charity scrimped and iced
> In the name of a cautious, statistical Christ.[24]

William T. Stead observed that nothing could be more admirable than the principles to which the societies were dedicated, and few things less satisfactory than the way in which they were conducted.[25] The conscientiousness with which agents of the local societies applied the doctrine of self-help often left them open to charges of harshness. At one point in the best seller, *Mrs. Wiggs of the Cabbage Patch* (1901), that long-suffering widow was so overburdened that she was tempted to register for aid with "The Organization." Jim, her thirteen-year-old son, objected:

> "Not yet, ma!" he said firmly. "It 'ud be with us like it was with the Hornbys; they didn't have nothin' to eat, an' they went to the organization an' the man asted 'em if they had a bed or table, 'an when they said yes, he said, 'well why don't you sell 'em!' "[26]

Poor Jim was such a believer in self-help that, rather than ask the rich society for assistance, he literally worked himself to death.

William Dean Howells also protested against the heartlessness of organized charity and the pharisaical spirit which he thought characterized its operations. Why should we be so hard on the poor, he asked, when we know by personal experience and statistics that thousands cannot obtain work and must suffer unless they beg? "Perhaps," he suggested, "it would be a fair division of the work if we let the deserving rich give only to the deserving poor, and kept the undeserving poor for ourselves who, if we are not rich, are not deserving either."[27]

As a trustee of the Cleveland C.O.S. Frederic C. Howe received a letter from a local clergyman denouncing the organization for its capitalistic bias and predilection to measure worthiness by business standards.

> Your society [wrote the clergyman], with its board of trustees made up of steel magnates, coal operators, and employers is not really interested in charity. If it were, it would stop the twelve-hour day; it would increase wages and put an end to the cruel killing and maiming of men. It is interested in getting its own wreckage out of sight. It isn't pleasant to see it begging on the streets.
>
> I doubt, as I read my New Testament, whether the Twelve Disciples would have been able to qualify as worthy according to your system. And Christ himself might have been turned over by you to the police department as a "vagrant without visible means of support."

Howe himself began to wonder whether charity, as practiced by the Society, was not "a business enterprise, designed to keep poverty out of sight and make life more comfortable for the rich."[28]

Part of the criticism of the charity organization movement stemmed from hostility to the growing professionalization of welfare work. During the eighties and nineties paid workers began to supplant volunteers as friendly visitors. In many communities there were simply not enough well-to-do ladies and gentlemen able and willing to give time day after day to difficult and arduous assignments in the slums.[29] The volunteers gradually retired to advisory and fund-raising committees, leaving the actual "case work" more and more in the hands of the professionals. Persons who were accustomed to think of charity as primarily a personal obligation regarded the notion that aid might be more efficiently dispensed by "paid clerks" as a heretical innovation. Advocates of one-hundred-per-cent charity were distressed by the fact that a portion of the money raised by contributions for the relief of the poor was used to pay salaries to persons who doled out the assistance. Men and women who gave slight thought to the hardships that may have resulted from their own neglect of charitable obligations and opportunities were outraged at reports of officious and inquisitorial conduct on the part of professional social workers.

Misunderstanding of the purpose of charity organization was another source of complaint against the movement. Unquestionably, in many cases, the harshness of the charity agents reflected their narrow experience and limited sympathies. In many other instances, however, their apparent hardness was simply the result of a sincere effort to do a difficult task in a competent manner. Their responsibility, as the agents saw it, was to help the poor, *really* help them—not just to give them food, clothing, coal, or alms to tide them over one emergency after another. Perhaps it was presumptuous to think and talk about "elevating" the victims of poverty, and yet it was a distinct advance in social thought to recognize that poverty was an abnormal condition, that it was unnecessary, that it was curable, and that its treatment required more fundamental changes than an increase in generosity on the part of the rich.

No one accused charity agents of radicalism; and yet, in the long run, their work undermined many cherished opinions regarding the cause and cure of poverty. The first and essential duty of case workers was to get the facts about the condition of persons who asked for charity. Writers such as Howells might take an occasional "East-Side Ramble" or Stephen Crane conduct an infrequent "Experiment in Misery," but it was the charity agents' daily job to collect and report data on the income, housing, employment, health, and habits of the depressed classes. It was their business to concern themselves with the welfare of widows and dependent children, aged persons, homeless men, vagrant boys, and wayward girls. When they went into a tenement it was not in search of "color" but to gather the plain gray facts about number of rooms, number of persons occupying them, possibility of ventilation, availability and condition of sinks and toilets—and the rent. In their investigations into the "worthiness" of a "case" they uncovered information about unemployment, industrial accidents, sickness, wages, and family expenditures. In nearly every city of any size these trained or partially trained observers compiled a fund of more reliable and comprehensive data on the economic and social problems of the very poor than had been available since the days of the close-knit village economy.[30]

In addition to specific information, agents of the organized charities contributed a technique of social research. The "case method" which they perfected was an attempt to treat each family or individual as a unique problem. This meant the rejection of preconceived notions about "the poor," "the depraved classes," or "the oppressed," and the substitution of efforts to discover pertinent and significant data about particular family histories. Case workers did not always succeed in emancipating themselves from prejudices of one sort or another any more than other social scientists did; but they worked with more concrete issues, and the inevitable tendency of scientific philanthropy was to emphasize an objective and factual rather than a deductive approach to the problems at hand.[31]

Even before the 1890's, and increasingly thereafter, social scientists utilized the facilities of charity organization societies in their research. At Johns Hopkins University Richard T. Ely assigned one of his graduate students, John R. Commons, to the Baltimore C.O.S. as a case worker and required him to report on his activities to the joint history and economics seminar.[32] During the nineties Columbia College and the New York C.O.S. entered into an agreement whereby Columbia's political-science students did field work in the Society's districts and obtained access to its files for statistical research. Simultaneously a committee on statistics of the New York C.O.S. prepared analyses of case records and compiled reports on homeless men and unemployment on the basis of data in the Society's files.[33] Amos G. Warner in studying the causes of poverty and John Koren in considering the economic aspects of the liquor problem both based their statistics on reports of the agents of the organized charities.[34] Similarly the records and reports of the charity organization societies provided a mass of documentary evidence to students of the housing of low-income groups.[35]

Beginning as the expression of a somewhat narrow, moralistic, and individualistic attitude toward poverty, the charity organization movement ultimately fostered the development of a more broadly social point of view. The obligation to obtain factual information about the economic situation of their clients, in practice, compelled charity agents to give attention to wages, conditions of work and unemployment, no less than to intemperance, improvidence, and shiftlessness. Knowledge of the misfortunes of hundreds of different families gained through experience as friendly visitors induced many representatives of the organized charities to regard the industrial causes of poverty as more important than the personal.

The emphasis of systematic charity on self-support and its prejudice against almsgiving as a remedy for the ills of the poor further disposed its practitioners to a sympathetic attitude toward labor. Charity agents' work brought them into frequent contact with suffering imposed by the subordination of labor to capital in industry; it made them acutely aware of the practical hardships that flowed from treating labor as a commodity in the service of private profit. From the beginning the aim of the charity organization movement had been, not to expand, but to restrict, the charitable impulse. Increasingly the agents of organized charity came to look upon the attainment of social justice as a more important field of endeavor than the administration of private benevolence.[36]

Neighbors of the Poor

In 1891 the rector of Holy Trinity Church in New York City publicly scoffed at the idea "that the Church must reach the masses, purify politics, elevate the laboring classes."[37] His view probably coincided with that of a great many other Protestant clergymen of the day, but there was a rising tide of dissent. W. S. Rainsford, himself the rector of the church at which J. P. Morgan worshiped, condemned the tendency of organized Protestantism to seek "comfort and ease in the society of the rich." He charged that as a result of indifference to the urban working class the Protestant churches had lost the initiative in the years between 1830 and 1890.[38]

Rainsford and other progressive clergymen sought to regain the initiative by restoring evangelical work among the poor to a more prominent place in the program of Protestant congregations. There had been an increase in home missionary activity ever since the third decade of the century, but much of this work had been directed toward spreading the gospel into sparsely settled areas of the West and toward stimulating religious observance among the middle classes.[39] By the eighties and nineties concern over the growth of Roman Catholicism, worry about the antagonism between capital and labor, and the example of the Salvation Army convinced Protestant groups all over the country of the need for intensified missionary labor in the roaring wilderness of American cities.

Interest in the evangelization of slum dwellers in Boston and

New York led to the establishment of missions in those cities at an earlier date than in other parts of the country.[40] To some extent the nationwide concern with the sinfulness of New York City and the eagerness of outsiders to promote missionary work there may have diverted church groups in smaller cities from recognizing opportunities for similar work at home. In Paul Leicester Ford's *The Honorable Peter Stirling* (1894), the hero's mother thought that there were no serious social problems in the mill town where she lived because there were seats enough in church for all comers; in New York City, however, she understood that existing churches could accommodate only one fourth of the population, and saloons outnumbered churches ten to one. Her information came to her by way of a missionary who was soliciting contributions in small-town churches for the building of more religious edifices in the metropolis.[41]

By 1880 there were at least thirty undenominational societies supporting missions in the slums of different cities. In addition to their strictly religious activities the missions often attempted to alleviate the material condition of the poor by engaging in limited relief work. Some of them built model tenements and lodginghouses, provided facilities for training children in the trades and domestic occupations, equipped libraries and reading rooms, and promoted country vacations for boys and girls from the slums.[42] The best-known and most successful of the missions was the Five Points House of Industry in New York. Most students credit the regeneration of the vicious Five Points district to the civilizing and educational influence of this institution and its founder, Rev. Lewis M. Pease.[43]

The Broome Street Tabernacle in New York City organized a mission society in the 1880's to conduct gospel meetings for inhabitants of the cheap lodginghouses that lined the Bowery. Alexander Irvine, a former British marine, was employed as a missionary by this society for several years around 1890. He made his home in just such a bunkhouse as Stephen Crane described in "An Experiment in Misery"; it functioned as a combination soup kitchen, employment agency, and old-clothes depot.[44] Every afternoon Irvine toured the neighborhood, conversing with destitute and homeless men, discovering in the process that "there was one gospel they were looking for and willing to accept—it was the gospel of work." Irvine's close association with outcast men acquainted him with a rich variety of human personalities. Where outsiders saw the Bowery bums only as objects of scorn or ridicule, Irvine, the missionary, took them seriously, listened to them with sympathy, and sought to understand the causes of their failure in life.[45]

The institutional church movement, which made considerable headway in the 1880's and 1890's, was closely related to city mission work. Some of the churches engaging in community service, such as the Broome Street Tabernacle, were erected through the efforts of mission and tract societies; others found it necessary, as a result of population shifts, to adopt welfare functions that had not been needed when the church membership was largely composed of persons in comfortable circumstances.[46] As defined by Josiah Strong, the institutional church was simply one that did whatever was most needed in the locality where it was placed. This usually meant expanding church facilities to include a gymnasium, baths, library, and rooms for clubs and classes.[47]

The pioneer of the institutional church movement was William A. Mühlenberg, rector of the Church of the Holy Communion in New York City, who organized various charitable enterprises, including St. Luke's Hospital, in the 1840's and 1850's.[48] Russell H. Conwell was one of the best known of the later exponents of the "teaching, healing, and preaching church." His Baptist Temple in Philadelphia instituted a night school for working people in 1884 which burgeoned into Temple University, and founded Samaritan Hospital with its auxiliary dispensaries and visiting-nurse services.[49] St. George's Church, situated at the edge of a congested tenement neighborhood in New York City, increased its membership more than fifty times in the fifteen years between 1882 and 1897 through the strenuous labor of its rector, W. S. Rainsford—even though Rainsford's liberalism (he permitted dancing in the parish hall) and his emphasis on the humanitarian aspects of religion cost the church some of its old communicants, including Captain Alfred Thayer Mahan.[50]

Institutional church workers, like Y.M.C.A. officials, often found it desirable to make either formal or informal surveys of social conditions in the community. Before assuming the pastorate of the Central Congregational Church in Topeka, Kansas, Charles M. Sheldon, author of *In His Steps,* familiarized himself with the city by living for brief periods with different economic and nationality groups and studying labor problems as they affected the people of the town. In 1889 Graham Taylor, then a professor at Hartford Theological Seminary, supervised his students in making an analysis of the population of Hartford by nationality and church denomination and in taking a census of the "destructive forces," such as saloons, and "preventive agencies," such as the Young Men's and Young Women's Christian Associations operating in the city. On an even broader scale the Federation of Churches and Christian Workers in New York began, in the late nineties, to make sociological surveys of various districts of the city. The Federation acted as a clearing-house in making the knowledge it had accumulated on housing, employment, and related information available to religious and secular welfare organizations.[51]

The settlement, like the charity organization movement, was an English innovation widely and rapidly copied in the United States. In 1883 the London Congregational Union published *The Bitter Cry of Outcast London*, a moving account of the condition of the poor in East London and an appeal for funds to establish mission halls in the district. The report began on this challenging note:

> Whilst we have been building our churches, and solacing ourselves with our religion, and dreaming that the millennium was coming, the poor have been growing poorer, the wretched more miserable, and the immoral more corrupt; the gulf has been daily widening which separates the lowest classes of the community from our churches and chapels, and from all decency and civilization.[52]

Among those stimulated to action by *The Bitter Cry* was Samuel A. Barnett, vicar of St. Jude's, Whitechapel, a parish that the Bishop of London acknowledged to be the worst in his diocese. In 1884 Barnett and his wife converted their rectory into a social center for the people of the community. They named the center Toynbee Hall in memory of Barnett's friend, Arnold Toynbee, a young Oxford tutor who had tried, as far as his academic duties permitted, to live like a workingman, and they invited university men to settle in the Hall, participate in its educational and recreational programs, and become, not occasional visitors to, but friends and neighbors of, the poverty-stricken inhabitants of the surrounding area.

The first American settlement houses were founded in the late 1880's by men and women such as Stanton Coit and Jane Addams who admired, and in some cases had observed at firsthand, the work being conducted at Toynbee Hall. In their turn the Neighborhood Guild (later known as the University Settlement), the College Settlement in New York City, and Hull House in Chicago became the models for numerous other settlements established in this country during the nineties. The idea was taken up so enthusiastically that within fifteen years after Coit had organized the Neighborhood Guild in New York's East Side about one hundred settlement houses were operating in American cities.

On the surface there was little that was radically new in the settlement movement. Missions contributed the idea of lighthouses in the slums to help the poor find their way to better lives; institutional churches suggested the community-center program which the settlements adopted; and charitable organizations promoted interest in voluntary service as the noblest form of philanthropy. Even the idea of "settling" in the slums was not entirely new. The occupation of tenements by well-to-do landlords was frequently advocated and occasionally practiced; and in some of the model tenements there were resident directors such as Charles B. Stover, later an associate of Coit at the Neighborhood Guild, who organized clubs and classes for the tenants.[53] The real novelty of the movement lay in the buoyant spirit, the fresh outlook, and the new attitudes its leaders introduced into philanthropic work.

From the start the settlement idea appealed to youth. The pioneers in the field were all young people. They were born too late for Brook Farm and, in most cases, a little too early for Greenwich Village. For the most part they were children of middle- or upper-class households, well born and well educated. Success in conventional business or professional careers and the achievement of assured social position offered less of a challenge to them than to the offspring of less fortunately endowed families. Instead, they found the call to altruistic service irresistible, and they gravitated toward poverty, a condition foreign to their personal experience. Had they lived in a different age or in a different country, religion, politics, or even revolutionary intrigue might have been their métier. Some of them, in fact, had once planned to become missionaries in remote corners of the world and were only deflected from that aim by becoming aware of the opportunities for service in neglected areas of their own communities.[54]

Most nineteenth-century philanthropists urged the rich to engage in friendly visiting and other voluntary charitable activities in order that the poor might be improved by coming into contact with superior beings. Brace, for example, rejoiced that through the volunteer teachers in the Children's Aid Society Industrial Schools "the refinement, education, and Christian enthusiasm of the better classes" were brought to bear on slum children.[55] Settlement leaders, on the other hand, emphasized the reciprocal advantages which they thought resulted from the association of persons of different economic and social levels. The aim of the University Settlement in New York City, as stated in its constitution, was "to bring men and women of education into closer relations with the laboring classes for their mutual benefit."[56] Graham Taylor intended the Chicago Commons to be "a common center where representatives of the masses and classes could meet and mingle as fellow men. . . ."[57] The settlement pioneers were very anxious to provide the poor with facilities for recreation, aesthetic enjoyment, and self-improvement; but they were no less desirous of making their settlements serve as kinds of graduate schools where young men and women from sheltered homes might study life in the raw and become acquainted with, and learn from, people and situations that they would not otherwise have known.

The twofold objective of the settlements gave rise to a good deal of uncertainty about their exact function. The story was told of a society matron who, lorgnette in hand, inspected one of the college settlements from top to bottom. "Well!" she exclaimed, at the conclusion of her visit, "I do think you young ladies down here are doing a magnificent work—*whatever it is!*"[58] Like many others she could admire the courage displayed by young ladies who went into voluntary exile in the slums, but it was difficult for her to grasp the real purpose of their "magnificent work." In fact, the settlement's mission was not to *do* any one thing, but to provide an atmosphere in which ties of understanding and sympathy could be established between people of very different backgrounds and material conditions.

Ideally, the settlement house was not an institution, but a home, a comfortable sociable annex to each drab tenement flat. "Its books and pictures," wrote Graham Taylor, "the nursery and play space, the lobby and the parlor, the music and flowers, the cheery fireplace and lamp, the dancing floor and place of assembly, are an extension of the all-too-scant home equipment of its neighbors."[59]

In the early days some of the settlement houses were scarcely less meager in appointments than other homes in the area they served. When Coit opened the Neighborhood Guild it was located in a dilapidated tenement. The Guild's librarian later recalled that the floors were uncarpeted, the windows curtainless, and the gas jets without globes. A piano, some books, a few photographs of Rome, and a Turkish hanging did something, but not much, to relieve the bareness of the place.[60] As late as 1895 the University Settlement was housed in an ancient four-story building so rickety that the police would not allow the settlement to hold dances in it or entertain more than a few children at a time.[61]

Clubs were the heart of the settlement program. Originally some of the houses were little more than meeting places for different neighborhood organizations. At the Neighborhood Guild the principal boys' club was called the O.I.F., the initials standing for Order, Improvement, and Friendship; the girls gave their clubs more romantic names: The Lady Belvedere, The Rosebud, The Lady Aroma, and The Four Hundred Social.[62] At the nearby College Settlement members of the Hero Club listened to stories of the lives of great men, and then discussed the reasons for their heroes' success in life.[63] Most settlements also encouraged the formation of social-science or social-reform clubs for adults and of literary, gymnastic, and singing societies.

Other features were added as the need for them became apparent or in response to the interests of patrons and residents of the house. Most settlements maintained playgrounds, kindergartens, day nurseries, baths, and classes in music, art, and domestic science. Some offered baby clinics, workrooms for the unemployed, penny provident banks, and meeting rooms for labor unions. Henry Street Settlement had its visiting nurses; the Commons housed a church; and Hull House sheltered a branch of the public library and operated a boardinghouse for working girls.

Miss Addams explained how it happened that the settlements became involved in such a variety of services:

> In Chicago . . . we have a day nursery at Hull House. We would a great deal rather have someone else establish the nursery, and use our money for something else; but we have it because there are not enough nurseries in that part of the city. We have a free kindergarten, because we cannot get enough of them in the public schools

> of our ward. We have a coffeehouse, from which we sell cheap foods in winter at cost, not because that sort of thing is what the settlement started out to do, but because we feel the pressure for it. One of the residents goes every day to the court, and has the children handed over to her probational care when they are first arrested —not because we want to do that, but because we have no children's court and no probation officer.[64]

In her opinion the settlement house should be a place for experimentation. Instead of concentrating on one line of work it should try out new ventures, demonstrate their worth or futility, and, if possible, get the city to take over the task of running the worthwhile ones.[65]

The settlement workers' close and neighborly relations with the poor enabled them to undertake detailed and realistic investigations of various phases of the poverty problem. The typical settlement study dealt with a specific question, such as the incomes and expenditures of a certain nationality or occupational group in a given district; often it had a homely, down-to-earth quality which contrasted sharply with the more ambitious but also more abstract and doctrinaire analyses of social and economic issues prepared by bookish academicians. Even for those not consciously engaged in research, settlement life offered training in the social sciences; many of the residents took on voluntary assignments—sanitary inspection of tenement houses, for example—which made them thoroughly familiar with conditions in the community. When outsiders, such as the novelist in Brander Matthews' "In Search of Local Color," wanted to explore the slums, they frequently called on settlement workers to be their guides.[66] "In those days," wrote Mary Simkhovitch of the late nineties, "there were few 'surveys.' The people who really knew the neighborhood best were the priests, the politicians, and the settlement residents."[67]

Because settlement workers were so well acquainted with the needs and problems of the people in their neighborhoods, they tended to place greater emphasis upon social reform than upon individual improvement. Without in the least disparaging self-help, they sought, through their clubs, lectures, and forums to encourage cooperative efforts toward community betterment. At their best the settlement houses were centers of discussion and information as well as of recreation. Their residents were particularly interested in securing

ILLUSTRATIONS

Lewis W. Hine, "The Spinner," 1913. The Child Labor Bulletin, *II (August, 1913), 20. (Reproduced by courtesy of the George Eastman House.)*

Thure de Thulstrup, "Where Two Ends Meet," 1891.
Harper's Weekly, *XXXV (1891), 616-17.*

Charles Graham, "West Gotham Court, Cherry Street," 1879. Harper's Weekly, *XXIII (1879), 245.*

W. Bengough, "Mulberry Bend," 1895. Harper's Weekly, *XXXIX (1895), 607.*

Thomas Pollock Anshutz, *"Steelworkers, Noon Time," 1890.* Design. The Creative **Art** Magazine, *LIII (1952), 195. (Reproduced by courtesy of Mr. and Mrs. Lawrence* ***Fleishchman and*** Design. The Creative Art Magazine.)

Charles Haag, "*Organized Labor*," *1907*. Charities and the Commons, *XVII (1906-7), 611.*

Eugene Higgins, untitled painting, c. *1905*. The Craftsman, *XII (1907), 144.*

John Sloan, "*Roofs–Summer Night*," *1906*. The Craftsman, *XV (1908-9), 562.*

LEFT: *Glenn O. Coleman, "The Shop Girl At Home," c. 1909.* The Craftsman, *XVII (1909), 146.*

RIGHT: *Art Young, "Holy Trinity," 1908. John Nicholas Beffel, ed.,* Art Young, His Life and Times *(New York, 1939), p. 280. (Reproduced by permission.)*

LEFT: *William Balfour Ker, "From the Depths," 1905. John Ames Mitchell,* The Silent War *(New York, 1906).*

Art Young, "Pigs and Children," c. *1910. (Reproduced by courtesy of The Vanguard Press from Art Young,* The Best of Art Young, *copyright 1936, by The Vanguard Press, Inc.)*

Puck, 1909

A contemporary is publishing a series of pictures entitled "American Mothers." Don't forget this one at the right.

Art Young, "American Mothers," 1909. Beffel, ed., Art Young, His Life and Times, *p. 259. (Reproduced by permission.)*

ABOVE: *Lewis W. Hine, "Wash-Day in a Homestead Court,"* c. *1908. Margaret F. Byington,* Homestead. The Households of a Mill Town *(New York, 1910), facing p. 141.* BELOW: *Lewis W. Hine, "The North Carolina Legislature in 1913 Declared That the Commercial Interest of the State Required Such as These in Cotton Mills," 1913.* The Child Labor Bulletin, *II (May 1913), frontispiece.*

more public parks and playgrounds, better schools, more public-health services, and improved tenement-house laws. Jacob Riis called the settlement houses fulcrums for the lever of reform and testified that whenever a good cause was proposed, the settlements contributed "young enthusiasts to collect the facts" and urge them on reluctant city officials.[68]

Not all the settlements were as successful as some in widening the areas of understanding between persons of different backgrounds, and not all were active in promoting reform projects. Some remained unilateral philanthropies whose residents, as Malcolm Cowley has suggested, seemed anxious to reach down and help the poor climb not quite up to the level of their benefactors.[69] Frederic Howe, a serious-minded and somewhat self-conscious reformer, found his experience in a Cleveland settlement house at the turn of the century "anything but fruitful." He felt uncomfortable as a friendly visitor in the tenements, ill equipped to lead boys' clubs, and awkward when dancing with heavy-footed immigrant women; he was so oppressed by the miserableness of the district in which the settlement was located that he could manifest little enthusiasm for its ineffective ventures in reform.[70]

Jack London, who had gained his knowledge of poverty the hard way, was even more contemptuous than Howe of "These people who try to help!" London's dislike of settlement workers reflected his hatred for the capitalist class:

> As someone has said, they do everything for the poor except get off their backs. The very money they dribble out in their child's schemes has been wrung from the poor. They come from a race of successful and predatory bipeds who stand between the worker and his wages, and they try to tell the worker what he shall do with the pitiful balance left to him.[71]

London was convinced that the settlements were a failure. "They have worked faithfully," he acknowledged, "but beyond relieving an infinitesimal fraction of misery and collecting a certain amount of data which might otherwise have been more scientifically and less expensively collected, they have achieved nothing."[72]

Perhaps the last word on the subject was spoken even before the settlement movement, as such, originated. Matthew Hale Smith wrote of the city missionaries in 1869: "Few are fitted to labor in such . . . work. Patience, a loving heart, and warm sympathy for the distressed are essential."[73] Men and women possessed of these qualities–and the combination is a rare one–found settlement life rewarding. "You know the poor, if you take the pains to know them," said Jane Addams, "and you do not know the poor, if you do not take the pains to know them."[74] In contrast to the workers attached to charitable societies, who ordinarily visited tenement families only in time of trouble, settlement residents saw nearly all sides of tenement life, the brave and joyful as well as the sordid. "We knew not only poverty and crime," wrote Mary Simkhovitch, "but also the intelligence and ability and charm of our neighbor."[75]

Through friendly contact with the poor, settlement workers acquired, not just a knowledge, but an understanding of the daily life and trials of the urban masses. The best of them identified their own interests with the welfare of their neighbors. Where others thought of the people of the slums as miserable wretches deserving either pity or correction, settlement residents knew them as fellow human beings–and insisted that they were as much entitled to respect as any other members of the community. Numerous young men and women who lived and worked in the settlements during the 1890's carried this attitude with them into later careers in social work, business, government service, or the arts. It was the most important single contribution of the settlement movement; and it was destined to exert a great influence on the course of both social work and social reform in the twentieth century.

CHAPTER 5

The Condition of the Poor; Late Nineteenth-Century Social Investigations

> The helpful result of our study should be to renew the search for the preventive causes of degeneration, and to re-instill a consciousness of the necessity of improving both character and conditions.
>
> AMOS G. WARNER, *American Charities. A Study in Philanthropy and Economics.*

THE information on urban social conditions gathered by settlement residents, institutional churchmen, Y.M.C.A. secretaries, and agents of charitable societies was usually obtained as an incident to other activities. Surveys and monographs undertaken by these groups influenced workers in the movements involved and were sometimes consulted by students and teachers of sociology; but as a general rule they were not intended for, or readily accessible to, the general public. Such knowledge as the average citizen possessed on the subject of poverty he acquired (if not by personal experience) from popular journalistic treatments of the problem.

There was no lack of curiosity about the existence of slum dwellers in the latter half of the nineteenth century, much of it excited by the peculiar depravity which was assumed to characterize that life. For a half century after 1842, when Charles Dickens startled the country with his description of the coarse and bloated faces of the inhabitants of the Five Points, a succession of books rolled off the press purporting to expose the mysteries and miseries of metropolitan life.[1] Not infrequently these sensational works, some of them written by authors of dime novels, appealed to prurience behind a mask of outraged respectability, and nearly all of them capitalized on public interest in the details of vice and crime. Yet even the most lurid of these "inside stories" of sin in the big cities recognized that "The deserving poor are a multitude . . ." and acknowledged that "amid all this crime and pestilential influence there are found true hearts beating under breasts of spotless purity. . . ."[2]

On a higher level, newspapers such as the *New York Tribune* and the *Daily Graphic* and periodicals such as *Frank Leslie*'s and *Harper's Weekly* devoted considerable space to articles describing life in the slums. *Harper's Weekly* was particularly interested in the tenement-house problem, and during the seventies and eighties it ran several series of papers on Bottle Alley, Gotham Court, Ragpickers Court, and other picturesque but miserable districts in New York City. The article on Bottle Alley told of the enterprising family which occupied one small room in a rear tenement: the family regularly took in from eight to twelve lodgers a night at five cents a head, and also sold sour beer at two cents a pint or three cents a quart.[3] Of Ragpickers Court the *Harper's* correspondent wrote: "The men who live in these wretched hovels pay from five to six dollars a month rent out of earnings that hardly ever exceed fifty cents a day. The agent who lets the property lives in New Jersey. The owner—well, if the name were mentioned it would surprise the people of New York City."[4]

By far the most influential of the popular writers on slum life was Jacob Riis. Through years of experience as a police reporter he had acquired an unrivaled store of anecdotes about the people of the tenements, and he made liberal use of these in his books and articles. In a typical chapter Riis explained the problem of child vagrancy by telling this story: The remains of Harry Quill, aged fifteen, were discovered at the bottom of an air shaft in the tenement where his parents lived; investigation disclosed that two months earlier Harry, while drunk, had attacked another boy on the roof of the building; in the struggle the youth pushed Harry into the air shaft, but felt it best to say nothing about the occurrence; at the time the body was discovered Harry's parents had not yet notified the police that their son was missing.[5]

The best known of Riis's books was *How the Other Half Lives* (1890), a reporter's sketchbook which had the good fortune to be published in the same year as Ward McAllister's picture of the pleasures of the idle rich, *Society as I Found It*, and General Booth's *In Darkest England*, an exploration of the social depths in London. Riis appealed not only to the sympathy but also to the self-interest of his middle-class readers. The strength of his book lay less in the novelty of his material—for by 1890 there had been at least a generation of intermittent discussion of the tenements and slums—than in the journalistic skill that made his description of existing evils seem so authentic and his plea for reform so compelling. He denied that the poor lived in slums simply because they were lazy, immoral, intemperate, and dirty, but, except in the cases of children and virtuous women, he displayed little sympathy for the economic underdog and voiced no protest against the arrangement of society which consigned masses of men to mean lives. His was no cry for social justice, but a call to the propertied classes to bestir themselves lest the crime engendered in the slums and the diseases bred there invade the comfortable quarters where ladies and gentlemen resided.

During the hard times of the nineties serious magazines such as *The Forum* printed numerous essays on philanthropic experiments and on improved methods of dealing with dependency. *The Arena*, edited by B. O. Flower, was especially receptive to articles on social problems. The first issue of the magazine carried a symposium on the causes of the increase in poverty, in which one contributor suggested that not poverty itself but consciousness of it was on the rise.[6] Helen Gardener's "Thrown in with the City's Dead," which appeared in *The Arena* in 1890, was an excellent early example of muckraking. "Suppose you chanced to be very poor and to die in New York," the article began. "We are fond of saying that death levels all distinctions. Let us see." There followed a harrowing report on conditions on tiny Blackwell's Island, to which the city of New York consigned its insane, its "medium term" prisoners, and its pauper dead.[7] Flower himself was the author of *Civilization's Inferno; or Studies in the Social Cellar* (1893), in which he attempted to do for Boston's slums what Riis had done for Manhattan's, and also to plead more vigorously for social justice for the laboring classes.

A series of articles appearing in *Scribner's Magazine* in 1892 and 1893 under the general title "The Poor in Great Cities" was a pioneer effort to examine urban poverty in a broad frame of reference. The introduction referred to the condition of the poor as "the central subject of all social questions" and cited relief of suffering and improvement in the standard of living of the masses as necessary forerunners of all other reforms. "What we need to know," said the editor, "is what is doing, here and elsewhere, in the general and efficient activity that has been the growth of the last few years; and especially, what are the facts with which our own efforts are to deal, and how facts elsewhere compare with them."[8] Articles in the series examined the extent of misery and the preventive and ameliorative activities under way in London, Paris, Naples, New York, Boston, and Chicago. The contributors included Riis, who wrote on the children of the poor, Robert A. Woods, a Boston settlement leader, and William T. Elsing, a city missionary and pastor of a large institutional church in New York City.

The popular books and articles mentioned above were important primarily as indications of a mounting interest in social questions. The best of them admittedly grazed only the surface of the problems examined. Based on personal observation or impressions, they were often intensely, and intentionally, subjective in their approach. As late as 1892 Washington Gladden protested that there was little "definite and reliable" information on poverty in America in print and complained that popular ignorance on the subject was "profound and universal."[9]

One reason why there was such a paucity of systematic knowledge about poverty in America was the widely shared assumption that being poor was a self-inflicted mortification. This attitude had the result of directing toward pauperism and crime most of the sociological research undertaken in the United States prior to the 1890's. Robert L. Dugdale's *The Jukes* (1877), for example, expressed both the contemporary concern regarding the "dangerous classes" and the proclivity to lump dependency in the same category as criminality. The Secretary of the Prison Association of New York introduced Dugdale's book with the observation that "out of the same social soil from which spring the majority of the criminals there also chiefly grow up the vagrants and paupers—the ignorant and vicious and incapable."[10] Even *American Charities* (1894) by Amos Warner, which incorporated the most recent findings of

European and American research, treated poverty, no matter what the cause, as synonymous with "degeneration." To the nineteenth-century American few crimes were more reprehensible than inability to make a living.

Preoccupation with the moral and fiscal aspects of pauperism (that is, dependence upon charity for support) long prevented Americans from making serious studies of the causes and results of poverty. The English investigator, Charles Booth, was perhaps more influential than any other intellectual factor in bringing about a shift in the emphasis of social research in the United States. His painstaking study of the *Life and Labour of the People of London*, which began to appear in the late 1880's, was soon well known and highly regarded in this country. To a very considerable extent Booth set the pattern for later American sociological investigations.[11] Like many of his contemporaries he had a tendency to subject persons in lowly economic circumstances to moralistic tests. Nevertheless, the ultimate result of his analysis of London's population was to direct attention away from moral considerations and toward economic factors such as occupations and wages.

Booth had a passion for facts. He was dissatisfied with guesses about the amount of poverty, with theorizing about its probable causes, and with melodramatic descriptions of isolated instances of misery. By means of school-board visitors and other voluntary and official agencies he made a street-by-street canvass of various London districts, obtaining data on the employment, earnings, and housing of a sizable portion of the city's population. On the basis of what he believed to be reliable and pertinent statistics collected in this fashion, Booth estimated that about 30 per cent of the people of London lived in poverty. This conclusion, and also his finding that intemperance was an unimportant cause of poverty as compared to illness and unemployment, awakened great interest in his work. In the long run, however, the lesson of Booth's study was its demonstration that poverty was not an amorphous, intangible, pseudoreligious problem, but a concrete situation capable of economic definition and worthy of scientific scrutiny.

Notable advances were scored in the field of social statistics during the last three decades of the nineteenth century. The Census Bureau, state bureaus of labor statistics, congressional committees, the federal Commissioner of Labor, and the Department of Agriculture compiled and published reports on a multitude of subjects ranging from wages and prices to the incidence of divorce. As a result of the data supplied by these agencies no less a student than Charles B. Spahr asserted in 1896: "In the United States, despite the absence of income-tax returns, we find perhaps the most complete and satisfactory statistics in the world regarding the aggregate of the national income."[12] It is noteworthy, however, that when Spahr estimated the distribution of income among various classes he relied heavily on "common observation" and contended that "upon matters coming within its field the common observation of common people is more trustworthy than the statistical investigations of the most unprejudiced experts."[13]

At the close of the century there were in fact (as there long remained) vast gaps in statistical information on some pressing economic and social issues. For example, in 1891 when Richard T. Ely attempted to ascertain the number of paupers in the United States he discovered that neither the states nor the federal government had accurate records showing the number of persons in public institutions or receiving outdoor relief.[14]

Inadequacies in technique were only partly responsible for the incomplete and unreliable statistical information available at the end of the century. By 1900 only about half the states had established labor bureaus and fewer than half had developed factory-inspection systems. Whether state or federal, legislation creating fact-finding agencies, to say nothing of regulatory bodies, was often so weak that employers were under no compulsion to answer questionnaires or, if they did reply, to submit accurate data.[15] Furthermore, the appropriations granted the bureaus were seldom sufficient to permit them to do a thorough piece of work.[16] Thus in 1892 Congress passed a resolution calling on the Commissioner of Labor to conduct an investigation into the slums of cities with populations of 200,000 or over—and appropriated $20,000 for the task. The number of cities in the category designated was sixteen, but the sum appropriated was barely enough to enable the Commissioner's staff to look into some of the slums in four cities.[17] Another example of congressional parsimony occurred in the mid-nineties when the Commissioner of Labor was "authorized and directed" to make a full-dress survey of the employment of women and children, subject to the provision that the investigation be carried out under the regular appropriation of the office.[18]

Some of the state labor bureaus were weakened by patronage appointments of dubious qualification. At least one was placed under the supervision of a director who had been notoriously hostile to the establishment of the agency. Not infrequently statistical findings were shaped by political pressures. The Michigan labor bureau, by selecting counties in which property ownership was much more concentrated than in the state as a whole, was able to demonstrate that "one two hundredth" of the population owned 60 per cent of the real estate of Michigan. In 1893 the Senate Finance Committee, by garbling the figures submitted to it by employers, managed to show a nearly seventy-per-cent increase in wages between 1860 and 1891.[19] Similarly, as his critics were quick to point out, Carroll D. Wright's summaries of the investigations conducted by his office (Department of Labor) were not always consistent with the observations and statistical data contained in the bodies of the reports. No doubt thirty years of experience as a state and federal officeholder had taught Wright the value of ambiguity in the discussion of controversial issues.[20]

The incomplete and unsatisfactory character of late nineteenth-century statistical inquiries into industrial issues is well illustrated by conflicting estimates of the extent of unemployment. In 1878, when some calculations placed the number of jobless in Massachusetts at as high as 300,000, the director of the state bureau of labor statistics, basing his figures on the returns of police officials and tax assessors, asserted that the actual number was less than 30,000.[21]

Wright devoted his first annual report (1886) as United States Commissioner of Labor to a study of industrial depressions in the United States and Europe in the half century since 1837; and in 1895 a Massachusetts commission prepared a notable report on unemployment relief.[22] In general, however, studies of unemployment long suffered both from inadequate coverage and from a want of scientific spirit. Many seem to have been undertaken less to ascertain the facts than to assure a troubled people that the problem was not really serious at all.

For all their shortcomings, the early reports of the state and federal labor bureaus introduced a greater degree of objectivity into discussions of social and economic questions. In a commentary on studies of unemployment made by various agencies in the eighties and early nineties, the economist Davis R. Dewey listed ten factors which he said were "generally recognized as contributary causes making for nonemployment," not one of which referred to personal defects in the jobless.[23] E. W. Bemis used the statistics on wages and unemployment compiled by the Ohio labor bureau in his inquiry into the standard of living of miners in the Hocking Valley in the mid-eighties. Bemis assigned the major responsibility for the high incidence of unemployment in the region to management's policy of keeping a surplus of labor on hand; and he showed that owing to low wages and frequent layoffs the average yearly expenditure per person in miners' families must have been less than the amount spent by the state of Ohio for the maintenance of an inmate in its asylums or prisons.[24]

Industrial accidents and occupational diseases were among the problems conspicuously avoided by most state labor bureaus.[25] Nevertheless, the Interstate Commerce Commission recorded and published in its annual statistical summary the grisly total of employees killed and injured on the nation's railroads. President Benjamin Harrison, calling attention to this "cruel and largely needless sacrifice," declared in 1889: "It is a reproach to our civilization that any class of American workmen should in the pursuit of a necessary and useful vocation be subjected to a peril of life and limb as great as that of a soldier in time of war."[26] In each of his annual messages to Congress Harrison recommended the passage of legislation, finally adopted in 1893, requiring gradual installation of air brakes and automatic couplers on railway cars employed in interstate transportation.[27] Meanwhile, approximately half of the states had enacted laws of varying effectiveness providing for the use of safety devices and appliances on railways within their jurisdictions.[28]

Much of the credit for arousing public interest in railway safety belongs to a Baptist clergyman, Lorenzo S. Coffin. Beginning in his native Iowa in the 1880's, he gathered such facts as were available regarding work accidents on the railroads and launched a campaign for the adoption of automatic couplers and air brakes. He interviewed railroad executives in an attempt to awaken their consciences, wrote articles, delivered lectures, and preached sermons on the need for protecting brakemen and other railroaders. In one day Coffin is reported to have mailed more than 2,000 letters to prominent citizens in different parts of the country explaining the pressing need for remedial action.[29]

Case workers for charity organizations were among the first persons, aside from the victims and their families, to recognize the part played by industrial accidents in producing poverty. W. F. Willoughby, who made a survey of workingmen's insurance in Europe and America in the 1890's, observed that in no other field of reform was the United States more backward than in legislation regularizing compensation for work accidents.[30] In 1890 only half-a-dozen states required factory accidents to be reported, and only one, Massachusetts, had an employers' liability law of any efficiency.[31] By the middle of the decade one out of seven railroad workers was protected against injury or death at work through insurance schemes voluntarily established by their employers.[32] For the great mass of workers in transportation and industry, however, there was bitter truth in an investigator's statement that in America human life was ordinarily regarded as cheaper than the small cost of protecting it.[33]

The plight of workingwomen was a favorite subject of discussion among mid-century reformers and feminists. A brief review of the problem in 1844 by a Boston clergyman, R. C. Waterston, struck a modern note by examining piece rates paid in garment shops and calculating the impossible number of hours it would be necessary for a hand sewer to work in order to support herself by making shirts at six or seven cents each and pants at twenty-five cents a pair. The author, whose remarks were addressed to the Society for the Prevention of Pauperism, warned that "inadequate wages—both because they are inadequate and because they discourage—have proved to many a source of pauperism."[34] Louisa May Alcott's *Work*, although not published until 1873, described conditions in a number of different women's occupations in the 1850's. To a modern reader its tone is distressingly sentimental, but, in one passage at least, Miss Alcott spoke with evident sincerity: the best reply to people who advise young girls to go to work as servants or factory hands, she said, was "Try it."[35]

After the Civil War both official agencies and private individuals made rather frequent investigations of female labor. Wright's reports from the Massachusetts Bureau of Labor Statistics were the first trustworthy accounts of the status of women wage earners in

American industry, and when he became United States Commissioner of Labor he continued to explore the question. His *Fourth Annual Report* (1889), covering more than 17,000 workingwomen in twenty-two cities, offered valuable data on wages, standards of living, and sanitary provisions in factories. The New York and other state labor bureaus undertook similar studies in the eighties and nineties.

Elizabeth Stuart Phelps obtained the framework for her novel of industrial life, *The Silent Partner* (1871), from the reports of the Massachusetts Bureau of Labor Statistics. Fifteen years later, and in a more realistic spirit, Helen Campbell's *Prisoners of Poverty* (1887) exposed the precarious and ill-rewarded labor of women in New York's needle trades and department stores. Although the style was emotional, Mrs. Campbell's book was marked by a very practical concern with earnings, budgets, and health. She showed how declining piece rates unsettled standards of living, and she presented numerous case records to reveal what it meant, in terms of household economy, to try to exist on three dollars a week. In a later work she described factory employment for women as valuable only as preparation "for the hospital, the workhouse, and the prison," since the workers so often were "inoculated with trade diseases, mutilated by trade appliances, and corrupted by trade associates."[36]

Where Miss Phelps, in *The Silent Partner*, had preached moral reform to manufacturers Mrs. Campbell maintained that the pursuit of "bargains" by well-to-do shoppers forced employers to depress wages below the subsistence level. Her disclosure of the human cost of bargain-counter finery was one of the factors that inspired the formation of consumers' leagues in several cities during the 1890's. These shoppers' organizations investigated wages and working conditions in retail establishments and published white lists recommending patronage of those which met the standards of a fair house. The national organization of the Consumers' League, as will be made clear in a later chapter, was one of the most active forces in working for improved factory legislation to protect women and children and in providing the legal defense when the constitutionality of the statutes was challenged in the courts.

Fairly numerous, but not necessarily effective, legal restrictions on the employment of minors testify that the question of child labor was by no means ignored in the late nineteenth century.[37] Yet on no issue, with the possible exceptions of unemployment and industrial accidents, was factual information more difficult to obtain. Prior to 1870 the federal census did not differentiate between child and adult workers in its statistics on wage earners; thereafter the totals were broken down so as to indicate the number over and under fifteen years of age. These figures did not represent an actual count of working children, since they did not include the large group that was not technically employed but regularly "helped" parents in sweatshops and mines.[38] For obvious reasons state labor bureaus found it almost impossible to get employers to submit accurate data on the employment of young children in their establishments. Those statistics that were available in 1890, however, indicated that the wage earners under fifteen were increasing at a more rapid rate than the adult workers.[39]

Popular attitudes toward child labor may be gauged by the frequency and enthusiasm with which the heroes of magazine fiction and dime novels assumed the economic burdens of manhood at a tender age. Charles Morris, not so well known as Horatio Alger, but equally devoted to the gospel of youthful endeavor, had one of his model youths, Harry Handy, complain to his employer that he was not worked hard enough.[40] From time to time a novelist wrote of working children with compassion; Elizabeth Oakes Smith described a group of newsboys, some of them dozing, in the pit of the Bowery Theater:

> You look at them, so thin, so like little old men, sharp, eager, self-reliant when awake, and then when sleep comes and muscles relax, and the overtaxed nerve yields to inaction, they grow children again, weary, suffering, hard-wrought children they look, and you gaze at their emaciated forms, the angular shoulders peeping from the ragged shirt, the hollow temple and thin nostril, with an indescribable pang. You feel how pitiful is the childhood of the poor.[41]

For the most part, however, Americans took it for granted that poor children had to work and assumed that, within reason, it was good for them to do so.

The legislation on the subject enacted in about half the states before 1896 was consistent with this view. Ordinarily the laws applied only to manufacturing, excluded only very young children (under ten in some states, twelve or fourteen in others) from employment, and permitted older ones to work ten hours a day. It was common knowledge that statutory restrictions were frequently violated through falsification of age. Compulsory-education laws designed to keep minors out of factories and mines until they had gained at least a common school education were, in most states, so loosely drawn and laxly enforced that, according to one investigator, they were "a farce."[42]

Charles Loring Brace, founder of the Children's Aid Society, devoted one chapter of *The Dangerous Classes of New York* (1872) to "Factory Children." Brace made one of the earliest surveys of child labor when he inquired into the employment of the boys and girls attending the Society's night-school classes.[43] He was far from a doctrinaire opponent of child labor. His society presented a bill to the New York legislature in 1872 which would have authorized factory labor of children over ten years of age for a maximum of sixty hours a week. Nevertheless, Brace was one of the most important figures in the post-Civil War era in the movement for better education for working children. He feared that, unless more attention were paid to their instruction, the child laborers would swell the ranks of the dangerous classes upon reaching maturity.

Critics of child labor became more outspoken during the eighties and the nineties. Clara Potter reported on the working conditions of children in New York City for the *Christian Union*, giving special attention to industrial accidents in which youthful workers were maimed and crippled. Because of the legal fiction that they were employed at their own risk, the children almost never received damages for these injuries.[44] Clare de Graffenried, who investigated the employment of minors in a wide range of retail and manufacturing enterprises in 1889, blamed the large number of cases of tuberculosis among working girls on premature work, unsanitary factory conditions, and poor nourishment.[45] Willoughby, discussing the social aspects of child labor, commented that public opinion would be inflamed if any state subjected the children in its reformatories and poorhouses to the kind of treatment which they received as a matter of course, and without public outcry, in many factories.[46]

Both Miss de Graffenried and Willoughby argued that permitting a young child to work usually meant dooming him to a lifetime of drudgery and helpless incompetence. They believed that boys and girls who went into the factories, mines, stores, and offices when they should have been at school wore out their energies in routine and repetitive tasks without acquiring the skills that would later enable them to earn decent wages. Child laborers consequently entered maturity under such a heavy handicap of ignorance and physical debility that many could never become self-supporting.[47] Several years earlier a writer in a metropolitan newspaper had arrived at a somewhat similar conclusion regarding children employed in the street trades. "It is a popular fallacy that bootblacks and newsboys grow up to be major generals and millionaires," he observed. "The majority of them, on the contrary, become porters and barkeepers."[48]

The best-informed student of child labor in the United States during the 1890's was Florence Kelley, a resident of Hull House and chief factory inspector of the state of Illinois. Mrs. Kelley collaborated with Alzina P. Stevens on a chapter about wage-earning children for *Hull-House Maps and Papers.* Their paper was a fighting document which asserted that "it is not where labor is scarce, but where competition for work is keenest that the per cent of children is largest in the total number of employed" and that "children are found in greatest number where the conditions of labor are most dangerous to life and health."[49]

In 1896 Mrs. Kelley told the National Conference of Charities and Correction that three years of experience as a factory inspector had convinced her that regulation of child labor was impossible; the only way to end the evils connected with it was to prohibit entirely the employment of children under sixteen.[50] Like Helen Campbell, who had urged that it was as necessary to rescue children from the factories as from the slums, Mrs. Kelley denied that child labor was either desirable or necessary.[51] "Why have newsboys?" she asked. "Why not let the unemployed men sell the papers and the newsboys go to school, as our own children do?" She contended that if parents could not provide children with maintenance and education, the state should assume responsibility for their care and instruction. In this paper, read before a meeting of professional philanthropists, Mrs. Kelley recognized that manufacturers' associations, department stores, and the telegraph company (then the largest employer of child labor in the world) would oppose the abolition of child labor; she predicted, however, that the fiercest opponents of such a reform would be the self-righteous, tax-conscious philanthropists. Prophetically, in view of the history of the proposed child-labor amendment in the 1920's, she forecast that the philosophy of self-help, appeals to the stern puritan virtues, and the argument of economy would all be adduced to justify the continuance of child labor.[52]

In the nineteenth century concern with poverty was usually accompanied by hostility to liquor; conversely, concern with intemperance frequently, as in the instance of Robert Hartley, led to interest in poverty. Not always, but in a number of cases (as, for example, Frances Willard), antisaloon sentiment went hand in hand with economic radicalism. To many persons "the liquor interests" represented plutocracy in its most insolent and insidious guise.[53] The temperance crusade also drew adherents from men and women who regarded indulgence in drink as not necessarily a vice but an expensive and dangerous pastime. "What a great amount of time, and strength, and money might multitudes gain for self-improvement by strict sobriety!" exclaimed Channing. "That cheap remedy, pure water, would cure the chief evils in very many families of the ignorant and poor."[54]

Throughout the century the idea was accepted that drink was one of the most important causes, if not the sole cause, of poverty. Those who held to this point of view could point to numerous examples that seemed to prove their point. As the years went by, however, students of poverty—as opposed to the general public—assigned a less prominent role to alcohol as a factor in producing want. In the 1830's Joseph Tuckerman estimated that 75 per cent of American pauperism resulted from drink; in the 1890's, on the other hand, the charity organization societies' records consulted by Amos Warner indicated that intemperance was the cause of distress in only 5 to 22 per cent of the cases investigated by the agencies.[55] By the closing decade of the century, as noted in a previous chapter, there was a growing tendency to think intemperance as much a result as a cause of poverty.[56]

The formation in 1893 of the Committee of Fifty for the Investigation of the Liquor Problem marked the emergence of a more detached and scientific attitude toward this particular social issue than had been apparent in most earlier discussions of it. The Committee was composed of college presidents, prominent clergymen, and well-known social scientists; its announced purpose was "to secure a body of facts which may serve as a basis for intelligent public and private actions."[57] In the ten years after its organization the Committee published five books, one a summary of its work and the others dealing with the physiological, legislative, ethical, and economic aspects of the liquor question.

In gathering data for several of these volumes the Committee utilized the services of charity agents, settlement residents, and teachers and students of economics and sociology. The study of the economic phase of the problem was based on special reports submitted by thirty-three charity organization societies for each "case" handled over periods of from three to twelve months. These reports, as analyzed by the Committee's staff, revealed a higher percentage of want attributable to intemperance (25 per cent) than had been shown in Warner's study of the regular case records.[58] The significance of this finding was undermined, however, by the growing conviction among professional social workers that it was unrealistic to attempt to pick out any single factor as solely responsible for distress.

The inquiry entitled *Substitutes for the Saloon* (1901) contained information furnished the Committee by a variety of correspondents on different grades of drinking establishments in seventeen cities. This report began with a frank recognition that the saloon performed a necessary function in society: "Its hold on the community does not wholly proceed from its satisfying the thirst for drink. It satisfies the thirst for sociability."[59] As the Committee saw it, the problem was to devise other institutions capable of meeting the social needs of working people as effectively as the saloon. Laying prejudice aside, the staff of investigators sought to learn from the saloon by analyzing its nonalcoholic appeal. Altogether it was a unique and enlightening presentation which, if its message had been heeded, might have brought a more realistic spirit into the temperance movement. Present-day students can find in it a wealth of information, not only on turn-of-the-century saloons, but also on the quantity and quality of other recreational institutions then available to the public in representative cities.[60]

In the latter part of the century the tenement problem awakened much interest, partly because of the traditional regard for the home as the bulwark of society, and partly because of the supposed connection between tenements and saloons. "Foul homes" and "intoxicating drink" were the twin causes of poverty, according to Robert Treat Paine, head of the Associated Charities of Boston. He thought that each led to the other and that improvement of the homes of the poor was a necessary preliminary to the elimination of intemperance.[61] E. R. L. Gould, a statistician in the federal labor bureau, expressed similar views in *The Housing of the Working People* (1895). "Bad housing is a terribly expensive thing to any community," he warned, "for its cost is drunkenness, poverty, crime, and other forms of social decline."[62] The reporter and fiction writer, Julian Ralph, who was not entirely sympathetic in his attitude toward tenement dwellers, nevertheless remarked that frequent visits to the saloon must be expected among people who lived in quarters too cramped to encourage use for any purposes save eating and sleeping.[63] Riis pointed out that because of scant water connections it was often easier to get beer than water in the tenements. In his opinion "the scandalous scarcity of water in the hot summer" was the one most important cause of drunkenness among the poor.[64]

State and city boards of health were usually charged with the administration of such tenement laws or ordinances as were adopted prior to 1900.[65] The reports of these agencies provide the most authoritative descriptions of slum and tenement conditions during the last third of the nineteenth century. Their findings, which were rather widely publicized in magazines and newspapers of the period, showed that one of the consequences of being poor was greater than average susceptibility to illness and death. Seventy out of every one hundred deaths in New York City befell residents of the tenement houses; in some notorious rookeries, such as Gotham Court on Cherry Street, the annual death rate was almost 20 per cent—seven times as high as the average in the city as a whole.[66] The mortality rates for the children of the poor were even more shocking than those for adults. A writer in *The Christian Union* cited two New York alleys where the death rates showed that nearly three out of four infants succumbed before reaching five years of age.[67]

Allusions to the depravity of slum dwellers persisted to the end of the century; but, especially in the 1890's, this view was challenged by numerous students. In *The Housing of the Poor* (1893) Marcus T. Reynolds drew together material on the economic condition of tenement dwellers from state labor bureaus, boards of health, tenement commissions, and charity organization societies; the slum investigation conducted by the staff of the United States Commissioner of Labor in 1894 contained almost 250 pages of statistics on earnings, unemployment, and rents paid by residents of slums in four large cities; and Gould's *Housing of the Working People* examined the experience of European and American communities in providing decent low-cost housing for wage earners through public or private initiative. Factual investigations of this sort disclosed that the problem of the slum and the tenement involved the housing of productive elements, not just the dregs, of industrial society.

In itself this was hardly a startling discovery. Fifty years earlier men such as Griscom, Hartley, and Channing had made the point that the tenements were nothing less or more than the homes of the urban working class. Yet the earlier reformers, no matter how sharply they had criticized the bad, expensive, and unhealthful housing of the poor, had usually asserted that the "fault or ignorance of the sufferers" was chiefly responsible for the evils they decried; and they had assumed that the remedy lay in "the elevation of the mind and character of the laborer."[68]

This may have been a valid diagnosis of the situation in the 1840's. A half century later the problem had become much more complex; its solution impinged on all the other issues—wages, working conditions, industrial accidents, health, and unemployment—affecting the standard of living of the urban masses. Relatively little positive action had as yet been taken to rectify the ills and injustices to which tenement dwellers were exposed, but improvement in housing was nevertheless seen to be dependent on economic and legal rather than moral reform.

At the end of the nineteenth century Americans were still ignorant as to the actual extent of poverty in their midst. Only rough estimates based on limited data could be hazarded. Charity organization records, the number of evictions, and pauper burials occurring in a given period were all used as an index of want. Projecting his conclusion from such data, Jacob Riis estimated in 1892 that from 20 to 30 per cent of New York's population lived in penury.[69] Charles B. Spahr's investigation of the distribution of property and income, which indicated a narrower and narrower concentration of wealth, also implied that the number of the poor was disturbingly large.[70]

Although only slight progress had been made in determining the amount of poverty in America, much attention had been given to its causes. The trend of informed opinion was away from the individualistic interpretation of want, and the ground had been prepared for an inductive approach to the problem. There was growing acceptance of the view that no single explanation yet advanced was in itself sufficient to stand the test of facts. Amos G. Warner, a very influential figure in the development of social work in the United States, noted in 1894 that in modern society, "where the individual suffers not only from his own mistakes and defects, but also from the mistakes and defects of a large number of other people," we must expect the causes of destitution to be "indefinitely numerous and complicated."[71]

The opinion that was becoming current among social scientists here and abroad was that poverty could not be studied as a separate phenomenon, isolated from other economic and social maladjustments. Rather, as a Canadian student suggested, poverty must be scrutinized as "a part of the study of the economic life of the people as a whole."[72] This conviction brought with it an eagerness to discover "what life is and how it is now lived by the people."[73] E. B. Andrews criticized both *laissez-faire* and socialist theoreticians for being "in too great haste to generalize." The business of the present, he advised, was "the analysis of social conditions—deep, patient, and undogmatic."[74]

It was not merely disinterested curiosity that led the publicists of the eighties and nineties to tear aside the veil of ignorance and indifference that concealed the suffering of the poor from public view. Men and women such as Riis, Flower, Helen Campbell, and Florence Kelley were propagandists who hoped to alter conditions by rousing the conscience of the nation. Like the muckrakers who followed them they sincerely believed that once the "plain bald statement of facts" had been submitted to the public judgment, nothing could stand in the way of reform.

Perhaps they erred on the side of optimism. Realism in social science was no better received by the polite classes than its counterpart in literature and art. The powerful alignment of groups with a stake in the perpetuation of social wrongs did not disintegrate when its malefactions were exposed. But it was placed on the defensive. In a liberal democracy it is literally true that the first step toward the achievement of reform is the exploration of and diffusion of knowledge about the realities of the prevailing situation. By the latter part of the 1890's a start had been made toward the accumulation of social facts; after the turn of the century the study of mankind was to be carried forward with a vigor and zest that imparted a characteristic tone to the intellectual climate of the Progressive era.

CHAPTER 6

The Discovery of Poverty in Literature

There is a greater army,
That besets us round with strife,
A starving, numberless army,
At all the gates of life.

The poverty-stricken millions
Who challenge our wine and bread,
And impeach us all as traitors
Both the living and the dead.

HENRY WADSWORTH LONGFELLOW, "The Challenge" (1873).

There is more true romance in a New York tenement than there ever was in a baron's tower—braver battles, truer loves, nobler sacrifices. Romance is all about us, but we must have eyes for it.

PAUL LEICESTER FORD, *The Honorable Peter Stirling.*

SOMETHING as old and omnipresent as poverty can hardly be said to have been discovered by writers at any particular time. It is just one of the elements the storyteller weaves into his tale along with birth and love and war and death. But the emphasis and approach to want vary with the writer, the social environment in which he lives, and the audience to whom his production is directed. Thus, in countless romances, old and new, poverty figures as the difference in economic status creating a temporary barrier to the mating of otherwise marriageable couples. It is the shadow from which heroes and heroines emerge by hook or crook or chance to lives of opulence and power. Scenes of humble life are frequently introduced into stories of the rich and wellborn for comic relief, homely philosophy, tragic contrast, or social protest. Here, however, we are concerned with depictions of poverty as a permanent, chronic condition in which people live out their lives—noble, sordid, or something of both.

Such a presentation of poverty first appeared in American literature in noticeable quantity in the late 1840's. Earlier writers had sometimes advertised their intention to record "the short and simple annals of the poor" and had asserted that noble hearts might beat under mean garments. In practice, however, few of them had departed from the convention that the heroes and heroines of fiction should come exclusively from the ranks of the upper classes. When they did, it was the homely virtues of the common man, not the sufferings of the uncommonly poor, that they described.

A possible explanation for the comparative neglect of the very poor in our literature during the first part of the nineteenth century is that the misery and destitution accompanying industrialization and immigration did not become clearly apparent in this country until about mid-century. There were, however, areas of pronounced wretchedness in the larger cities at a much earlier date; and during periods of depression severe hardship was common throughout the nation. If American writers failed to reflect these matters, the reason was not that poverty and hard times were unknown, but that authors did not deem them worthy of notice in literature.[1]

This attitude was related to the fact that the creative writers, to an equal or even greater degree than students of social conditions, were believers in the philosophy of democratic individualism. Generally speaking, they were more interested in moral questions than in economic issues. Mind and character struck them as infinitely more important than material circumstances. "The man, not the condition, imports," declared the youthful Emerson in 1832.[2] Shortly after the onset of the depression of 1837 he wrote that it was easy for the "philosophic class" to be poor; the only real sufferers from poverty, he implied, were those persons who, lacking the consolation of books, conversation, and thought, depended on outward display to demonstrate their inward merit.[3] Ten years later the author of a novel about the Lowell factory girls expressed Emerson's ideas in a slightly vulgarized form. Virtue is the only basis for human distinction, said

A. I. Cummings. Without nobility of character the millionaire is poor; if possessed of those "gems of true value—the virtues," factory girls are rich as queens.[4]

The man who was most responsible for interesting American writers in poverty was Charles Dickens. He proved that powerful and popular works of art could be fashioned from the dross of human experience, showed that adventure, pathos, comedy, and romance abounded in the shabbiest walks of life, and disclosed the color and variety of incident that could be discovered in such unlikely places as "the haunts of hunger and disease," "foul and frowsy dens," and "cold, wet, shelterless midnight streets."[5] Dickens peopled his stories with waifs, paupers, criminals, and followers of lowly and sometimes disreputable occupations. For readers he opened a new and populous world where exciting adventures befell people as familiar and peculiar as one's next-door neighbors; for writers he uncovered a vein of rich and readily accessible literary material.

Dickens' influence was not confined to questions of style, plot, subject matter, and locale: he also introduced a strain of radical humanitarianism into the literary treatment of low life. "He was more truly democratic than any American who had yet written fiction," observed William Dean Howells in *My Literary Passions* (1895). Through all his work ran "the strong drift of a genuine emotion, a sympathy, deep and sincere, with the poor, the lowly, the unfortunate."[6] Dickens combined pity for the underdog with a hatred, bitter and outspoken, for all the brutal acts that degraded the poor and for all the harsh theories that justified or excused their mistreatment. He did his share of moralizing, but he was not content to bid people living in want to cultivate their minds and improve their character. Unlike the American romantics, Dickens *was* interested in the material surroundings of the poor. He described them minutely and demanded that they be bettered.[7]

In the hands of some of his American imitators, Dickens' feeling for the lowly lost its sharp edge and degenerated into sentimentality. Yet he communicated both to readers and writers certain critical attitudes that did much to stimulate interest in reform. Dickens poked fun at manufacturers who claimed they would be ruined if required to send factory children to school or to protect workmen against dangerous machinery. He ridiculed philanthropists so intent on rescuing heathens in faraway corners of the world that they could not see the misery under their noses. He told temperance advocates that the saloons would cease to be problems when the poor received other and better escapes from hunger, filth, and foul air. He reminded those indifferent to the neglect and mistreatment of children that boys and girls robbed of their childhood would not respond, as adults, to reason and persuasion; and he warned society that every slum would visit retribution upon the community that permitted breeding places of ignorance, vice, disease, and despair to exist.

Partly in imitation of Dickens, partly because they regarded the misery that was developing in the fast-growing cities as an unwelcome phenomenon in American life, the writers who dealt with urban poverty in the 1840's and 1850's emphasized the lurid and sensational aspects of the subject. The short and simple annals of the poor were first explored in cheap serialized thrillers such as George Lippard's *Quaker City* (1844) and Ned Buntline's *Mysteries and Miseries of New York* (1848). These were allegedly factual exposures of vice and crime in the big cities. Frankly directed toward a popular reading public, they were spiced with knowing descriptions of gambling dens and brothels and larded with warnings of the temptations that lured unsuspecting youths and maidens to moral and financial ruin.

Lippard, before he died in 1854 at the age of thirty-two, wrote a dozen books, including historical romances and legends of the Revolution as well as sketches of contemporary urban life. An enemy of capitalism, he organized a secret society whose members pledged themselves to work for the eradication of the social evils that produced crime and poverty. In one of his last books, which bore the title *New York: Its Upper Ten and Lower Million* (1854), he contended that "the true Word" enjoined "the establishment of the kingdom of God, *on earth*, in the physical and intellectual welfare of the greatest portion of mankind."[8] Although Lippard's works enjoyed wide popularity, they were not taken very seriously by critics. Horace Greeley refused to review, or to read, one of his novels, even though the author described it as "an earnest effort on behalf of the poor." Greeley advised Lippard that he would render the poor a greater service by raising potatoes "than by writing novels from July to Eternity."[9]

Buntline, a flashy and disreputable figure whose real name was

Edward Zane Carroll Judson, has been called "the patriarch of blood-and-thunder romancers."[10] In the course of a half century of sub-literary activity extending from the 1830's to the 1880's he produced more than two hundred action stories of the sea, the city streets, and the Wild West. *Mysteries and Miseries of New York* appeared shortly before the author was sentenced to a year in prison for his part in the Astor Place riot and about twenty years before he discovered and popularized Buffalo Bill. The plots of the several stories comprising the narrative are less interesting today than the preface and appendices of the book, in which Buntline contrasted social conditions in New York City with those of a generation earlier, surveyed the extent of destitution in the metropolis, and argued for stricter law enforcement and curbs on immigration as remedies for the evils he described.

Both Lippard's *Quaker City* and Buntline's *Mysteries and Miseries of New York* were adapted for the stage soon after their publication. It was in the theater, in fact, that the melodramatic approach to poverty, especially the representation of slums as adjuncts of the criminal or near-criminal underworld, found its abiding home. The vogue of the play dealing with the seamy side of metropolitan life has been traced back as far as 1823, when *Life in London* was first produced in New York City and Philadelphia. By the 1830's the locale had been shifted to the New World in such topical skits as *Life in Philadelphia* (1833) and *Life in New York* (1834).[11] Beginning in the late forties and continuing until after the Civil War there was an epidemic of New York plays. Benjamin A. Baker's *A Glance at New York* (1848), Dion Boucicault's *The Poor of New York* (1857), and Augustin Daly's *Under the Gas Light* (1867) were only the best known of a group of offerings that included *New York as It Is*, *Out of the Streets*, and *New York Burglars; or Wedded by Moonlight*. Baker's *A Glance at New York* detailed the experiences of a greenhorn in the slums and criminal districts of Gotham. The hero was Mose, a "fire b'hoy," the idol of the democracy not only because of his brave calling, but also because of his prowess in beating the criminal element at its own game.[12]

Most of these fugitive melodramas were concerned with the surface excitement of crime and disaster, but the titles of several—*Life's Struggles in a Great City*, *The Upper Ten and the Lower Twenty*, and *Democracy and Aristocracy, or Rich and Poor in New*

York—suggest that both playwrights and playgoers sympathized with the hard lot of the poor and deplored the sharp contrasts between wealth and poverty. The point should not be pressed too far, however. Despite their titles, a number of the plays had to do, not with the chronically poor, but with persons of means who were suddenly, and usually briefly, reduced to want by deceit or misfortune. In Boucicault's *Poor of New York*, for example, the hero was a rich young man ruined by the panic of 1857. At one point in the play all action stopped while he addressed the audience as follows:

> The poor—whom do you call the poor? Do you know them? do you see them? they are more frequently found under a black coat than under a red shirt. The poor man is a clerk with a family, forced to maintain a decent suit of clothes, paid for out of the hunger of his children. The poor man is the artist who is obliged to pledge the tools of his trade to buy medicine for his sick wife. The lawyer, who, craving for employment, buttons up his thin paletot to hide his shirtless breast. These needy wretches are poorer than the poor, for they are obliged to conceal their poverty with the false mask of content. . . . These are the most miserable of the Poor of New York.[13]

In popular fiction, as in the drama, writers often found it expedient to follow a middle course between low and high life. They set their stories amid scenes of dire poverty and exposed their characters to privation and humiliation; then, as the plots unfolded, they revealed that the protagonists had somehow become separated from wealthy parents or otherwise deprived of their rightful inheritances. The heroes and heroines were really gentlemen and ladies, but it required complicated and lengthy maneuverings to prove the fact. Meanwhile, Oliver or Gertrude suffered—all the more exquisitely because made of finer clay than the multitude. This formula guaranteed both tears and a happy ending. Dickens used it, and so did a host of his American followers.[14]

Heroes drawn from the ranks of the people, like Mose the fireman, were nevertheless elbowing their way on to the stage and into the pages of novels. In *The Newsboy* (1854) Elizabeth Oakes Smith, wife of the Yankee humorist Seba Smith, made no pretense that Bob, the key figure of her story, was anything but a homeless orphan, entirely on his own. She liked him for what he was, a self-reliant boy, "all real . . . nature down to his heels."[15] Her sympathy went out to boys such as Bob, but they did not impress her, as they did

Charles Loring Brace, as potential members of the dangerous classes. To prove how far they were from being pauperized, she told of one little fellow who, on being asked if his feet were not cold, replied: "What in hell is that to you?"

At mid-century writers such as Mrs. Smith, who possessed strong democratic inclinations, honestly admired the self-made man, and they were much less critical of social and economic conditions than their successors were to be a generation later. In *Song of Myself* (1855) Whitman announced his identification with "what is commonest, cheapest, nearest, easiest"; judging by the long list of occupations and conditions of life out of which he said his song was woven, however, Whitman associated himself most closely with the active and prosperous doers and builders, the strong-muscled carpenters, blacksmiths, drovers, and farmers. There was no hint of exploitation in his description of a file of laborers carrying hods. Each man in the line was apparently destined to rise into the ranks of skilled tradesmen. When he wrote of the "Yankee girl . . . with her sewing machine or in the factory or mill," it was her clean hair that attracted his notice, not her hours or wages.

To the extent that it was expressed in the literature of the period, social criticism emanated more often from spokesmen of the conservative classes than from champions of the common man. It was Melville's Redburn, carefully identified as a "gentleman's son," who asked himself, after viewing the slums of Liverpool: "What right had any body in the wide world to smile and be glad when sights like this were to be seen?"[16] It was proslavery Southerners, such as William J. Grayson, author of *The Hireling and the Slave* (1855), who most frequently attacked the inhumanities of the factory system. And it was James Russell Lowell, heir to the New England patrician tradition, who, in "A Parable" (1848), raised the objection to the materialistic tendencies of capitalism which nearly all later critics would repeat.

Lowell's poem described Christ's return to earth. Although greeted with honor and displays of wealth, the Saviour heard bitter groans wherever He went.

> And in church, and palace, and judgment-hall,
> He marked great fissures that rent the wall,

And opened wider and yet more wide
As the living foundation heaved and sighed.

Accusingly, Jesus asked men:

"Have ye founded your thrones and altars, then,
On the bodies and souls of living men?
And think ye that building shall endure,
Which shelters the noble and crushes the poor?"

"The chief priests and rulers" denied any guilt. They had built as their fathers built, and their only concerns were to hold the earth forever the same and to keep His images "sovereign and sole" throughout the land.

Then Christ sought out an artisan,
A low-browed, stunted, haggard man,
And a motherless girl whose fingers thin
Crushed from her faintly want and sin.

These set he in the midst of them,
And as they drew back their garment hem
For fear of defilement, "Lo, here," said he,
"The images ye have made of me."[17]

Forty-five years after its publication "A Parable" gave William T. Stead the idea for *If Christ Came to Chicago* (1894). Still later it was quoted with approval by Jack London in *The People of the Abyss* (1903).[18] Lowell's position, however, was quite different from that of some of the admirers of his poem. He was moved less by fellow feeling for the "low-browed, stunted" artisan than by contempt for "the chief priests and rulers," the money worshipers whose religion and law were profit. Not because he believed in the equality of men, but because he recognized their inequality, Lowell thought that the able and the strong were duty bound to conduct themselves toward the less fortunate in a decent and responsible manner. The rich and the powerful were false to their trust when they used their superior strength to enslave and destroy Wealth and authority were corrupt unless employed positively and beneficently in the interests of mankind.[19]

As industrialism waxed during and after the Civil War a fairly numerous group of writers examined the effect of economic hardship and industrial oppression on society. They exposed the horrors of mill towns and called on the upper and middle classes to take the lead in remedying evils that threatened to produce social disintegration or provoke social upheaval. One of the earliest of this didactic school was Rebecca Harding Davis, mother of the famous reporter. In *A Story of To-Day*, serialized in *The Atlantic Monthly* in 1861 and 1862, she asked her readers to dig into the commonplace, vulgar American life, look at the so-called dregs of society, and see if they did not agree with her that this life had "a new and awful significance." To a nation whose major attention was already fastening on the battlefields of the Civil War she counseled: "Go down into this common everyday drudgery and consider if there might not be in it also a great warfare."[20] What she saw was

> the slow stream of human life creeping past, night and morning, to the great mills. Masses of men, with dull, besotted faces bent to the ground, sharpened here or there by pain or cunning; skin and muscle and flesh begrimed with smoke and ashes; stooping all night over boiling cauldrons of metal, laired by day in dens of drunkenness and infamy; breathing from infancy to death an air saturated with fog and grease and soot, vileness for soul and body.[21]

Mrs. Davis described a textile mill in which most of the operatives and some of the office help were women. In those establishments, she observed, women could perform any job except that of overseer—they were "too hard with the hands for that." She was no less critical of the men in the plant, describing the laborers on the loading dock as "red faced and pale, whiskey-bloated and heavy-brained, . . . with souls half asleep somewhere, and the destiny of a nation in their grasp. . . ."[22]

Elizabeth Stuart Phelps, daughter of the president of Andover Theological Seminary and author of several popular novels, usually with a religious tinge, wrote at least one book and a well-known short story dealing with labor problems. "The Tenth of January" (1868) was a fictionized account of the collapse and burning of a Lawrence textile mill in 1860—a disaster that cost the lives of nearly ninety employees. The story opened quietly enough, but then the author made this startling observation:

> Of the twenty-five thousand souls who inhabit that city, ten thousand are prisoners—prisoners of factories perhaps the most healthfully, considerately and generously conducted of any in this country, but factories just the same. Dust, whir, crash, clang; dizziness, peril, exhaustion, discontent—that is what the word means taken at its best.

> Of these ten thousand two-thirds are girls: voluntary captives, indeed; but what is the practical difference? It is an old story—that of going to jail for want of bread.[23]

Her novel *The Silent Partner* (1871) presented a more detailed picture of working conditions in the mills. William Cullen Bryant, who touched on some of the same problems in his long poem *The Song of the Sower* (1871), suggested somewhat vaguely, and in allegorical terms, that the solution lay in a more equitable distribution of the world's goods. Miss Phelps, however, like most of the other writers of the day, was of the opinion that the only cure for industrial ills was an increase in benevolence and piety on the part of employers.[24]

In "The Symphony" (1875) Sidney Lanier exclaimed:

> Look up the land, look down the land—
> The poor, the poor, the poor, they stand
> Wedged by the pressing of trade's hand
> Against an inward opening door
> That pressure tightens evermore. . . .

Lanier, who once likened the Civil War to a tournament, despised industrialism as only a countryman, poet, musician, moralist, cavalier, and Southern patriot, all rolled into one, could despise it. In some respects his poem harked back to earlier Southern attacks on wage slavery, but it anticipated Markham's "The Man with the Hoe" and Vachel Lindsay's "The Leaden-Eyed" by many years in comparing the plight of the poor to that of beasts:

> "Each day, all day" (these poor folks say),
> "In the same old year-long drear-long way,
> We weave in the mills and heave in the kilns,
> We sieve mine-meshes under the hills, . . .
> The beasts, they hunger and eat and die;
> And so do we, and the world's a sty."[25]

With the exception of Lanier, who wrote from an agrarian rather than a proletarian point of view, few writers of the seventies and early eighties expressed open hostility to capitalism. Although kindly disposed to the poor, they identified themselves and their interests with the well-to-do. They were frightened by the estrangement of classes that was dividing society into hostile and unfeeling camps. The lesson they sought to impart was the need for mutual understanding and sympathy on the part of labor and capital or, as they would have said, the rich and the poor, to knit together the dangerous rent in the social fabric. Believing that the comfortable classes, although currently the more powerful, were potentially the more vulnerable, they felt it was incumbent upon the rich to acquaint themselves with the discontent of the poor and to do what they could to alleviate it.

This attitude was well expressed by George T. Dowling in *The Wreckers* (1886), a novel that combined the elements of a Sunday-school lesson and a detective story. The Dickensian plot involved a lost child adopted, after her cup of sorrow had been filled almost to the brim, by a good and very wealthy family. The story did not end at this point, however. There were a bank robbery, a murder, and a murder trial yet to come, and also sufficient discussion of industrial issues to justify the book's subtitle, *A Social Study*. Nevertheless, the author maintained that his theme was "the dignity of the commonplace." After all, he said, Jesus was "only a poor peasant." The wreckers referred to in the title were "the intentionally vicious" (a wicked foreigner), "the systematically tyrannical" (a harsh employer), "the thoughtlessly frivolous" (an idle society woman), and "those who lie to, frighten, and mistreat children." The author's philosophy was stated by one character:

> "That there's bad people among the rich I don't doubt, just as there is among the poor. But it ain't riches or poverty that makes 'em bad; it's the kind o' heart they've got inside of 'em."

"God help us all deal tenderly with one another while we may," he concluded. "Soon we shall lie down together in the dust, and it will all be over."[26]

In the mid-century melodramas the novelty of urban poverty constituted its chief claim to dramatic interest. The slums appealed to dramatists and audiences alike as fitting backdrops for crime and violence. By a generation later the slum and its denizens had become sufficiently well established to permit Edward Harrigan to write and produce a long series of popular comedies based on the recognizable types and situations of New York low life. A native New Yorker and graduate of the variety halls, Harrigan delighted in the color and variety of everyday life among the poorer classes of the city. He amused theatergoers of the late seventies and eighties by showing them the familiar rather than the sensational aspects of slum life; his plots, he said, described occurrences that were "simple and natural—just like what happens around us every day."[27]

Frankly acknowledging his interest in the box office, Harrigan defended his preoccupation with the lower orders of society on both economic and artistic grounds:

> It may be that I have struck a new idea in confining my work to the daily life of the common people. Why some other playwright does not try the same experiment, I cannot say. Their trials and troubles, hopes and fears, joys and sorrows are more varied and more numerous than those of the Upper Ten. Whoever puts them on the stage appeals to an audience of a million. . . . And human nature is very much the same the world over. It thins out and loses all strength and flavor under the pressure of riches and luxury. It is most virile and aggressive among those who know only poverty and ignorance. It is also then the most humorous and odd.[28]

His plays—musical comedies really, with music by his father-in-law, Dave Braham—were rowdy and rollicking sketches of political rivalries, social climbing, antagonisms, and alliances among the tenement population.

Harrigan did not ignore the discomforts under which his characters lived. Like the people he wrote about, however, he made the best of things as they were, whenever possible turning hardships into a joke. One of his songs, "Mulberry Springs," began with the observation that when the rich went to Saratoga, Long Branch, or Newport the poor also repaired to summer resorts—the roofs and fire escapes of tenements.

> The heat is intense, and the crowd is
> immense, all praying and whistling for wings,
> To get up and fly to the clouds in the
> sky, the boarders at Mulberry Springs.[29]

The chorus of "McNally's Row of Flats" ran:

> Ireland and Italy, Jerusalem and Germany,
> Chinamen and Nagurs, and a paradise for cats
> Jumbled up together in snow or rainy weather,
> They represent the tenants in McNally's row of flats.

One verse bluntly described the misery of the tenants:

> Bags of rags and papers, tramps and other slapers,
> Italian lazzaronies, with lots of other rats,

Laying on the benches and dying there by inches
From the open ventilation in McNally's row of flats.[30]

But cheery hospitality was the rule in "Maggie Murphy's Home" (1890):

Behind a grammar schoolhouse,
In a double tenement,
I live with my old mother,
And always pay the rent.
A bedroom and a parlor
Is all we call our own,
And you're welcome every evening
At Maggie Murphy's home.[31]

Irish-American, Negro, and German and Italian immigrant types were Harrigan's stock in trade. In the old tradition of comedy he sought to create typical representatives of a class or group, rather than individual personalities. Within this limitation he strove to make his characterizations authentic, not only in external details of costume and make-up, but also in the more difficult matter of "vices and virtues, habits and customs." As painstaking in setting his stage as in limning his characters, Harrigan copied the barroom scene in the *Mulligan* series from a saloon on Roosevelt Street and modeled the dive in *Waddy Googan* after an establishment near the Bowery. His aim, he asserted, was to make each of his plays "a series of photographs of life today in the empire city."[32]

Contemporary literary figures watched Harrigan's work with keen interest. Brander Matthews, devoted student of the French theater, proudly took the great Coquelin to see Harrigan in *Waddy Googan* in 1888.[33] Howells hailed his productions as part of "the great tendency toward the faithful representation of life which is now animating fiction"; and Hamlin Garland, writing in 1894, looked on Harrigan as the precursor of a school of urban local colorists who would describe city life closely and sympathetically, but in a matter-of-fact spirit, without consciously striving for the picturesque.[34]

The picturesque, however, was precisely the quality of Harrigan's subject matter that most appealed to many of his admirers; and it was in search of the picturesque, the quaint, the droll, and the oddly touching that writers of fiction began to explore the slums. The first and most enthusiastic of literary slummers was H. C.

Bunner, editor of *Puck* from 1878 to 1896. As early as 1878 he penned a triolet about a pitcher of mignonette in a tenement window; later, in "The Love Letters of Smith" (1890), he wrote with affectionate humor of the silent and ungrammatical courtship of "the little seamstress" who lived "in the story over the top story of the great brick tenement house." From his office window Bunner watched the daily routine of tenement dwellers, finding in their comings and goings and brief diversions the material for a charming essay.[35] He called himself "an ardent collector of slums" and thought Mulberry Bend "the most picturesque and interesting" one he had ever seen. Color was its strong point, he decided, for every tint and hue was represented in the clothes, foodstuffs, and candy displayed in the stalls along the street. There were shades to set your teeth on edge, "pure arsenical tones," greens that nature could not invent, and a profusion of reds and yellows so bright that "you could warm your hands" on them.[36]

In his discussion of the urban local color movement Garland had declared: "The novel of the slums must be written by one who has played there as a child. . . . It cannot be done from above nor from the outside."[37] In practice, few if any of the writers then invading the slums in search of local color were native to the region. Bunner had spent his boyhood in a moderately prosperous environment; his friend and colleague in putting New York on the literary map, Brander Matthews, was the son of a millionaire, as much at home in Paris or London as New York. Nevertheless, Matthews had a genuine feeling for the city, and in "Before the Break of Day" (1894) he offered a delightful vignette (his own word) of East Side life. He could describe the locale expertly:

> She lived in a little wooden house on the corner of the street huddled in the shadow of two towering tenements. There are a few frail buildings of this sort still left in that part of the city, half a mile east of the Bowery and a mile south of Tompkins Square, where the architecture is as irregular, as crowded, and as little cared for as the population.[38]

The people, however, were beyond his ken. An author who might have been Matthews himself figured in one of his sketches. This man asked a settlement worker to escort him around the slums and help him meet some poor people. "I can describe a first night at the theater or a panic in the street," he explained, "but I've pretty nearly exhausted the people I know, and I thought I would come down here and get introduced to a set I didn't know."[39]

Newspapermen, regardless of family background, had less reason than Matthews' novelist to complain of lack of familiarity with the people of the slums. Their assignments acquainted them with the strange accidents and odd deaths that so often befell inhabitants of the picturesque districts of the large cities. Reporting murders, fires, accidents, fights, and trials was all part of the day's or night's work for them. So, too, was attending political rallies, excursions, weddings, wakes, funerals, and evictions. For many aspiring authors journalism was an education in itself, not the least part of which was the experience it afforded to write about actual people in real situations. Yet in the nineties the newspapermen who wrote fiction had little opportunity to use their professional experience. To be more exact, they received little encouragement in the form of acceptances if they wrote about the slums in a truthful vein. Business is business, said magazine editors; stories are stories—fiction, not fact.

"Avoid offense" was the watchword of the quality magazines, a policy that James L. Ford, onetime editor of the weekly *Truth*, called "better for the counting room than for the making of good literature."[40] For a long time "Avoid offense" was almost synonymous with "Reject low life." So scrupulously was this rule observed that Ford once speculated whether Dickens could have sold *Oliver Twist* to *Century* or *Scribner's*.[41] "What a rush of literary boomers there would be to this new Oklahoma should this old barrier be torn down!" he exclaimed in 1894.[42]

Even as Ford wrote the rush was under way. The old barriers of prejudice against low life in fiction had been, not torn down, but breached at several points. The picturesqueness of the slums had proved as irresistible to editors and readers as to writers. Heroes and heroines were now permitted, even encouraged, to live in tenement houses, but they were required to hide their poverty behind a sunny smile and to avoid unnecessary references to it. Although the stories might occasionally be sad, the shadow of adverse circumstances must never be allowed to darken the glow of loving hearts. Low life, in other words, was acceptable provided it was not presented in a low or vulgar way. Whether happy or sad, the picture must always be pretty.

"Good bad stuff" was Ford's name for the intentionally false treatment of low life that found favor with editors and presumably with the reading public. This species of fiction was usually written in an arch style, and it nearly always adhered to certain conventions. One of these was that the people in the tenements were not really poor. The hero of Bunner's "Love Letters of Smith" received good wages; he lived where he did because it was cheap and he was saving money to return to Maine and buy an interest in a shipbuilding business. The seventeen-year-old Elsa in Julian Ralph's "Love in the Big Barracks" (1896) shared a four-room flat with six other members of her family and a lodger, but this inconvenience received less attention than Elsa's quaint superstitions and her touching love for Yank.[43] In another story of tenement folk Ralph reassured his readers that

> . . . they are not so poor as most of us think! Many are not poor at all; many are poor only as they make themselves so. As a rule, each family includes several wage-earners, worth to the common treasury five dollars a week apiece. The rent of each flat is little; the cost of food is less than most of us would believe possible, for these people only eat to live. There is plenty of money for dress, cheap life insurance, father-land societies, for charity to organ grinders and beggars, for the church, funerals, festivals—and beer.[44]

If beggars appeared in the stories they were invariably frauds, and the heroes dealt with them accordingly. The admirable Smith in Bunner's tale collared two of them and kicked them "with deliberate, ponderous, alternate kicks, until they writhed in ineffable agony." This performance put color in the little seamstress' wan cheeks and made her look very pretty.[45] Richard Harding Davis' aristocratic Van Bibber, who lived in style on inherited wealth, treated a panhandler with equal but more refined cruelty.[46]

In "good bad stuff" child laborers were bright-eyed, keen-witted, and heroic. The newspaper office boy in Davis' "Gallegher" (1891) worked until two o'clock every morning; he did not get home until four and sometimes not at all. If he had ever attended school the experience had left no mark on him.

> He could not tell you who the Pilgrim Fathers were, nor could he name the thirteen original States, but he knew all the officers of the twenty-second police district by name, and he could distinguish the clang of a fire engine's gong from that of a patrol-wagon or an ambulance fully two blocks distant.[47]

All Gallegher knew he had learned on the street. This apparently included pickpocketing; for it was through this art, no less than by his courage and endurance, that the boy was able to beat the town with a sensational scoop. Where was Gallegher at the end of the story? Sitting on the managing editor's lap with his head resting comfortably on the older man's shoulder.

The popular delineations of low life frequently showed criminals in a surprisingly sympathetic light. The authors' intention, of course, was not to glorify crime but to prettify it. Human nature, rather than criminal psychology, was what interested them, and they liked to demonstrate that there was good in nearly everybody. In "The Trailer for Room No. 8" Davis wrote of another child worker, Snipes, a vagrant employed as a spy by a crook. Such was the honor among thieves, Davis implied, that the brave little lad, out of loyalty to the gang, rejected an offer of a good home with a kindly farm family. Rags in Davis' "My Disreputable Friend, Mr. Raegan" might have been Snipes grown up. This tough, having killed an old enemy, escaped from the police and took refuge in a tenement house. He was safe as long as he stayed there. But in the house he found an abandoned baby. The baby was hungry and weak, growing weaker every minute. The disreputable Raegan proved his essential goodness by giving himself up to the police in order to save the baby's life.

It would have been strange indeed if the literature of a period marked by industrial and agricultural depression, political ferment, and serious labor unrest had been characterized only by romanticized versions of poverty. Edward Bellamy and Howells, unlike some of their colleagues who made lightheartedness a profession, did not seek to minimize the ugliness and suffering caused by poverty. Rather they sought, to the best of their abilities, to convey to readers their own conviction that no issue was more important than the eradication of needless want. Had everyone been poor, poverty might not have struck them as a serious matter; what distressed them was the glaring contrast between luxury and misery, the seeming heedlessness of the fortunate toward the unfortunate, and the utter hopelessness of fundamental improvement under competitive conditions. Julian West, the narrator of Bellamy's *Looking Backward* (1888), was shocked by the differences in dress and circumstance of persons who brushed against one another on the sidewalk in nineteenth-century Boston. The teeming hovels of the slums lay so near the mansions of the rich that West was surprised that the other guests at a fashionable dinner party were not disturbed by the grievous voices of the poor. The guests were used to the sound; it was the accompaniment to their every banquet; they indicted their society by assuming that the noise was natural.

In Howells' novel of the economic chance world, *A Hazard of New Fortunes* (1890), Basil March and his wife were accosted by a bum. Instead of kicking or making sport of him, as Smith or Van Bibber would have done, March gave him a coin. When his wife suggested that the man might have been an impostor, March (and through him, Howells) replied:

> Oh, I don't say he was an impostor. Perhaps he really was hungry; but if he wasn't, what do you think of a civilization that makes the opportunity for such a fraud? that gives us all such a bad conscience for the need which is, that we weaken to the need which isn't? Suppose that poor fellow wasn't personally founded on fact; nevertheless, he represented the truth. . . .[48]

Mr. Homos, the enlightened visitor in *A Traveller from Altruria* (1894), was another of Howells' spokesmen. He recalled stokers in the depths of steamships who "fed the fires with their lives," of mines that were the source of wealth and the graves of men, and of so-called labor-saving machines that were really monsters wasting men and devouring women and children.[49] In a poem entitled "Society" (1895) Howells compared the social order to "a splendid pageantry of beautiful women and lordly men" dancing and cavorting on flowers that barely covered the bleeding faces and mangled bodies of the poor.

> And now and then from out the dreadful floor
> An arm or brow was lifted from the rest,
> As if to strike in madness, or implore
> For mercy; and anon some suffering breast
> Heaved from the mass and sank; and as before
> The revellers above them thronged and prest.[50]

Here again was "the living foundation" of which Lowell had written in "A Parable," supporting now, not thrones and altars, but a dancing floor.

It was quite impossible for men afflicted with such troubled social consciences to find anything picturesque in the cheerless life of hard-working impoverished people. The Main-Travelled Roads that Garland wrote about (1891) had "a dull little town at one end and a home of toil at the other." One of his characters who had been fortunate enough to escape from this dreary environment felt his heart sink when he revisited the scenes of his boyhood. The typical farm home was "a grim and horrible shed," "a bare, blank, cold, drab-colored shelter from the rain," and farm life itself seemed chiefly characterized by "sordidness, dullness, triviality, and . . . endless drudgeries."[51]

As for the local color of the city slums, it impressed these writers as a dark and ugly hue. Howells admitted that at first glance a row of tenements, decorated with the iron balconies of fire escapes and festooned with lines of clothes fluttering like banners, might appear to possess "a false air of gaiety." In a picture or from a distance it might be very effective.

> But to be in it, and not have the distance, is to inhale the stenches of the neglected street, and to catch the yet fouler and dreadfuller poverty-smell which breathes from the open doorways. It is to see the children quarrelling in their games, and beating each other in the face, and rolling each other in the gutter, like the little savage outlaws they are. It is to see the work-worn look of mothers, the squalor of the babes, the haggish ugliness of the old women, the slovenly frowziness of the young girls.[52]

Certainly there was nothing quaint or humorous, nothing at all exciting in Stephen Crane's description of a night spent in a seven-cent lodginghouse on the Bowery. The mingled stenches of a hundred men's breaths and bodies, their fitful tossing, and their coughs, snores, and other night noises made the venture just what Crane called it, "An Experiment in Misery." It had nothing to attract the reader—except truthfulness to reality.

Those writers who admitted that poverty, whether urban or rural, was in fact very offensive in aspect did not therefore reject it as the stuff of literature. But they did reject the light touch, the spurious felicity and optimism of the fabricators of popular fiction. "Life's a failure for ninety-nine per cent of us," cried a farmer in one of Garland's stories. Of an old woman in the same story Garland wrote: "There was sorrow, resignation, and a sort of dumb despair in her attitude."[53] Charles Dudley Warner introduced a seamstress into his problem novel, *The Golden House* (1894); this woman lived in a tenement house, but she had no time to exchange love notes with her neighbor. She was busy finishing pants at five cents a pair from six in the morning until midnight.[54] Edward W. Townsend, who appreciated the lively colors of Mulberry Bend as much as Bunner, sketched a very somber picture of nearby Baxter Street, where the sweatshop workers lived:

> The people, from the youngest to the oldest, were speechless and grave and hopeless-looking. Men staggered past, their bodies bent almost double under what seemed impossible loads of clothing they were carrying to and from the sweaters' and the workshop-homes; women carrying similar bundles on their heads, or perhaps a bundle of wood from some builder's waste, not speaking to those they passed; none of the children seen was much more than a baby in years, and they were silent, too, and had no games: they were in the street because while the sweaters' work went on there was no room for them in their homes. In the dress of none was any bright color, and the only sounds were the occasional cry of a hurt child, the snarling of the low-browed men who solicited trade for the clothing stores, quarrelling for the possession of a chance victim; and always, as the grinding ocean surf mutters an accompaniment to all other shore sounds—always, always, always!—was heard the whirring monotone of the sewing-machine.[55]

On the copy of *Maggie* that he sent to a clergyman Crane wrote that the book tried "to show that environment is a tremendous thing in this world, and often shapes lives regardlessly."[56] In the story, however, Crane depicted Maggie as a victim rather than as a product of her environment. The locale was Rum Alley, a far more sordid slum than Baxter Street, not unlike some of the areas Jacob Riis photographed in the late eighties, and strikingly similar to the Ash Can Alley that Lincoln Steffens used in his brief and brutal sketch, "Extermination" (1897).[57] There were no pitchers of mignonette on the windowsills here—only empty bottles to throw at the cats. The inhabitants, although not necessarily criminal, were mean and vicious and scornful. They saved their pity and indulgence for themselves. In such a place and among such people weakness was an invitation to attack. Had Maggie been hard and calculating she might have adjusted to her surroundings as readily as her parents and neighbors. But as far as we can tell from the rather thin characterization of her provided by Crane, Maggie had defied all the rules by growing up to be a decent, gentle girl. The very qualities that might have brought her happiness in a different sphere were her undoing in the neighborhood of Rum Alley and Devil's Row, for the slum would not tolerate such a deviation from the norm. Like Lenny, the crazy boy in Steffens' "Extermination," Maggie was unfit to survive in a bestial habitat; when the pack turned on her, the river was her only escape.

If Maggie and Lenny were victims of their environment, the neighbors who hounded and tormented them were the natural products of it. The behavior of the slum folk was not abnormal, but only what was to be expected of the people at the bottom of the pile in a brute struggle for existence and advantage. They were the debased end product of an inefficient economy that gave no thought to human needs, the logical results of a society that was as much and as profitlessly in love with gold as Trina in Frank Norris' *McTeague* (1899). And they were not much more cruel or coarse than persons in more fortunate circumstances; for nowhere, as things were (the writers implied), was the social environment amenable to decent and humane conduct. From bleak prairie farm to urban tenement the story was the same: the whole people squeezed and twisted out of shape by monstrous economic forces and suffering from a fearful insecurity that made all selfish and unfeeling. We were making wealth; but what kind of human beings were we producing in the process?

Edwin Markham offered an answer to the question in "The Man with the Hoe," an answer essentially the same as the one suggested much earlier by Lowell, Lanier, and Rebecca Harding Davis. Markham's poem, however, was inspired by Millet's painting of a work-sodden peasant, a universal rather than a national figure, and one representing, so Markham thought, "the slow but awful degradation of man through endless, hopeless, and joyless labor."[58] As Markham saw him, the Man was "a thing that grieves not and never hopes," "a brother to the ox"; his brow was slanted back, his jaw brutal. There was "the emptiness of ages on his face"; all intelligence had been extinguished in his brain; and he was "dead to rapture and despair." He was a "dread shape," and the fact of his existence was "a protest that is also prophecy."

> O masters, lords and rulers in all lands,
> Is this the handiwork you give to God,
> This monstrous thing distorted and soul-quencht?
> How will you ever straighten up this shape;
> Touch it again with immortality;

Give back the upward looking and the light;
Rebuild in it the music and the dream;
Make right the immemorial infamies,
Perfidious wrongs, immedicable woes?

O masters, lords and rulers in all lands,
How will the future reckon with this Man?
How answer his brute question in that hour
When whirlwinds of rebellion shake all shores?
How will it be with kingdoms and with kings—
With those who shaped him to the thing he is—
When this dumb Terror shall rise to judge the world,
After the silence of the centuries?

First printed in the *San Francisco Examiner* in January, 1899, the poem "flew eastward across the continent like a contagion." Temporarily Markham's pathetic yet terrifying monster took precedence over sporting events and crime in the daily press. It was the subject of countless editorials and of innumerable letters to editors; clergymen discussed it in their sermons; college students debated its message, lecturers analyzed it, and William Jennings Bryan contributed an exegesis to a Hearst paper.[59]

"The Hoe-man," as the newspapers dubbed Markham's toiler, smote the conscience of the nation. In Garland's words, the cry of the age became "What shall I do to be just? . . . My heart is aflame to be right."[60] All through the next decade "The Man with the Hoe" was to quicken the pulse of humanitarian reformers. It was one of the literary influences that, together with the gradual accumulation of sociological data on the condition of the poor, challenged the complacent assumption that things were bound to work out all right in the long run because human nature was the same at every level. Human nature may be the same, said Garland, Markham, and other writers and reformers, but conditions are not, and we must face the fact that personality and citizenship may retrograde under the pressure of extraordinary circumstances. We can put our trust in long-suffering human nature, they said, only when we provide for it a social environment conducive to the development of mankind's nobler rather than its baser qualities.

CHAPTER 7

The Poverty Theme in Art and Illustration

AMERICAN subjects are well enough, but hard to find you know—hard to find," remarked an impecunious young artist in Stephen Crane's novel *The Third Violet* (1897). He was pretending to be a fashionable painter showing off his wares at a smart studio tea. Here was a pretty little thing, a peasant woman in sabots; over there, a sketch of an Arab squatting in a doorway; and next to it a delightful study of a gondolier leaning on his oar. "Morocco, Venice, Brittany, Holland—all oblige with color, you know—quaint form—all that," the impersonator continued. "We are so hideously modern over here; and, besides, nobody has painted us much. How the devil can I paint America when nobody has done it before me?"[1]

This attitude was common among artists in the 1890's, but it had not always been so, for there was a long tradition of interest in the native scene in American art. Fifty years earlier painting America had been a flourishing enterprise, and representations of the homely incidents and occupations of everyday life rivaled portraits and landscapes in popularity. The painters of the 1840's and 1850's had usually chosen to depict the pleasanter aspects of the American scene, but they had not complained of a dearth of subjects, nor had they scorned to record the characteristic experiences and emotions of ordinary people. By the final decades of the century, however, both the artists and the nation had changed. The painters who then dominated the field had been trained in the best European schools. Devoted to beauty, conscious and proud of the dignity of their high calling, interested in technique and in displays of virtuosity, they found the average American environment distressingly ugly.

In fact, it very often *was* ugly. Water fronts that had been picturesque in the days of sailing ships seemed prosaic in an era of steam and steel. Cities, towns, and villages whose individual peculiarities had once bestowed on them a kind of awkward charm were giving way to raw industrial agglomerations differing from one another, according to Lord Bryce, only in that some were built more with brick than wood, others more with wood than brick. Fanatical Greenbackers, hard-bitten Prohibitionists, and gaunt Populists lent themselves to caricature more readily than to the sympathetic treatment painters of genre had given farmers forty years earlier. The immigrants who worked in the steel plants were a far cry from the village blacksmiths; their sisters in the box factories did not look or behave like the young girls who answered the morning bell at a mill in one of Winslow Homer's early canvases. A certain geniality had gone out of American life, or at least seemed to be fast disappearing. It was hard for men whose business was conceded to be the fabrication of things of beauty to find their inspiration in the commonplaces of American experience.

If the artists were becoming more sophisticated, so were their patrons. Ironically enough, as American life became progressively uglier, public sensibilities became more refined. Year by year the number of the wealthy, the cultured, and the educated increased until gentility was so firmly enshrined as a national virtue that, as someone said, to cause a blush was deemed more reprehensible than to break a heart. There was no lack of interest in art. Museums, home-study courses, libraries, and magazines assiduously spread the gospel of good taste. Inevitably these institutions gave the impression that art was what pleased the eye of the initiated. Of course it was remote from everyday life, like literature and religion, an escape from mundane affairs.

Toward the end of the nineties Henry B. Fuller observed that American taste seemed to be composed of alternate layers of slush and grit—sometimes one was exposed, sometimes the other.[2] At the moment, as for several decades before, the layer of slush was on top. When not engaged in painting portraits of the fashionable or decorating public buildings with allegorical murals, artists sought to satisfy the demand for charm and beauty with idyllic landscapes and representations of mythological, historical, or literary events and personages. The huge panoramas popular some years previously, in which "one could see every spectacular feature for miles and at the same time count every leaf," had been supplanted by smaller and daintier scenes of gardens, graveyards, and bazaars.[3] Pastoral subjects, however, remained so much in vogue that one aspiring art critic concluded that familiarity with the different breeds of livestock was essential to success in the profession.[4]

Figure painting had come to mean a discreetly draped maiden posed in a treetop ("Spring"), or firmly planted on a haystack ("Autumn").[5] It was the era of "ideal heads," an art form greatly admired by Trina in *McTeague*. Norris, a former art student, described these as pictures of "lovely girls with flowing straw-colored hair and immense upturned eyes." They were invariably given names such as "Reverie," "An Idyll," or "Dreams of Love."[6] Painters of genre had ceased to pretend that their works offered truthful glimpses of actual life. Instead, they used their brushes and paints to tell stories. The point of the anecdote was usually obvious, but to make absolutely certain that no viewer was left in the dark, the title explained what the picture said. Thus under a picture of a little boy wearing oversize spectacles and pulling on an enormous pipe, large black letters spelled out the message, "I'm Grandpa."[7]

One of the most successful painters of the day was John George Brown, a former prize fighter who was reputed to be William Jennings Bryan's favorite artist. He had perfected a sure-fire formula for his innumerable renderings of newsboys and bootblacks: ideally pretty faces combined with photographically exact representations of tools and clothes. "Sympathy," for example, showed a mongrel dog comforting a pensive bootblack; the boy's brushes and polish were spread out in front of his copper-toed shoes and the sagging stockings on his sturdy legs sported a prominent hole.[8] From the sale of originals and reproductions of such "good bad stuff" Brown derived an income of around $40,000 a year.

Oddly enough, the age of Brown was also the era of America's most truthful and independent artists, Winslow Homer and Thomas Eakins. Homer began his career as an illustrator, an occupation he followed for nearly fifteen years after he began to paint. As a young man he drew street scenes in Boston and New York for the pictorial magazines, and in 1859 contributed a Christmas drawing to *Harper's Weekly* in which he contrasted the celebration of the holiday season on Fifth Avenue with its observance among the poor Irish squatters of Shantytown.[9] Later he drew a factory girl at her loom to illustrate a passage in Bryant's *The Song of the Sower*. But neither the slum nor the factory was his sphere; both as illustrator and painter Homer preferred to depict rural or outdoor scenes and healthy, vigorous people. The latter, whatever their other problems, do not give the impression of being troubled by financial worries. Homer's distinction, as Henry James acutely but somewhat ruefully observed in 1875, was that he treated his homely American subjects "as if they *were* pictorial, as if they were every inch as good as Capri or Tangiers. . . ."[10] Perhaps for that very reason it is significant that, as he grew older, Homer apparently found less to please him, either as a man or as an artist, in the American social scene. It had become too urban, too artificial, too economic for his taste. He devoted himself more and more to the study of the untamed forces of nature, especially the sea, gradually almost eliminating the human element from his compositions.

With Eakins the human element was always dominant. His subjects, however, except for professional oarsmen and pugilists, and a few cowboys, were drawn from a rather narrow segment of humanity. This was not the result of exclusiveness in taste or temperament, but because the everyday life of the middle class was the life Eakins knew, and the materials were ready at hand. Subject, as such, was relatively unimportant to him. He did not have to track down the quaint and the picturesque in out-of-the-way places. There was beauty enough, interest enough, in the real and the ordinary to satisfy him. Eakins did not himself paint low life, but by his teaching and example he helped break down the convention that only the pretty and the pleasant were fit subjects for art.

Contemporary critics, although not universally hostile, customarily expressed certain reservations about the work of Homer and Eakins. Even a critic who praised Homer warmly remarked that his pictures were "not wholly pleasing" and "not quite refined." James admitted that one of Homer's canvases was "a very honest, and vivid, and manly piece of work," but he went on to complain that it was "damnably ugly."[11] Eakins fared less well. The "Gross Clinic," for example, was denounced as a "morbid exhibition" and as an example of "the horrible in art." Why it was painted in the first place and why it was exhibited in the second mystified one critic. Another remarked that to "sensitive and instinctively artistic natures" the picture could not appear otherwise than as "a degradation of Art."[12]

There was one point, however, on which critics were inclined to support Homer and Eakins. That was their preference for American subjects. W. Mackay Laffan baldly asserted in 1880 that there was more to be admired in one "truthful and dirty tenement," "unaffected sugar refinery," or "vulgar but unostentatious coal wharf" than in "ninety and nine mosques of St. Sophia, Golden Horns, Normandy Cathedrals, and all the rest of the holy conventionalities and orthodox bosh. . . ."[13] Few of his contemporaries would have gone quite so far, but several chided American artists for being so occupied with "Naples Sketches" and "Cairo Streets" that they neglected the picturesque at home. E. W. Townsend, writing in 1895, regretted that Mulberry Bend seemed destined to be transformed into a park without having been painted by any American artist. Should anyone condescend to paint "the Bend," said Townsend, he might call the picture "Street Scenes in an Italian Town"—and sell it.[14]

Neither Homer nor Eakins was addicted to "Naples Sketches," but, as already noted, neither was inclined to seek out the picturesque in American slums and factory districts. Nevertheless, well before Townsend called attention to the artistic potentialities of Mulberry Bend a few artists had intermittently exploited the local color of the tenement districts. Louis C. Tiffany, later famous as the discoverer of a new formula for making decorative glass, and painter of pictures bearing titles such as "Street Scene in Tangiers" and "Feeding the Flamingoes," portrayed the ramshackle houses and sagging store fronts of "Old New York" in 1878. At a water-color show in 1882 F. Hopkinson Smith, who subsequently achieved popularity with sketches of romantic European cities, exhibited "Under the Towers," a view of the slums below the New York approach to Brooklyn Bridge. "Forty-third Street West of Ninth Avenue" (1883), by Louis Maurer, would have been branded "ash-can art" had it been painted twenty-five years later, for the scene depicted was a bleak city street with a man emptying a can of ashes into a refuse cart.[15]

In somewhat similar fashion painters who ordinarily selected more conventional subjects occasionally turned their attention toward working-class life. John F. Weir, a friend of Homer who became director of the Yale School of Fine Arts, painted two exciting and informative industrial studies in the late sixties, "The Gun Foundry" and "Forging the Shaft." In 1879 Brown interrupted his profitable production of street urchins long enough to make an interesting picture of a group of longshoremen of different nationalities loafing and exchanging stories during the noonday rest. Charles F. Ulrich displayed a similar interest in immigrant types in "The Land of Promise" (1885), a view of the crowded interior of the immigration depot at Castle Garden; and in another painting he rendered the details of the glass blower's trade with minute accuracy.[16]

The best of the industrial genre was "Steelworkers, Noontime," painted about 1890 by Thomas P. Anshutz, a student and colleague of Eakins, and himself the teacher of Robert Henri, John Sloan, and William Glackens.[17] The picture was as natural and forthright as the scene it depicted: a group of men and boys, some washing, two or three scuffling, but most of them just standing in the sunshine outside of a huge mill. It had no story to tell, no humorous or exotic types to portray, and no mysterious labors to describe. The scene could have been duplicated outside any large plant in the country. Or could it? For Anshutz somehow made it plain that each man or boy in the picture was a distinct being, possessed of a history and destiny all his own. It was a typical scene, but a unique one, showing real people in a moment of their lives that would never return.

Paintings such as those just mentioned were the exception rather than the rule in the eighties and nineties. So, too, was the critic Charles W. Larned's injunction that "in man's humanity lie the noblest subjects of art." His advice, "Go out into the highways of life, artists of today, and paint us the tragedies, the comedies, beauties, hopes, aspirations, and fears that live; 'bring in the poor, and maimed, and the halt, and the blind,' with the rest, and let us see the panorama of life more before us," seemingly fell on deaf ears.[18] Yet in one branch of art, illustration, the daily panorama of life was being recorded. It was the illustrator, much more than the painter, who delineated the contemporary scene in a realistic manner. The reason was plain. The painter's function, as most artists, critics, and laymen saw it, was to create objects of aesthetic loveliness. The illustrator's job was more prosaic. He earned his bread and butter by representing actual places, people, and events as faithfully and accurately as possible.

Throughout most of the latter half of the century *Harper's Weekly* was the illustrator's best market for topical drawings. Liberal by the standards of its time, with a national audience and a wide range of interests, the magazine balanced serious news pictures of train wrecks and Mississippi floods with numerous scenes of humble life. Yellowing in old issues are illustrations of a woman choosing a hired girl from the immigrants at the Castle Garden labor exchange in 1875; the catfish woman, the crabman, and other Philadelphia street traders in 1876; and tramps sawing wood in a newly opened Wayfarers Lodge in 1884.[19] One of *Harper's Weekly's* star performers was a student of Eakins, A. B. Frost, who is best remembered as the illustrator of *Uncle Remus*. Sometimes his contributions were genre done in black and white. "Good Intentions," a typical example, was a humorous but sympathetic drawing of a workman trying to decide whether to stay on the wagon or yield to the temptation of a hospitable saloon.[20]

Some of Frost's earlier work, along with the drawings of two other prominent illustrators, W. A. Rogers and E. W. Kemble, appeared in the *Daily Graphic*, published in New York in the seventies and eighties. This was the first fully-illustrated daily newspaper in the country and, like *Harper's Weekly*, it devoted almost as much space to human interest as to news pictures. In an early issue the paper carried an illustrated story on "The Private Life of the Gamin" and a full page of drawings depicting "The Rag Pickers of New York." Both were realistic and unsentimental in approach. The first told of boys who spent the whole day on the streets, first selling the morning papers, next shining shoes, and finally, in the late afternoon, hawking the evening papers. In one of the ragpicker cuts women rummaged through ash cans; in another an old woman and a dog wrestled for a bone. American ragpickers, the text apologized, lacked the romantic attributes of Parisian chiffoniers.[21] Several weeks later the *Daily Graphic* published Rogers' "Lunch-Time on the Wharf," a picture very similar in subject, at least, to the "Longshoremen's Noon" Brown subsequently painted.[22] The paper had the distinction of being the first American newspaper to print a half-tone photoengraving. Characteristically, for the *Graphic*, the photograph selected to be thus reproduced was "A Scene in Shantytown."[23]

Despite the high quality of its art work the *Daily Graphic* was never a commercial success. Most newspapers looked upon illustrations as an expensive luxury, and few made any regular use of them until the late eighties. Illustrations did not really become common in newspapers until the nineties, when the spread of sensational journalism and increasing competition forced publishers to adopt pictures and other circulation-stimulating features. Then for a brief period, until photoengraving processes were further perfected and the photographer began to supplant the illustrator, newspaper artists made drawings from photographs and sketched murder scenes, fires, meetings, and sporting events. They were quick to respond to the passing show of urban life; and sometimes, as in the case of John T. McCutcheon, who illustrated George Ade's column in the *Chicago Record*, they were regularly called upon to depict atmospheric corners and queer characters of their cities.[24]

The slums and their inhabitants provided illustrators with an inexhaustible fund of material, all the more so because the subject could be approached from several different angles. Tenement scenes were often depicted simply because they were "interesting." For example, Charles Graham's "On the Roof of a Tenement House" (1885) was introduced by the comment: "It is an interesting sight to see a roof which covers a whole block and is two acres in extent turned into the playground or the resting place of the hundreds of men, women, and children who live under it."[25] Sometimes, as in Graham's "Sketches in the Fourth Ward," the interest was primarily historical. Here the illustrator displayed Gotham Court, New York's first great tenement building, a structure 30 feet wide and 300 long, erected in 1850; on the same page he pictured a little house more than two hundred years old that currently sheltered from fifteen to twenty lodgers a night at ten cents a head.[26] More frequently men such as F. Barnard, who had illustrated an American edition of Dickens' *Bleak House*, consciously sought out picturesque episodes in the lives of the animated, oddly dressed inhabitants of ruinous buildings.[27]

W. A. Rogers, although not indifferent to the odd and colorful aspects of the tenement scene, inclined toward a more documentary style. He sometimes accompanied Health Department physicians on their tours of inspection in the slums and sketched their activities.[28] Likewise factual in approach was W. H. Drake, some of whose drawings were used to illustrate the *Annual Report* of the New York A.I.C.P. in 1884. Since one of the original aims of the Association had been to promote friendly visits to the poor it is interesting to note that the secretary now explained that Drake's pictures were designed to show members "how and where the poor of New York live" and thereby to "obviate the necessity of . . . personal exploration of these unwholesome depths."[29]

There was enough unpleasantness in these pictures to satisfy the most uncompromising realist, and the horrors they revealed were confirmed in the photographs Riis used to document his case against the slums. Not infrequently, however, the editorial comment that accompanied the illustrations took the sting out of the drawings by asserting that the chief responsibility for the conditions displayed lay with the occupants of the tenements. They were drunken, improvident, and dirty, and they made their environment as bad as themselves. Dan Beard, a pioneer in radical cartooning as in the scouting movement, took no chance that his attack on the Trinity Church tenements would be misconstrued. At the top of his page a minister mouthed platitudes against corruption; at the bottom the Grim Reaper stalked through the church's dilapidated properties, cutting down children and old people. Beard pictured Trinity as Janus-faced: one side was a pious preacher, the other a grasping landlord.[30]

Low life made as strong an appeal to illustrators as to writers. Early in his career Charles Dana Gibson, whose beautiful girls and Van Bibberlike young men were to be idolized by a generation of Americans, contributed to *Life* a series of drawings entitled "Salons of New York." In these sketches Gibson obliquely satirized the pretensions of the Four Hundred by portraying receptions and balls in the humbler social circles of the metropolis. The best of the group was the memorable "Evening with the Gentlemen's Sons' Chowder Club," a drawing that might have been an illustration of a scene from one of Harrigan's comedies. There was nothing colorful or cute, however, about Charles H. Johnson's "What Is Going on When the Clock Strikes Twelve" (1892). He drew a "sport" drinking with his girl; a tenement woman, tired from a long day's labor, sent out for beer by her no-good husband; and a prostitute approaching a young man on the street.[31]

Perhaps the most realistic and certainly the most comprehensive collection of drawings of low life was the set of illustrations E. W. Kemble prepared in 1895 for Townsend's *Daughter of the Tenements.* Kemble was best known as the illustrator of *Huckleberry Finn* and as a delineator of Negro types. Here, however, he presented a gallery of East Side scenes and types–sweatshop workers, fruit peddlers, beer-hall entertainers, street urchins, and bums. They were straightforward pictures, showing an appreciation of the distinctive flavor of the region, but not seeking to make the place or the people more colorful than they were in life.

Several illustrators made a specialty of depicting slum children. Some of their characterizations seem to have been strongly influenced by Brown. Dickens had described Jo, the crossing sweeper in *Bleak House,* as "dirty, ugly, disagreeable to all the senses," covered with sores and devoured by vermin, but Barnard presented him as a handsome and pitiable little boy.[32] Sol Eytinge reflected less of Brown's and more of Dickens' spirit in drawings such as "The Hearthstone of the Poor" (1876), in which street children huddled over a steam grating, and "A Tragic Story," wherein ragged newsboys and bootblacks enacted a sad scene from a popular melodrama.[33]

M. A. Woolf's tenement kids were as characteristic of *Life* as the Gibson Girl, and as many as three or four of his drawings of the amusing and pathetic adventures of city children appeared in a single issue. Woolf's affectionate portrayal of youth in the slums mirrored the philanthropic attitude of John Ames Mitchell, the editor of *Life,* who maintained a farm camp for underprivileged children. The boys and girls he drew were frayed and undernourished, often forlorn, but never downright wretched, and, although mischievous, they were never presented as actually or potentially vicious. They bore little resemblance either to Brace's dangerous classes or to the little monsters that Crane and Steffens described in their stories of slum life. On the contrary, they were appealing youngsters, just as endlessly involved in affairs of the heart as their older, healthier, and better-dressed cousins in Gibson's society drawings.[34]

"Hogan's Alley," the most famous of the early comic strips, also emphasized the genial side of tenement life. After Hearst lured R. F. Outcault, the originator of the strip and the creator of the Yellow Kid, to the *New York Journal,* George Luks drew "Hogan's

Alley" for the *World*. Always exuberant, Luks attempted to outdo Outcault by introducing the Yellow Twins into the cartoon. Both Outcault and Luks had earlier contributed sketches of low life to *Truth*, and both relished the earthy and physical kind of humor that seemed more abundant among uninhibited poor people than in refined and prosperous circles.[35]

The contrast between rich and poor, a theme that Eytinge broached in several drawings, was strikingly illustrated by Thure de Thulstrup in "Where Two Ends Meet" (1891). Earlier attempts to state the problem in pictorial terms often gave the impression of being contrived, but De Thulstrup's drawing revealed a scene from life. The place was Bellevue Wharf in New York, a pier that served both as a yacht landing and as the terminus of the ferries that ran to the islands in the East River where the city's charitable and correctional institutions were located. At one side of the pier stood a knot of well-dressed and handsome people awaiting the arrival of the rest of their yachting party. At the other side, and only a step or two away, a file of dispirited men and women shuffled and hobbled to the boat that was to carry them to the almshouse or the workhouse. The idle rich and the idle poor were going for boat rides.[36]

De Thulstrup's drawing was perhaps not intended to convey any specific message. It simply recorded a fact. But on the title page of B. O. Flower's *Civilization's Inferno* (1893) an unidentified artist used the contrast theme in a symbolic cross section of the social structure. As he pictured it, society's top story was a luxurious room in which the rich danced and made merry; at the street level workmen crowded around a factory; in the basement widows and orphans, representing the deserving poor, struggled to maintain life and self-respect; and down below, in the cavernous subbasement, lighted only by the faint rays of a policeman's lantern, lurked the desperate and vicious classes.

Like other students of the contemporary scene, illustrators often seemed more interested in existence in the social basement and subbasement than at the street level. Nevertheless, they did not entirely ignore working-class problems in their drawings, and some of them expressed strong sympathy for labor. Magazine and newspaper artists depicted working conditions of miners, stokers, and stevedores as well as turbulent episodes in strikes.[37] As early as 1859 *Harper's Weekly* published a cartoon criticizing the railroads for disregard of their employees' safety, and in the seventies the *Daily Graphic* waged a spirited pictorial campaign in behalf of a Saturday half holiday for working girls.[38]

In these and other drawings illustrators and cartoonists, by prodding the consciences of employers and of the middle class in general, sought to induce them to treat deserving workers more benevolently. Gradually, however, a more radical note entered the cartoons. Walt McDougall introduced the conflict between predatory wealth and involuntary poverty into the political arena in the campaign of 1884. His "Royal Feast of Belshazzar Blaine and the Money Kings" showed Blaine and his bedizened millionaire supporters seated at a table laden with Monopoly Soup, Lobby Pudding, Gould Pie, and Patronage Cake; in front of the table, but ignored by the diners, stood a tattered workman pleading in vain for food for his wife and child.[39] By a decade later, according to a cartoon by Beard, workmen were no longer content to beg for crumbs. Now Labor was attacking Monopoly with the club of Trade-Union; Monopoly, well protected by an armor made of Police, Sheriff, Military and Vested Wrongs, struck back with the sword of Starvation and the dagger of Pinkerton.[40]

Even though the validity of Beard's presentation of the problem of industrial unrest might be challenged, no one disputed the right of a cartoonist to deal with controversial topics. Nor did anyone accuse De Thulstrup of impropriety when he drew even so unlovely an incident as the meeting of the rich and poor at Bellevue Wharf. Cartoonists and illustrators were expected to concern themselves with such matters. Their business was life, not art. Not so with artists. Beauty was their realm. Good taste circumscribed the subject matter of their work; aesthetics demanded the observance of certain niceties in its execution. Their products need not be beautiful or grand, but they must be artistic, a delight to the eye and a consolation to the spirit.

As the century drew to a close the reign of pretty falsification seemed secure. Never had the output of ideal heads, allegorical maidens, and nuzzling sheep been larger. Yet a revolution in subject matter was shortly to burst upon the placid art world, and the first stirrings of that revolution were already visible in the nineties. In 1891 a Chicagoan named Krausz issued a portfolio of photographs of street types—"Tough," "Ditch Digger," and "Iceman."[41] Shortly thereafter Alfred Stieglitz returned from a lengthy stay abroad and began a series of painstaking camera studies of wet streets, horsecar terminals, and railroad yards in New York.[42] Meanwhile, Jerome Myers was painting the people and buildings of the East Side, not as an occasional diversion, but as a daily labor of love. George Luks's fondness for low life was sufficiently well known in 1892 to attract friendly satire in a cartoon called "The Glorification of the Tramp."[43] In Philadelphia John Sloan, Everett Shinn, and William Glackens, like Luks, were drawing for the newspapers and in off hours discussing the philosophy and practice of art with Robert Henri.

If American subjects were hard to find, these men did not know it. What they bemoaned was not paucity of pictorial material in modern America but the lack of interest in it manifested by artists. This indifference, they thought, extended not only to native subjects, but to all the real issues of life. It was the want of vitality and truth much more than the lack of Americanism that they decried in the artistic tendencies of the day. Their careers were only beginning in the nineties, and neither their work nor their ideas received much notice until after the turn of the century. Then, in a time of protest and reform, they sought to prove that the province of art is as wide as life.

Part Two

THE SEARCH FOR TRUTH, c. 1897-1917

CHAPTER 8

The New View of Poverty

> . . . a vast army of the poor in this country are not in poverty because they want to be, but because they have not been able to avoid slipping down into the economic slough of despond. For the hard-working father of a large family, who has been inadequately educated, or who has indeed entered the world but poorly equipped physically to fight the battle of life, it is natural that an industrial panic, that high rents, that dust-breathing trades, that industrial accidents from unprotected machinery, that disease and other ills must almost inevitably bring poverty. And when poverty comes in at the door many of the customary virtues go out through the window . . . Deception, falsehood, unreliability, intemperance follow naturally in the wake of poverty.
>
> "The Conquest of Poverty," *Metropolitan Magazine*, October, 1909.

ALTHOUGH the Victorian era was marked by mounting concern for the poor, few nineteenth-century students of social questions were really interested in poverty. Until quite late in the century "the poor" was used to denote persons receiving or in need of charity. Literary and political hacks heaped praise on the "honest" or self-supporting poor, but social scientists paid this group scant heed. In an age of *laissez faire* it was taken for granted that dependency was the only phase of the poverty problem that affected society, or with which society was competent to deal. According to the prevailing view, a man's economic condition was nobody's business but his own—until he "degenerated," ceased to be independent, and became a charge on society. Throughout most of the nineteenth century, therefore, pauperism rather than poverty engaged the attention of students, and the energies of reformers were directed less at the abolition of want than at devising methods of relieving distress.

One of the peculiarities of late-nineteenth-century philanthropy was an intense dislike for charity on the part of those who dispensed it. Scientific philanthropy began as a revolt against the old-fashioned spendthrift almsgiving. Its supporters regarded chronic dependency as a pernicious social disease; they operated on the theory that people ought to be self-supporting and that those who were not must be led or driven into taking care of themselves. They thought that charitable assistance should be provided, not abundantly in a spirit of loving-kindness, but reluctantly, and only as a matter of stern necessity. Their object was to induce prosperous America to mobilize its charitable resources for legitimate need instead of squandering that precious reserve on casual benevolence. Above all, they insisted on thorough investigation of each individual and family applying for assistance. Verify the applicant's need for aid, ascertain the exact circumstances of his case (ran their creed), and, on the basis of the knowledge so acquired, help the recipient of charity find his way back to the path of independence.

In the course of these painstaking investigations the men and women who were the most active in scientific philanthropy uncovered evidence of a host of poverty-producing factors that forced a radical revision in the original assumptions of their work. By the end of the 1890's agents of charity organization societies, settlement-house residents, professors and students of political economy, and supervisors of public-welfare institutions were all coming to believe that pauperism was as much a result as a cause of social ills. Their experience and research had convinced them that the evils attendant on pauperism could not be brought within manageable limits until the more fundamental problem of poverty, even, and especially "honest" poverty, had been attacked. Social workers, as they were beginning to call themselves, continued to regard efficient administration of relief as their particular responsibility; but to a much greater extent than ever before they were aware of the need for identifying and eradicating the destructive forces that bred the misery they daily, and often vainly, sought to succor.

The new view of poverty, which became current around 1900, was a product of the earlier interest in scientific philanthropy. The new view departed from the old, not in any slackening of hostility toward pauperism, but in defining the problem in terms of insufficiency and insecurity rather than exclusively as a matter of dependency. Robert Hunter, a leading settlement worker and author of one of the first estimates of the actual extent of poverty in the United States, was as adamant in his attitude toward paupers as any nineteenth-century poor-law reformer. Hunter contended, however, that many families who were in no sense pauperized must be included in any census of the poor. Only the most miserable of the needy are destitute, said Hunter; much more numerous are the men and women who, although self-supporting, are unable to secure the goods and services essential to a state of physical efficiency. These are the real poor of any community, he maintained, and their poverty consists simply in receiving "too little of the common necessities to keep themselves at their best. . . ."[1]

This more inclusive definition of poverty won rapid acceptance in the first two decades of the twentieth century, among both practicing social workers and academic economists and sociologists. A widely used college text published at the end of the period adopted inability to maintain a decent standard of living as the test of poverty.[2] Perhaps the most explicit and succinct statement of the modern attitude appeared in 1914 in Jacob Hollander's *Abolition of Poverty*. The author, a professor of political economy at Johns Hopkins and an adviser to several Republican presidents, identified the poor simply as the portion of the population that was "inadequately fed, clad, and sheltered."[3]

Once want had been distinguished from dependency it was possible to extend the concept of poverty from present to prospective need; that is, from insufficiency to insecurity. Hunter referred to the poor as "the large class in any industrial nation who are on the verge of distress," and Hollander likened poverty to a treacherous path encircling the morass of pauperism. "Those who tread it," he said, "are in constant danger, even with the exercise of care and foresight, of falling or of slipping or of being crowded off."[4] Is it surprising, he continued, that people subsisting on miserable wages should be unable to take precaution against mishap and calamity?[5] Agents of charitable societies who had formerly assumed that example and exhortation were sufficient to lift paupers to economic independence now despaired of rehabilitating clients whose lives were darkened by uncertainty. A report on widows' pensions issued by the New York A.I.C.P. in 1914 began with the significant declaration: "Until the income *needed* for the maintenance of a fair standard of life is *assured*, there can be no foundation upon which the visitor from the relief organization, the nurse, the dietitian can work.[6]

Defining the issue in terms of insufficiency and insecurity brought a changed attitude toward the supposed utility of poverty. In earlier eras most Americans, while acting as if poverty were the worst fate that could befall them, gave lip service to the doctrine that a dose of adversity was good medicine for the individual as well as for society. Throughout the greater part of the nineteenth century it had been an article of faith with dime novelists, Sunday-school teachers, and millionaires that poverty strengthened character, stimulated incentive, and punished sloth. Andrew Carnegie, for one, had written eloquently on the curse of wealth and the blessings of poverty.[7] The advantages accruing from severely straitened circumstances were less apparent, however, to twentieth-century students, who saw poverty as "the supply source of pauperism" and who believed that low incomes meant "insufficiency of food, lack of clothing, and improper and unfit housing."[8] To their way of thinking poverty was neither desirable nor necessary, but unnatural and intolerable.[9]

It was a sign that a new day had arrived when, in 1903, the editor of *Gunton's Magazine* had the temerity to argue that Lincoln was a great man in spite of, rather than because of, the economic hardships he faced early in life.[10] Three years later *The Outlook* denounced "that curse of want which today condemns countless children of the poor from their birth."[11] Lester Ward's *Applied Sociology* (1906) contained the flat assertion: "Indigence is an effective bar to opportunity";[12] and Edward T. Devine, the dean of American social workers, observed that although temporary lack of wealth might serve as a wholesome inducement to labor, chronic poverty meant a low standard of living, overwork, overcrowding, disease, and friendlessness.[13]

Walter Rauschenbusch, whose *Christianity and the Social Crisis* (1907) was the most influential exposition of the social gospel, emphasized the debilitating effects of want. His contention was that "Constant underfeeding and frequent exhaustion make the physical tissues flabby and the brain prone to depression and vacillation, incapable of holding tenaciously to a distant aim." Far from acting as a moral tonic, said Rauschenbusch, "Poverty teaches men to live from hand to mouth, and for the moment."[14]

Two monographs published by the Russell Sage Foundation in 1914 examined the influence of a miserable economic environment on children. *The Neglected Girl* began on a somber note:

> It [poverty] does not kill perhaps but it stunts. It does not come as an overwhelming catastrophe; but steadily it saps the vigor of the young as well as of the old. . . . With the less fortunate, poverty takes the form of a slow, chronic contest against everlasting odds.[15]

The companion volume, *Boyhood and Lawlessness*, also made the point that poverty destroyed the possibilities for normal development: "The tenement child runs his race, but it is always a handicap."[16]

The view of poverty as a stultifying experience, debasing to body, mind, and character, found its way into the species of popular literature that had long sung of the bracing mental and moral results of hard, ill-rewarded toil.[17] In *The Wisdom of the Simple* Owen Kildare defied propriety by presenting honest poverty in an unfavorable light. Wittle Street in lower New York, the locale of the story, was no paupers' alley. Each house or flat had its breadwinner. Every household was supplied with the indispensable minimum of furniture, although in some instances the beds were "surpassed in comfort and sanitary detail by the cots in ten-cent lodginghouses peopled nightly by the scum of the city."[18] Nor were the Wittle Street folk lazy. They had "the confirmed habit of working for every bite of bread and every drop of whiskey they consumed."[19] They had their hard, heartless independence—and precious little else. "It would have been better for them had they been poor, abjectly poor and depending on charity," declared Kildare.[20]

By all the tests of civilized thought and behavior the working-class families on Wittle Street lived in a primitive state. They were quarrelsome, cruel, superstitious, and suspicious, and they demanded conformity to their mean pattern. Kildare's explanation was that years of struggle to obtain the bare essentials of existence had smothered every aspiration for a better life and taught the people of Wittle Street to be fiercely content with what they had. The standard of living available to them was simply incapable of supporting more than a brute existence.

Yet even as Kildare prepared this indictment, another and more reputable novelist argued that privation was by no means the worst of being poor. Much deadlier, in William Dean Howells' opinion, was the sense of insecurity that corroded the lives of both the idle and the industrious. In *A Hazard of New Fortunes* (1890) Howells had described and expressed the bafflement of the white-collar class in the economic chance world. Shortly after the turn of the century he contributed an editorial to *Harper's Weekly* in which he averred that the curse of modern society was fear of want, a dreadful uncertainty so exhausting to the spirit that want itself, when it finally overtook its victims, was embraced almost with a feeling of deliverance. With the barbed urbanity characteristic of his social criticism, Howells commented that the United States was so abundantly supplied with organized benevolences that destitution could easily be confronted and overcome. "The community has amply the wealth and will for that," he said. "It is the fear of want, the lurking fear, the hidden fear, which cannot always be met, and which remains through all the struggle of life to harass and hamper the victim."[21]

The shift in emphasis in studies of poverty from dependency to insecurity and inadequate living standards reflected an improvement in fundamental economic conditions. It had been pointless to rail against want and uncertainty as long as man's incapacity and the niggardliness of nature kept the supply of economic goods too meager to meet the clamorous demand for them. Only satirists and philosophers had then dared dream of a society in which there would be sufficiency for all. Yet somewhere in the nineteenth century, or even earlier, perhaps, the balance had begun to change. By the start of the twentieth century, at least in fortunately endowed regions of the world, industry and agriculture had advanced to a point where there was at last a favorable relationship between human needs and the possibility of satisfying them.

The dawning realization of this momentous change injected a buoyant spirit into the study of economics. "Political Economy is radiant with hope," wrote Henry George in the closing paragraphs of *Progress and Poverty*.[22] In England Seebohm Rowntree rejoiced in the passing of "the dark shadow of Malthusian philosophy"; in the United States Simon N. Patten hailed the emergence of an economy of plenty as "a new basis of civilization."[23] Walter Lippmann lent his youthful voice to the happy chorus. Resignation may have been an appropriate attitude for mankind to assume during the long centuries when the world was poised uncertainly on the edge of starvation, Lippmann wrote in 1914. "But in the midst of plenty the imagination becomes ambitious, rebellion against misery is at last justified, and dreams have a basis in fact."[24]

Even social workers succumbed to the infectious optimism of the new century. "We are living in an age of economic surplus," boasted one of Robert Hartley's successors as general agent of the New York A.I.C.P., "in an age when labor harnessed by science produces more of the necessities of life than the race requires for its bodily sustenance." There is wealth enough in the world to make successful war on poverty, he exulted—wealth enough to abolish brutalizing tenements, provide for the physical well-being of the entire working population, and replace ignorance with enlightenment.[25]

This conviction of abundance was the wellspring of the humanitarian movements of the Progressive era. To Walter Weyl the "disequilibrium between social surplus and social misery" seemed at once the irritant of popular unrest and the maker of uneasy social consciences. "Our surplus has made us as sensitive to misery, preventable death, sickness, hunger, and deprivation as is a photographic plate to light," Weyl wrote in *The New Democracy* (1912).[26] Devine believed that "the sting of modern poverty in prosperous communities is precisely that it is not necessary . . ."; and Hollander was of a similar opinion: "It is because the whole loaf is large enough to satisfy the hunger of all who must be fed that individual want is intolerable."[27] The views of these men appeared to be borne out by the findings of the federal Commission on Industrial Relations, whose eleven-volume report was submitted to Congress in 1916. Basil M. Manly, director of research for the Commission, reported that lengthy investigation had revealed no "natural reason" why any able-bodied American workman should be unable to rear a family of moderate size in comfort, health, and security.[28]

Advances in medical knowledge gave further impetus to the tendency to view poverty as an abnormal manifestation. The latter part of the nineteenth century saw several communicable diseases, long accepted as unwelcome but unavoidable impositions on the human family, arrested or wiped out entirely. A generation that had seen typhus, typhoid, and smallpox brought under control, that was eliminating yellow fever from large areas and was embarking on a campaign against tuberculosis, was strongly disposed to regard the scourge of poverty as similarly vulnerable.

Agents of charitable societies were well aware of the connection between sickness and dependency. They were heartened by the belief that if preventable diseases were checked, the incidence of poverty would decline. In view of the emphasis medical scientists placed on unsanitary living conditions as a source of disease it was only natural that social scientists came to regard poor environment as their major problem.[29] The new school of reformers thought of poverty itself as a kind of malady, largely environmental in cause and cure.[30] They confidently referred to indigence as "a social disease as surely curable as tuberculosis, typhoid and yellow fever"; and they deemed "an epidemic of avoidable poverty" as disgraceful to the community tolerating it as an epidemic of any other preventable disease.[31]

This attitude contrasted sharply with the traditional religious explanation of want as an affliction visited upon humanity by the inscrutable will of God. For years Jesus' admonition "the poor always ye have with you" had served as the text for innumerable sermons and editorials designed either to encourage charity or discourage social reform. In 1904 J. G. Phelps Stokes, brother-in-law of Robert Hunter and himself the founder of the extremely successful Hartley House settlement, challenged the customary interpretation of this oft-repeated phrase. He suggested that Jesus' words might be regarded, not as a prophetic utterance, but simply as a description of conditions prevailing at the time they were spoken. After all, said Stokes (who had once aspired to be a missionary), "Jesus used the present tense, not the future. . . ."[32]

The heart of the matter was that in the secular atmosphere of the twentieth century, the idea that mankind was eternally and inevitably caught in the toils of misery seemed unscientific. To a confident and pragmatic generation such a view was part and parcel of outworn and discredited postulates.[33] A leading social worker confessed that even in the hard times following the panic of 1907 he and his colleagues went about their work cheerfully, fired by the conviction that poverty was "a relic of barbarism, man-made and not God-made, unnecessary and preventable."[34] The New View was itself taking the form of a gospel. One of its clearest statements was contained in an obscure book bearing the significant title, *Poverty; The Challenge to the Church*, which began: "Poverty is no longer an inevitable condition to be accepted and endured; it is a problem of economic and social life which demands solution."[35]

To Americans there was little that was novel in the idea that poverty was unnatural and unnecessary. For generations they had boasted that in their uniquely favored land any man able and willing to work was certain to achieve a fair living. The point of divergence between the new view and the old was the different explanation offered for the residue of misery that persisted despite the favorable opportunities America freely extended to all comers. During most of the nineteenth century the prevailing theory was that if an individual failed to obtain a competence, the fault lay in some weakness or defect in his own character. The experience of the last quarter of the century, however, produced ample evidence to bring this thesis into disrepute. By 1900 there was a widespread conviction that the causes of failure were to be found, in most cases, in circumstances outside and beyond the control of individual personality. Robert Hunter voiced the opinion of nearly all the reformers of the Progressive generation when he declared that twentieth-century poverty was due "to certain social evils which must be remedied and certain social wrongs which must be put right."[36]

One of the most important of the numerous factors occasioning this change of thought regarding the causes of poverty was a shift in public attitudes toward wealth. The average American of the Civil War generation deemed wealth the measure of virtue and ability. His school readers no less than his elders' conversations indoctrinated him with the idea that affluence was both attainable and admirable. When a rich man came to town he heard his parents say, "He is rich," much as the ancients might have said, "He is a God."[37] In an age of extraordinary economic opportunities it had seemed axiomatic that if a man were rich it was because he possessed more than ordinary intelligence and resolution. Men who, starting life with no advantages other than their native resources, triumphed over all obstacles to amass large fortunes were patriotic symbols. "They illustrated with a peculiar glory the land of opportunity."[38]

After the 1890's conditions were less conducive than formerly to adulation of wealth. Twice within the span of even a young man's lifetime severe depressions had engulfed the nation. The growth of monopoly and the closing of the frontier had seemingly curtailed opportunities, not only for achieving immense wealth, but also for establishing successful individual enterprises. In the decade and a half before World War I the American economy appeared to many observers to have reached maturity. The demand of the times was for conservation rather than exploitation, distribution rather than accumulation. The economic climate had undergone such a change that success no longer seemed easily possible for all.[39] Nothing was more remote from the American consciousness than despair; nevertheless, as the new century broke, a strong current of criticism began to supplant the earlier complacent and unquestioning reverence for material success.

Even in the heyday of the Gilded Age thoughtful men and women had condemned the relentless intensity with which their contemporaries pursued wealth, but a stigma of radicalism had often been attached to their criticism. Under the altered circumstances prevailing in the Progressive era it became more respectable and popular to belabor "malefactors of great wealth." Where the earlier critics had attacked materialism in general terms, their successors were more specific in their charges. Muckrakers documented instances of malpractices in business and finance and exposed concrete examples of the use of economic power to corrupt politics on the local, state, and national levels. In the past pulpit and press had often denounced the ostentatious extravagance with which wealth was dissipated in lavish entertainments; now writers as diverse in their points of view as Gustavus Myers and William Allen White subjected the methods by which riches were garnered to close and critical scrutiny.[40] Fortunes that had been admired for their very bigness were presently shown to have been acquired in ways "that not only grazed the prison gate but imposed burdens and disadvantages upon the rest of the community."[41] No man could "make" $20,000,000 in a whole series of lifetimes, said the poet and journalist, Ernest Crosby; the foundation of such wealth, he maintained, was "not the ability to *create* but the ability to *annex*."[42]

Clergymen of the social-gospel persuasion were particularly troubled by the moral implications of huge fortunes obtained under the conditions of competitive capitalism. Rauschenbusch spoke for the liberal wing of Protestantism when he objected that a social system that lifted a small minority to great wealth and submerged vast numbers in poverty was inimical to the interests of the church.[43] More bluntly, the aging Washington Gladden lashed out at the forces he called "predatory wealth." He touched off a controversy within the religious community of the nation in 1905 by protesting against the acceptance by the Congregational Board of Foreign Missions of a gift of "tainted money" from John D. Rockefeller. The gift was accepted despite Gladden's protest, and in his autobiography, published several years after the episode, Gladden continued the attack vigorously:

> It is impossible to deny the existence of a considerable class of persons who have obtained great wealth by predatory methods, by evasion and defiance of the law, by the practice of vast extortions, by getting unfair and generally unlawful advantages over their neighbors, by secret agreements, and the manipulation of railway and government officials; . . . by manifold arts that tend to corrupt the character and destroy the foundations of the social order.[44]

Gladden held that the duty of the churches and the universities was to make practices of this kind "abhorrent and detestable" in the eyes of youth, and he questioned their ability to do so if they succumbed to the temptation of enriching themselves by taking endowments from monopolists.

Growing concern with the sins of wealth induced a greater willingness to apply a common standard of morality to all men, regardless of their position in society. Progressive literature abounded in exhortations to judge people by what they *did* and *were* rather than by what they *had* or *wore*.[45] Alfred Henry Lewis, author of the Wolfville stories and an aggressive individualist in politics and economics, was only applying this doctrine in reverse when he asserted that he had found the poor to be "as thievish, as mendacious, as tyrannical within their narrower power . . . as the rich."[46] More typical of the Progressive emphasis was the concluding sentence in a temperance tract issued by a charitable society in 1916: "John Tenement Barleycorn and John Mansion Barleycorn differ only in the houses they live in and the clothes they wear."[47] Mary E. Richmond, a decisive figure in the development of professional standards in social work, advised her students that the classification of humankind into workers and parasites was as appropriate for the wealthy as for the needy.[48] Rauschenbusch contended that luxury was as responsible as penury for the production of degenerate types, for both conditions fostered "the love of idleness, vagrant habits, the dislike of self-restraint, and the inclination to indulge in passing emotions."[49]

Once it was agreed that virtue and vice knew no class lines, interest in the so-called moral causes of poverty began to decline. Students of social conditions no longer deemed it profitable to exercise themselves about the precise amount of distress properly attributable to various categories of undesirable behavior. "All these can exist and do exist where there is no poverty," commented a labor spokesman.[50] Amos Warner's *American Charities*, published in the early nineties, had devoted a full chapter to "Personal Causes of Individual Degeneracy"; but Charles R. Henderson's *Modern Methods of Charity*, which appeared a decade after Warner's book, dismissed the moral causes in one sentence: "The more individual and personal causes of poverty . . . are to be found not alone in any one class of the community, but infect the whole social body, deadening that spirit of devotion to social tasks by which alone men become strong."[51]

The new school of reformers did not deny that individual frailties contributed materially to want and insecurity, but they insisted that social rather than individual weaknesses were the basic causes of poverty. In existing circumstances, they said, character is of only secondary importance in determining a man's economic status. In the opinion of these students poverty was not so much a mark of personal failure as an incident of society's imperfect methods of producing and distributing goods. They believed that misery was more often imposed on people by external forces than generated by inadequacies within the sufferers. Consequently, in seeking to explain the causes of distress they gave more and more attention to the impersonal economic factors and less and less to the personal, moral considerations.

In the economic interpretation of poverty unemployment, low wages, and high living costs took the central place assigned to idleness, improvidence, and intemperance in the moralistic view of the problem. Basil Manly cited the findings of the Industrial Relations Commission as evidence that lack of work and miserable pay had reduced part of the nation's industrial population to a dangerously low level.[52] Louis Brandeis' brief in support of the Oregon minimum-wage law contained a section headed "Underpayment the Root of Poverty" and argued that underpaying industries were parasitic in nature, subsidized by the employees, their families, and society as a whole.[53] In a study of the standard of living in certain working-class households Robert Coit Chapin concluded that, regardless of personal habits or ability to adhere to a budget, the economic well-being of a family varied as the two jaws of the vise, wages and prices, contracted and relaxed.[54] Quite properly, however, it was an avowed socialist who delivered the sharpest thrust against wage slavery. "People are poor," said Scott Nearing in 1916, "because the rate of wages paid by the industries of the United States will not permit them to be anything but poor."[55]

Although "dying wages" and "famine for work" were the most frequently cited of the economic causes of poverty, the list was capable of almost indefinite expansion.[56] Various students elaborated it to include overwork, unhealthful and dangerous occupations, industrial accident and disease, unsanitary dwellings and workshops, congestion, child labor, and immigration.[57] In 1910 Henry R. Seager of Columbia University attempted to encompass many of these factors in an arraignment of the "five great misfortunes"—illness, accident, premature death, unemployment, and old age. He estimated that each year a half million Americans were victimized by personally unavoidable contingencies.[58]

The idea that poverty stemmed from economic forces over which the individual had little control, and for the effects of which he ought not to be held responsible, was not new. Yet never before had it been so frequently advanced or so widely accepted as in the first decade and a half of the twentieth century. It suited the secular spirit of the Progressive era better than any other explanation of want, and it was both a reflection of, and a stimulus to, contemporary movements for social justice. Most significant of all, the increasing emphasis placed on the economic (as opposed to the moral) causes of poverty denoted that the historic interest in the condition of the poor was giving way to a newly aroused concern with the rights and grievances of the working class.

The new view of poverty affected opinion regarding the cure no less than the cause of want. Individual reform, the traditional remedy recommended to persons suffering from economic distress, seemed ineffective to men and women who believed that "the mass of the poor . . . are bred of miserable and unjust social conditions, which punish the good and the pure, the faithful and industrious, the slothful and the vicious, all alike."[59] Many Americans agreed with R. H. Tawney in his observation that unemployment, short time, and low wages fell impartially upon the just and the unjust; and like the brilliant English student the Americans were inclined to take an irreverent attitude toward proposals to eliminate poverty by improving the morals of the poor. "Improve the character of individuals by all means—if you feel competent to do so" (said Tawney), "especially of those whose excessive incomes expose them to peculiar temptations."[60]

The younger reformers deemed social reform a more urgent task than the elevation of personal morality. They tended to be more tolerant of personal derelictions than their predecessors had been, because, in their opinion, poverty originated in adverse circumstances too powerful for any individual to alter. On the other hand, confidence that society could correct these adverse circumstances if it chose to do so made them extremely critical of social failures or inaction.

The target of their attack was "social maladjustment." Devine declared that behind every form of degeneration and dependence "there is apt to be some entrenched pecuniary interest which it is desirable to discover and expose and with which it is the duty of society to deal."[61] Hollander claimed that "the misdirections, not the normal workings" of twentieth-century industrialism left a portion of the community in receipt of less than enough to maintain itself in decency. "Now, in our own day," he asserted, "the conquest of poverty looms up as an economic possibility, definitely within our reach—if only society desire it sufficiently and will pay enough to achieve it."[62]

Would society be willing to pay the price? Or would the effort and the inconvenience involved, not to mention the material costs, seem too onerous? The reformers' problem was to rouse the public from its lethargy, make consciences uneasy, and stir genial good will into enthusiasm for social betterment. Their first step was to lay bare the responsibility of the community for needless suffering. With a unanimity rare among their kind, the reformers emphasized the same point: society, by callous inaction, countenances cruelties that few men, as individuals, would perpetrate.

One of the best examples of the hortatory approach appeared in 1906 in an unsigned article entitled "The Struggle against Social Despotism" in Lyman Abbott's magazine, *The Outlook*. The author praised John Spargo's *The Bitter Cry of the Children* and Florence Kelley's *Some Ethical Gains Through Legislation* for their forthrightness in placing the blame for the evils described "upon the social system under which we live." He remarked that when Americans read about Armenian massacres or slavery in the Congo they cried out in horror and demanded that these crimes against humanity cease. In such instances it was easy to see how innocent people were crushed by conscienceless desire for wealth and power. "In the meantime," the writer continued, "before our eyes there are whole classes of people who are as truly subject to the tyranny of death, disease, want, vice, and crime as any Armenian or Congo native to his master." But in these cases it is harder for us to recognize the forces of evil. "We have no sultan or king we can call to account, we see no murderer with sword or gun whose hand we can stay, and we ignore the fact that the responsibility rests upon ourselves."[63]

Charles Edward Russell aimed a similar blow at public apathy in the Christmas issue of *Everybody's Magazine* in 1907. He reproduced an album of drawings depicting drab and sorrowful scenes in the slums during the holiday season. "Look at these pictures," Russell urged, "and reflect that for all these things not the ways of Providence are responsible, nor inevitable conditions, nor the vain imaginings wherewith we salve our consciences, but merely you and I."[64]

Several years later a student who investigated juvenile delinquency in a poverty-stricken metropolitan district suggested that the indictments issued against the youthful offenders should have been directed at the municipality itself "for allowing any of its children to start the battle of life so poorly equipped and so handicapped for becoming efficient American citizens."[65] Ruth S. True, in a parallel study of neglected girls in the same blighted neighborhood, recalled that she had once found a crippled baby, cold and miserable, in a barren tenement room. "She was as helpless and defenceless a little creature as could well be met," reported Miss True. "But this was the treatment an indifferent community tolerated for her. And she was only one."[66]

The cure for poverty suggested by the Progressive reformers (that is, those who reached maturity around 1900) was simply correction of unjust and degrading conditions of work and living. Specifically they proposed legislative action to establish and maintain fair standards of wages, hours, and housing; prohibition of child labor and regulation of dangerous trades; compensation of labor for unemployment, accidents, sickness, and old age; organization of more vigorous and more effective public-health programs; institution of more abundant recreational facilities and a more practical system of public education; and restriction of immigration.[67]

Nearly all of these reforms involved limitations on private-property rights and extension of public authority into areas previously regarded as the exclusive preserve of individual initiative. Taken one by one the proposals were neither novel nor drastic. Collectively, however, they implied that a new attitude toward politics and economics was taking shape. In particular they demonstrated a strong tendency to substitute public benefit for private profit as the measure of industrial efficiency. At the time of its formulation supporters of the program called it "preventive social work."[68] Today, when most of it has been adopted, we recognize it as the core of "the welfare state."

Preventive social work continued the distaste for charity which had characterized the earlier scientific philanthropy. "Charity is not a balm with which to shrive our souls, but a blot on our enlightenment and civilization," declared Lee K. Frankel, manager of the United Hebrew Charities of New York City.[69] The new movement placed less emphasis than the older one on the rescue of individual victims of social maladjustment, stressing, instead, the need for battling with the forces that every day added new recruits to the army of the miserable. Reduced to its simplest terms, preventive social work meant improving the environment of the economically weaker members of society. "Let it be this," urged Hunter, "rather than a barren relief system, administered by those who must stand by, watching the struggle, lifting no hand to aid the toilers, but ever succoring those who flee and those who are bruised and beaten."[70]

The use of the phrase "aid the toilers" was not merely poetic. Like Josephine Shaw Lowell (who had been the preceptress of several of them) the younger reformers were increasingly of the opinion that the poverty problem and the labor problem were inextricably interwoven. They doubted whether the former could be handled until more satisfactory solutions had been found for the latter. Frankel told an audience of social workers in 1906:

> The basis of all philanthropic effort must rest, not upon a maudlin sentimentality directed toward the victims of our own near-sighted and narrow policy, but shall be expressed in terms of exact justice. The opportunity must be given to all individuals to earn their living (it is true by the sweat of their brow), but under conditions which permit of decent living, proper housing, wholesome nourishment, and providing for the proverbial rainy day.[71]

Tawney voiced the same opinion in his inaugural address as director of a British foundation for the elimination of poverty.

> The problem of preventing poverty is not primarily to assist individuals who are exceptionally unfortunate. It is to make the normal conditions under which masses of men work and live such that they may lead a healthy, independent, and self-respecting life when they are *not* exceptionally unfortunate; so that when they *are* exceptionally unfortunate, misfortune may not descend upon them with the crushing weight with which it falls today upon large sections of the working classes....[72]

Advocates of the new view contended that the environment of the working classes, at work, at home, and at play was still inadequate to meet the material and spiritual needs of human life. They deemed it both necessary and possible for society to raise the standard, and thereby eradicate the social causes of poverty. They did not suppose that, even then, want would entirely disappear. They believed, however, that individuals would be in a much better position to achieve the station in life to which their energies and talents entitled them if, by joint action, men thrust aside the obstacles that no man alone could move. When people are freer than at present to control the material conditions of their own lives, said the spokesmen of the new view, they may be poor, but they will not be a social problem, and the shadow of their suffering will no longer lie so dark and heavy across the conscience of the nation.[73]

CHAPTER 9

A Factual Generation

The beautiful industrial idyls of half a century ago, the charming inculcation of thrift to the desperately poor, the stories of the astounding progress of the newsboy and the grocer's clerk (who inevitably marries the daughter of his employer), have given way to somber investigations of newsboys, messenger boys, grocers' clerks, *et al.*, and to a very wide bookshelf on the influence of evil industrial conditions upon the virtues and vices of the industrial classes.

WALTER WEYL, *The New Democracy*.

There is only one sure basis of social reform and that is Truth—a careful detailed knowledge of the essential facts of each social problem. Without this there is no logical starting place for reform and uplift.

W. E. BURGHARDT DU BOIS and AUGUSTUS GRANVILLE DILL, *The Negro Artisan*.

FACTS, facts piled up to the point of dry certitude, was what the American people then needed and wanted," wrote Ray Stannard Baker in explanation and justification of the muckraking movement.[1] A muckraker himself, Baker was one of the most resolutely objective observers of American life in the early years of the twentieth century. His comment has a bearing not only on prewar journalism, but also on the general spirit of the Progressive era. It was a time when realism influenced, if it did not entirely dominate, many aspects of American culture. Religion, philosophy, the arts, politics, and philanthropy were all agitated by efforts to discover and disclose the tangible truths of actual life.

Perplexity and suspicion sharpened the public demand for facts. At the turn of the century a generation born and raised on farms or in small towns was attempting to make the best of an environment that was more urban, cosmopolitan, and industrial than Americans had been accustomed to regard as normal. Many people were discontented with conditions and circumstances that seemed not of their own making. Harassed by rising living costs and troubled by a sense of insecurity, they were eager to have light shed on problems that baffled them. For decades critics had been condemning the growth of monopoly, the arrogance of the plutocracy, and the pervasive corruption of politics. If these oft-repeated animadversions accomplished nothing else they whetted the public appetite for more specific evidence of malfeasance in business and government.

Quite apart from the concern aroused by such darker speculations, a lively interest in the contemporary scene was stirring in the nation. The everyday environment of the average American had changed and was continuing to so rapidly that those who sought to describe it approached the task with the zest of adventurers exploring a newly discovered continent. Their enthusiasm for the freshness and vitality of the scene was catching. All agreed that a new civilization was taking shape, but none knew what its form was or would be. Not only among artists and writers, but also in the people as a whole, there was a feeling of participation in events of more than passing importance and of sharing experiences that deserved to be recorded accurately.

Curiosity regarding the facts of American social life contributed to the vogue of confession literature in the late nineties. The Lexow Committee's investigation of police corruption in New York City and William T. Stead's exposure of civic immorality in Chicago imparted a certain respectability to the ever present interest in the mysteries and miseries of the urban underworld. Rumors and occasional revelations of similar conditions in other cities made it seem almost a mark of good citizenship to be well informed about the extent of vice and crime in one's community. Magazines that still shied away from fiction dealing realistically with social outcasts vied with one another to print the memoirs of hobos, beggars, and ex-criminals. Although usually presented in the guise of moral tracts, these confessions were often unblushingly realistic in style and content. Rightly or wrongly—for the veracity of some is questionable

—they were accepted as truthful records of experience in the seamy side of life. As such, they helped to bridge the chasm between Victorian gentility and twentieth-century frankness.

In the nineties few issues excited more interest than vagrancy. In that depression-ridden decade the tramp problem reached alarming proportions. To many observers the hobo seemed the most obvious manifestation of the economic dislocations and social maladjustments of the times. He was ubiquitous and easily identifiable—the least common denominator of unemployment, parasitism, crime, and vice. Moreover, he was the best example that the age afforded of the individual's protest against social pressures. The tramp was a voluntary exile from society; his mode of life and standard of values contrasted sharply with those of ordinary mortals. Where other men surrendered their lives to the pursuit of comfort and security, he held fast to man's choicest possession, freedom. Not infrequently, therefore, a measure of grudging respect was mingled with the scorn that an outraged society heaped on him.

Appropriately enough the most influential of the confession writers, Josiah Flynt, gained his reputation by a series of sketches of hobo life. Although he was later hailed as the originator of "realistic sociology" and ultimately awarded the title of "the first muckraker,"[2] it was in no spirit of scientific inquiry that Flynt began the wanderings he described in *Tramping with Tramps* (1901). The son of a Chicago newspaperman and the nephew of Frances Willard in whose Evanston home he spent part of his restless boyhood, Flynt was the victim of psychological conflicts that made it impossible for him to accept the discipline or assume the responsibilities of normal life. Instead, he ran away; he rode the freights, begged handouts, slept in haystacks, served a brief jail sentence, and tasted the other hardships and pleasures of an outlaw existence.

Flynt was a bona-fide hobo for only about eight months, in 1889. After the publication of his first article on the subject in 1891 his excursions into hoboland were undertaken, ostensibly, at least, for purposes of research. Short though it was, this early experience equipped him with an understanding of tramping as a way of life. He had the true hobo's disdain for "enforced vagrants"; that is, migratory workers and the itinerant unemployed. His interest was centered exclusively on the men who had chosen vagabondage in preference to more conventional professions. He maintained that these "voluntary vagrants" were more interesting and worthy of study than the larger group of men who had been driven into vagabondage by the pressure of adverse economic conditions.[3] Flynt's point of view, unfortunately, was as characteristic of middle-class opinion as of the attitude of the tramps themselves.

Although Flynt called the real tramps "human parasites" and "discouraged criminals," his description of their life was remarkably free from censure. He told how hobos duped kindhearted citizens and evaded the forces of the law as though the sly and cynical dodges they practiced were the most natural things in the world. Nothing about their mode of existence surprised or shocked him unless it was society's willingness to put up with the expense and nuisance of supporting large numbers of idle, homeless, and useless persons. He had a fellow craftsman's admiration for those members of the guild who excelled at their calling, and in one typical passage he asserted that success in tramping demanded the same combination of "diligence, patience, nerve, and politeness" as eminence in any other field of endeavor.[4]

The distinction of Flynt's work lay in its flavor of authenticity. Flynt had lived with tramps and he wrote as an insider. His matter-of-fact account of tramping adventures was absorbing, not because the story was either moving or exciting, but because it bore the stamp of truth. Flynt's method was realistic; where others had studied the problem academically, he had examined it "on its own grounds and in its peculiar conditions and environment."[5] He had arrived at the method by chance rather than design, but his success with it convinced other investigators that the scientific approach to social research was through firsthand explorations of life in the lower depths.

What Flynt had done for tramps Owen Kildare sought to do for the related but not identical class of city bums. Like Flynt, Kildare had intimate personal knowledge of his subject matter. Unlike Flynt, however, Kildare was not a fugitive from respectability, but an eager convert to it. Orphaned while still a baby, thrust on the street to forage for himself when a boy of seven, he had grown to manhood in the debauched Bowery district during the 1870's and 1880's. For more than twenty years, according to his own report, he led an existence that was as depraved as his environment. Kildare's regeneration was effected by a young schoolteacher whom he met in 1894. She taught him not only to read and write, but also inspired him to give up, at the age of thirty, his old associations and to find respectable employment. After numerous tribulations, which he described in his popular autobiography, *My Mamie Rose* (1903), Kildare became a feature writer for the Sunday supplements, a reporter for several New York newspapers, and a frequent contributor to the family magazines.

Kildare's most informative book was *My Old Bailiwick* (1906), a circumstantial exposé of the haunts and habits of the 50,000 bums who inhabited New York's cheap lodginghouses. Some of his contemporaries were already beginning to regard these shambling, defeated men with a certain tolerance and sympathy. Not so Kildare, whose social attitudes had been strongly influenced by the genteel schoolteacher who had reshaped his own life. To him they were "has-beens," "human junk," and "wrecks of their own folly"—objects of concern but not fit subjects for pity. He was a reformer as well as a journalist, and his aim was to awaken in his readers a sense of responsibility for eliminating a public nuisance.

The thesis of Kildare's book was that, far from being unduly harsh, the life of the "has-been" was enervatingly soft. This was precisely the point that advocates of scientific philanthropy had been making for fifty years or more, but Kildare buttressed the argument with a wealth of detail gained from his own experiences as a Bowery bum. He challenged the popular notion that flophouses were vermin-infested dens of iniquity, asserting, to the contrary, that although drab and depressing, they were seldom either particularly dirty or peculiarly wicked.[6] Their chief characteristic, and their worst danger, as he saw it, was cheapness. Like everything else the "has-beens" required to stay alive, shelter could be obtained for a pittance. It was not necessary for them to seek regular work because they could live on the small sums obtained from begging or occasional odd jobs. The bare essentials of existence cost these confirmed idlers so little that they were able to spend a larger proportion of their incomes on dissipation than any other group in the population. Hence, Kildare concluded, they had no economic incentive to reform.

In *My Old Bailiwick* Kildare proposed the application of a rigorous work test to all vagrants. We must "assay this mass of useless humanity with the acid of honest work," he declared.[7] "Work for those who will, reformatories for those who will not" was his slogan. It is apparent from his other writings, however, that Kildare recognized that work alone was an inadequate answer to the problem. In his novel *The Wisdom of the Simple* (1905) he described the honest poverty of low-income working-class families as a brutish state; and in his autobiography he confessed that his own regeneration had been accomplished by love and understanding rather than by stern warnings to work or go to jail.

The real message of Kildare's work was that indifference, even more than laziness, was at the root of the "has-been" problem. Existence for the bums had deteriorated into "a drifting, a sliding to nowhere."[8] They had lost the will to aspire toward a better life; they were content with too little. In this sense their indifference was but another form of a malaise that infected all society. "We, the more fortunate, are also afflicted with that dread disease, carelessness, and so long as we get 'ours'—no matter how we get it—we do not care much for aught else."[9] Were it not for a kind of social sickness we would not permit human wrecks to drift through our communities as aimlessly, helplessly, and dangerously as derelicts on the sea. In our own way, he suggested, the rest of us are very nearly as indifferent to the possibility of a more wholesome society and as little inclined to work for it as the most wretched of the dispirited men we call bums.

In the same year (1891) as Flynt published his first article on tramps a young Princeton graduate embarked on what he called "an experiment in reality." Walter Wyckoff, a widely traveled son of Presbyterian missionaries to India, became convinced in his mid-twenties that the "slender book-learned lore" acquired in his formal education had failed to provide him with "vital knowledge of men and the principles by which they live and work."[10] His experiment consisted of going to work as an unskilled laborer. It lasted for eighteen months, during which he beat his way from Connecticut to California.

"I am vastly ignorant of the labor problem and am trying to learn by experience," Wyckoff wrote at the outset of his sojourn among the workers. Starting as a day laborer on a construction gang, he worked successively as hotel porter, ditchdigger, farm hand, and teamster's helper in a logging camp. In Chicago, between spells of unemployment, he obtained an unskilled job in a factory and worked on a road-building crew at the World's Fair grounds. West of Chicago he passed from one odd job to another until he reached the Pacific coast.

Wyckoff's sampling of manual occupations was necessarily haphazard, and he stayed on no job long enough to acquire more than a superficial understanding of the workers' problems. His "experiment in reality" was a courageous personal undertaking and, from the author's point of view, a rewarding spiritual exercise; but it was not a systematic survey of labor problems. Nevertheless, when Wyckoff published *The Workers* (1897 and 1899), a lengthy report of his experiences as an unskilled laborer, the book was immediately, and justly, hailed as an important contribution to sociology. Like Flynt, Wyckoff broke new ground both in subject matter and methodology. He directed attention to a segment of the population that had been largely ignored by previous writers, and he demonstrated that the way to investigate living issues was to consult life, not books.

Wyckoff's example was soon followed by numerous students. Lillian Pettengill, identifying herself as "a college woman," became a domestic servant in order to obtain "a look upon the ups and downs of this particular dog-life from the dog's end of the chain."[11] Other researchers, assuming disguises appropriate to the task, infiltrated beggardom, Southern mining and lumber camps, and the ranks of the unemployed.[12] Even persons such as Jack London, with much less reason than Wyckoff to bemoan lack of worldly knowledge, engaged in role playing to secure data for books and articles.[13]

The Woman Who Toils (1903) by Bessie and Marie Van Vorst was a companion volume to Wyckoff's study of unskilled male workers. Its subtitle, *Being the Experiences of Two Gentlewomen as Factory Girls*, conveys something of the tone and contents but does the work less than justice. As a picture of industrial conditions the Van Vorsts' book marked an advance over Wyckoff's effort because it devoted more space to factory employment, covered a wider range of jobs, and was more critical in approach. When a friend asked whether it was not true that factory girls were generally happy, Marie Van Vorst replied with an asperity foreign to Wyckoff:

> Is it a satisfaction to the leisure class, to the capitalist and employer, to feel that a woman poorly housed, ill fed, in imminent moral danger, . . . overworked, overstrained by labour varying from

> ten to thirteen hours a day, by all-night labour, and destruction of body and soul *is happy?*
>
> Do you wish her to be so? Is the existence ideal?[14]

The chief weakness of *The Woman Who Toils*, as of other books of its kind, was that the situations described were artificial. It was neither a scholarly work nor an authentic record of working-class life. The Van Vorsts were rich women on a temporary excursion into poverty. They could, and they apparently did, escape from privation whenever they chose by changing their clothes and resuming their proper stations in society. They could not experience the anxiety of real workingwomen who were unable, except in dreams, to transform themselves into ladies. Nor could these two gentlewomen, by working at a few jobs in several scattered cities, obtain the data necessary for a comprehensive analysis of women's work. When the authors attempted to generalize on the basis of their limited observations, their conclusions were suspect because the supporting evidence was fragmentary, the experience factitious.

Unlike the numerous accounts of contrived adventure, *The Long Day* (1905) was—or at least professed to be—the true story of an honest-to-goodness working girl related by herself. Published anonymously, but attributed to Dorothy Richardson, *The Long Day* chronicled the experiences of an eighteen-year-old girl from rural Pennsylvania who came to New York to earn a living. She had no family at home, no friends in the city, and very limited funds. Her search for decent lodging at a price she could pay acquainted her with slovenly boardinghouses, rented rooms in tenement flats, and appalling institutional "homes" for working girls. "Work or starve, work or starve" was the refrain that drummed in her ears as she made the rounds of factories and shops. She found, to her dismay, that it was possible both to work and to go hungry, for, although jobs were available, it was not always possible to support oneself on the wages offered inexperienced help.

For several years "Rose Fortune," as the writer called herself, spent the long day in factories making paper boxes, artificial flowers, jewel cases, and underwear. She "shook" in a laundry and demonstrated wares in a ten-cent store. While thus engaged she became familiar with the literary and musical tastes of her coworkers, their slang, recreation, and moral standards. She also came to know the fatigue, the layoffs, the danger of fires, accidents, and occupational illness to which all of them were sometimes exposed. Her experiences and observations were not unlike those of the Van Vorsts, but instead of being a sequence of arbitrarily terminated incidents, *The Long Day* provided a connected narrative of one woman's adjustment to the task of supporting herself.

The Long Day was a success story. Not that Rose Fortune married a duke or a millionaire, but she did manage to summon enough energy after the day's work to study shorthand and typing, so that eventually she was able to obtain a responsible secretarial position. Implicit in the book, however, was the recognition that for many working girls the ending was less happy. They did not have the health, the education, or the will to surmount the obstacles and withstand the temptations that confronted them. Few of them ever found the key to even such a modest success as Rose Fortune achieved: learning to work instead of being worked.

Narratives of personal experience popularized and humanized sociological literature, but they were individual case histories, not finished examples of social research. The writings of Wyckoff, the Van Vorsts, and Miss Richardson, in common with nearly all studies of working-class life undertaken around the turn of the century, tended to be descriptive rather than analytical. Labor was still such a largely unexplored subject that books about it, even by experienced investigators, often resembled travelogues. In *America's Working People* (1900) Charles B. Spahr made an ambitious but not entirely successful attempt to survey the labor scene in the nation as a whole. Like a conscientious sight-seer Spahr covered all the high spots on a well-planned itinerary, but he executed the project in such a hasty and summary fashion that his book did little more than convey a sense of the enormous complexity of American economic life.[15] Working on a smaller canvas, A. M. Simons, in *Packingtown* (1899), presented a brutally realistic picture of bad working and worse living conditions in the Chicago stockyards district. The coal strike of 1902 called forth both an official investigation and numerous journalistic accounts of life in the coal fields.[16] Shortly thereafter Peter Roberts described the people and social institutions of Pennsylvania's "islands of anthracite" as minutely as though the region were a remote archipelago in the South Seas.[17]

Very gradually more consciously analytical studies began to take their place beside the volumes of description. W. E. B. DuBois at Atlanta University and Mary White Ovington in New York launched the inquiries that were to yield the first scientific knowledge of the status of the Negro in American society.[18] Government statisticians and agents of private philanthropic societies made several careful attempts to ascertain the economic condition of immigrant groups.[19] The settlement houses conducted block-by-block surveys of poverty-stricken neighborhoods and encouraged young college graduates to examine the homes, health, budgets, and employment of families living in the vicinity of the settlements.[20] With each year official or semiofficial tenement-house investigations became more frequent and thorough, providing interested students with a new fund of information on the housing—and inferentially on the home life—of the poorer classes.[21]

Of all these undertakings the one that was to exert the greatest influence on later social research was the New York tenement-house investigation of 1900. Although carried out by a state commission, the enterprise was almost entirely a project of the Charity Organization Society of New York. In 1898 the Society had established a tenement-house committee whose members included such well-known and experienced advocates of housing reform as Felix Adler, Richard Watson Gilder, E. R. L. Gould, and Jacob Riis. Failing in an attempt to obtain adoption of improved construction standards in the metropolitan building code adopted in 1899, the committee prepared and held a tenement-house exhibition in the spring of 1900. It was this exhibition, which acquainted both the public and influential officials of the state government with the seriousness of existing conditions, that prompted Governor Theodore Roosevelt to appoint the New York State Tenement House Commission.

The exhibition was itself a notable achievement in graphic presentation of sociological data. It was hardly news to any New Yorker that housing in the slums was appallingly bad, but never before had so many facts about the problem been assembled in so informative a way. Arranged by Lawrence Veiller, secretary of the tenement-house committee, the exhibits included more than a thousand photographs, detailed maps of slum districts, numerous statistical tables and charts, and papier-mâché representations of tenement blocks. These displays not only showed how many tenement rooms were without outside light or ventilation, but also correlated information on pauperism and disease with housing conditions. Among the most alarming revelations was that even worse buildings than were to be found in the historic slum districts were being erected at the rate of several thousand a year in new areas of the expanding city. Veiller's purpose in the exhibition was to make clear that working-class families were more poorly housed in New York than in any other city of the civilized world, and that they were required to pay more in rent—approximately one fourth of their earnings—than was demanded of workers for better homes in other communities.[22]

Many of the data originally compiled for the exhibition were incorporated in *The Tenement House Problem* (1903), the two-volume report that Robert W. De Forest and Veiller submitted in the name of the State Tenement House Commission. De Forest, chairman of the Commission and president of the C.O.S., was a corporation lawyer who had been drawn into philanthropy, and in a sense into the reform movement, through the influence of Josephine Shaw Lowell.[23] Veiller, who was secretary of the Commission, contributed an essay tracing the history of the tenement problem since the 1830's, analyzing earlier attempts to deal with it, and describing the present condition of the tenement population. Once again, as in the C.O.S. exhibition, he made the point that the tenements housed not only "the drunken, the dissolute, the improvident, the diseased," but also "the great mass of the respectable workingmen" and their families.[24] Technical experts employed by the Commission called attention to defects in the type of tenements then being constructed in respect to light, ventilation, sanitation, fire danger, and privacy. The report also contained detailed recommendations for changes in the existing tenement-house laws, specified improvements and alterations necessary to bring existing structures to a minimum standard of safety and decency, and suggested administrative machinery to make the tenement laws enforceable.

All the recommendations contained in the report were put into effect.[25] *The Tenement House Problem* was thus not only the most thorough and constructive examination yet made of the housing situation in any American city, but also the most effective in securing remedial action. For almost a decade De Forest's and Veiller's report stood as a model of social research, impressive equally in methodology and practical results. It demonstrated that social evils long denounced in general terms could be analyzed factually, that specific remedies for their correction could be prescribed, and that those remedies would be applied if convincing evidence of their need and appropriateness was presented to the public. The lesson of the tenement-house investigation seemed to be that the path to reform lay through research.

Robert Hunter's *Poverty* (1904), like the books by Flynt, Kildare, Wyckoff, the Van Vorsts, and Miss Richardson, was based in large part on the author's own experiences and observations. The experiences on which Hunter drew, however, were quite different from those of the writers mentioned. In the eight and a half years that intervened between his graduation from Indiana University and the publication of *Poverty*, Hunter had lived in close contact with the poorest and most degraded elements in the population, but he had lived among them as a social worker and settlement resident. He wrote, therefore, as a professional rather than as an amateur sociologist—as a trained and sympathetic observer, but not as a direct participant in the struggles of the poor.

Hunter explained that his book did not pretend to be a scientific or exhaustive study of all the conditions, causes, and problems of poverty. Nevertheless, his approach to the topic was broader and his handling of the material much more searching than his disclaimer would suggest. His purpose, as he put it, was to "state the problem"; that is, to define poverty, estimate its extent, reveal the evils it produced, and suggest remedial measures that society might adopt to deal with it. *Poverty* was therefore hardly the "modest undertaking" that Hunter called it. Regardless of its limitations it was the most comprehensive as well as the most controversial treatment of the subject yet attempted in the United States.

Much of the controversy was provoked by Hunter's assertion that even in fairly prosperous times no fewer than 10,000,000 persons in the United States lived in poverty. Nearly all readers were shocked by this figure, and many were inclined to believe that Hunter had erred in placing the number of the poor so high. Conservatives, in particular, were unwilling to admit that distress was anywhere nearly as prevalent as Hunter indicated. Liberals, on the other hand, accepted his statement as proof of the need for reform. Hunter himself admitted that his estimate was a guess derived from such statistics as were available on pauperism, case loads of charitable societies, evictions, pauper burials, unemployment, industrial accidents, and wage rates. He contended that if a truly scientific census of the poor were taken the results would probably show that many more than 10,000,000 persons were in a condition of poverty.[26]

The argument between those who thought Hunter's estimate too high and those who believed it substantially correct was not easily resolved, because neither side was in possession of facts to support its position. In the absence of factual knowledge, opinion regarding the extent of poverty was necessarily determined by personal bias, temperament, and casual observation. Nevertheless, the dispute was by no means barren of results. It revealed how little reliable information on the condition of the poor and of the working class was available even to specialists in the field and demonstrated that no generally satisfactory conclusions on the extent of poverty in the United States could be drawn until a great many more basic data had been accumulated.

This result was not entirely accidental. In one sense Hunter's whole book was a plea for recognition of the nation's obligation to ascertain how well or badly its people fared. Neglect even to inquire into the amount of distress in the state struck him as symptomatic of "the grossest moral insensitiveness" on the part of society.[27] He observed that Americans, although they spent more money on statistical investigations than any other people, knew less about the economic circumstances of their fellow citizens. We do not know how many of the poor we have; we do not know whether their number is increasing or decreasing; we cannot be sure whether, in proportion to population, we have more or fewer of them than other countries. "But ought we not to know?" he demanded. Until we do, he said, all our boasts that we have no real poverty problem in the United States must be taken as evidence of either ignorance or indifference.

Twenty years before Hunter wrote *Poverty* William Graham Sumner had objected that there was no possible definition of "a poor man." He deplored the use of the phrase because he deemed it dangerously elastic and capable of covering a host of "social fallacies."[28] Unlike Sumner, Hunter and many other social scientists active in the decade and a half before World War I believed that poverty could be defined in arithmetical terms. To them "a poor man" meant any person who, for whatever reason, was unable to provide himself and his dependents with a decent standard of living. They maintained that it was possible to determine the components of a decent living and also to compute the income required to obtain it. According to their definition, therefore, the poor were simply those members of society whose incomes fell below the established minimum.

In *A Living Wage* (1906) the Catholic economist John A. Ryan formulated a statement of a fair standard of living that was consistent with progressive thought on the matter. His contention was that an American family deserved more than just enough food, clothing, and shelter to support life on a subsistence level. The essential physical requirements should be provided in such quantity and quality as to enable the family to maintain both health and self-respect. The family budget should provide for savings and insurance; it should also permit expenditures for "mental and spiritual culture"—education, reading, modest recreation, and membership in church, labor union, and clubs. These things should be paid for from the father's earnings. It should not be necessary for the wife or the children under sixteen to work outside the home.[29]

Ryan adopted $600 a year as a rough approximation of a living wage for the head of a family of moderate size in the United States in 1905.[30] This figure was necessarily arrived at in a somewhat arbitrary and deductive fashion. At approximately the same time, however, studies of the cost of living and of the actual expenditures of working-class families were being made by settlement workers and statisticians employed by state and federal bureaus. These inquiries confirmed Ryan's view that anything less than $600 a year was not a living wage and indicated that in the larger cities an annual income of from $650 to $800 was needed to support a family of normal size.[31]

More difficult to ascertain, but equally important to know, was the proportion of American workers who failed to obtain a living wage. Ryan estimated that at least 60 per cent of the adult male wage earners received less than $600 annually.[32] Other economists who worked on the same problem in the next few years came to an almost identical conclusion. Generally speaking, they found that adult male workers in the leading industries seldom received less than $450 or more than $600 a year and that the average annual wage was between $500 and $600. Their figures indicated that from one half to two thirds of the workers earned less than enough to provide a family with the vaunted American standard of living.[33]

In the new view of poverty these underpaid workers comprised the most numerous of the poor. It was the dearth of exact and reliable information on their way of life, betraying an apparent indifference toward their plight, that Hunter thought disgraceful. The organization of the Charities Publication Committee in 1905 attested that other prominent social workers shared his opinion. The new group was composed of Jane Addams, Jacob Riis, and influential representatives of the organized charity and settlement movements; it served as an editorial board for the magazine *Charities;* and its primary objective was "the undertaking of important pieces of social investigation not provided for by any existing organization."[34]

Under the skillful direction of Edward T. Devine and Paul U. Kellogg, *Charities*, which had originated as the house organ of the New York C.O.S., had rapidly developed into the leading American journal of social work. Even before 1905 the magazine had sponsored several social surveys, but, as Devine admitted, these were "adolescent gymnastics" compared to the comprehensive program of research inaugurated after the formation of the Publications Committee. In the first year of the Committee's existence *Charities and the Commons* (as the magazine was known after 1905) published two special issues: "The Negro in the Cities of the North" and "Next Door to Congress."[35] Both were significant studies, but the latter, a seventy-page report on housing, health, education, and child labor in Washington, D. C., was more in harmony with the muckraking spirit and seems to have attracted greater public interest. One of its principal points was that Congress had neglected to provide the District of Columbia with a child-labor law, a compulsory-education law, and with other legislation "now deemed essential in modern communities." Devine later boasted that more social legislation was enacted for the District in the five months following the appearance of "Next Door to Congress" than in the five years preceding it.[36]

Encouraged by the favorable reception accorded the Washington issue, the Publications Committee accepted the suggestion offered by an official of the Allegheny County (Pennsylvania) Juvenile Court that a similar study be made of Pittsburgh. A distinguished staff headed by Paul Kellogg and including Florence Kelley, John

R. Commons, and Robert A. Woods was recruited to conduct the survey. The Russell Sage Foundation, whose president was the ubiquitous Robert W. De Forest, assumed the major share of the considerable costs of the venture. Field work, carried out in 1907 and 1908, was sufficiently near completion by November of the latter year to make possible an exhibition, patterned after the New York tenement-house exhibition of 1900, to display the findings of the survey staff to the people of Pittsburgh. Devine summed up these findings at a joint session of the American Economic Association and the American Sociological Society in December, 1908; and an abbreviated version of the survey report appeared in special issues of *Charities and the Commons* in the winter of 1909.[37]

The Pittsburgh survey was the first attempt made in the United States to examine thoroughly and at close range the conditions under which working people spent their lives in a modern industrial community.[38] The survey staff put the steel district under a microscope, and the facts revealed were far from pleasant. So far as the findings are susceptible of brief summary, they showed an incredible amount of overwork, reaching the extreme of a twelve-hour day and seven-day work week in the steel mills and railroad switchyards; wages that, though not lower than in other cities, were adjusted to the requirements of a single man rather than to the needs of a responsible head of a family; still lower wages for women, averaging about one half to one third the earnings of men; an absentee capitalism with social and economic results similar to those produced by absentee landlordism; and the destruction of family life under the combined pressures of the extraordinary demands of work on men, women, and children, the prevalence of preventable diseases such as typhoid fever, and the cruelly high toll of industrial accidents.[39]

The total picture that emerged from the laboriously compiled volumes of the survey was one of appalling waste resulting from social timidity and disinclination to interfere with the rites of money-making. In Pittsburgh, lives, health, strength, education, even the industrial efficiency of workmen were treated as things of little worth. The important matters were output, time, cost, and profit. In comparison to these considerations human lives and happiness were relatively unimportant. "Make do, wear out, use up, replace, discard" applied no less to men and women than to other expendable items in the industrial process. It was easier and cheaper to do business that way, and it did not seem to matter much that this false economy imposed unnecessary hardship and suffering both on individual families and on the entire community.

The Pittsburgh survey was by far the most important of the prewar social investigations. It was discussed and studied not only in Pittsburgh but throughout the country. To its influence Jane Addams attributed "the veritable zeal for reform" that agitated the United States between 1909 and 1914.[40] Supporters of nearly every good cause drew inspiration and ammunition from its pages; yet it was not a propagandistic or polemical work. It commanded respect because it was an outstanding piece of research—honest, informative, reliable. The facts it disclosed were their own best advocates. The survey findings, especially as they related to the waste of human resources, were taken to heart by a nation just awakening to the realization that conservation was as vital to its future as exploitation had been characteristic of its past.

In the years following the Pittsburgh survey social research flourished as never before and seldom since. A considerable part of this activity was subsidized by the Russell Sage Foundation. Incorporated in 1907, the Foundation was pledged by the terms of its charter to use an endowment of $10,000,000 for "the improvement of social and living conditions in the United States." That the Russell Sage Foundation was not to be a charitable organization of the old-fashioned alms-dispensing type was made clear by its first president. "The Foundation will not attempt to relieve individual or family need," De Forest announced. "Its function is to eradicate so far as possible the causes of poverty and ignorance, rather than to relieve the sufferings of those who are poor and ignorant."[41] A contribution toward the support of the Pittsburgh survey was the first substantial grant made by the Foundation in pursuance of its objective. In the next ten years it made grants totaling almost $2,000,000 to encourage research and published nearly fifty volumes, among which, in addition to *The Pittsburgh Survey*, were Lawrence Veiller's *Housing Reform* (1911) and Mary E. Richmond's textbook of social case work, *Social Diagnosis* (1917).

The Sage Foundation organized its own surveys and exhibits department in 1912 and carried out community surveys, on the Pittsburgh model, in St. Paul, Scranton, Topeka, Ithaca, Atlanta, and Springfield, Illinois.[42] Meanwhile, with *Charities and the Commons* significantly retitled *The Survey*, the Charities Publication Committee made a social study of Birmingham, Alabama, and followed up the Pittsburgh survey with a review of labor problems in all the major steel centers of the country.[43] Enthusiastic support for the community survey idea came from the "Men and Religion Forward" movement, a nationally organized effort to stimulate interest in social service among churchgoing men. Through this movement laymen in numerous cities were induced to make a systematic canvass of social conditions in the neighborhood of their churches.[44]

The state and federal governments responded to the factual temper of the times, or at least to the pressure of what was called "the social welfare lobby," by creating new fact-finding agencies and by appointing an unprecedented number of official investigatory commissions. The prewar years were, indeed, the golden age of commissions. It was a time when the solution to every difficult problem seemed to lie in submitting it to a group of good citizens and disinterested experts who were expected to examine the question from all sides and then recommend suitable legislation. In practice legislatures did not always heed the recommendations of the advisory groups, but very few reforms were enacted until after one or more commissions had conducted lengthy hearings into the need for and practicability of the proposed remedies. Regardless of immediate political consequences, some of the commissions made valuable contributions to research. Thus, in 1908, Frances Kellor and Lillian Wald participated in an official inquiry into "the condition, welfare, and industrial opportunities of aliens in the State of New York"—topics about which there was a plethora of talk but little knowledge; and in 1910 the governor of Illinois named Charles R. Henderson and Dr. Alice Hamilton to a commission charged with exploring the previously neglected field of occupational disease.[45]

An outpouring of reports on the condition of labor and the standard of living reflected the mounting interest and activity in social research on the part of agencies of the national government. Reports of federal investigations not only became more voluminous and broader in scope than before, but also more specific in presentation and more critical in tone. These tendencies were especially marked after Charles P. Neill succeeded the politic Carroll D. Wright as Commissioner of Labor in 1905. Wright's annual and special reports had often been couched in such cautious language that their meaning was ambiguous, but Neill did not hesitate to speak the truth bluntly. The new commissioner showed his colors in 1906 when he and the New York social worker James B. Reynolds prepared a scathing account of unsavory conditions in the meat-packing industry.[46] The tenor of the reports of the Bureau of Labor during Neill's administration is indicated by a typical passage from one of them:

> The female workers in the confectionery industry are largely unskilled, they are usually young, to a considerable extent they are foreigners, and they are unorganized. Consequently they are peculiarly unable to have any effective voice in fixing their wages. They take what they can get and, at least in the establishments covered by this investigation, the majority were plainly getting less than a living wage.[47]

Under Neill's direction agents of the Bureau of Labor conducted the most thorough investigations yet attempted in the United States of social insurance and of the condition of working women and children. As will be shown in later chapters both of these studies exercised a strong influence on contemporary reform movements.

The last volume of the report on woman and child labor had scarcely appeared when the newly organized Children's Bureau began a series of investigations of infant mortality. Little was known about the death rate of American babies because, owing to incomplete birth registration in most states, there was no reliable information on the birth rate for the nation as a whole. Julia Lathrop, a former Hull House resident who was the first director of the Children's Bureau, proposed a novel method of inquiry. Her agents began their investigations with infants' births rather than with their deaths. They studied the social, economic, and civic environment of each child born in a given community in a given year and traced the baby's history through the first year of its life, or through that portion of a year that it lived. After these studies were under way the Bureau also began to collect and interpret statistics on maternal mortality. Josephine Goldmark, herself a skilled research worker, has described the shock the early Children's Bureau reports administered to the nation's complacency:

> We had taken for granted American superiority in sanitation and health. American plumbing was the sign and symbol, the world over, of our national pre-eminence in physical care. Now for the first time, in this house-to-house canvass, was disclosed a very different and horrifying state of affairs. Babies under one year were dying at a rate unthought of: for the United States as a whole, a quarter of a million babies were dying each year. The maternal death rate was also shocking, higher than the deaths of women from any other cause except tuberculosis, higher than in any other civilized country of the world.[48]

The reports bore out the charge made half a century earlier by Horace Greeley that poverty was both the mother and murderer of children.[49] They showed that it was twice and, in some circumstances, more than three times as dangerous to be born into a poor family as in one of comfortable economic circumstances.[50]

On the same day as the Children's Bureau began operations—August 23, 1912—President Taft gave his approval to an act authorizing the appointment of a Commission on Industrial Relations. The measure had been proposed and drafted by a group of economists and social workers, headed by Devine, who were anxious to have an impartial but official body conduct a nationwide survey of the deeper causes of industrial unrest.[51] Controversy between Taft and Congress over the composition of the Commission delayed the start of the investigation until after the Wilson administration took office. When the Commission at length began its work the nine members, representing industry, labor, and the public, faced a difficult assignment. They were to "inquire into the general condition of labor in the principal industries of the United States, including agriculture," and to "seek to discover the underlying causes of dissatisfaction in the industrial situation."[52] To gather data on these controversial topics the Commission held numerous public hearings, many of them quite heated, in cities throughout the country, and listened to the often-contradictory testimony of hundreds of witnesses.

Members of the Commission, seriously divided in their sympathies and social philosophies, were unable to agree on the conclusions to be drawn from the evidence submitted. However, in the opinion of Basil Manly, director of research and investigation, the hearings showed that the incomes of from one third to one half of the families of wage earners in manufacturing and mining were inadequate to support "anything like a comfortable and decent condition."[53] He stated that there were four basic causes of labor unrest: unjust distribution of wealth and income; unemployment and denial of opportunity to earn a living; partiality toward employers in the writing, administration, and adjudication of law; and denial to employees of the right and opportunity to form effective labor organizations.[54] Testimony received by the Commission on the last point was voluminous and eloquent.[55]

The Commission's report, *Industrial Relations* (1916), contains a wealth of information and opinion on the status of industrial democracy in the United States on the eve of World War I. It is interesting not only as a summary of the amount and kind of data on working-class problems available to students at the close of the Progressive era, but also as an encyclopedia of the varying sentiments toward labor then current. The advance registered since the turn of the century both in the accumulation of specific information and in the development of enlightened attitudes was impressive. Nevertheless, the eleven volumes of *Industrial Relations* are quite as interesting for the gaps in knowledge that they reveal as for the positive information presented.

One area in which knowledge was still very sketchy became apparent shortly after the Commission began its hearings. During the winter of 1913–14 reports of widespread unemployment began to be received from several large cities. In this instance foes of the Wilson administration were inclined to give credence to estimates placing the number of the jobless at astronomical figures, while administration supporters tended to minimize the seriousness of the problem. Much of the testimony submitted at the Commission's hearings related to unemployment; but because of the failure of Congress to appropriate funds to complete the tabulation of the portions of the census of 1910 dealing with unemployment, the most recent comprehensive data on the subject were fourteen years old. The Commission asked police officers in various cities to make a count of the jobless, a method that a well-qualified expert characterized as hurried, ill advised, and subject to political pressures.[56] In the absence of any national machinery for collecting current statistics on unemployment, *Industrial Relations* could offer no reliable data on the actual number of people in the United States who were out of work. It could only report that want of work was a major cause of discontent.

The need for more serious study of this vital problem was the theme of Frances Kellor's *Out of Work* (1915). On the subject of unemployment, she remarked, "research is limited, knowledge circumscribed, and literature local or indefinite." While creating committees or commissions to investigate almost every other problem, she continued, we have permitted the wilderness of unemployment to remain unexplored, have allowed its waste to go unchecked, and have suffered its causes to remain obscure.[57] Miss Kellor carefully examined all the existing sources of information on unemployment and shrewdly analyzed the defects in prevailing methods of gathering data. Her point was that no trustworthy statement on the extent of joblessness could be made as long as neither states nor the federal government required employers to furnish employment records.[58]

As Miss Kellor well realized, the fundamental problem was much more complex. What was needed was not simply improvement in reporting methods and statistical techniques, but a keener awareness than had yet developed of the fact that unemployment was a genuine and constant problem even in prosperous America. No book, no matter how penetrating, could create that awareness. Despite all the demonstrations and protestations of economists and sociologists to the contrary, the notion still persisted that any man willing to work could find a steady job—somewhere. Not literature but bitter experience would finally be required to destroy that happy delusion.

The foregoing recital of the piling up of inquiry upon inquiry, survey after survey, raises certain difficult questions. Were not the friends of reform mistaken in assuming that repeated investigations of the same old problems signified progress? Was not the bustling activity in social research but a form of busywork that was at best a substitute for positive remedial action? That reform was effected in spite of the penchant for meticulous, time-consuming investigations will be shown in subsequent chapters. Nevertheless, it is all too true that the appointment of a commission to inquire further into an obvious evil may mean that reform is being sidetracked rather than advanced. To demand "an objective, impartial re-examination of all the issues involved" is a favorite method of halting reform. The resulting investigation is not research but a device to kill time and destroy interest. It satisfies the popular clamor—loud but short-lived—that "something must be done" without seriously disturbing the privileged groups that are determined that nothing detrimental to their interest shall be done.

In 1913 R. H. Tawney delivered some remarks on the status of social research in England that were very nearly as applicable to the American as to the British situation.

> Social research has in the last ten years become an industry. Whilst progress was undoubtedly retarded in the 19th century through the contempt of our grandfathers for economic investigation, there seems some danger that it may be paralysed in the 20th through a superstitious reverence for accumulated facts. . . . There are, it is true, a considerable number of matters where practical action is delayed by the absence of sufficient knowledge. There are more, perhaps, where our knowledge is sufficient to occupy us for the next 20 years, and where the continuance of social evils is not due to the fact that we do not know what is right, but to the fact that we prefer to continue doing what is wrong.

All that economic inquiry can do, Tawney concluded, is to give society the information upon which to found reasonable judgments, and thereby to deprive it of excuses for either inaction or unwise action.[59]

In the United States, as in Tawney's England, the great outburst of interest in social investigation came during a period of political liberalism. Conversely, the development of political progressivism coincided with the rise of social research. The two movements were so closely related that it is almost impossible to separate one from the other. Disembodied ideals of justice, fair play, and democracy were not sufficient to cope with the complex issues of modern industrial society. Reform could no more be effected by platitudinous avowals of righteousness than by generalized denunciations of evil. Nor could research alone accomplish reform. Mere exposure of wrongdoing did not automatically produce remedial action. But until practices long tolerated had been clearly demonstrated to be unnatural, unnecessary, and detrimental to society scant attention was paid to them. Even then action sometimes faltered. On the whole, however, the first decade and a half of the twentieth century was unusually productive of social reform. It was a time when the will to improve conditions was guided and strengthened by knowledge gained from factual inquiry, when the zeal to do good was matched by eagerness to learn how and what to do.

CHAPTER 10

The Literary Record

> But what, asked the wanderer insistently, does LIFE mean in this vast gray labor-house?
>
> ROBERT HERRICK, *A Life for a Life.*

> By learning the sufferings and burdens of men, I became aware as never before of the life-power that has survived the forces of darkness, the power which, though never completely victorious, is continuously conquering. The very fact that we are still here carrying on the contest against the hosts of annihilation proves that on the whole the battle has gone for humanity.
>
> HELEN KELLER, *Out of the Dark.*

DURING the Progressive era the life and condition of the poor received almost as much attention in imaginative literature as in factual social research. From the 1890's onward American writers were less and less content to chronicle only the affairs of the polite and prosperous classes and became increasingly interested in describing the adventures of the unrefined and underprivileged members of society. Many authors sought to depict the romance of poverty; others presented realistic accounts of lower-class life; and still others attacked the sins of society and glorified individual or class protests against injustice.

One of the characteristics of the literature of the period was an unusual emphasis upon strength and vitality. In its cruder forms this amounted almost to a worship of force. In its better manifestations it expressed itself in enthusiasm for humanity in the mass and reverence for the life power in individuals. There was a close connection between this literary tendency and the political and economic struggles of the time. As American democracy broadened and strengthened its base, American literature expanded its horizons to include consideration of types, classes, ways of life, and social issues that, for the most part, had previously been excluded from its compass.

In an unfavorable but not entirely hostile review of Frank Norris' *McTeague* (1899) a critic remarked that the book dealt with "a class of people that story-tellers generally avoid or at least seldom select for their chief characters."[1] There was a good deal of truth in this observation. Popular writers had already begun to exploit low life and to search out the local color of the tenements, but they had not yet shown much interest in the lower middle class, the stratum of society to which Norris' hero and heroine belonged.

The McTeagues were not poor in the ordinary meaning of the word. Mac was an unlicensed dentist with a fair practice; Trina, his wife, was the pretty daughter of a frugal and respectable immigrant family. They lived in a small apartment in a business block, a modest but neat and comfortable home. Both husband and wife were industrious, and for several years after their marriage they prospered. Like others in their position, however, Mac and Trina were economically insecure. Thoughts of money were hardly ever out of their minds. In the best of times they had to skimp and be cautious in their spending. A misfortune such as sickness or loss of work might thrust them into real want.

The critics acknowledged that the minutely detailed picture Norris drew of the McTeagues' domestic economy was an accurate rendering of the way of life of people who lived above, but dangerously near, the poverty line. The realism of the setting, however, was one of the critics' chief objections to the book. Instead of praising Norris for exploring a new literary milieu, they scolded him for wasting undisputed talent on unworthy and disagreeable material. "It is about the most unpleasant American story that anybody has ever ventured to write," complained one reviewer. With few exceptions the critics expressed the hope that Norris' next plot would fall in "more pleasant places" and that in the future his books would be "not less true but a good deal more agreeable."[2]

The popular literature of the day contained many heroes and heroines who were poorer than Mac and Trina, who lived in more sordid environments, and who suffered crueler blows of fate. There were, for example, the Jewish peddlers and sweatshop workers in the stories of Abraham Cahan, I. K. Friedman, and Myra Kelly, compared to whom the McTeagues were affluent. The confessions of beggars, bums, and thieves, which enjoyed wide popularity around the turn of the century, introduced readers to persons whose occupations were less reputable and whose morals were worse than Trina's and Mac's. As for a disagreeable plot, what could be more depressing than the tale Alice Hegan Rice unfolded in *Mrs. Wiggs of the Cabbage Patch* (1901)? The setting was a shanty in a miserable district on the outskirts of a Southern city, the heroine an impoverished widow who tried in vain to support her five children by taking in laundry. Reduced to its essentials this extremely popular and highly regarded novel was the record of a poor family's battle against starvation, with the eldest child, a boy of fifteen, sacrificing his youth, his health, and eventually his life in the unequal struggle.

Despite the wretchedness and sorrow they described, works such as *Mrs. Wiggs of the Cabbage Patch* were acceptable both to the critics and the reading public because, unlike *McTeague*, they were suffused with optimism. One could read them with assurance that love would conquer all and that everything, or nearly everything, would turn out right in the end. Mrs. Wiggs's philosophy of life, "keeping the dust off rose-colored glasses," was shared by other heroes and heroines of popular fiction. They met adversity bravely and resourcefully—and they could be helped. If criminals, they could be reformed by appeals to their better instincts; if poor, they could be lifted out of the slough of despond by kind treatment. James L. Ford attributed the success of books of this type to the authors' ability "to make the reader feel benevolent without spending a cent." He confessed that he had read *Mrs. Wiggs* with moistened eyes, and laid it down with the conviction that "if I had Rockefeller's money I would give that woman all our family washing."[3]

Trina and Mac differed from Mrs. Wiggs not only in class, but also in psychological make-up. Norris once defined romance as "the kind of fiction that takes cognizance of variations from the type of normal life."[4] In this sense *McTeague* was a romantic novel, for the leading characters were abnormal persons. The mischances Mac and Trina encountered were not all of their own making, but their inability to surmount these reverses resulted from their personal peculiarities. Being the kinds of individuals they were, they could neither help themselves nor be assisted by others. Their doom was sealed from the instant they met. From the author's point of view the deterioration of the McTeagues' fortunes was important mainly because, with each downward step, the basic elements of their characters became more obvious. Their personalities were not so much shaped as revealed by a succession of disasters. At last, when they had sunk about as low in the social scale as they could go, the McTeagues showed themselves to one another, and to the reader, in their true colors: Trina a miser and Mac a brute.

Norris was not alone in believing that people in poverty were more "real" and "natural" than those in prosperous circumstances. This was a widely held view, and it was a major factor in arousing literary and artistic interest in the poor. *McTeague* was out of step with the literary trend of the time because in it Norris made the bad characters of his hero and heroine the central theme of the book. Most of the literary treatments of poverty contemporaneous with *McTeague* dealt with good people in bad environments. Some writers searched the ranks of the poor to find individuals who departed from the type of normal life, not in depravity, but in unusual virtue and heroism. Mrs. Rice declared: "Looking for the nobility that lay hidden in the most unpromising personality became for me a spiritual treasure hunt."[5] Others, however, were content with less extraordinary figures; they attempted only to show that the poor were very much like people at other levels of society. Thus, in *The Good of the Wicked* (1904) Owen Kildare stated that his purpose was "to demonstrate that beneath the rough manner and language of my people of the tenements emotions and sentiments common to all humankind are stirring."[6]

Nearly everyone could subscribe to the dictum that human nature was basically the same at every economic level. In practice, however, most popular writers continued to regard the poor with pity strongly tinged with condescension. They portrayed the victims of poverty indulgently, delighting in their childlike simplicity, ignorance, and uncouthness—in all the outward signs of their inferiority. There was something humorous about the usually ill-fated efforts of the poor to become like other people; that is, to obtain education, respectability, and security. It was even funnier when they fell in love; for to storytellers the very notion of Cupid going slumming was comical. Besides, the uninhibited poor were true romantics who could be counted on to do anything for the sake of love. In "The Uses of Adversity" Myra Kelly wrote with seeming approval of a tenement girl who exposed her unruly younger brothers to one disease after another. While the boys were shut up in the charity ward of a hospital the girl was free to pursue her romance with a pushcart peddler.[7]

The chief difference between fiction of this sort and O. Henry's stories of "the four million" was that the former gratified the reader's sense of superiority, the latter appealed to man's fellow feeling for others of his kind. O. Henry did not patronize the shopgirls, typists, waitresses, and lonely transients he wrote about. He could not, for he was nearly of a piece with them. It was not a matter of indifference to him that working girls lived in tiny rooms whose walls closed in upon them like the sides of coffins, that they were expected to get along on six dollars a week, or that they sometimes went hungry. It did not strike him as ridiculous that the poor should seek pleasure, crave affection, spend money foolishly, or hold fast to quixotic ideals. In these respects they were no different from the rich. But their stories seemed to him more moving. They worked harder; they paid more dearly for their follies; their standards were more difficult to maintain; and they gave more freely of themselves.

At his best O. Henry could stir depths of compassion in the reader that his rivals in the field of light fiction could not even touch. Quite often he peopled his weekly stories with stereotypes, but (as Vachel Lindsay observed) in some of his tales

> The masks fall off for one queer instant there
> And show real faces: faces full of care
> And desperate longing: love that's hot or cold;
> And subtle thoughts, and countenances bold.[8]

In "The Cop and the Anthem," for example, the hero was a bum, and O. Henry drew him to conform to the standard literary specifications of the type. The man's name was Soapy; he didn't like to bathe; he was lazy and shiftless; he actually *wanted* to be arrested so that he could be sent to the workhouse to while away the winter at the taxpayers' expense. But "for one queer instant" Soapy's mask dropped. He saw clearly "the degraded days, unworthy desires, dead hopes, wrecked faculties, and base motives that made up his existence." He resolved to reform, and at that very moment, of course, was arrested. His earlier wish was realized, his later resolution shattered beyond repair.[9]

Soapy was regenerated, but he was not saved; for O. Henry, although ever hopeful and always willing to respond to the best that was in his characters, was not so determinedly optimistic as the other purveyors of commercial fiction. His stories were not all compounded of sweetness and light. "The Furnished Room" told of a suicide in one of the most frightful chambers in American literature. And it was not only love that drove O. Henry's people to despair. "Of what she earned, Dulcie received six dollars per week," he observed at the start of "An Unfinished Story." This was an unfinished tale, he said, because the future of a girl who had to manage on such a precarious budget was not very certain. He hated skinflint employers and those other oppressors of the poor, landladies and middle-aged mashers. One rooming-house keeper reminded him of "an unwholesome, surfeited worm that had eaten its nut to a hollow shell and now sought to fill the vacancy with edible lodgers."[10] Piggy, a would-be seducer of shopgirls, was such an expert in his line that he could look at a prospective conquest "and tell you to an hour how long it had been since she had eaten anything more nourishing than marshmallows and tea."[11]

O. Henry proved the thesis that authors had long asserted: that the lives of the poorer classes were as abundantly endowed with the elements of romance as those of the well-to-do. He read between the lines in what he would have called "the book of life" and found ideas for stories in individuals and incidents that others would have dismissed as unimportant. One reason for his success in finding romance in unexpected places was that he pursued the chase relentlessly. It was his stock in trade, and he had a story to write, not when the mood struck, but every week of the year. He had "the sense of the marvelous," but it was a faculty cultivated and developed by necessity as well as by inclination. Nevertheless, O. Henry was uniquely suited by temperament to be a romancer. Where others merely said, "Romance is all about us," he believed it sincerely. There was something at once humble and chivalrous in his attitude toward people. If a plain waitress imagined herself a sleeping beauty, or a piano salesman fancied himself Sir Galahad, O. Henry was willing to give each the benefit of the doubt. There was always the faint possibility that they might be right; but if they were mistaken, their dreams were, nevertheless, deserving of respect. And when the magic gates failed to open, when the court slumbered on, or the knight fell off his horse—when all that happened was disappointment and heartbreak—that, too, was a tragedy to be felt and recorded.

One of the canons of commercial fiction, observed even by writers such as O. Henry who were truly sympathetic with the poor, was that poverty was unimportant. The important matters, in literature as in life, were romance, comedy, tragedy, and nobility of character. These were constants, existing independent of economic circumstances, and it was the storyteller's task to find them wherever they occurred. If they were discoverable among people in humble walks of life, so much the better, for the locale was relatively new, the material fresh and interesting. The poverty of the characters, although incidental to the main theme of romance, contributed atmosphere, poignancy, and a pathetic quality to the narrative.

Theodore Dreiser rejected this approach to literature. He thought the writer's function was to tell the truth about human affairs, not to find or fabricate romance. He described *Sister Carrie* (1901) as "a picture of conditions done as simply and effectively as the English language will permit." After the publication of *Jennie Gerhardt* (1911) he said: "My own ambition is to represent my world, to conform to the large, truthful lines of life."[12] Dreiser was unsophisticated enough to believe that honesty was the best policy in art. His attitude toward his craft may have been influenced by preliminary training as a newspaper reporter and as a contributor of factual articles to the magazines. It seems to have been strongly affected by his admiration for realism in the graphic arts; and it is quite possible that he consciously strove to introduce into fiction that same fidelity to life that some of his contemporaries were bringing to painting.[13]

Neither as a man nor as an artist could Dreiser believe that the economic circumstances of people counted for little. His own experience and observation taught him just the opposite. Possession or lack of money seemed to him to make a lot of difference—sometimes all the difference—in the way people behaved and were treated. He knew that being poor meant going without the decencies, comforts, and pleasures that human beings wanted and needed if their lives were to have any meaning.

Dreiser, no less than O. Henry, was moved by the morning

spectacle of "typewriter girls in almost stage or society costumes entering shabby offices," and "boys and men made up to look like actors or millionaires turning in to the humblest institutions."[14] The notion that the lives of the lower classes abounded in romance and adventure, however, impressed him as false. "Humdrum," "barren," "lean," "narrow," and "pointless" were the words he used most frequently to describe the drab and cheerless existence of the poor. The poor, he knew, did not smile bravely through their tears: they sweated and strained and cursed. Some of them had "a lean, pinched appearance as though they were but poorly nourished or greatly enervated." Others wore "a furtive, hurried look, as though the problem of rent and food and clothing were inexplicable and they were thinking about it all the time."[15] Most of them were marking time, struggling not so much to get ahead as to make ends meet. The poverty they suffered was not "interesting" or "colorful." It blighted, when it did not entirely destroy, love, joy, kindness, and beauty.

Dreiser's attitude toward poverty coincided with that of the literary realists of the 1890's and also with opinions expressed by social workers after the turn of the century. His view, however, was more the product of personal familiarity with the problem than of reading or disinterested analysis of social conditions. "Unlike yourself," he once told H. L. Mencken, "I am biased. I was born poor."[16] Dreiser was an immigrant's son who had grown up in shabby neighborhoods among disreputable people. He could recall a time in his boyhood when his father had been out of work for more than a year. As a youth he had worked at a succession of casual low-paid jobs. On at least two occasions in his formative years he had experienced spells of unemployment and mental depression that nearly destroyed him. He was an authority on the "curious shifts of the poor" because he was better schooled in poverty than in any other subject.

Dreiser's characters often indulged in daydreams, not about Prince Charmings or Good Fairies, but about "belonging," "having a good time," wearing fine clothes, dining in expensive restaurants, and obtaining responsible positions. These reveries were only a part of their lives, however, for usually they were caught up in some serious practical financial dilemma. If their dreams were tawdry, the problems they faced were real enough. His first heroine, Carrie Meeber, came to Chicago to find a job. Without training or experience to qualify for any employment except the poorest paid, she had to go to work in a shoe factory at four dollars and fifty cents a week. After paying for her room and board she had fifty cents of her weekly earnings left to spend on clothes and recreation. Even ten cents a day for carfare was a luxury beyond her means. When she missed work for three days because of illness she knew her job was gone and she did not even return to the factory. "The winter was near at hand, she had no clothes, and now she was out of work."[17] It was a stroke of luck for her that a genial salesman, frankly described as a masher, offered to make her his mistress.

As related by Dreiser, the annals of the Gerhardt family read like a case record prepared by a charity agent. At the start the father was ill and unemployed. The Gerhardts "lived from day to day, each hour hoping that the father would get well and that the glassworks would soon start up." Jennie and her mother went to work as maids in a hotel. Then a brother was arrested for stealing coal and, soon after, Jennie herself got into trouble. Nobody was responsible for the Gerhardts' misfortunes. They were the kinds of things that regularly happened to the poor. Later, with the family resettled and everybody except the mother and the very youngest children hard at work, "the closeness with which their expenses were matching their income was an ever present menace." Dreiser studied the Gerhardt budget carefully; he showed how much each member contributed, and explained how the total was paid out for rent, coal, light, food, clothes, medical expenses, and installment payments on the furniture. The family might have scraped through, leading a "straitened, humdrum life," had Mr. Gerhardt not been injured in an accident at work. Now there was five dollars less a week coming into the treasury and a larger outgo for medical care. "Either more money must come from some source or the family must beg for credit and suffer the old tortures of want."[18] It was at this point that Jennie, like Carrie before her, accepted the advances of a generous man.

Like many of his contemporaries Dreiser was intrigued by tramps, whom he compared to "gulls or moles, or some different and unsocial animal" that still found in man its rightful prey. They did not suggest want or poverty to him so much as "a kind of devil-may-care indifference and even contempt for all that society as we know it prizes so highly."[19] His special interest and sympathy, however, went out to those individuals who were less self-reliant, who took life seriously and hence were tortured by it. For the men and women who did the work of the world, and who, in trying to get along as best they could, so often stumbled or made mistakes, he had the tenderest compassion. Most of his characters were attempting to rise out of the dreary environs of poverty into more spacious and easy economic domains. Yet he was always conscious of the failures and the "has-beens," whose paths turned downward and who no longer had the will or the ability to reverse their course.

Dreiser's account, in *Sister Carrie*, of Hurstwood's sinking into the sea of the forgotten men of the Bowery was remarkable both for its detail and its restraint. He told the story objectively, as if the facts alone were sufficient and needed no comment. Hurstwood's decline was a slow process, and Dreiser recorded it minutely: the man's growing lethargy and unsuspected diffidence, the hotel lobbies he frequented, the jobs he obtained, the charities he patronized, the weary miles he walked, the flophouses he slept in—even the ironic circumstance that at the outset his good appearance and decent clothes were a handicap in his fruitless search for a cheap "business opportunity." Often Hurstwood thought that "the game was up" and that he would "end his troubles"; but then he either had no money to rent a room where he could turn on the gas, or, if someone gave him a quarter or a dime, he remembered that he was hungry. "It was only when he could get nothing but insults that death seemed worth while." The time came at last, though, when Hurstwood turned out the gas, then turned it on again, and applied no match. " 'What's the use?' he said weakly, as he stretched himself to rest."[20]

Dreiser did not constantly and self-consciously insist, as did so many other writers of the day, that humanity was the same regardless of rank. He took that for granted. What impressed him were not the obvious similarities between human beings but the astounding disparities in their material conditions. He thought the peculiar "color" of modern life was imparted to it by the vivid contrasts between extremes of wealth and poverty. The social contrast gave cities "a gross and cruel and mechanical look"; its presence made society seem "so harsh and indifferent" that Dreiser said he felt numbed by it.[21] Until relatively late in his career he assumed that the contrast in conditions was not only unavoidable, but unexplainable. "The rich were rich and the poor poor, but all were in the grip of imperial forces whose ruthless purposes or lack of them made all men ridiculous, pathetic, or magnificent as you choose."[22] Only in this sense, in their helplessness in the hands of an uncertain fate, were men truly equal and alike.

To Dreiser, a truthful picture of the struggle of men and women against unequal odds was beautiful in itself. It did not have to be sweetened and prettified, as the popular writers tried to do; nor did the drama need to be heightened by use of "variations from the type of normal life." The romance, the comedy, and the tragedy were in the reality of human experience—in the urgency of the effort, the emptiness of the goal, and in the inevitable but ever unexpected intervention of death. "We toil so much, we dream so richly, we hasten so fast, and lo! the green door is opened. We are through it, and its grassy surface has sealed us forever from all which apparently we so much crave—even as, breathlessly, we are still running."[23]

Considering the subjects they dealt with, the writers thus far discussed voiced remarkably little protest against social injustice. Alice Rice and O. Henry employed economic distress mainly as an atmospheric background for romance. For all his interest in poverty, Dreiser was even more concerned with the larger mystery of life. There was no suggestion of social criticism in *McTeague*, and although *The Octopus* (1901) tended strongly in the opposite direction, Norris' conclusion was that protest was fruitless. In *The Octopus* six men were killed in a pitched battle between agents of the railroad company and the ranchers who were being turned off their land; one woman died of starvation, and another was reduced to prostitution; an upright rancher was forced to resort to bribery; a faithful workman was turned into a hunted criminal; and an inoffensive poet was driven to attempt murder. Norris showed that all of these tragedies resulted from the policies pursued by the railroad company. Yet, at the end, he insisted that they were but trivial incidents in the growth, harvest, and marketing of the "nourisher of nations," the wheat. The wheat was a "mighty world-force" that neither ranchers nor railroad could control; and Norris, despite his recital of evil, professed that "all things, surely, inevitably, and resistlessly work together for good."[24]

The note of criticism and protest that Norris sounded and then muffled in *The Octopus* became almost the dominant one in the literature of the following decade and a half. Numerous poets, dramatists, and novelists brought to their work the reformer's ardor and the muckraker's passion for facts. They were less given to pondering the mysterious workings of the universe than to attacking the inequities of a social system that imposed enormous disadvantages on the many while conferring extraordinary privileges on the few. The protests they raised were directed at man's inhumanity to man, preventable cruelties, specific wrongs, and identifiable abuses. In contrast to "The Man with the Hoe," which had fastened the reader's gaze on the end product of economic oppression, their novels, stories, plays, and poems bade the reader consider the social processes that made the poor, in Vachel Lindsay's phrase, "oxlike, limp, and leaden-eyed." Figuratively speaking, they examined the social, legal, economic, and moral environment of the Hoe-man and his children. They described the miserable hovel that served him as a home, the loathsome, deadening toil that was his job, his misadventures in the economic chance world, and the ramification of these circumstances and events upon his progeny.

A contemporary critic objected that these authors made economic hardship play the role Greek dramatists had assigned to fate. Most of the writers did, in fact, regard poverty as an almost insurmountable obstacle that charity could not ameliorate nor individual pluck overcome. Their characters succumbed to poverty, or triumphed over it only by chance or selfish disregard for others. But if the men and women they wrote about were often weak, they were no weaker than the ordinary run of mortals; and the "imperial forces" that shaped their destinies were man-made, not supernatural. Typically, their heroes and heroines were caught and crushed in the cogs of a social machine that was inefficient, poorly tended, and, in terms of human costs, very expensive to operate.

It was the human costs that the literary radicals, like the reformers of the Progressive era, counted. Carl Sandburg spoke for all of them when, at the end of the period, he chanted "Pittsburgh, Youngstown, Gary—they make their steel with men."[25] Twenty years earlier, in "Gloucester Moors" (1900), William Vaughn Moody likened the earth to a ship that was "blind astray" and captained by "a haggard and ruthless few" who kept the masses penned below deck. When asked to relieve the suffering of their human cargo, the masters replied:

> "Let be:
> Our ship sails faster thus."[26]

In "The Brute" (1901) Moody compared the factory system to a monster that fed on the limbs and brains of men, the souls of children, and the hearts of women. He declared that mankind would obtain no good from the brute—that is, industry—until it had been tamed and tethered and "made to give each man his portion, each his pride and worthy place."[27]

Robert Herrick, a colleague of Moody at the University of Chicago, sent the hero of his novel *A Life for a Life* (1910) on a voyage through the industrial regions. In the course of his wanderings he

> breathed the deadly fumes of smelter and glass works, saw where men were burned in great converters, or torn limb from limb upon the whirling teeth of swift machines,—done to death in this way and that, or maimed and cast useless upon the rubbish heap of humanity, —waste product of the process.

The reason for all this suffering, according to the young man's guide, was that "in this country, where Property is sacred, nothing is cheaper than human life."[28] Upton Sinclair analyzed the problem similarly. He called Packingtown a jungle because "there was not a place in it where a man counted for anything against a dollar."[29] In quieter vein the Yiddish poet Morris Rosenfeld told the sad story of a poor old woman who was neglected in life but pitied and prayed for in death:

> The rich and the pious are nobly behaved:
> A body—what matters? But souls must be saved.[30]

The body was worth exactly $100, according to Reginald Wright Kauffman. In *The House of Bondage* (1910) he wrote circumstantially of an employer's offer of that sum to the widow of a man killed at work "as full payment for whatever inconvenience she might have been occasioned by her husband's demise."[31]

One of the most frequently recurring themes in the literature of protest was hatred of "toil." Earlier poets had sung of the dignity of labor, but Rosenfeld cried, "Oh, horrible toil! born of Need and of Dread," and he asserted

> This life crushing labor has ever supprest
> The noblest and finest, the truest and richest
> The deepest, the highest and humanly best.[32]

At one point in Jack London's semiautobiographical novel *Martin Eden* (1909) the hero was forced to take a job in a laundry. For a time he lived in "the unending limbo of toil," working before breakfast, all day long, and far into the night. He had no time to read, to write, or even to think. All he had energy left to do was get drunk on the weekends. During one of his drinking bouts he realized "the beast he was making of himself—not by the drink, but by the work."[33]

Sandburg's poem "The Right to Grief" (1916) showed how devoid of dignity labor could become. It was about a "stockyards hunky" who made his living (a dollar and seventy cents a day, when he worked) by sweeping blood off the killing floor. All he did the livelong day, said Sandburg, was "keep on shoving hog blood ahead of him with a broom."[34] Another stockyards worker, Jurgis Rudkus, in Sinclair's *The Jungle* (1906), discovered that "most of the men *hated* their work. . . . They hated the bosses and they hated the owners; they hated the whole place, the whole neighborhood—even the whole city. . . ." But their hatred was only partly engendered by the hardness and unpleasantness of their work. Mainly it stemmed from their conviction that the plants were crooked, rotten through and through. There was no place for decency and loyalty in them. The bosses grafted off the men, and the men grafted off each other. Worse than the revolting labor was the certainty that "nobody rose in Packingtown by doing good work . . . —if you met a man who was rising in Packingtown, you met a knave."[35]

The low esteem in which the writers held the prevailing social order led them to condone unconventional and even lawless behavior on the part of their heroes and heroines. Unlike the literati of earlier generations they did not look upon the poor as a morally debased, quasi-criminal element. On the contrary, they thought them a good deal better behaved than their environment warranted. Appalled by the corruption of the plutocracy and by the hypocrisy of existing legal and economic institutions, they seldom presented immorality, intemperance, and outbursts of violence among the lowly as peculiarly reprehensible. If, as often happened, their leading characters committed antisocial acts, the responsibility—as the authors saw it—lay in the unjust organization of society. Brand Whitlock voiced the suspicions of the whole school when he asked whether poverty was not the one offense that society was sure to punish.

The tendency to deal lightly with the crimes of the poor was well illustrated in Charles Kenyon's play *Kindling* (1911). Maggie Schultz, the heroine of the piece, lived in a vile tenement; her husband, a stevedore, was on strike. Discovering that she was pregnant, and determined to obtain the means of giving her unborn child a fair start in life, Maggie robbed her employer, a rich society matron who was also the owner of the tenement in which Maggie and her husband lived. The problem of the play was which was the more culpable, the thief or her victim? the tenement dweller or the tenement owner? the woman who took property that did not belong to her or the one who compelled her tenants to live under hazardous and unhealthful conditions by disregarding housing, fire, and sanitary ordinances? The playwright obviously believed the tenement owner was the more disreputable of the two, and he did his best to make his audience concur in his judgment.

Even more frequently than in novels or plays, the early movie scripts treated criminality on the part of the poor as the logical result of deplorable social conditions. Edward S. Porter, who brought the story film to the American screen, examined the problem in *The Ex-Convict* (1905). The plot concerned a reformed criminal whose police record made it impossible for him to obtain honest employment. Porter contrasted the barren room in which the poor man and his family lived with the luxurious establishment of the rich manufacturer who fired the ex-convict from his job. Although a heroic type, as attested by his rescue of the manufacturer's daughter from almost certain death under the wheels of an automobile, the ex-convict was so oppressed by the hunger and illness of his family that he returned to crime, the one means of livelihood left open to him by a vengeful society. Only fortuitous and, needless to say, extremely unlikely circumstances permitted a happy ending for this sad tale.

Porter's *Kleptomaniac* (1905) compared the justice meted out by the courts to rich and poor offenders. In this movie two women were arrested for theft. One, a banker's wife, was accused of shoplifting in a department store; the other, a poor woman, of stealing a loaf of bread. When brought to trial, the poor woman's appeal for mercy went unheeded and she was sentenced to jail. The rich woman, zealously defended by an expensive lawyer and treated considerately by the judge, was released with apologies. In an epilogue Porter drove the message home remorselessly: money outweighs bread in the scales of justice; for justice has but one eye and it is fixed unwinkingly on gold.[36]

Not only Porter but other movie producers dealt frankly with economic and legal maladjustments in the days when the picture shows catered mainly to working-class audiences. For a few years, during which the movies were subject neither to official censorship nor to policing by the industry itself, the ever present and everlasting need for more money than was at hand, the uncertainty and insecurity of employment, the drain of sickness, the calamity of accidents, and the anxiety wrought by the unequal operation of the law provided the plot for many a screen play. Sometimes, as in *The Eviction* (1907), a personal factor such as intemperance was acknowledged to be the cause of poverty, and individual regeneration was advanced as its cure. Frequently, however, as in *The River Tragedy* and *The Eleventh Hour*, tragedy struck, not because of any moral defect in the protagonists, but in spite of their virtue and in consequence of their helplessness. Some films, such as *The Miser's Hoard*, allowed pure chance to rescue the poor from their misery. In an astonishing number, however, including *The Need of Gold* (1907) and *Desperate Encounter* (1907), violence was presented as the only way out of apparently hopeless economic situations. Far from condemning the poor for their transgressions, the early movies often excused their acts of violence as evidence of manly or womanly character.[37]

These rugged individualists who took the law into their own hands were shown in a quite different light from the goodhearted criminals of the 1890's. The latter had a soft side, a sentimental streak that made them, so the authors declared, almost as human as respectable, law-abiding citizens. But the rebellious heroes and heroines of the plays, films, and literature of protest were made to seem morally better than their low-spirited neighbors. The trouble with most of the poor, said Vachel Lindsay in "The Leaden-Eyed," was

Not that they starve, but starve so dreamlessly,
Not that they sow, but that they seldom reap,
Not that they serve, but have no gods to serve,
Not that they die, but that they die like sheep.[38]

People such as Maggie Schultz in *Kindling* and the ex-convict in Porter's film were not resigned to misery like dumb beasts. They were alive, vigorous, and purposeful, and they struck back against blows that less vital persons supinely accepted.

At first glance the cult of vitality and the adulation of the rebel seem anachronistic in an age characterized by high concentration of economic and political authority, an age in which, practically speaking, individual protest counted for little. Nevertheless, though we may talk glibly of the need for social action, it remains true that all social movements have their origin in individual remonstrance. Behind every reform are men and women too sensitive or too proud to abide things as they are and brave or foolhardy enough to demand that wrongs be rectified. The soundings of dissent were symptoms of health, not only in American literature, but also in American society. It was well that writers should recognize and emphasize the causes of discontent; and it was a hopeful sign that their point of view, however critical, was positive—that they put a high value on life, believed that justice could yet be done, and admired the courage of men and women who stood up for their rights.

During the first half of the Progressive era most of the radical writers, with a few exceptions such as Sinclair, were more interested in the individual than in the class response to social and economic pressures. Their position was similar to that of Dreiser, who maintained for a long time that he "didn't care a damn for the masses"—individuals were his only concern. Nevertheless, while the literature of protest honored the strong man who struggled against injustice, it was suspicious of the doctrine of individualism; for the writers all declared that under existing conditions the fruits of personal success, however and by whomever gathered, were bitter.[39]

No American author of the period was more torn between admiration for the bold and lawless individual and allegiance to the principle of class solidarity than Jack London. He confessed that in his youth he had "no outlook, but an uplook rather."[40] In *Martin*

Eden London wrote about a young man, very much like himself, who aspired to "win to the heights," who decided at an early age to "fight his way on and up higher," and who boasted that "the race is to the swift, the battle to the strong."[41] Martin refused to remain a "toil-beast"; he scorned "herd-creatures" with their "slave morality"; he sneered at the stupid bourgeoisie and loathed the contemptible crowd. He laughed at a rich man who had "robbed himself of life" in youth for the sake of an income of $30,000 a year in his dyspeptic old age. But in his arrogance Martin cut himself off from humanity. He could establish no kinship either with the poor or the rich, the slaves or their masters. The end of the story found Martin quite literally robbing himself of life by committing suicide.

London, too, was disillusioned by the barrenness of success. The people with whom he mingled on the "parlor floor of society" seemed to him insipid. Some were good, and some were mean, but the fault with all of them was that "they were not *alive*." Unlike Martin Eden, however, London attempted to bind himself to life by embracing socialism. "I went back to the working class in which I had been born and where I belonged," he said.[42] He resolved his personal "thought-chaos" by asserting that the only worth-while purpose to which the exceptional man could put his talents was service in behalf of the less able. The year before he died London wrote that the strong man must "devote his strength, not to the debasement and defilement of his weaker fellows, but to the making of opportunity for them to make themselves into men rather than into slaves and beasts."[43]

Around 1910 American literature, like American politics, took a turn to the left. Only a few of the writers could say, as Dreiser did, that they had been born in poverty, or maintain, with London, that they belonged to the working class by right of birth. Many of them, however, were unconsciously and almost unwillingly swept along on the tide of radicalism. A settlement worker in Arthur Bullard's *A Man's World* (1912) explained their predicament:

> I had seen so much I could never forget. It was something from which there was no escape. No matter how glorious the open fields, there would always be the remembered stink of the tenements in my nostrils. The vision of a sunken cheeked, tuberculosis ridden pauper would always rise between me and the beauty of the sunset. A crowd

of hurrying ghosts—the ghosts of the slaughtered babies—would follow me everywhere, crying, "Coward," if I ran away. The slums had taken me captive.[44]

Who could be neutral in a contest that arrayed flesh and spirit against dollars and cents? A sizable number of prominent authors now joined Sinclair and London in the Socialist party. Even among those who remained outside the party there were some who were so disgusted with the waste and inhumanity of "the system" that they were half-convinced that any change would be for the better; and numerous writers, whether sympathetic to the movement or not, accepted the eventual triumph of socialism as inevitable.

The shift in the writers' attitude was reflected in their work in a growing emphasis on class, as opposed to individual protest. London had made class war the theme of *The Iron Heel* (1908), and even earlier, in *The Silent War* (1906), John Ames Mitchell had described a giant workers' conspiracy to force millionaires to submit to blackmail or suffer assassination. London's novel was set in the future; Mitchell's was a curious and improbable blend of social criticism and sentimental romance, climaxed, as the advertisements for it proclaimed, by having "love and gratitude rise superior to issues of world importance."[45] There was no need for such far-fetched plots when public attention was focused on the Wobblies and their free-speech fights, the garment workers' strikes in New York and Chicago, the Lawrence and Paterson strikes, and the Ludlow massacre. Here were concrete examples of working-class protest against industrial oppression. In view of the actual labor strife of the time it is not surprising that the strike should loom as the "revolutionary situation" in nearly all of the proletarian novels after 1910. Strike leaders assumed heroic proportions; strikers became dauntless crusaders for justice; and the strikes themselves were presented as battles in the cause of humanity. "There ain't no difference between one strike and another," cried the girl strike leader in Bullard's *Comrade Yetta* (1913). The issue in each was identical: "People fighting so they won't be so much slaves like they was before." The "People in Bondage," said Comrade Yetta, were "starting out for the Promised Land."[46]

The most ambitious of the proletarian novels, and the most successful in showing the revolutionary implications of industrial strife, was *The Harbor* (1915) by Ernest Poole. A Princeton graduate who had continued his education at the University Settlement in New York, Poole, like his friend Bullard and several other settlement associates, had been converted from social work to socialism. *The Harbor* was written from the standpoint of a journalist who, at first an interested but more or less objective observer of the labor movement, found himself being drawn into and at length actively and enthusiastically taking part in a maritime strike. The title of the book might better have been given a plural ending, for it was the story of the changing harbors of the port of New York that the narrator, Bill, had known in the first thirty or thirty-five years of his life. In his boyhood, from his home in Brooklyn Heights, Bill had watched the harbor of sailing ships. This gave way, in his young manhood, to the harbor of steam and steel, of efficient engineers and large-visioned business executives whose success stories he chronicled for admiring magazines. It was also the harbor of dockers and stokers, of overburdened marine workers driven to revolt (that is, to strike) by labor conditions that left them little better than galley slaves. The third harbor was the one that was still struggling to be born. It was the harbor of the workers, whose awakening consciousness and overpowering vitality Bill sensed during the great shipping strike.

Part of the impressiveness of *The Harbor* lay in the weight of factual information about maritime operations that the author skillfully presented to the reader. As he had demonstrated in his earlier studies of the ravages of tuberculosis in the tenement districts and of the effect of street trades on the health, morality, and occupational opportunities of the children engaged in them, Poole was an able and conscientious investigator. Furthermore, despite his hero's sympathy with the strikers, Poole gave the impression of fairness. He refrained from telling the story in simple black-and-white terms, with wicked industrialists bent on crushing the good toilers. Nevertheless, Poole was very sensitive to the social contrast, and he described it graphically. In the first chapter he explained how sod had been laid and flowers planted on the roof of a tenement to provide a back yard for a comfortable dwelling built in front of and on a higher level than the tenement. Once a drunken dock worker opened a trapdoor in the roof of the tenement and thrust his dirty presence into the quiet garden. At the end of the story Poole depicted a great liner putting out to sea. The rich passengers idled on the decks and in their cabins, while, far down in the bottom of the ship, stokers shoveled coal in time to the clang of a gong.

Poole's book was less an account of violence and injustice than the record of a young writer's shifting allegiances in his search for values. Perhaps it was this, more than anything else, that lifted *The Harbor* out of the usual category of strike novels and gave it a distinct place in literary history. Bill's earliest god was art; the next was efficiency at whose shrine he worshiped alongside the businessmen and engineers; the last was the masses—"a huge new god, whose feet stood deep in poverty and in whose head were all the dreams of all the toilers of the earth. . . ."[47] During his years as a journalist Bill had trained himself to observe and describe individuals, big men, and persons who, for one reason or another, were newsworthy. Life had then seemed an endless procession of "figures emerging from dark obscure multitudes into a bright circle of light." But in the strike he had to pay attention to and seek to understand the multitudes. Gradually the crowd took on the form of an "awakening giant," and Bill began to feel "What It wanted, what It hated, how It planned and how It acted."[48] Not the harbor, but the crowd—slowly developing a sense of unity, haltingly learning to pull together, beginning to realize and to use its power—was the real subject of his narrative.

With the appearance of *The Harbor* the literary revolution, at least, was accomplished. Poole's protagonist reversed the usual course of fictional heroes. Instead of seeking to rise superior to the mob, he found his identity by immersing himself in it. The "dangerous classes" were not dangerous at all: collectively they were the hope of the world; individually they were "people as human as yourself, or rather much more human," because they lived "close to the deep rough tides of life."[49] No longer helpless victims of conditions, the members of the crowd were helping each other and themselves. They were not waiting for the operation of natural laws, divine intervention, or human kindness to improve their lot, but were remaking society by their own efforts. They were to be envied, rather than pitied or patronized; they held the future in their grip; and they had "life power," a "boundless fresh vitality," a capacity to survive defeat and emerge from each conflict stronger and more resolute than before. This strike or that one might be broken, but in the end the crowd would prevail, for it had what individual men lacked: unlimited time and unflagging energy.

CHAPTER 11

Art for Life's Sake

> A concern with the abstract beauty of forms, the objective quality of lines, planes, and colors is not sufficient to create art. The artist must have an interest in life, curiosity and penetrating inquiry into the livingness of things. I don't believe in art for art's sake.
>
> JOHN SLOAN, *Gist of Art.*

> What we need is more sense of the wonder of life and less of this business of making a picture.
>
> ROBERT HENRI, *The Art Spirit.*

IN the periodic controversies that have shaken the American art world the advantage has usually lain with the defenders of art for art's sake and against the advocates of art for life's sake. This has remained true despite repeated pronouncements by critics and others in favor of an "American" or a "democratic" art. The principal reason seems to be that in this country, contrary to common belief, we hold art in very high esteem. We think of it as something apart from and superior to the concerns of everyday life, and we are affronted when those concerns intrude into art and thereby degrade it to the level of the commonplace. For most of us art is so serious a matter that we approach it with deference and are quite willing to believe that its mysteries can be appreciated only by the knowing and discerning few. Realism, in the sense of truthful rendering of the facts and issues of actual life, has no place in this toplofty conception of art. Its language is too coarse for the sensitive and refined; it speaks too plainly to suit the sophisticated. Only when we forget about art and concentrate our thoughts and energies on the problem of living does art for life's sake flourish.

At the turn of the century no convention seemed more firmly established in art circles than the rule that art and life, particularly American life, were separate and incompatible. It was the settled conviction of many artists, and of art patrons as well, that the American environment was, for the most part, hopelessly inartistic. Furthermore, if the purpose of art was "to delight" and "to give joy," as the leaders of the profession seemed to believe, it followed that artists must be even more careful than writers to avoid depicting the unpleasant and "the low." "It is not the mission of art to grope in the gutter in search of nasty things which have been swept there out of the way of cleanly people," declared a columnist in an art journal in 1905. "When an artist paints, not the pig sty—that might be picturesque—but people and things only fit to be housed in it," he continued, "I contend he is tainting the whole atmosphere of art, and ought to be suppressed."[1]

The estrangement of art from life did not go unnoticed by the critics, and some of them decried the lack of interest shown by artists in native and contemporary themes. In 1900 Sadakichi Hartmann issued a "Plea for the Picturesqueness of New York" in which he suggested to photographers that "many a portfolio could be filled with pictures of our slums" and reminded them that "the art signifying most in respect to the characteristics of its age is that which ultimately becomes classic."[2] John Corbin, writing in *Scribner's Magazine* in 1903, observed that what American cities most needed to make them seem beautiful was an artist capable of revealing "to our duller eyes the beauties already there."[3] The critic of the *New York Evening Post* called for a revival of genre in order that some worthy memory of American life in a time of emerging national greatness might be bequeathed to posterity.[4] Another writer warned that if the savants of the future had to obtain their knowledge of American civilization solely from pictures displayed at one of the exhibitions of the National Academy of Design, they would be led to believe that twentieth-century Americans plowed their fields with oxen, entertained haloed angels in their homes, and regularly encountered nymphs, mermaids, Pan, and Venus on their rambles.[5]

It was the beauty and wholesomeness of American life that the critics wanted the artists to record, and it was the snobbish assumption that American subjects were not good enough to paint that they deplored. Consequently, some of them were shocked and angered when, around 1905, the work of a group of realists, later dubbed the "ash-can school," came to their notice. Instead of dwelling on the pleasant aspects of the American scene, the realists chose to emphasize the least pictorial and most unlovely phases of it. Not the campus, the suburb, and the summer resort, not the architectural wonders or the engineering triumphs, but the dirty back streets and the tenement house, the coal wharf and the saloon were the kinds of subjects painters such as Robert Henri, John Sloan, and George Luks selected to record for posterity. There were protests that Henri and his cohorts were derivative in style, that they had "a slapdash way of laying color on," and that their palettes were so dark that they might as well have painted in soot. For the most part, however, criticism of their work was directed less at the *way* than at *what* they painted. To one startled observer it seemed that the Henri group "deliberately and conscientiously" depicted "the ugly" wherever it occurred; and another raised the inevitable question of who would want to hang such canvases on his living-room walls. "Is it fine art to exhibit our sores?" he asked.[6]

Like certain of their contemporaries in literature, the realistic painters irritated conventional people by giving an unwonted share of their attention to the lowly and disreputable elements of society whose existence was barely acknowledged by the more conservative practitioners of the arts. The attitude of the critics, however, was by no means entirely hostile to this development. James Huneker admired the "absolute sincerity" of the realists and praised them for perceiving that "character, too, is beauty."[7] Others hailed Henri, Luks, Sloan, William Glackens, and Jerome Myers as "men with something affirmative and stimulating to communicate"; and one champion of realism commented on the queer state of a public taste that could simultaneously wax sentimental over pictures of French peasants and scornfully reject frank depictions of American workingmen and their children.[8]

The most serious opposition to realism in art came, not from the critics, but from semiofficial bodies such as the National Academy of Design. Dominated by men of established reputations, these organizations were strongholds of artistic conservatism. They could, and they did, exclude from their annual exhibitions the work of artists whose originality and individualism were distasteful to them. As a result the younger realists found it extremely difficult to exhibit, and for a long time they were almost unknown to the public. B. O. Flower of *The Arena*, an enemy of monopoly in every sphere, saw the struggle between the independents and the academicians as part of the nationwide conflict between democracy and privilege. On the one hand, he said, stood the men who believed in artistic freedom and who sought to express in their work "the larger, truer life of our day." Opposed to them were reactionary forces who "would form a trust where the measuring rod of mediocrity would become paramount, and where favoritism or subserviency to the ruling spirits of the organization would be essential to success."[9]

The acknowledged leader of the realists in their revolt against the conservative tendencies of the Academy was Robert Henri, a dynamic teacher who for more than thirty years occupied strategic positions at some of the most prominent art schools of the country. The heart of his teaching was that the beauty of a work of art lay in its execution rather than in its subject. In the hands of some painters this doctrine has led to an extremely esoteric kind of expression, but in Henri's case it was accompanied by an injunction that a work of art must be inspired by and must communicate an emotion drawn directly from life. "The cause of revolution in art," he said, "is, that, at times, feeling drops out of the work and it must fight to get back in again." He believed that the great artists were those who were alert and responsive to life, who took a keen interest in the occurrences of their own time, and who had the skill to express the vital quality of their interest in their work. The kind of pictures he recommended to his classes were the ones that seemed to carry with them "the feel and the way of life as it happened, and as it was seen and understood by the artist."[10]

The alleged "cult of the ugly" inaugurated by Henri and the other realists was, to the painters, the cult of the actual. Although these men differed from one another in many respects they had in common an objective rather than an introspective turn of mind. They were curious about their surroundings and their fellow men, and they relished the urban scene all the more because it was not pretty. In the streets, the markets, the water fronts, and tenement districts they saw a vigorous, lively quality which they admired more than charm or quaintness. It was characteristic of them to speak seriously of "the wonder of life" and "the marvel of existence." They often called their paintings "human documents," "human histories," or "chapters out of life." Once an artist has grasped the reality of beauty in man and nature as they are (ran their doctrine) he does not need to falsify to make his subjects romantic, or sentimentalize to make them movingly beautiful. This reverence for life colored their vision of reality. Today, after the passage of half a century, the love they felt for their world, their sympathy for the common man, and their delight in revealing unsuspected beauty in hitherto-unexplored areas of American life are even more apparent than "realism" in their work. "It has beauty, I'll not deny it," Sloan wrote of one of his pictures which showed two young women in a dingy gaslit room; "it must be that human life is beautiful."[11]

The realists, just as they preferred the excitement and sweat of the streets to the refined atmosphere of the drawing room, also liked to paint low life better than high. They were ready to admit that human nature was much the same wherever found, and that human beings were worth study and wonder at any social level, no matter how exalted. In practice, however, they usually chose their subjects from the poorer classes. They thought the poor were more natural and genuine—in short, more human—than the rich. The reason was not that poor folk were more virtuous or in any other fundamental sense different from wealthy people, but that they were, or seemed to be, less bound by convention and appearances. Luks, for example, maintained that prosperity was like a protective garment, almost a disguise. He thought that under the pressure of hardship men and women, whether they willed it or not, demonstrated their true natures. In poverty character took on "edge"; people displayed individuality in dress and conduct and cast caution and reserve aside. The slum was an "art bonanza," for there was life in the raw, human nature as undraped as models in the life class, and a multitude of persons "as undefiled by good taste, etiquette or behaviour" as newborn babes.[12]

This happy-go-lucky, indulgent attitude toward the slum and its people was based in part on a superficial observation of the life of the urban poor. It was not very realistic at all, for it overlooked hard and sorrowful economic facts, ignored the many pressures for conformity that operated in the slums, and failed to recognize that poverty more often distorted personality than allowed it free and normal development. Yet there was more to these artistic expeditions into poverty than a search for unconventional types. The painters were looking for truth and sincerity, for men and women in whom dignity of life was manifest. They might have addressed themselves to individuals in any class. But where better could the human drama be studied and understood than among the people who, because of their poverty, were in constant touch with the vital, elemental problems of existence? Where else was the game played more intensely, or for higher stakes? "Each day they matched their wits against destiny," Jerome Myers said of the people of the East Side, whom he painted for so many years. They were rewarding subjects because, if they had gained nothing else, they possessed "a vast experience in the adventure of life."[13] On their faces and in their bodies both the joy and travail of living were plainly disclosed.

Some of the ash-can painters, notably John Sloan, were active members of the Socialist party, and most of them were to the left of center in their political and economic views. Because of their affiliation with radical causes and their attacks on the Academy, and especially because they so often painted low life, observers sometimes interpreted their work as social criticism. John Spargo found Luks's "Little Gray Girl" "a perfect symphony of sorrow and mute protest." Another enthusiast pronounced a Luks canvas "a terrible indictment of our own cities in its pitiless truth to nature," and declared that Myers' East Side studies showed the growing sympathy for "the great crowds for whom there can be no hope under present conditions."[14]

Although social criticism may be read into their pictures, it was not in fact always intended as such by the artists. Sloan's characterization of his early paintings as "unconsciously social conscious" applies fairly well to the work of the rest of the Henri group. They were intent on painting the truth as they saw it, and when the truth was unpleasant they did not hesitate to state the facts bluntly. But, being men of good temper, they delineated the bright side of everyday life quite as often as the dark. Furthermore, their very realism made them more concerned with specific individuals and situations than with generalizations about social conditions. Thus when Everett Shinn chose "labor" as the theme of his most ambitious mural, he treated the subject in a factual instead of an allegorical or proletarian vein. He studied actual workers in a pottery and steel mill, came to know the men and their jobs, and painted them at their tasks. The only message his mural was intended to convey was admiration for the skill and character of the men depicted and appreciation for the value and seriousness of their labor.[15]

On occasion the realists purposely satirized the foibles of society. For the most part, however, they were not protesting against injustice in their paintings so much as affirming the artistic and human worth of their subjects. For all the social content of their work, the men remained artists rather than propagandists. Their aim was to produce "human documents," not tracts. Their greatest service was to disregard the artificial standards of taste and propriety that had made art "an orchid-like parasite" on life.[16] In doing this they not only freed American art from the iron grip of officialdom and the cloying embrace of gentility, but also, by broadening the range of artistic vision to include the lives and activities of the masses, restored American art to its proper democratic course.

Social criticism, which, if present at all, was usually only implied in the paintings of the ash-can school, was voiced explicitly in the works of Eugene Higgins. Born in 1874, Higgins grew up in a succession of boardinghouses in dismal neighborhoods near the railroad yards in St. Louis. According to his own account he was unfamiliar with Daumier, who is often thought to have influenced him, until after his own style had crystallized. It was Millet, first encountered in reproductions printed in *St. Nicholas Magazine,* whom Higgins admired and imitated when he began to sketch and paint. As an art student in Paris at the turn of the century Higgins experienced the privations of extreme poverty. Partly because circumstances made it impossible for him to do otherwise he found his models among the beggars and derelicts of the shadowy underworld of the city. His pictures of social outcasts won some attention in Paris, and on his return to the United States he continued to work in the same vein. In 1907 he was discovered by Spargo, who described him as "a Gorky in paint." Edwin Markham, a fellow admirer of Millet, hailed Higgins as "the painter who gives us the pathos of the street and hovel and morgue, as Millet gave us the pathos of the field."[17]

On the surface there was a good deal of similarity between the work of Higgins and that of Jerome Myers. But where Myers was content to reveal the distinctive character of the slums and slum dwellers of Manhattan, Higgins attempted to depict the broader theme of poverty itself. Moreover, there was a world of difference in the social attitudes of the two men. The kindly, warmhearted Myers, accepting conditions as they were and taking hardship for granted, described the slums as "habitations of a people . . . rich in spirit and effort," and he seldom failed to discover attributes of courage and dignity in his subjects.[18] Higgins, on the contrary, hated the economic forces that he believed debased the poor. When asked what life in the slums was like he replied: "There is struggle and strife, horrible suffering, livid agony of soul and body, want, misery, and despair going on there in monotonous, killing repetition."[19] Like Myers, Higgins was moved by "the patient suffering, the long and stolid endurance, the enormous capacity for misery" of the poor. Characteristically, however, he added: "How unjust it all is! How terrible are the meek, the lowly! I never stop wondering at these things and trying to express them."[20]

Higgins' art was didactic. His purpose was to expose the hideousness of poverty and to show the tragic human wreckage it left in its wake. The faceless people he drew were mere shadows of broken lives. They were too sunk in shame and defeat to be able to rise again; but he hoped that his pictures might shock society into taking action to correct the conditions that produced such hopeless, helpless shapes.

While painters such as Higgins and Myers were variously expressing sympathy for the poor, the Swedish-born sculptor Charles Haag was introducing a more militant kind of social protest into American art. Haag, who came to the United States in 1903 at the age of thirty-five, had been a factory worker in Europe, and he regarded the class struggle as an established fact. Not the dignity of toil, nor the need for charity, but the determination of labor to rectify injustice through collective action was the theme of his work. The workers he modeled were not hopeless and helpless except when they meekly accepted their lot. They were brutish only when they fought against each other like beasts. When they stood together, united in purpose—as in "The Strike" or "Organized Labor"—they were resolute and confident.

"Haag depicts labor in revolt," wrote Spargo approvingly. "Almost all his work aims to be a protest against the degradation and exploitation of the proletariat."[21] That Haag's art should have been highly recommended to labor and to socialists was not surprising. What was more significant was that it was called to the attention of social workers in the pages of their journal, *Charities and the Commons*. Crystal Eastman, who shortly afterward conducted one of the most important phases of the Pittsburgh survey, wrote in 1906 that there were two separate forces attacking social problems in the United States. "One of these," she said, "seems to be reaching down from a place of comparative safety to investigate, help and prevent. . . . The other . . . seems to be blindly struggling up from beneath, bound to break through and find the light." The forces were social work and organized labor; and Miss Eastman believed that Haag's sculpture might foster better understanding between the two, because through study of Haag's pieces social workers could gain knowledge of "the forceful idealism of the working-class movement." Although his art was class-conscious, it was not, in her opinion, socially disruptive in effect. Instead, it disclosed "the nobility that comes to everyday men when they have for a time lost sight of individual gain and are standing for some common good."[22]

Some of the drawings of the illustrator William Balfour Ker were more propagandistic in intention and more revolutionary in theme than Haag's statues. Much of Ker's work appeared in John Ames Mitchell's *Life*, and the greater part of his contributions to the magazine were sentimental fancies like "The Blind Leading the Blind" (a blindfolded Cupid leading a pair of lovers down a twisting path between gaping chasms) and "The Tattle Tale"–Cupid whispering something in the ear of Dr. Stork. "The Hurry Call," one of his most popular drawings, showed a doctor in a buggy racing the stork down a country road. Ker frequently drew pictures of the unfortunate children of the city for whom his editor felt such strong sympathy. In "Wish I Was a Dog" a newsboy huddled in the snow watched a rich woman carry her lapdog from a dress shop to a waiting carriage; and in "Nothing Left" Santa sadly showed an empty bag to two pathetic children in a miserable garret.[23] Ker's own views were more radical than these efforts would suggest. He was a socialist, and he once confided to Art Young his determination to prove that a painter could "use his brush like the splendid weapon it is, and as hundreds have used their pens, for freedom and light. . . . Socialism makes us think big things and long to do them whether we can or not."[24]

Ker is best known for "From the Depths," a drawing he prepared to illustrate Mitchell's novel *The Silent War* (1906). It pictured the panic that broke out in a fashionable ballroom when one of the oppressed toilers, whose task it was to support the structure of luxury, revolted and succeeded in thrusting his fist through the tiled floor. *Life* sold copies of the picture, advertised as suitable for framing, at one dollar apiece. Socialists renamed it "The Hand of Fate" and gave it wide publicity; and it has since been widely reproduced to document the social unrest of the Progressive era.[25]

In "King Canute," another illustration Ker drew for Mitchell, a businessman seated in a thronelike chair on the ocean shore vainly commanded the onrushing tide of humanity to halt. In the spume of the wave Ker made faintly visible the faces and arms of the masses who he believed were about to inundate the modern Canute and his entourage of policemen, soldiers, politicians, and clergymen. Ker expressed the same idea in different terms in his contribution to a symposium on "The Message of Proletaire." Comparing the workers to a sleeping giant "whom pygmies pillage as he sleeps," he warned that the colossus was stirring and would soon be fully aroused. Then, unless his rights were granted him, he would take them by force. "The giant is clenching his teeth. He is snarling ominously, maddened by the wrongs of the ages, and his snarl says 'Beware.' "[26]

Ker's friend Art Young was the most effective propagandist for social reform among the artists. A fellow student of Henri at the Académie Julian in Paris, Young was the first daily newspaper cartoonist in the Midwest. In a career that extended from the 1880's to the 1940's, during which he drew for *The Saturday Evening Post* and the Hearst papers as well as for *The Masses* and a long list of radical publications, Young traveled from the political right to the left. He campaigned for Benjamin Harrison in 1892 and for Norman Thomas in 1936; designed a cover for a tract upholding the conviction of the Haymarket anarchists in the eighties, and defended Sacco and Vanzetti in *New Masses* cartoons in the twenties; supported the Spanish-American War in 1898 and was indicted and tried under the Espionage Act twenty years later for alleged complicity in a "conspiracy to obstruct the recruitment and enlistment service of the United States."

The range of Young's work was as broad as his period of activity was long. He was equally at home in social satire, political commentary, nostalgic reminiscence of small-town life, allegory, and fantasy. One of his favorite themes was hell. Gustave Doré had been the idol of his youth, and Young continued the Frenchman's explorations of the nether regions in his own fashion in several books and magazine series. "Having Their Fling," the antiwar cartoon that incensed the Department of Justice in 1917, displayed capitalist, editor, politician, and preacher cavorting to the music of a satanic orchestra. Poverty occupied Young's attention no less often than hell. Perhaps this, too, was the result of Doré's influence, for Doré had pictured the contemporary hell of London slums as well as the remoter one of Dante's Inferno. Young himself was of the opinion that his political cartoons represented his best work, but he prided himself that he had not wasted time on "the trivial turns in current politics." His text, he said, was "the one important issue of this era the world over: Plutocracy versus the principles of Socialism. . . ."[27]

Young's militancy made him impatient with less propagandistic artists, including other socialists such as Sloan, whom he accused (during a squabble over the artistic policies of *The Masses*) of wanting "to run pictures of ash cans and girls hitching up their skirts . . . –regardless of ideas and without title."[28] In Young's work the idea was all-important and the title or caption was often essential to make the point of the drawing clear. Some of his works, such as the famous cartoon in which a woman told her husband that he had no right to complain of being tired when he had worked all day in "a nice cool sewer"–while she had been slaving over a hot stove–were illustrated jokes. Others, such as the picture showing two slum children admiring the night sky, with one observing that the stars were "thick as bedbugs," might have stood alone as drawings, but they took on added meaning as a result of the captions.[29] As his message became more radical, Young sometimes had to change his captions. Once he made the mistake of labeling a top-hatted villain in a drawing for Hearst's *Sunday American* "capitalism." "We can't do that," the editor, Arthur Brisbane, told him. "Call him *Greed*. That means the same thing and it won't get us into trouble."[30]

Young was a formidable social critic because he combined a strong comic sense with a deep strain of moral earnestness. Most of his shafts were directed at hypocrisy. He attacked self-righteousness wherever he found it, whether in individuals, institutions, or society. "Holy Trinity" (1908) showed a clergyman conducting a service in a beautiful church supported by tenements on Squalor Street, Bacteria Court, Thug Corner, Tuberculosis Alley, and Filth Lane. In

"American Mothers" (1909) he reproduced a picture of a society matron and her children such as might have adorned the cover of *Town and Country;* beside it he placed a view of a tenement home where the mother ironed, one daughter washed clothes, another cared for the baby, and a little boy, too young to work and too old to be tended, stood forlorn and neglected. "Poverty develops character," asserted a pompous businessman in another drawing; an impertinent youth replied: "Then, of course, you will bring up *your* children in poverty." "Pigs and Children" compared the advice given in a Department of Agriculture bulletin to allow piglets sunshine, fresh air, and space to run and play, with living conditions in the slums and working conditions in factories employing child labor.[31]

There was humor of a sort in nearly all of Young's work, but usually it was better calculated to make men wince than laugh. His aim was to indict, not to amuse. In his opinion the prime requirement of an artist was altruism. "An artist is one who can put himself in another's place," he wrote toward the end of his long career. "The better the artist the more intensely he feels. He is sympathetic and imaginative to a degree that makes him 'queer' to the world of 'normal' human beings. Seeing others in despair is his own despair."[32]

Like Young, the photographer Lewis W. Hine enlisted his talent in the service of reform. He had been trained as a sociologist and was teaching at the Ethical Culture School in New York when he took up photography. His original purpose was to gather illustrative material for use in the classroom, and, although he soon made camera work his full-time occupation, he never ceased to regard himself as primarily a social investigator. Hine first attracted attention in 1906 when he collaborated with Charles Weller in photographing alley dwellings and their occupants for the *Charities and the Commons* special issue on Washington, D. C.[33] He was a member of the Pittsburgh survey staff, contributing to the report of the survey a portfolio of pictorial documents of industrial life. Around 1908 he began a lengthy investigation of child labor for the National Child Labor Committee. In carrying out this project he sometimes found it necessary to smuggle his bulky camera into hostile factories, "steal" his pictures, and take notes with his writing hand concealed in his pocket.[34] Subsequently he prepared a photographic study of tenement homework for the New York State Factory Investigating Commission and took pictures of the children of New York's West Side slums for the Russell Sage Foundation inquiry, *Boyhood and Lawlessness* (1914).

Hine persevered in his photographic investigations through good times and bad, mainly the latter as far as his personal fortunes were concerned, until his death in 1940. His pictures recorded vital aspects of changing social conditions in the United States from before the panic of 1907 until near the close of the New Deal. Through them it is possible to follow immigrants from their arrival at Ellis Island to the homes and jobs they eventually found or made for themselves in America. His photographs show the circumstances in which 2,000,000 American children at the start of the century labored in textile mills, coal mines, glass factories, canneries, in their homes, and on the streets. Hine's camera revealed the arduousness of the twelve-hour day in the steel mills and the dangers to which men, women, and children were casually subjected in their work. He provided graphic evidence that was used effectively by social workers and humanitarian reformers in their attempts to awaken the public to the incongruous contrast between ostentatious wealth and desperate poverty in democratic America. Charles Edward Russell called Hine's child-labor photographs "witnesses against ourselves"; for they exhibited faces and bodies that testified to the ugly towns, squalid houses, unwholesome meals, monotonous tasks, and vicious recreations that made up many of the children's whole existence.[35] But Hine also chronicled the gradual improvement of conditions in many areas, as, for example, the change for the better accomplished at Ellis Island between 1905 and 1926; and his camera recorded the progress made by and as a result of the activities of public and private welfare agencies.

Unlike his contemporary, Alfred Stieglitz, Hine was not a conscious artist. Although very much aware of the color and pathos of the material he photographed, he was more interested in human lives than in problems of design. He seems to have given little thought to art other than to do his best to make accurate and convincing renderings of matters that deeply moved him. Perhaps it was because art was to him subordinate to social justice that he was so often able to create images of life that were at once truthful, appealing, and challenging.

Charles Caffin's observation, made in 1913, that "the artistic expression of a people varies according as its ideals incline to the aristocratic or democratic" may not have universal validity, but it does have some pertinence to artistic developments in the United States in the early twentieth century. Art for life's sake was both a product and a manifestation of what Henri called "the great fresh ideas" that coursed through the United States in the Progressive era.[36] It was not just by accident that the revival of realism and the emergence of social protest in art coincided with the appearance of similar movements in literature, with the development of factualism in social science, and with efforts to achieve a better realization of democracy in American political and economic life. The fascination the poor exercised over the artists mirrored the national concern with the problem of poverty; the artists' preoccupation with the lower classes reflected the interest displayed in other fields in the way the masses lived and died, did their work, and sought their pleasure. "Society is in ferment with new Hope," rejoiced Caffin. The hope was in the possibility of guaranteeing "the right of all to a chance of fair and wholesome living, both spiritual and material."[37] The artists expressed in graphic terms the democratic spirit that produced the hope and ferment of the age: belief in the primacy of human values, founded in respect and consideration for all men regardless of station in life.

Part Three

SOCIAL STRIVING, c. 1897-1925

A Note on the Role of Social Workers in the Reform Movement

Toward the end of the 1890's the United States entered an era which, in retrospect, appears to have been one of the most fruitful epochs in American history. The two decades preceding our entry into World War I were relatively, although not uninterruptedly, prosperous. They were happy years, not because sore spots in the nation's economic and political structure were either absent or ignored, but because there was abounding confidence that old evils could be eradicated and a more wholesome society achieved. The atmosphere was charged with unrest, but it was vigorous discontent rather than despair or cynicism that characterized the times. Seldom in American experience have criticism and confidence, protest and affirmation, coalesced more completely. Out of their mingling emerged an attitude of aggressive optimism that was uniquely favorable to constructive social endeavor.

The most audacious belief of the age was in the possibility of abolishing poverty. The social causes of misery were to be discovered and rooted out; the personal causes were to be dealt with by providing an environment less likely to drive men and women into vicious habits and more conducive to the development of good character. All of the more fundamental reform movements of the Progressive era were dedicated to these ends. Campaigns for better housing, public health, stricter child-labor and compulsory-education laws, more adequate protection for employed women, compensation for work accidents, more stringent regulation of the liquor trade, and a host of other measures were all parts of a broad attack on the problem of poverty.

For all the enthusiasm with which the fight was waged the ultimate goal of the abolition of want was not yet attained. But to have begun the struggle was itself a major achievement, and the immediate results, the elimination of specific abuses and the securing of long-overdue reforms in industry and government, were not inconsiderable. These early victories have served as precedents and have provided the inspiration for all our later conscious efforts to obtain a fuller measure of economic security.

The initial impulse for the battle against poverty came from the new profession of social work. Labor unions, women's clubs, religious and academic organizations, and various civic associations all made vitally important contributions to the reform movement, but none of these groups was more consistently active in promoting action for community betterment than the social workers. Their daily tasks brought them into frequent and regular contact with the less fortunate members of society; their major occupation was to ascertain and to relieve need; all their activities were directly related to human welfare. If charity agents and settlement residents regularly took their places in the vanguard of reform it was less because of any theoretical radicalism on their part than because they were better informed about the actual situation of the poor and more keenly aware than others of the necessity for improving social conditions.

Perhaps the chief accomplishment of men and women such as Edward T. Devine, Robert Hunter, Mrs. Josephine Shaw Lowell, and Miss Jane Addams was to communicate to workers in other fields, and in no small degree to the public as a whole, a sense of the great need and the vast opportunities for humanitarian service. Teaching had long been recognized as the central tendency of philanthropy. The "friendly visitors" of the early charitable associations had sought to uplift the poor by instructing them in the ways of temperance and frugality. Subsequently the charity organization movement had attempted to educate the well-to-do away from indiscriminate almsgiving and toward more scientific philanthropic practices. In the morning years of the twentieth century many social workers, without giving up their interest in developing better methods of charity, became propagandists of higher living standards and crusaders for social justice. They ceased to be exclusively preceptors of the poor and advisers of the rich and became, instead, teachers of a more wholesome way of life to the entire community.

The fact that social workers so often took the lead in reform movements helps to explain the pragmatic character of prewar liberalism. The aims of their profession, well expressed in a slogan carried on the cover of a philanthropic journal, "Charity today may be justice tomorrow," were visionary enough; but its methods were neither utopian nor radical. By temperament and experience case workers and settlement residents were convinced that persuasion and education were the most effective methods of obtaining improvement. Their everyday job was to bridge the chasm between rich and poor, and in their labors for reform they tended to emphasize the harmony rather than the conflict of class interests.

Individual social workers represented many different shades of opinion, including socialism. In their professional capacity, however, they were practicing humanitarians, not doctrinaire advocates of any particular economic system. Hence they made their appeal to altruism rather than to ideology. Generally speaking, they were content with piecemeal progress. It was typical of their attitude to regard "the greatest good of the greatest number" as too vague an ideal to serve as a program of action. Their approach was just the opposite. Abolish the misery of the most miserable, they counseled, and repeat the process as long as want and suffering persist.

CHAPTER 12

The Home and the Child

> It takes a lot of telling to make a city know when it is doing wrong. However, that was what I was there for. When it didn't seem to help, I would go and look at a stonecutter hammering away at his rock perhaps a hundred times without as much as a crack showing in it. Yet at the hundred and first blow it would split in two, and I knew it was not that blow that did it, but all that had gone before. . . .
>
> JACOB A. RIIS, *The Making of an American.*

Tenement-House Reform

THE movement for tenement-house reform was the first major venture in social amelioration in the United States in the twentieth century and the one that, in the long run, was destined to be the most instructive. By the turn of the century the influence of the settlements and the frequent exploitation of slum scenes and personalities in literature had begun to affect popular attitudes toward tenement dwellers. The older loathing for the people of the slums began to give way to sympathy and even respect. They were less often lumped with the vicious and criminal classes and more frequently considered particularly unfortunate members of the working class. It became something of a commonplace to remark that they were obliged to pay high rents for accommodations that compared unfavorably with the stables of beasts. "You are liable to arrest if you allow your stable to become filthy and a nuisance," commented a writer in *Scribner's Magazine*. "The landlord may do pretty much what he pleases with his tenements."[1]

If opinion regarding the residents of the tenements was mellowing, criticism of the tenements themselves was becoming sharper than ever before. There was general agreement that the tenement house was the nexus of all the evils associated with the slum. In an appeal for funds to finance the famous tenement-house exhibition of 1900 the New York C.O.S. argued that the crime, pauperism, disease, and intemperance of urban communities were directly traceable to the deplorable environment created by the tenements.[2] Ernest Poole's pamphlet *The Plague in Its Stronghold* (1903), written while the author was a resident of the University Settlement, recounted story after story of the largely preventable and unnecessary suffering caused by tuberculosis in the slums and exposed conditions in tenement houses—such as a so-called air shaft six feet long, twelve inches wide, and six stories deep—that contributed to the spread of the disease.[3] At the suggestion of Maud Nathan of the Consumers' League, Theodore Roosevelt admonished an audience gathered to celebrate the opening of a charity rest home for tubercular patients that eliminating tenement sweatshops would be a more effective method of dealing with the problem.[4] Even more pointedly, in 1907, Charles Edward Russell warned the readers of a muckraking magazine that cities could not sow slums without reaping epidemics, that society could not allow masses of people to dwell in cellars and attics without breeding national weakness, and that someday there would have to be "an accounting for every rotten tenement, every foul alley, every reeking court, every life without light."[5]

In accordance with the established pattern of liberal reform, investigation of existing conditions was the initial step in the campaign against the tenements. "Light is a very effective moral disinfectant," declared Charles R. Henderson of the University of Chicago. "Information about abuses is often the only remedy that is required."[6] Henderson's view was shared by several generations of American students. For years they occupied themselves in compiling an impressive store of data on the housing of the poor. The facts were laid before the public by the popular writings and illustrated lectures of Jacob Riis, by intrepid clubwomen such as Albion Fellows Bacon of Indiana, by publications of the federal Commissioner of Labor, by numerous state investigating commissions, and by surveys undertaken by charitable societies, settlement houses, research foundations, and schools of social work.[7] The facts were that, as of about 1917, roughly one third of the people of the United States lived in houses that were bad by any standard, and approximately one tenth of them occupied dwellings that constituted an acute menace to health, morals, and family life.[8]

Despite the expectations of some reformers, the tenement did not disappear even after its evils had become a matter of common knowledge. For all the light thrown upon it, the housing problem remained "almost as immovable as the Sphinx."[9] One housing report was much like another in that whatever city was surveyed the same conditions were found to prevail—overcrowded lots and overoccupied rooms, dark rooms, no running water, no toilets, excessive fire risk, and miserable "apartments" in basements and cellars.[10] Edith Abbott, a colleague of Henderson at the University of Chicago and one of the most experienced housing investigators in the nation, eventually came to the conclusion that the repeated tenement surveys conducted in Chicago provided "only further demonstrations of the futility of such investigations."[11]

Not popular indifference, not even the bitter-end hostility displayed over the years by landlords and groups associated with them entirely explain the slow progress of tenement reform. The average citizen was honestly perplexed by the magnitude and complexity of the problem. "He trun' up bote hands!" exclaimed an interested East Side observer in describing the behavior of Richard Watson Gilder when that dignitary toured the sweatshops of Ludlow Street in connection with his duties as chairman of the New York Tenement House Committee of 1894.[12] Society, too, figuratively threw up both hands when confronted by the sordid spectacle of the slums. It was, after all, one thing to recognize and demand the elimination of bad housing and quite another to accomplish the task by democratic means in a capitalistic economy.

A frequently proposed and occasionally implemented remedy for the housing problem was the erection of model tenements by limited-dividend corporations. The plan appealed to many moderate reformers because it avoided governmental compulsion and seemed to provide a voluntary and almost automatic method of improvement. Not only would the model dwellings make larger and better accommodations available at low cost to a portion of the poor, but, it was assumed, they would also set a standard that other landlords would have to meet, either because of the pressure of public opinion or through the operation of the law of competition.

Beginning in the 1850's, in greater numbers after the 1870's, and still more frequently after 1900, model tenements were built in New York, Brooklyn, Boston, Washington, Philadelphia, Baltimore, and Cincinnati. The earliest of these, the "Big Flat," erected by the New York Association for Improving the Condition of the Poor in 1855, proved to be a model of the worst type of housing.[13] Had it not been for the more successful experiments of Alfred T. White of Brooklyn during the seventies and eighties advocates of the model-tenement idea might have been permanently discouraged. White's work, however, seemed to demonstrate the feasibility of "philanthropy plus 5 per cent"—decent working-class homes yielding investors a modest return on their capital.[14] In 1896 the A.I.C.P. helped organize the City and Suburban Homes Association, capitalized at $1,000,000, which was the largest builder of model tenements in the United States. The president of the Association was E. R. L. Gould, author of *The Housing of the Working People* (1895). In the prewar years he and General George M. Sternberg of Washington, D. C., former Surgeon General of the United States, were the leading American proponents of limited-dividend housing; and the comparative success of the enterprises they headed awakened enthusiasm and emulation in many parts of the country.[15]

Closely related to the model-tenement movement was the suggestion that better management of rental properties would produce improvement in slum conditions. Resident directors were installed in a few of the model dwellings, and, following the example of Octavia Hill of London, a few American landlords either took up residence in the tenements they owned or personally collected rent from their tenants.[16] Henderson waxed enthusiastic about the good works performed by the "landlord missionaries"; by combining business with philanthropy, they "transformed the houses and the people at the same time." A quite different opinion was expressed several years later by the dramatist Charles Kenyon, who, in *Kindling* (1911), pilloried a landlady bountiful for her presumption and hypocrisy.[17]

In its best expression, however, improved management was less an attempt to uplift tenants than to reform landlords. Robert Hunter asserted that the few followers of Octavia Hill had exposed the indifference of the majority of tenement owners and shown that the worst abuses in slum dwellings were by no means entirely the fault of the tenants.[18] A signally successful application of the idea began in 1909 when the Trinity Corporation, whose tenement properties in lower Manhattan had long been notorious, experienced a belated conversion to higher standards of management. The wealthy church had previously fought the efforts of housing reformers and had once succeeded in delaying for eight years the enforcement of a regulation requiring the installation of running water on each story of a tenement house. Repeated criticism, especially the savage pictorial and editorial attacks of Art Young and Charles Edward Russell, at length proved too much for even this citadel of self-righteousness to withstand. The Trinity Corporation employed the secretary of the tenement-house committee of the New York C.O.S. as supervisor of its houses and embarked on a new career as a model landlord.[19]

Neither the building of model tenements nor the labors of "landlord missionaries" brought about a general improvement in urban housing standards. Types of buildings that were known to be unsatisfactory in every respect continued to be erected; old ones in advanced stages of decrepitude remained profitably rented, often more profitably than those kept in good repair. A few model houses, returning 5 or 6 per cent on the capital invested, offered no serious competition to the more numerous bad and neglected ones that earned higher dividends. Nor did good example or the pressure of public opinion exert much influence on the impersonal "estates" that held so many of the dwellings of the poor in mortmain. Nowhere did the number of model dwellings even begin to meet the need, and not infrequently the higher costs of building and operating them necessitated the charging of rentals that put them out of the reach of the poor.[20]

Long before the end of the nineteenth century the failure of voluntary methods of reform led states and municipalities to enact building and sanitary codes regulating the construction and maintenance of tenement houses. These pioneer interferences with private enterprise were seldom stringent. They imposed only minimum standards, avoided precise specifications, distributed administrative authority among several different boards or departments, and in effect permitted enforcement agencies to nullify the laws by exemptions from the code requirements.[21] The laws were gradually strengthened, so that by the late nineties New York, Boston, and Chicago had secured authority to seize and demolish dangerous tenements. Nevertheless, flagrant violations were common, because inspectors, where present at all, were very few. Enforcement would have been still weaker had not the omnipresent charity agents supplemented the work of the official inspectors, reported instances of evasions of the laws, and prodded civic authorities into taking action against some of the violations.[22]

Substantial improvements in the housing laws were made around 1900 when both New York and Chicago, following thorough and well-publicized investigations, obtained more stringent legislation. The New York Tenement House Law of 1901, one of the proudest achievements of the C.O.S., was the earlier and the more influential of the two measures. It established higher standards than had formerly prevailed for new construction, required alterations and improvements in existing structures, and provided for inspection of all dwellings housing three or more families. By amendment to the city charter, responsibility for enforcement was centralized in a new tenement-house department. The C.O.S. committee, through whose efforts the law of 1901 had been adopted, fought later efforts to weaken it, lobbied for new legislation to strengthen weak spots in the code, and worked unremittingly for an honest administration of the measure. In somewhat similar fashion the Hull House group and the School of Social Service of the University of Chicago sought to safeguard, extend, and translate into reality the legal gains recorded in Chicago's ordinance of 1902.[23]

In the next decade and a half eleven states and more than forty cities enacted new tenement-house codes or revised existing building and sanitary regulations. Nearly every one of these measures was patterned either after the New York statute, whose principal author was Lawrence Veiller, or after a later model law also drafted by Veiller.[24] At the time the passage of these laws was hailed as a great victory for reform. Events were soon to prove, however, that the battle had only begun. Opponents secured the repeal or modification of some of the new codes; others were declared unconstitutional by the courts; appropriations for administering them were usually meager, and the number of inspectors was seldom adequate. Friends of reform were not always in control of city governments. When they were, commercial housing interests displayed the wiliest ingenuity in evading regulation; when they were not, city authorities made no genuine effort to enforce the codes.

In New York, where, with the exception of one brief period, the administration of the laws was more effective than elsewhere in the nation, owners of "old law" tenements converted their properties into lodginghouses to escape the necessity of conforming with the higher standards imposed on tenement houses. In Chicago, more than thirty years after the passage of the ordinance of 1902, investigators found that numerous provisions of the statute were still being flouted.[25] Similar evasions or violations of local building and sanitary codes persisted in every large city in which the demand for houses was greater than the supply.

Enforcement was the nub of the problem, but not simply because civic authorities deemed it bad politics to insist that landlords make expensive structural changes in tenements. Very frequently officials were humanely reluctant to order poor families to vacate miserable homes when there were no better ones available at prices they could afford to pay.[26] The degree of enforcement, in other words, was necessarily conditioned by the fact that although regulatory legislation might "outlaw" bad houses it did not provide good ones.[27]

To say that such amelioration of slum conditions as was effected in the first third of the twentieth century came primarily as an incidental result of the general progress of invention, the substitution of automobiles for horse-drawn vehicles, and the curtailment of immigration, is not to disparage the tenement-house laws.[28] They were needed, and a stricter enforcement of them would have been desirable. At best, however, they were negative remedies. Although it was not recognized until later, the major contribution of the prewar years toward the solution of the tenement evil was to demonstrate the inefficacy of traditional methods of dealing with the problem. Fundamental improvement awaited the adoption of more positive programs of action.

In the middle of the nineteenth century Theodore Parker had suggested that if capitalists neglected their responsibilities, municipalities should undertake to provide adequate and cheap homes for the poor.[29] Forty years later, in the course of "An East Side Ramble,"

William Dean Howells mused that as long as housing was left to private interests "the very poorest must always be housed as they are now." Cannily avoiding too specific a statement, Howells averred that "nothing but public control in some form or other" could secure for the poor shelters fit for human beings.[30] Similar expressions of opinion were not uncommon around the turn of the century, and pictures of municipally owned workingmen's homes in European cities were displayed at the New York tenement-house exhibit of 1900. Tentative interest in extending public ownership into the field of housing was temporarily suppressed, however, by the hostile pronouncements against it in De Forest and Veiller's influential and authoritative volumes on *The Tenement House Problem* (1903) and in Veiller's subsequent writings.[31]

Veiller's animosity toward municipal housing arose mainly from suspicion of the honesty and competency of public officials. In view of this attitude his strong advocacy of public regulation was not entirely logical; but, like many of his contemporaries, he deemed regulation the sensible middle ground between the dangerous extremes of *laissez faire* and socialism. In spite of this widely shared opinion, evidence of the failure of regulatory legislation to solve the housing problem mounted. In 1913 an official commission advised the Massachusetts legislature that "In no country has private enterprise been equal to the task of properly housing the inhabitants. In nearly every country of standing among the civilized nations the government has actively aided and encouraged the creation of a larger supply of good homes."[32] The next year a bulletin issued by the United States Bureau of Labor Statistics affirmed that a satisfactory housing program required "systematic Government regulation, encouragement, and financial aid."[33]

Organized labor, representing the portion of the population that suffered the most from bad housing, was the first sizable group to advocate government subsidies for housing. Delegates to the national convention of the A.F.L. in 1914 adopted a resolution calling on the federal government to make loans for financing municipal and private ownership of "sanitary homes."[34] In the following year the voters of Massachusetts ratified a constitutional amendment, backed by organized labor, that authorized the Commonwealth to build and sell low-cost homes.[35]

With the exception of the emergency projects erected by the

federal government during World War I, little progress in public housing was made until the 1930's. By then several decades of research had made it clear that bad housing was above all else a consequence of low wages. Until the wage structure was fundamentally altered the only alternative to permitting large numbers of the poorly paid to dwell in houses dangerous to their own and the community's welfare appeared to be the adoption of a permanent housing subsidy paid from public funds.

Recognition of the absolute necessity of publicly financed housing programs was made easier by depression conditions. The conclusion was by no means the inspiration of the moment, however, and it had not been arrived at easily or quickly. Its acceptance was a response to fact, not a triumph of theory. Public housing was adopted because successive generations of informed, public-spirited citizens who had been wrestling with the problem in dead earnest for the better part of a century had been unable to find any other solution that worked.

The Crusade Against Child Labor

Much of the history of philanthropy and social reform can be written in terms of efforts to rescue the children of the poor from the bad consequences of their poverty. In a sense the long agitation for improved housing and the elimination of the slum was part of, and a continuation of, the "child saving" movement of the nineteenth century. Sunday schools, missions in the slums, denominational orphan homes, children's aid societies, and neighborhood settlements were all attempts to deal with the problem of neglected and potentially wayward children. Like the campaigns to take youthful paupers out of the almshouses, to establish reformatories for juvenile offenders, and to create a system of public education, tenement-house reform was intended to obtain better surroundings and opportunities for the [illegible]ng of poor families.[36]

[illegible]sons for the continuing interest in the children of the poor are not hard to discover. Being more numerous than adults, especially in an era when large families were the rule, children formed the largest group in the ranks of poverty.[37] Their sufferings were the most grievous and their own responsibility for their condition the least apparent. Of all the poor they were the most deserving of sympathy and the most entitled to generous assistance. Moreover, an improvement in their lot was essential to society. In 1854 Charles Loring Brace had warned his generation to beware the day when "the outcast, vicious, reckless multitude of New York boys, swarming now in every foul alley and low street, come to know their power and *use it!*"[38] Half a century later, and with working rather than idle children in mind, Edwin Markham called attention to "the terrible truth that drudgery yoked with misery always begets a degraded and degrading humanity."[39]

Such warnings carried unusual weight in the prewar years; for the renewed faith in democracy that characterized the Progressive era placed a premium on the development of good citizenship. The goals of progressivism, a larger degree of popular control over government, and the conferring of greater regulatory authority on the agencies of government had value only if future generations possessed the strength of mind and character to assume the burdens of democratic rule.[40]

As in the past, child saving took many different forms. Bills seeking to curtail infant mortality through improved milk supplies, organizing juvenile court and probation systems, establishing small parks, playgrounds, and public baths, authorizing mothers' pensions, and imposing a longer period of compulsory school attendance crowded the calendars of state legislatures and city councils. The most typical expression of the early twentieth-century interest in child welfare, however, was the crusade against child labor. It was in this struggle that the progressive reformers scored some of their most notable victories; it was in this field, also, that they experienced their most humiliating defeat.

Opinion regarding child labor shifted with changing attitudes toward poverty. As long as poverty itself was regarded as either a blessing in disguise or an unfortunate but inevitable necessity, the employment of boys and girls at gainful occupations in industry or trade was countenanced and sometimes defended as a positive good. But with the coming of the new view of poverty child labor seemed absurd and reprehensible.

The main lines of theoretical attack on child labor were that it was not necessary, that it was harmful to the child, and that to permit it to exist was contrary to the best interests of the community. To the argument that it was essential for children of the poor to earn money to help support their families, reformers replied that the burden of financial responsibility should not be thrust upon the shoulders of youth. They accused some parents of undue dependence on the labor of offspring, charging that all too often children were put to work in order that adults might enjoy idleness. In any event, the reformers contended, it would not be necessary for boys and girls to seek employment at an early age if the natural wage earner, the father, were paid a living wage. They suspected, and in various studies proved, that the number of poor widows supported by the pittances earned by their sons or daughters was much smaller than was popularly supposed. In those comparatively few instances in which widows actually were dependent on the wages of young children, the reformers suggested that either the state or private philanthropy should relieve the children of the task of supporting the family.[41]

In *The Bitter Cry of the Children* (1906) John Spargo estimated the number of working children in the United States at two and a quarter million; he alleged that they were employed mainly because it was cheaper to use them than to hire adults or install machinery. "Such child labor," Spargo declared, "has no other objective than the increase of employers' profits; it has nothing to do with training the child for the work of life."[42] S. W. Woodward, a prominent Washington merchant, wrote from a more conservative point of view than Spargo, but he also emphasized that employment at too early an age blighted a child's economic prospects: "It may be stated as a safe proposition that for every dollar earned by a child under fourteen years of age tenfold will be taken from its earning capacity in later years."[43] The child laborers of today will be the paupers of tom[illegible]ow, predicted Jane Addams; they are the boys and girls who [illegible]w up without either formal schooling or knowledge of a [illegible]ner or later, their youthful energies exhausted, they will [illegible]ll, shiftless drifters.[44]

Ernest Poole presented facts and figures to disprove the cherished legend that newsboys were plucky "little merchants" learning the lessons of industry and enterprise in the spine-stiffening school of hard knocks. His research indicated that street work not only failed to provide useful training for later trade or business, but that it also bred habits of irregularity and restlessness that were positive handicaps to steady employment in manhood. He found that such of its graduates as did not grow up to be unskilled and low-paid laborers more often became pimps, gamblers, petty thieves, and professional toughs than successful citizens.[45] Poole's view of the matter was endorsed by Charles P. Neill, United States Commissioner of Labor, who branded newspaper selling as "a training in either knavery or mendicancy." Nowhere else, he said, was "the unfortunate lesson so early learned that dishonesty and trickery are more profitable than honesty, and that sympathy coins more pennies than does industry."[46]

Robert Hunter told of a confirmed vagrant who explained and excused his refusal to work on the ground that day after day, year in and year out, all through his youth he had been compelled to repeat one simple operation in a textile mill. "I done that," the tramp said, making a motion with one hand, "for sixteen years." The moral Hunter drew from this and similar tales was

> You cannot rob children of their play, any more than you can forget and neglect the children at their play, as we now do in the tenement district, without at some time paying the penalty. When children are robbed of playtime, they too often reassert their right to it in manhood, as vagabonds, criminals, and prostitutes.[47]

The reformers' argument was thus not compounded entirely of sentiment. The leaders of the movement were concerned with the bad economic and social consequences of child labor as well as with its present inhumanity. They pointed to its effect on wages: men received less than a living wage because it was expected that their wives and children would also work; the women and children received even less than the men because it was not expected that they would be self-supporting; and meanwhile the presence of children in the labor market depressed the wages of adults who were forced to compete with them for jobs.[48]

Taking advantage of the waxing enthusiasm for conservation of natural resources, critics of child labor pointed out that careless, unregulated exploitation could exhaust the nation's working force as readily and as irreparably as its timber and mineral reserves.[49] Child labor "robs the assets of the community," said Miss Addams; "it uses up those resources which should have kept industry going on for many years."[50] If for no other reason than hardheaded national self-interest the children must be saved. The shortsighted and extravagant economic practice of child slavery must be brought under control.

Fundamentally, however, the reformers' outlook was ethical rather than coldly economic. Again and again they returned to the humanitarian aspects of the problem. John Spargo cried out in horror: "This great nation in its commercial madness devours its babes."[51] Felix Adler observed that superstition once decreed the sacrifice of a child's life to insure that a temple, a city wall, or a bridge should stand. "We must not return to those ancient barbarisms," he admonished. "We must not allow this new frenzy, this obsession, this mania of money-making at any cost to lead us into similar frightful aberrations."[52] Less rhetorically, but with the quiet conviction that often made it seem as though the conscience of the nation spoke through her voice, Jane Addams summed up the case against child labor: ". . . it confuses our sense of value, so that we come to think that a bolt of cheap cotton is more to be prized than a child properly nourished, educated, and prepared to take his place in life."[53]

By 1900 the dangers inherent in unregulated child labor had become so well recognized that twenty-eight states had adopted some, but by no means adequate, legal protection for working children. Among the states that had not yet done so were North Carolina, South Carolina, Georgia, and Alabama. These four states, although not unique in their dereliction, had a more serious child-labor problem than the other commonwealths that had failed to enact legislation on the subject. They were the principal centers of cotton-textile manufacturing in the South; and for more than a century that industry had been notorious wherever it flourished as a user and abuser of boys and girls.

During the 1890's the number of children employed in Southern mills increased more than 160 per cent; persons under sixteen years of age, many of them much younger, comprised nearly 30 per cent of the labor force of the mills. In the absence of either statutory restraints or effective employee organizations they were worked such hours by day or night and paid such wages as were consistent with the impersonal demands of profit. The harshness of this arbitrary taskmaster was sometimes mitigated, but also occasionally aggravated, by the paternalistic management of the textile enterprises.

The situation in the South was complicated by the underlying poverty of the region. No matter how deplorable conditions in the mills and mill villages might appear to be, they could always be defended as superior to the misery prevailing in the wretched hills and barrens whence the children came. Local opinion tended to regard rapid industrialization, at whatever human cost and regardless of the limited enjoyment of its immediate benefits, as essential to the welfare of the South. So the clarion call for cheap labor, blown on factory whistles, rang through the Piedmont, and a "gaunt goblin army" of children answered the summons to duty. The interrupted advance of the Great South was resumed on a new front with "pygmy people sucked in from the hills" marching in the front ranks.[54]

One of the Southern textile states, Alabama, had once passed a statute fixing a minimum age for factory employment, but repealed it in the 1890's. In 1901, however, child-labor bills backed by the state federations of labor, supported by important political figures, and endorsed by newspaper editorials were introduced in the legislatures of all four of the leading textile states. The foremost champion of child-labor legislation in the South was Edgar Gardner Murphy, an Episcopalian clergyman who founded the Alabama Child Labor Committee, the first organization of its kind in the country. Through a series of newspaper articles and widely circulated pamphlets Murphy succeeded in arousing public sentiment to the evils of unregulated child labor. Not the least effective of his points was that representatives of Northern capital were leading the opposition to the enactment of child-labor bills in the South. In one of his pamphlets he demolished the ingenious argument that children were better off working in the mills than idling on the streets by asking: "Are the probable iniquities of little children under twelve so great that we can save them only by the antidote of sustained labor in the factory for ten or twelve hours a day?"[55]

Within a few years after 1901, but not without a hard struggle, Alabama, Georgia, the Carolinas, and several other Southern states enacted measures establishing a legal minimum age for child workers in manufacturing establishments. In the textile states the mill interests, although unable to prevent the passage of the acts, were influential enough to keep them weak. In Alabama, for example, the minimum age was twelve and the maximum work week was sixty-six hours. The laws permitted children below the legal age to work if their earnings were needed to support themselves, widowed mothers, or disabled fathers. In some cases no provision was made for enforcement; where it was made, enforcement was vitiated by making the affidavit or statement of parents the only required proof of age. Experience in the Northern states had already proved that parents who were willing to put their children to work did not scruple to perjure themselves in stating the children's ages.[56]

Meanwhile efforts were under way in the North to broaden the coverage and strengthen the enforcement features of child-labor laws passed before the turn of the century. The reformers, aided by the vigorous support of organized labor, scored impressive victories in New Jersey in 1902 and in New York, Illinois, and Wisconsin in 1903. The labor unions had been active in the movement since the days of the Knights of Labor in the 1880's, and Gompers only slightly exaggerated the facts when he declared: "There is not a child labor law on the statute books of the United States but has been put there by the efforts of the trade-union movement."[57] It is unlikely, however, that the campaign against child labor would have made such rapid headway after 1900 had it not been for the pressure brought to bear on both public opinion and legislatures by voluntary groups such as the consumers' leagues, state charities aid associations, federations of women's clubs, and the child-labor committees. It was the New York Child Labor Committee, organized by settlement workers and headed by Hunter, that drafted the act of 1903 and contrived to push the measure through the legislature after it appeared to be headed for certain defeat.[58]

At the meeting of the National Conference of Charities and Correction held in Atlanta in 1903 Murphy delivered an address entitled "Child Labor as a National Problem." He did not deny the culpability of the South in permitting large numbers of boys and girls to work too long and at too early an age, but he asserted that Northern investors had a responsibility for fastening the system of child labor on the South; he also pointed out that if the proportion of child to adult laborers was larger in the South than elsewhere in the nation, the actual number of working children was greater in the one state of Pennsylvania than in all the Southern states combined.[59] A few months later Murphy joined with members of the New York Child Labor Committee in issuing a call for a conference to discuss the possibility of establishing a national organization to promote child-labor legislation. It was at this meeting in 1904 that the National Child Labor Committee was founded.[60]

The National Committee established its headquarters at a familiar New York address, the United Charities Building, which also sheltered the A.I.C.P., the C.O.S., the Children's Aid Society, and the National Consumers' League. No less familiar were the names listed on its roster of officers and board of trustees. Felix Adler of Columbia University, founder of the Ethical Culture movement and long-time crusader for tenement-house reform, was its chairman; Florence Kelley, Jane Addams, Lillian Wald, Murphy, Devine, and De Forest were on the board of trustees. The original purpose of the organization was to work for better state regulation of child labor. To this end it investigated and publicized the facts concerning child workers in textile mills, glass factories, berry fields, canneries, the street trades, and messenger service. It drew up a model child-labor bill, encouraged the formation of state and local committees, pointed out failures in enforcement of existing statutes, and lobbied for the enactment of more stringent and enforceable laws.[61]

The standards recommended by the National Child Labor Committee called for a minimum age of fourteen in manufacturing and sixteen in mining; a maximum working day of eight hours; prohibition of night work; and documentary proof of age. At the time of the Committee's organization in 1904 no state had legislation that met all these requirements, and many fell far below the standard. There were still a few states without minimum age requirements, some that imposed no limit on the number of hours a child might work, and several that had no compulsory-education laws.

In the decade after 1904 very considerable progress was made in stamping out some of the most flagrant abuses of child labor, but these advances were made only with extreme difficulty and were often accompanied by disheartening reverses. If employers in the Carolinas were adamant in opposing the adoption of fourteen years as the minimum age for employment, manufacturers in Pennsylvania and Massachusetts were no less hostile to the establishment of eight hours as the maximum working day for children.[62] In Pennsylvania, "that state of colossal industrial crimes," the glass factories secured exemption from the law prohibiting night work for children, although —or perhaps because—they were the worst offenders in this practice.[63] Florence Kelley computed the average cost of violating the child-labor laws in Pennsylvania at twenty-three cents.[64] It was in Pennsylvania that officials fought proposals to substitute documentary proof of age for parents' affidavits, despite the fact that coroners' inquests revealed children of ten and eleven among the victims of mine disasters.[65]

Canneries sought and obtained exclusion from child-labor statutes on the ground that their work was light and wholesome and that children worked in the sheds "for the fun of the thing and to earn pocket money"—much as they might have sold lemonade at their own doorsteps.[66] Everywhere child labor in agriculture and domestic service escaped regulation except as affected by compulsory-education laws. Poverty permits and authorizations to work outside of school hours or during school vacations kept the number of child laborers at a high level even in those states that prided themselves on the stringency of their laws.[67]

A continuing obstacle in the path of reform was the popular belief that "child labor" meant factory work. Census figures showed that the overwhelming majority of child workers—somewhere in the neighborhood of 85 per cent—labored outside the factories in occupations that, because of legal exemptions or loopholes in the laws, were often unregulated by statute. The street trades in general and newspaper selling in particular were cases in point. In the eyes of the law the newsboys, bootblacks, and peddlers were "independent contractors," not employees, and hence outside the scope of the regular child-labor laws.[68] A few efforts were made to control the street trades through licensing systems, but the results were mostly so unsatisfactory that many reformers came to believe that child labor on the streets was an evil requiring prohibition, not regulation.

For the first ten years that it was in existence the National Child Labor Committee withheld its support from proposals for federal regulation of child labor. Very shortly after its formation, however, officers of the National Committee began to feel that much of the energies and resources of the Committee was being expended in collecting information that might better and more appropriately be obtained by a government agency. The idea of establishing such an agency actually antedated the founding of the Committee. Florence Kelley had lectured on the desirability of a national commission for children as early as 1900, and Lillian Wald had first proposed the creation of a permanent children's bureau in one of the federal departments in 1903. It was not until 1906, however, that the Child Labor Committee was able to secure the introduction into Congress of a bill providing for the establishment of the bureau, and public hearings on it did not begin until three years later. In the interim members of the Committee sought to drum up support for the plan in and out of Congress. They were responsible for the calling of the White House Conference on the Care of Dependent Children in 1909, a meeting that appears to have been designed primarily to influence Congress to pass the children's bureau bill.[69]

At the conclusion of the conference President Roosevelt sent a special message to Congress urging favorable action on the measure. The functions proposed for the new bureau were to

> . . . investigate and report . . . upon all matters pertaining to the welfare of children and child life among all classes of our people, and . . . especially . . . the questions of infant mortality, the birth rate, orphanage, juvenile courts, desertion, dangerous occupations, accidents and diseases of children, employment, legislation affecting children in the several States and Territories.[70]

Congress finally passed the act creating a Children's Bureau in the Department of Commerce and Labor in 1912; but even after it had done so appropriations for the new agency were miserly. Nevertheless, the very establishment of the Bureau represented a victory, not just for the Child Labor Committee, but for the profession of social work. There had been no dearth of fact-finding agencies and investigating commissions in the past, but the institution of a permanent bureau whose continuing task was to keep the nation informed on the conditions under which children lived, worked, were injured, became delinquent, and died in infancy marked a new departure in governmental policy.[71] Acceptance of the obligation to seek and disseminate facts about child life signified that the federal government was consciously, albeit cautiously, entering the broad field of welfare services.

An unexpected result of the White House Conference of 1909 was the impetus the meeting gave to the movement for mothers' or widows' pensions. Among other topics the Conference debated home versus institutional care for dependent children. Despite the embarrassing objection that the homes of the poor were far from satisfactory, the delegates went on record as favoring keeping the children of worthy parents in their own homes rather than placing them in institutions. They recommended, however, that the necessary financial aid be furnished by private charity instead of by public relief.[72]

The latter recommendation attracted much less notice than the Conference's pronouncement, "Home life is the highest and finest product of civilization"—a sentiment heartily endorsed by President Roosevelt in his special message to Congress on the children's bureau bill. In the next few years state after state (twenty by 1913) enacted laws authorizing financial assistance from public funds to widowed or abandoned mothers of young children. The theory was that it was preferable to give to the mother, for use in maintaining her family at home, the money that the state would otherwise have to expend in supporting children in public institutions. The payments were modest, ranging from $2.00 a week to $15 a month for the first child, with smaller grants for each additional one. These allowances were granted only after careful examination of the home and proof of the mother's need; generally speaking, the payments ceased after the children reached the legal working age.[73] In practice the laws were sometimes less inclusive than their titles implied: they might apply only to "cities of the first class" and be only permissive; that is, communities were authorized to make the payments if they chose to do so and provided they were able to finance the program, in whole or part, from local funds.[74]

Social workers were divided in their attitude toward the mothers' pension movement. The historic insistence of scientific philanthropy that assistance should be given in kind rather than in cash was beginning to break down.[75] As indicated by the recommendation of the White House Conference, however, many professional welfare workers retained a lingering suspicion of public outdoor relief.

Critics of mothers' pensions also protested that in spite of the name of the program, the payments constituted arbitrarily determined grants for children and were not geared to the needs of the mother or of the home.[76]

An even more fundamental objection was that mothers' pensions were only temporizing devices. They were not attempts to remedy the underlying causes of distress. They did not stop the preventable deaths that made widows; they did nothing to block the forces that made families destitute; they did not require the payment of higher wages or provide security against sickness, accident, or unemployment. All that the mothers' pensions did, and all that they were intended to do, was to provide a tiny dole until such time as children reached the minimum working age.

These criticisms were, perhaps, unduly harsh. The enactment of the mothers' pension laws was a forward step in the battle against poverty; for their adoption involved recognition that the provision by the state of financial aid in the presence of want has positive value and is not merely an irksome necessity.[77] The ire of the more radical reformers was directed not so much at the pension laws themselves as at the uncritical attitude of mind that was satisfied with palliatives. From their point of view the chief danger was that, by easing consciences and providing a cheap outlet for sentimental talk, the mothers' pension movement might postpone consideration of more serious reforms. It did not surprise them that such well-intentioned but superficial proposals were passed with ease and alacrity while more basic issues were avoided. Mothers' pensions hurt no interests—and they cost very little.[78]

The first formal attempt to bring child labor under federal control was made in 1906 when Senator Albert J. Beveridge of Indiana and Congressman Herbert Parsons of New York introduced identical bills designed to prohibit the interstate transportation of articles produced in factories or mines employing child labor. Later in the same session Beveridge proposed his bill as an amendment to a measure for the regulation of child labor in the District of Columbia. To the considerable annoyance of his colleagues the Senator held the floor for four days, during which time he presented numerous affidavits on child-labor conditions prepared by field representatives of the A.F.L. and read lengthy passages from the writings of Mrs.

Kelley, Spargo, the Van Vorsts, and A. J. McKelway, secretary of the National Child Labor Committee for the Southern states. The burden of his address was that the states were incompetent to deal with the problem, a point that the National Child Labor Committee was not yet ready to concede. To the usual catalogue of the evils of child slavery Beveridge added a new and startling warning that the practice of putting children to work at tender ages was undermining white superiority: "Whereas the children of the white working people of the South are going to the mill and to decay, the Negro children are going to school and improvement."[79]

No action was taken on the Beveridge amendment, but on the day his oration came to a close the President signed an act directing the Secretary of Commerce and Labor to investigate and report

> . . . on the industrial, social, moral, educational, and physical condition of woman and child workers in the United States wherever employed with special reference to their age, hours of labor, terms of employment, health, illiteracy, sanitary and other conditions surrounding their occupation, and the means employed for the protection of their health, person, and morals.[80]

The nineteen volumes required to provide the requested information appeared between 1910 and 1913. The conditions revealed by the report, together with the census returns of 1910, which showed that some two million children under sixteen were at work in the United States, made the need for federal regulation more evident than it had been when Beveridge introduced his amendment.

Between 1906 and 1912 officers of the National Child Labor Committee hesitated to support proposals for federal child-labor legislation for fear that advocacy of such measures would jeopardize the passage of the children's bureau bill. Moreover, the National Committee contained Southern representatives such as Murphy who were opposed, on constitutional and emotional grounds, to national interference in a matter that lay within the traditional boundaries of state responsibility. By 1914, however, only nine states had met all the standards recommended by the Committee ten years earlier. Twenty-two commonwealths still permitted children under fourteen to be employed in factories; sixteen neglected to demand documentary proof of age for working children; twenty-eight permitted children to work more than eight hours a day; and twenty-three had failed to adopt adequate limitations on night work. Between states specializing in the same industries—Massachusetts and North Carolina, for example—there remained in child-labor standards wide differences that gave an unwholesome competitive advantage to those with the lower legal requirements. The more progressive states were becoming still more progressive; but the backward ones continued, by comparison, to be as resolutely and defiantly backward as ever.[81] Despite the opposition of the Southern members, many of whom left the organization, the Committee was forced to the conclusion that it was hopeless to expect uniform and moderately high child-labor standards to be achieved on a nationwide basis by state action.

A number of other organizations, including the A.F.L., the American Medical Association, the National Consumers' League, and the Federal Council of Churches of Christ in America joined the Child Labor Committee in urging the passage of the Palmer-Owen bill when it was introduced in Congress in 1914. Both major parties came out in favor of the measure in their 1916 platforms. Only the counsel of the National Association of Manufacturers and representatives of Southern textile interests appeared in opposition at the congressional hearings. As enacted in 1916 the federal law adopted the major recommendations of the National Child Labor Committee. It prohibited the shipment in interstate commerce of goods produced in factories or mines that employed children under fourteen years of age (sixteen in the mines), or worked children between fourteen and sixteen more than eight hours a day or at night.[82]

Supporters of federal regulation failed to reckon with the conservatism of the judiciary. Three days before the law was scheduled to go into effect a federal district judge in North Carolina issued an injunction staying its enforcement in order to protect the rights of Reuben and John Dagenhart, aged fourteen and twelve respectively, to work more than eight hours a day and before reaching the age of fourteen. The Supreme Court had previously upheld congressional use of the commerce clause to exclude impure food, the white-slave trade, and lotteries from interstate commerce; by a five-to-four decision handed down in 1918, however, the Court declared the child-labor law unconstitutional as an improper exercise of the power to regulate interstate commerce.[83]

Within a few months after the first law had been declared unconstitutional Congress passed a second child-labor law in the guise of an amendment to the Revenue Act of 1919. The standards governing the employment of children set forth in the earlier statute were repeated, but instead of excluding goods produced in violation of these requirements from interstate commerce, the new law made such goods subject to a tax of 10 per cent over and above all other taxes.

The fate that befell the first law soon overtook the second. The same federal judge enjoined the enforcement of the act, and when the Supreme Court ruled on the case it declared the law unconstitutional as an improper exercise of the taxing power. The Court had earlier given its sanction to the application of prohibitory taxes on phosphorus matches, narcotics, and yellow oleomargarine. Its attitude now appeared to be that some limitation must be placed on the taxing device lest Congress gain unlimited power to regulate.[84] To reformers it seemed singularly in keeping with the social viewpoint of the Court that its members should deem regulation of child labor the proper point at which to draw the line.

These two decisions left supporters of national regulation no alternative but to seek a constitutional amendment conferring on Congress power to protect working children. No serious difficulty was encountered in obtaining the consent of the Senate and the House to the proposed amendment granting Congress authority "to limit, regulate, and prohibit the labor of persons under eighteen years of age," and it was submitted to the states in 1924.[85] Obtaining state ratification proved to be an entirely different matter. During the first few months the issue was before the country three times as many states rejected the amendment as adopted it. Within little more than a year it was evident that the approval of the requisite number of states could not be obtained.[86]

Rejection of the amendment was the first and most serious defeat suffered by social reform in the United States in the twentieth century. There had been earlier setbacks in plenty, but these could be written off as merely temporary reverses attributable to judicial hairsplitting or legislative timidity. The defeat of the child-labor amendment was a much more fundamental blow to progressivism. It demonstrated, not only the strength of reactionary forces, which was well known, but also a quite unexpected susceptibility on the part of the public to abstract and irrational (or perhaps overrational) arguments.

It is important, but not at all easy, to explain the factors that made possible the defeat of the amendment. The postwar slump in idealism encouraged the revival of a species of lawless individualism at all levels of society. Federal regulation, never popular in some circles, and made less so by the imposition of extraordinary economic controls during the war, was further discredited by experience with the national prohibition amendment. Prohibition produced revulsion against reform and reformers within the ranks of liberals, and imparted new luster to the theory of states' rights, even in the eyes of persons who had not previously displayed much enthusiasm for the doctrine. Meanwhile, in an atmosphere of intense nationalism, "Americanism" took on a new meaning. To the superpatriots of the 1920's Americanism was not an evolving process of social improvement, but a static concept compatible only with the most extreme varieties of economic and political conservatism. In these circumstances, those who had a material interest in the maintenance of freedom from effective regulation of child labor were able to enlist widespread support in agricultural, industrial, and professedly patriotic groups, and by shrewdly developed techniques of misrepresentation they succeeded in rallying an effective segment of public opinion against the amendment.

None of the opponents of the amendment defended child labor. Some of them went so far as to pronounce idleness "the devil's best workshop." In general, however, they paid lip service to the ideals of the reformers, loudly proclaimed their own love of children and devotion to wise child-labor laws. Their argument was simply that child labor was "practically nonexistent." Having thus disposed of the real issue of the debate, they were free to denounce the amendment as the work of vicious plotters intent on destroying local self-government, nationalizing the children, and subverting the authority of the family, home, church, and school. They represented the sponsors of the measure as fanatics determined to stop young boys from the wholesome exertion of milking the family cow, to prevent young girls from the maidenly task of washing dishes, and to spare all children under eighteen from the nightly chore of school homework.[87]

That such arguments were presented at all indicates either an extremely theoretical turn of mind or a cynical contempt for truth and for public intelligence. That they were accepted in good faith by a considerable portion of the electorate bespeaks a naïveté bordering on gullibility, if not a more deep-seated preference of myth to reality. The reformers had trained themselves to deal in facts; they had confided their hopes in a belief that truth, disseminated widely, would inspire all good citizens to intelligent action. They had not yet learned the bitterest lesson of the twentieth century—that untruth, disseminated widely by forces possessing unlimited funds to expend on propaganda, is the most effective method yet devised to stem the advance of democratic reform.

Sooner or later advocates and opponents of housing and child-labor legislation reached agreement on one point. This was that neither the abolition of the slum nor the effective regulation of child labor was likely to be achieved without involving many other reforms. Every housing survey and each investigation of working children forced some consideration of the entire labor problem; every serious attempt to improve the home or save the children turned attention toward low wages, unemployment, industrial accidents, sickness, and the general atmosphere of economic insecurity.

The tendency of movements for the elimination of specific abuses to burst out of prescribed channels and merge with the larger stream of social amelioration distressed conservatives, but it only served to heighten the enthusiasm and zeal of progressive reformers. Felix Adler, first chairman of the National Child Labor Committee, frankly expressed the hope that the campaign against child labor would redound to the benefit of adult workers:

> . . . if once it comes to be an understood thing that a certain sacredness "doth hedge around" a child, that a child is industrially taboo, that to violate its rights is to touch profanely a holy thing, that it has a soul which must not be blighted for the prospect of mere gain; if this be once generally conceded with regard to the child the same essential reasoning will be found to apply also to adult workers; they, too, will not be looked upon as mere commodities, as mere instruments for the accumulation of riches; to them also a certain sacredness will be seen to attach, and certain human rights to belong, which may not be infringed.[88]

In 1909 Jane Addams suggested that desire to protect and preserve children from want might serve as the means of correcting American backwardness in social legislation.[89] Almost thirty years later, speaking with the authority of a half century of experience in welfare movements, Homer Folks reminded a younger generation of child-labor reformers that they discharged only a portion of their responsibilities to children when they worked for better regulatory legislation; they must in addition give active support "to all measures which will bring a greater degree of economic security to that third of our population which *still* is 'ill-housed, ill-clad, and ill-nourished,' and which turns to child labor as one source of added income."[90]

CHAPTER 13

Women's Hours and Wages

The courts here deal with statutes seeking to affect in a very concrete fashion the sternest actualities of modern life: the conduct of industry and the labor of human beings therein engaged. Yet the cases are decided, in the main, on abstract issues, on tenacious theories of economic and political philosophy.

FELIX FRANKFURTER, "Hours of Labor and Realism in Constitutional Law."

THE logical sequel to child-labor laws was regulation of the hours and conditions of women's work. Inspectors charged with enforcing legal restrictions on the employment of children repeatedly complained of the difficulty of securing compliance with those laws as long as girls below the minimum working age were able to obtain jobs by pretending to be a year or so older than they actually were. Reformers pointed out that if girls under fourteen were deemed too young to be allowed to work, "women" of fifteen or sixteen deserved protection against overwork.[1] Persons of widely varying political and economic outlooks recognized the need for state intervention to conserve the health and energies of workingwomen for the responsibilities of motherhood. The cause held an especial appeal for feminists, who inclined toward the view that woman had always performed the important work of the world and had always been exploited by the predatory male.[2] Workingmen, however, were scarcely less sympathetic; for it was readily apparent to them that the low wages and long hours that prevailed in industries employing large numbers of women and children dragged down the level of labor as a whole, made the achievement of better conditions for men difficult, and menaced the gains secured by collective bargaining in the organized trades.

Most of the laws regulating women's work enacted before 1900 stemmed directly or indirectly from the agitation of organized labor. Legislators unswayed by other arguments could not afford to be utterly indifferent to the power of workingmen at the ballot box and therefore sometimes gave favorable consideration to bills that might otherwise have received scant attention. Both humanitarian considerations and self-interest dictated that workingmen seek legal protection for—and from—workingwomen. Organized labor welcomed legislation for women that gave legal sanction to the shorter hours that the stronger unions had previously won from employers by collective bargaining. Men employed in the textile mills, where women and children comprised a large percentage of the labor force, fought gallantly for statutes limiting the workday of their sisters and protecting women from the rigors of night work—knowing full well that their own hours of work would be determined by the legal standards set for women. In a few instances craft unions sponsored legislation to exclude women from engaging in those trades in which male union members predominated.[3]

Although there was no lack of interest or want of support for women's hour legislation, little progress had been made in this reform by the late nineties. Only a fourth of the states had adopted maximum hour laws, and in only three of these were the limitations effective. The others had not provided for enforcement or had so phrased their statutes that employers could be punished only for "willful" violations or for "compelling" employees to work longer than the maximum number of hours. With few exceptions the legal limit was ten hours; only two states prohibited night work in manufacturing; and only one had extended its protection to women employed outside of factories.[4]

More serious than the paucity, limited coverage, and lax enforcement of the women's hour laws was the fact that after 1895 their constitutionality was open to question. In that year the Supreme Court of Illinois ruled a law fixing eight hours as the maximum working day for women invalid on the double grounds that the statute was class legislation and that it interfered with freedom of contract. This decision did not entirely discourage the enactment of hour laws in other states, but for more than a decade the constitutional issues it raised served as a fairly effective deterrent to further action and made the enforcement of existing laws difficult.[5]

The most important agency working to establish the legality of labor legislation for women was the National Consumers' League, whose general secretary and leading spirit was Florence Kelley. The socialist daughter of a long-time Republican congressman from Pennsylvania, a licensed attorney, and a veteran of many reform battles, Mrs. Kelley brought to the League a unique combination of radicalism, idealism, experience, and shrewdness. An early resident of Hull House, and later an associate of Lillian Wald at the Nurses' Settlement in New York City, she made the investigation of the condition of women and children employed in the manufacture of clothing in tenements and small subcontractors' sweatshops that led the Illinois legislature to pass the eight-hour law of 1893. As chief factory inspector of Illinois she vigorously enforced the act until it was set aside by the state Supreme Court in 1895.[6]

More clearly than some of her contemporaries Mrs. Kelley understood that reform consisted of a great deal more than the passing of laws. Her point was not that reformers should go slow, but that they must approach their tasks in a resolute and realistic spirit. Statutes, being only trial drafts until approved by the courts, must be so carefully drawn and so expertly defended that judges could not deny their validity. No less imperative, if the laws were to be enforced, was the preparation of the community, intellectually and ethically, to accept the reforms that legislation sought to establish. In her opinion there were already abundant examples of laws that communities were willing to place on their statute books but that they were reluctant to have enforced.[7]

The Consumers' League had begun as an attempt by Josephine Shaw Lowell and prominent society women in New York to obtain better wages, hours, and working conditions for clerks and cash girls in retail stores. Its original purpose was to organize purchasers into an association pledged to patronize only those establishments that dealt humanely and considerately with their employees.[8] By 1899, when the National League was organized, members of the local and state consumers' associations had become interested in labor and sanitary practices in factories as well as in stores. Under Mrs. Kelley's leadership the League gathered and published data on the condition of women and children in industry and on the effect of long hours and night work on their health and welfare. In pamphlet after pamphlet the League sought to educate public opinion to the need for better legislation, to the dangers present in the use of goods produced under sweatshop conditions, and to the buyer's responsibility for enforcing higher labor standards on producers and retailers.

The research on which these propaganda leaflets were based was carried out by Mrs. Kelley's principal lieutenant, Josephine Goldmark, a young social worker who had the good fortune to be the sister-in-law of both Felix Adler and Louis Brandeis. In addition to her duties as publications secretary, Miss Goldmark was chairman of the Consumers' League committee on the legal defense of labor laws. Like Brandeis, who had once observed that "a judge is presumed to know the elements of law, but there is no presumption that he knows the facts," she believed that in passing on the constitutionality of labor legislation the courts needed the guidance of testimony from physicians, sociologists, and economists.[9] As early as 1904, in a case involving the New York child labor law, Miss Goldmark had furnished the presiding judge with material from factory inspectors' reports to prove the social value of the legislation. By 1907 passages in various judicial opinions, including statements in decisions that held labor laws unconstitutional, had convinced her and Mrs. Kelley that women's hour legislation might be sustained by the courts if the legal briefs made "the facts" sufficiently clear to the justices.[10]

An opportunity to test this thesis arose when the constitutionality of the Oregon ten-hour law for women was challenged before the United States Supreme Court in 1907. The National Consumers' League undertook the defense of the statute and obtained the services of Brandeis to present the case to the Court. The famous "Brandeis brief" in *Muller* v. *Oregon* (1908) consisted of two pages of legal arguments and of more than a hundred pages outlining "the world's experience regarding women's hours of labor." Brandeis entrusted the preparation of the latter part of the brief to Miss Goldmark. She and a few assistants collected, analyzed, and organized excerpts from a mass of British, Continental, and American sources. They drew on reports of factory inspectors, bureaus of labor statistics, commissioners of hygiene, and official investigating committees as well as on the observations of physicians and economists. From this accumulation of material Miss Goldmark compiled a closely reasoned monograph demonstrating that everywhere in the civilized world long hours had been shown to be detrimental to the health, safety, and morals of employed women and harmful to the general interests of the community; whereas shorter hours instituted by law had been proved to have a beneficial effect on efficiency, output, morality, and welfare.[11]

The action of the Court in *Muller* v. *Oregon* bore out the prediction made by Mrs. Kelley a dozen years earlier; she had declared then that once the medical profession, the philanthropists, and the educators became thoroughly aware that a workday of reasonable length was, in literal truth, a matter of life and death to working people, the Illinois decision of 1895 would cease to carry weight even in legal circles.[12] By unanimous vote the members of the nation's highest tribunal pronounced the Oregon statute constitutional, thus establishing the validity of state efforts to protect women from excessive hours of labor. By their audacious brief, Brandeis and Miss Goldmark had "made the law grow a hundred years in a day."[13] Brandeis himself believed that the Court's ruling in this and several subsequent cases revealed that when judges could be persuaded to reason from life they arrived at conclusions different from those they reached when they reasoned entirely from abstract conceptions.[14] Victory for social legislation as a whole was still far from won, but the happy outcome of this skirmish strengthened the reformers in their conviction that factualism was the best weapon of humanitarianism.

The five years after the Muller decision saw activity in women's hour legislation reach its peak; during the same period there was a quickening of interest in the subject of women's wages. Social investigations played a major part in both developments and, as in a number of other reforms, the findings of the Pittsburgh survey were especially influential in creating an atmosphere of opinion congenial to social advance. The first volume of the survey to be published was *Women and the Trades* (1910) by Elizabeth Beardsley Butler, a former secretary of the Consumers' League of New Jersey. The author gave particular attention to the well-established custom of paying female employees less than enough to live on—a practice based on the theory that girls and women were rarely self-supporting and that they usually worked only for "pin money." A box manufacturer candidly admitted: "We try to employ girls who are members of families, for we don't pay the girls a living wage in this trade."[15]

Miss Butler showed that in the Pittsburgh district the employers' assumption that a father or some other relative would meet the difference between a young woman's wages and the cost of living was often without factual basis. "That a girl is one of a family group is quite as likely to indicate that she is chief breadwinner as that her family is her chief bulwark against the world," she concluded.[16] For the fairly large and increasing number of girls who did not live with their families but were entirely on their own the consequences of underpayment were equally serious. Some of them supplemented the scanty wages received from stores or factories by occasionally engaging in what Miss Butler called "unsocial employment." Most of them struggled along by systematically undereating and by practicing the most rigorous economies in housing. They could live and continue to work on a diet of coffee for breakfast, very little or no lunch at all, and two or three sandwiches for supper. She cited the case of a girl who paid three dollars a week for board and room, her "room" being a couch in the kitchen of a crowded tenement apartment. She also mentioned the five young women from an iron mill who cut expenses by sharing one room with five workmen from the same plant.[17]

In 1910 the Russell Sage Foundation, which had financed the Pittsburgh survey, established a Committee on Women's Work headed by Mary Van Kleeck. Miss Van Kleeck had previously written a report on the operation of the New York hour law in which she revealed that, owing to unenforceable features in the law, women were working as long as seventy-eight hours a week, although the legal maximum was sixty hours.[18] Her most important research for the Sage Foundation was a series of inquiries into women's labor in bookbinding, artificial flower making, and the millinery trade. In these studies she conclusively proved the fallacy of the pin-money theory and demonstrated that in case after case wages adjusted to the supposedly meager needs of the girl who "lived at home" were a major cause of poverty and an important factor in perpetuating it.[19] For obvious reasons her monographs were frequently cited by advocates of a legal minimum wage for women. It is worth noting, however, that by 1914 Miss Van Kleeck and other officials of the Russell Sage Foundation had become convinced that the problems of women in industry were largely phases of conditions affecting men as well as women. In recognition of this attitude the name of the Committee on Women's Work was changed in 1916 to the Division of Industrial Studies.[20]

Influential though the Butler and Van Kleeck studies were, they were overshadowed by the multivolume *Report on Condition of Woman and Child Wage Earners in the United States* published by the United States Bureau of Labor between 1910 and 1913. Despite its length, detail, and formidable array of statistical tables, portions of the report made lively reading. There were pages in the volume on the life of working girls in stores and factories that might almost have been lifted from an O. Henry story. An investigator told of one salesgirl, thin and pale, who bravely explained why she was eating only a two-cent dish of tapioca pudding for lunch: "You see, I'm dieting," she said. The real life working girls, however, enjoyed less privacy than O. Henry heroines. The investigator reported that single women living in rooming houses regularly shared rooms with members of the landlady's family; in extreme cases they slept in the same room with the landlady and her husband. Calling on one workingwoman early in the evening, the investigator was received in a room in which a male lodger had already retired for the night. "This seemed to be the only available sitting room and disconcerted no one save the agent."[21]

The most frequently recurring observation in the nineteen volumes of the report was that wages of women appeared to be totally unstandardized. The most incongruous and inexplicably wide variations in pay prevailed within the same industry for the same work. "In the main," remarked one of the agents, "the women were wholly unorganized and seemed to have no idea in regard to wages beyond taking what they could get. The determining factor seemed not so much what their services were worth or what the industry could afford as the individual employer's attitude upon the matter." Instances were not lacking of employers who desired to treat their employees justly; but neither was there any scarcity of employers who made it a practice to pay women and girls the very least they could be induced to accept. In almost no employment was there any generally accepted standard of a fair wage for women. "What a woman could earn by a week's work," concluded the agent, "seemed to depend fully as much upon extrinsic factors over which she had no possible control as upon her own ability or her own efforts."[22]

A strike originating among employees of the Triangle Waist Company in New York in 1909, but eventually spreading to at least 20,000 other women in the garment trades, aroused unusual public interest in the wage problem. During the strike it became known that waist makers working at top speed for as long as seventy hours earned only four or five dollars a week. The stirring of sympathy provoked by this disclosure was as nothing compared to the outburst of indignation that followed news that 148 persons, mostly girls and young women, had been burned, smothered, or trampled to death in a fire on the top floors of a loft building housing the Triangle Company. The firm had been as thoughtless of safety as it was stingy with wages. Carl Sandburg's elegy for the victim of another factory fire might have been written for the Triangle girls: "It is the hand of God and the lack of fire escapes."[23]

One positive result of the storm of protest aroused by the needless loss of life in the Triangle fire was the appointment of the New York State Factory Investigating Commission. For three years members of the investigating group examined all phases of industrial working conditions, weighed proposed methods of dealing with them, and prepared reports and recommendations for the guidance of the legislature. At the instigation of the Commission the legislature overhauled the existing industrial code of the state by enacting more than thirty-five new factory laws in the space of two years. The subsequent championing of labor legislation by Senator Robert F. Wagner and Governor Alfred E. Smith may be attributed in large part to the knowledge and experience the two men acquired as chairman and vice-chairman, respectively, of this Commission.[24]

In its *Second Report* (1913) the Factory Investigating Commission recommended passage of a law prohibiting the labor of women between the hours of 10 P.M. and 6 A.M. A similar law adopted in 1899 had been in effect until 1907, when it was declared unconstitutional by the New York Court of Appeals. The Commission therefore included in its report a brief, patterned after the one submitted in *Muller* v. *Oregon,* setting forth both the legal arguments and the " 'Facts of Common Knowledge' Concerning Night Work" in defense of the proposed statute.[25] Acting on the Commission's recommendation, the legislature adopted the measure. When the Court passed on the new law in 1915 it reversed its earlier decision, citing the information gathered by the Commission, and additional data supplied by Brandeis and Miss Goldmark, as grounds for justifying prohibition of night work for women. Once more it seemed to the friends of reform that factualism had scored a victory over legalism.[26]

Each investigation of women's work, whether conducted by private foundations, the federal government, or state commissions, brought to light shocking instances of underpayment and presented new evidence of the dangerous effects of miserable earnings on women's health and welfare. It could scarcely be denied that many women were poorly paid because they possessed no skill, training, or experience to make their services valuable to employers; they received substandard earnings because they were substandard workers. But this was not the only reason why women's wages were so often disgracefully low. There was, in addition, the convenient fiction that the majority of female employees had no real economic responsibilities and that the wages paid them were therefore matters of little consequence. There was also the fact that intense competition in some lines of manufacture forced all employers to make cheapness their goal and to sacrifice every other consideration to this end. And, quite aside from skill or the lack of it, there was the poverty of applicants for jobs. "It is the worker nearest starvation who is most likely to accept starvation wages," warned Mary Van Kleeck.[27] In the circumstances it sometimes appeared that the greed of the worst employers and the need of the poorest workers were the principal factors in determining rates of pay for women.

As a way out of the dilemma reformers suggested the establishment of a legal minimum wage for women. Support for this reform, first proposed in 1906 by Father John A. Ryan, developed rapidly after 1910.[28] Previously it had seemed unlikely that any American state would countenance so obvious a departure from *laissez faire*, but the adoption in England in 1909 of an act authorizing the appointment of wage boards to fix minimum rates of pay in the sweated trades attracted favorable attention in this country.[29] Recent progress in state regulation of women's hours further encouraged reformers to believe that state intervention in the field of women's wages was feasible. The Consumers' League from its founding had made the payment of a living wage one of the first requirements to be met by establishments placed on its approved list. After 1910 Florence Kelley and other national and state officials of the League, including Father Ryan and John R. Commons, placed minimum-wage legislation on the "must" list of the organization's program. About the same time, and partly through the influence of Mrs. Kelley, two other voluntary organizations, the American Association for Labor Legislation and the Women's Trade Union League, enlisted in the campaign for women's wage laws.[30]

A not altogether unfounded but perhaps exaggerated notion of the extent of white slavery in the United States did much to build up popular and legislative support for the minimum-wage idea. Beginning in the 1890's, and increasingly after 1900, civic groups in Chicago and New York had investigated prostitution, especially in its relationship to police graft, the saloons, and political corruption. George Kibbe Turner's article "The Daughters of the Poor" (1909) and Reginald Wright Kauffman's novel *The House of Bondage* (1910) added to the great wave of interest in the subject —an interest which, on the national level, led to the enactment of the Mann Act of 1910.[31] Nearly all the investigators of women's labor gave some attention to the connection between low wages and prostitution. Miss Butler's comment was typical: "So long as custom or fact renders the payment of a full living wage nonessential, economic needs impel many a girl toward a personally degrading life."[32] Where other arguments for the payment of a living wage—as valid as this one, or perhaps more valid—were ignored, the suggestion that low wages tempted or forced women into prostitution made a strong impression. In the opinion of one contemporary observer, fear of sexual immorality was a major factor in precipitating the sudden flood of minimum-wage bills in 1913.[33]

Popular concern over low wages, not the pressure of organized labor, was responsible for the passage of minimum-wage laws. Generally speaking, union leaders were suspicious of the principle of governmental interference in the province of wages and somewhat fearful that the legal minimum might in practice become the going rate. Except in California, state federations of labor did not actively oppose the bills, but their support was ordinarily only lukewarm. Labor disputes, however, were a factor in arousing sentiment for wage legislation. In Massachusetts, the first state to adopt a minimum-wage law, the Consumers' League and other voluntary associations prepared the ground for reform, but it was the Lawrence strike of 1912, precipitated by a cut in wages at the textile mills, that finally convinced public opinion that legislative action was necessary, if only to prevent recurrence of labor disorders of like magnitude.[34]

Following the lead of Massachusetts, fourteen states enacted laws affecting women's wages between 1913 and 1923. More than half of these laws were passed in 1913. Broadly considered, the statutes were of two kinds. In Massachusetts and Nebraska employers were free to accept or reject the wage established as a fair minimum by a state commission; there was no coercion except that the commission published the names of the firms that failed to pay women employees the approved minimum. In Oregon and most of the other states, however, compliance with the minimum determined by the industrial commission was made compulsory for all employers. The model bill drafted by the Consumers' League was of the mandatory type, and it was this measure that Congress enacted into law for the District of Columbia in 1918.[35]

The Oregon statute was the first of the minimum-wage laws to be challenged in the courts. The State Industrial Welfare Commission, whose secretary, Father Edwin V. O'Hara, had been the chairman of the Oregon Consumers' League, set the minimum wage for experienced adult women workers at eight dollars and sixty-four cents per week. A paper-box manufacturer and one of his employees, who professed satisfaction with her weekly earnings of eight dollars, moved to have the law set aside on the grounds that it interfered with "the operation of natural and economic laws" and destroyed property and employment without due process of law. At the request of the Industrial Welfare Commission Brandeis submitted a brief in support of the law before the Oregon Supreme Court and, following the favorable decision of that tribunal, argued the validity of the Oregon statute before the United States Supreme Court in 1914.

The case was not decided until 1917. By this time Brandeis had been elevated to the Bench, and he, of course, did not take part in the decision. His arguments in 1914, however, and the exhaustive array of sociological, medical, and economic data Miss

Goldmark gathered for his brief won the approval of half of the eight members of the Court who participated in the decision. The effect of the justices' four-to-four vote in *Stettler* v. *O'Hara* was to leave standing the Oregon Supreme Court's ruling that had pronounced the law constitutional.[36]

Some enthusiasts, mistakenly assuming that the Court's action had settled the constitutionality of the issue, expected that this judgment would give the same impetus to minimum-wage legislation that *Muller* v. *Oregon* had provided for women's hour laws. In fact, the Court's split decision did little to stimulate the further enactment of wage bills. Some few laws, including the federal statute for the District of Columbia, were passed after 1917, but even before the Stettler decision there were signs that the movement was losing momentum. The opposition had begun to stiffen as early as the legislative sessions of 1915; by 1917 important industrial states such as New York, Michigan, Ohio, and Missouri had already rejected or deferred action on minimum-wage bills. Thereafter it was increasingly difficult to maintain the earlier popular interest in the reform, especially when talk ran high about unprecedentedly high earnings enjoyed by unskilled workers in war industries.

Without the strong backing of middle-class opinion and denied the active support of organized labor, the reformers made slight headway against the thoroughly aroused opposition of merchants' and manufacturers' associations. These groups affirmed their complete adherence to the sound business policy of paying employees fair wages—and denounced all efforts, whether by statute or trade-union activity, to insure observance of this wholesome practice as certain to harm business. Compulsory minimum-wage laws, when not branded socialistic, were decried because they stifled the employer's humanitarian motives. Voluntary legislation was scarcely less reprehensible if it entailed "vicious publicity" for firms refusing to comply with the minimum rates. In the heat of the fight manufacturers' associations counseled members to make gifts to such organizations as the Y.W.C.A. contingent on the promise that no part of the contribution should be used to promote the passage of, or to carry on propaganda for, any "social-service labor program."[37]

During the controversy over the New York minimum wage bill (recommended by the Factory Investigating Commission but not passed by the legislature) Walter Lippmann commented that if it were not for the war, which had accustomed men and women to the sight of whole nations glowering at one another from "holes in the mud,"

> it would be hard to believe that America with all its riches could still be primitive enough to grunt and protest at a living wage—a living wage, mind you; not a wage so its women can live well, not enough to make life a rich and welcome experience, but just enough to secure existence amid drudgery in gray boardinghouses and cheap restaurants.

Alarmed conservatives protested that radical innovations such as minimum-wage laws would undermine the foundations of the Republic. "But you cannot ruin a country by conserving its life," Lippmann replied. "You can ruin a country only by its stupidity, waste, and greed."[38]

After the war opponents of minimum-wage legislation found a valuable ally in the federal judiciary. The manufacturers' associations prevented the passage of new laws; the courts undid the work of reformers in the states and territories that had already adopted them. In 1923 the United States Supreme Court held the District of Columbia minimum-wage law to be an illegal interference with the right of contract and hence unconstitutional. On the basis of this ruling six state minimum-wage statutes were found unconstitutional and the publicity provision of the voluntary act of Massachusetts was declared invalid. Justice George Sutherland spoke for the majority of the Court in *Adkins* v. *Children's Hospital* (1923), the leading decision.[39] He dismissed the compilation of reports of industrial investigations, expert opinion, and informed observations that Felix Frankfurter adduced in support of the law as "interesting but only mildly persuasive." If the Brandeis brief in *Muller* v. *Oregon* had "made the law grow a hundred years in a day," the Sutherland opinion caused it to retrograde as far in a single sentence. Returning to the narrowly legalistic opinion the court had abandoned fifteen years earlier, Sutherland asserted that the sociological data in the brief, although proper for the consideration of legislative bodies, had no standing in a court of law, since they shed no light on the issue of the law's constitutionality.[40]

The Sutherland opinion blocked further progress in minimum-wage legislation for a decade and a half. Its implications for other social reforms were no less ominous; for it signified not only a revival of extreme conservatism but also a repudiation of factualism. In rejecting the appeal of ascertained facts and avowing an almost aesthetic doctrine of law for law's sake, Justice Sutherland and the majority of the Supreme Court were doing more than turning the clock back: they were stopping it. The importance of the Adkins case rests not so much in the decision, later reversed, that minimum-wage laws were unconstitutional, as in the intellectual attitude expressed by the justices. This attitude is by no means confined to the judiciary or to persons who are called or call themselves conservative. It is the tendency to regard the practical issues of human welfare as immaterial and to endow abstract conceptions of rights and liberties with reality. Whenever this view prevails, reform is virtually impossible.

CHAPTER 14

The Common Welfare

> No society can surely be flourishing and happy, of which the far greater part of the members are poor and miserable. It is but equity, besides, that they who feed, cloath and lodge the whole body of the people, should have such a share of the produce of their own labor as to be themselves tolerably well fed, cloathed and lodged.
>
> ADAM SMITH, *An Inquiry into the Nature and Causes of the Wealth of Nations.*

> Justice is what we want, not patronage and condescension and pitiful helpfulness. . . . Every one of the great schemes of social uplift which are now so much debated by noble people amongst us is based, when rightly conceived, upon justice, not upon benevolence. It is based upon the right of men to breathe pure air, to live; upon the right of women to bear children, and not to be overburdened so that disease and breakdown will come upon them; upon the right of children to thrive and to grow up and be strong; upon all these fundamental things which appeal, indeed, to our hearts, but which our minds perceive to be part of the fundamental justice of life.
>
> WOODROW WILSON, *The New Freedom.*

Two Kinds of Voluntarism

THROUGHOUT most of the first three decades of the twentieth century organized labor, as represented by the American Federation of Labor, was in certain respects even more devoted to the theory of *laissez faire* than organized business. Samuel Gompers could, and frequently did, denounce governmental "intermeddling" in economic affairs with all the vehemence of a self-made industrialist. But while businessmen were willing to employ the machinery of government for the advancement of their own interests, Gompers advised workingmen to abstain from the debilitating practice of using politics for welfare purposes. Year in and year out, for more than a generation, he preached a new version of the philosophy of self-help. According to his view, labor's rights were to be secured, not by "the regulation and the discipline and the decision" of the state, but through the organization of strong and stable trade-unions competent to bargain with employers on a basis of equality.

"Voluntarism," the program espoused by Gompers and other leaders of the A.F.L., meant first of all allowing free play to "the lawful and natural functions of the trade-union movement." Gompers was by no means a doctrinaire opponent of all social legislation, but he resented and resisted measures that, in his opinion, seemed likely to weaken trade-unionism either by lessening the effectiveness of collective bargaining or by obscuring the need for organization. Maximum-hour and minimum-wage laws for adult male workers in private employment fell in this category, as did proposals for public health and unemployment insurance. On the other hand, Gompers and the A.F.L. worked for laws controlling immigration, limiting the use of injunctions in labor disputes, and offering protection to woman and child wage earners.[1]

Gompers' long and prominent identification with the trade-union movement at a time when most employers were bitterly opposed to the organization of labor led many persons to assume that his views reflected the general attitude of American workers. Actually, of course, Gompers spoke only for the tiny fraction of the nation's labor force that was organized or organizable under the terms of craft unionism. His program was frankly designed for the benefit of this relatively small group of skilled or semiskilled workmen; it was not intended, except indirectly, to improve the status of the great mass of the workers; and certain of his policies, such as opposition to eight-hour laws, were more in harmony with the wishes of the stronger unions within the A.F.L. than of the membership as a whole.[2]

Gompers' creed, compounded of nineteenth-century theory and experience, was not an easy one to apply in the rapidly changing economy of the United States in the twentieth century. Voluntarism, a late-blooming variety of old-fashioned liberalism, seems in retrospect to have been strangely out of place in an era of giant business combinations, increasing mechanization of industry, large-scale immigration, and open-shop employers. All these factors made collective bargaining extremely difficult, especially for labor unions organized on the craft basis.[3] During his lifetime Gompers' dynamic personality and his unshakable conviction of rectitude were sufficient to cover serious defects in his program. It is more than likely that without his resourceful leadership organized labor might have suffered even more seriously than it did from the pommeling of the courts and the employers' associations. Nevertheless, it is now evident that voluntarism had the unfortunate effect of detaching a considerable segment of organized workmen from the reform movement, and of thereby delaying the adoption of social measures for the prevention of poverty.

Assertions that "the best form of charity is to give men work and to pay them decent wages" are a commonplace of philanthropic literature.[4] In the nineteenth century it was often assumed that all labor problems would disappear if only employers could be persuaded voluntarily to follow this advice. Not infrequently philanthropists sought to bolster the plea for voluntary action by stressing the religious obligation of persons in positions of authority to deal generously with their inferiors. As might be expected, this view was especially prevalent among the nonemploying classes. Many employers also endorsed it warmly; they did not always find it convenient to put the theory into practice, but they invariably appealed to it to justify their refusal to bargain with employees and to explain their opposition to compulsory legislation. Although George F. Baer, president of the Philadelphia and Reading Railway and leading spokesman of the mine operators at the time of the coal strike of 1902, gave the doctrine its most extreme expression, he was by no means the only representative of capital who contended that God had delegated exclusive responsibility for the care of workmen to employers.[5]

This particular species of voluntarism was never in good repute with organized labor, and by the first decade of the twentieth century it was not uncommon for leading social workers and prominent clergymen to contend that labor deserved justice rather than kindness. Settlement residents were often stanch friends of the labor movement. James B. Reynolds invited union groups to hold their meetings in the University Settlement in New York; and Raymond Robins, active in Chicago settlements, told delegates to the National Conference of Charities and Correction that "the one main thing" they had to do was to aid workingmen in their struggle for fair wages, shorter hours, and security of employment.[6] A speaker at the White House Conference on the Care of Dependent Children in 1909 went even further in his praise of the labor movement. Father William J. White, supervisor of the Catholic Charities of Brooklyn, saluted organized labor as "an agency for social betterment" and hailed its achievements as contributions to the general welfare.[7]

These opinions contrasted sharply with the prevailing sentiment and practice of industry, which was insistence on unilateral control of the conditions of employment by management. In *The Steel Workers* (1910), one of the six volumes of the Pittsburgh survey, John A. Fitch made an extended study of the practical results of this approach to the problem. Much of the book related to the labor policies of the United States Steel Corporation, the largest employer of labor in Pittsburgh as well as in the United States as a whole. Those policies, which had become standard in the steel industry and were being adopted wherever possible by other employers, led the A.F.L. in 1909 to brand the Steel Corporation the worst enemy of organized labor in America. Fitch showed that in the efficient, profitable, and tariff-protected process of steelmaking wages had failed to keep pace with the increase in the cost of living, that the level of wages in the industry was lower than it was popularly believed to be, and that the earnings of skilled steelworkers had suffered a decline in the fifteen years since unionism had been banished from the mills.[8] He also contended that the elimination of the union had been followed by an increase in the working day. The majority of steelworkers labored twelve hours a day; many of them worked seven days a week, either without a full day of rest or with a free Sunday one week followed by the "long turn"—twenty-four hours of continuous duty—the next.[9]

Fitch concluded that the steel companies were taking advantage of their unrestricted power over employees "to exact far more of the worker than was expected of him years ago, and . . . far more than is expected now in other industries."[10] One reason why they exercised such dominance was that 60 per cent of the steelworkers were unskilled laborers—poverty-stricken immigrants for the most part—who had no choice but to accept employment on any terms offered them. The other reason was that the steel companies had perfected elaborate secret-service devices to ferret out any efforts at unionization. Spying is justified in time of war, said Fitch. "Does war exist in western Pennsylvania?"[11]

The effect of the companies' espionage systems on community life was disastrous. "I doubt whether you could find a more suspicious body of men than the employees of the United States Steel Corporation," Fitch commented. "They are suspicious of one another, of their neighbors, and of their friends."[12] Another investigator quoted an old resident of the steel district as saying: "If you want to talk in Homestead you must talk to yourself." Paul Kellogg, director of the survey, observed that it would mean instant dismissal for large numbers of men employed in the steel mills if they met to discuss methods of improving their working conditions "in the way that farmers would take up freight rates or the price of apples at a grange hall."[13] Fear and suspicion on the part of employees, censorship and repression on the part of employers, made freedom of speech and activity rare things in those portions of Allegheny County where the steelworkers lived. In the opinion of the survey staff the steel industry's frankly avowed policy of industrial dictatorship implied denial, not only of unionism and collective bargaining, but also of democracy itself.

The tendency of students such as Fitch and Kellogg to examine the political as well as the economic consequences of industrial practices was in keeping with the general trend of prewar reform. Progressivism was primarily a political movement, stemming from a renewed faith in democracy and expressing itself in efforts to solve social problems by democratic political processes. Progressive reformers were often ready to seek political remedies for industrial ills at an earlier date than the leaders of organized labor, who, under the sway of Gompers' voluntarism, preferred to rely mainly on economic action. The reformers did not question the need or the desirability of trade-union activity, but this alone did not satisfy them. They were mindful of the great mass of America's working people who were beyond the pale of the labor movement as it was then organized and who lived in or on the brink of want. In their opinion the poverty of this numerous class was the basic problem, the issue that took precedence over all others. Not one but many strong levers must be fashioned to raise the standard of living of the laboring poor to a level consistent with the dignity and responsibility of democratic citizenship.

Social Measures for the Prevention of Poverty

Social insurance, or workingmen's insurance as it was usually called, awakened relatively little enthusiasm in the United States until long after it had become fairly well established abroad. A few Americans studied and discussed German and other European experiments in this field as early as the 1890's, but even those who praised the general idea were skeptical of the possibility of introducing workingmen's insurance into this country.[14] Shortly before 1910, however, concern over industrial accidents in the United States and growing interest in the rapid development of European legislation led both the Russell Sage Foundation and the United States Bureau of Labor to prepare more detailed and informative surveys of foreign insurance and compensation systems than had previously been available to American students.[15] The publication of these authoritative works, together with the gradual acceptance of the new view of poverty and the emergence of the concept of preventive social work, produced a much more favorable attitude toward workingmen's insurance.

After 1910 the idea of preventing destitution through the adoption of public insurance against the major causes of poverty—accident, illness, premature death, old age, and unemployment—won rapid approval, at least in reform circles. In 1910 Henry R. Seager delivered a series of lectures at the New York School of Philanthropy urging the incorporation of social insurance in the program of social reform.[16] I. M. Rubinow's *Social Insurance* (1913), recognized as the standard textbook on the subject for more than twenty years, grew out of a similar course of lectures at the same institution in 1912. Brandeis unqualifiedly recommended the establishment in the United States of a comprehensive system of workingmen's insurance in an address before the 1911 meeting of the National Conference of Charities and Correction.[17] The following year a committee of the National Conference issued a report defining the position of social workers on contemporary economic issues. The report recommended, in addition to a long list of other reforms, workmen's compensation laws covering occupational diseases as well as industrial accidents, and compulsory old-age and unemployment insurance.[18] Apparently through the influence of Paul Kellogg, all of the recommendations contained in the report, including the insurance proposals, found their way into the "Social and Industrial Justice" plank of the Progressive party's platform in 1912.[19]

Workmen's compensation was the first form of social insurance to receive serious consideration in the United States. Prior to the adoption of the compensation system Americans injured in work accidents, unless employed by one of the few companies that had voluntarily installed accident-insurance plans for their employees, had no assurance that the loss and expenses occasioned by the accident would be compensated. Some received cash settlement from their employers; some carried small industrial-insurance policies of their own; and some were covered by the insurance programs of trade-unions or fraternal organizations. They could, theoretically, sue their employers for damages, but this was an uncertain, expensive, and time-consuming process; and where the common-law rule that the right of action for personal injury expired with the death of the injured person was still in force, the families of men killed in industrial accidents had no right to sue.

Under the common law an injured workman's suit for damages against his employer might be dismissed by the judge before it reached the jury unless the plaintiff's lawyer could prove to the judge's satisfaction that the employer had been negligent and that his negligence had been the proximate cause of the injury. Even if this were established, the injured workman might still lose the suit if it could be shown that his own or a fellow employee's negligence had contributed to the accident or that, by continuing to work under obviously dangerous conditions, the workman had voluntarily assumed the risk of the accident. In the unlikely event that the injured man was able to surmount all these obstacles and win a favorable judgment, the case might be appealed to a higher court, in which the decision might be reversed on some technical point of law. The amount of damages received depended on the whim of the jury. Whatever they were, a sizable portion, perhaps deservedly, went to the lawyer who had steered the case through the shoals of the law.[20]

The injustice and absurdity of some of the common-law rules of employers' liability were recognized as early as the 1850's; by a half century later nearly all the states had passed measures modifying these doctrines in such a way as to give the injured party a slightly better chance for success in damage suits.[21] Most of the enactments, however, applied only to accidents suffered by railway or mineworkers, and they left many of the more serious defects in the common-law system untouched. Recovery of damages was still dependent on proof of the employer's negligence; and recovery might still be denied, in most states and for the majority of workers, through the operation of fellow-servant and contributory-negligence principles. One careful investigator estimated that notwithstanding the passage of employers' liability statutes, nine tenths of the economic cost of work accidents fell upon the injured party and that only about one fourth of the sums paid out by employers in damages and liability premiums reached the victims of industrial accidents.[22]

As the inadequacy of employers' liability laws became more evident, criticism of the whole system of requiring sufferers from work accidents or their bereaved families to resort to suits at law for the collection of damages became more frequent. It was argued that it was unfair to shift the burden of the cost of accidents to the persons who already bore the physical suffering, and—worse than unfair—unwise, since the practice inevitably doomed large numbers of hard-working, self-respecting families to poverty. For families dependent on a father's daily earnings, which were usually too small to permit of savings or adequate insurance protection, any interruption of work, for whatever cause, meant hardship. When cessation of work was accompanied by unusual medical and hospital expenses, and when injury resulted, as it often did, in permanent impairment of earning power, the results might well be calamitous.

Another frequently voiced objection was that the prevailing system contributed to the extremely high rate of accidents in American industry. Employers, having little to fear from damage suits, had no incentive to install safety measures or devices in their plants.

They were not more indifferent to suffering than employers in other lands, but they were under less compulsion to eliminate the hazards of industrial employment.[23]

No one knew the precise number of industrial accidents occurring each year in the United States, because, before the passage of the workmen's compensation laws, some states did not require accidents to be reported, and no state's accident statistics were entirely reliable.[24] An insurance statistician, basing his figures on the fragmentary data at hand, estimated that in 1913 there were 25,000 fatal industrial accidents and 700,000 work injuries involving disability for four weeks or longer.[25] Enough was known on the subject to convince interested students not only that the rate of fatal industrial accidents in the United States was higher than in Europe, but also that between one third and one half of the American fatalities were preventable.[26] "If no nation in the world rivals the United States in the dash and energy of its business methods, no other nation is willing to pay the price in flesh and blood of citizens," wrote Ellery Sedgwick in a famous article entitled "The Land of Disasters." He alleged that "accidents" that were a daily occurrence in the United States would be impossible in countries that enforced respect for human life. "In America things are different. Here men mind their own business."[27]

Quite aside from its inhumanity "the wanton slaughter of the toilers," as an irate journalist denominated industrial accidents, was attacked as detrimental to the national interest.[28] Writing shortly after the Ballinger-Pinchot controversy, I. M. Rubinow observed: "There is a problem of preservation of human resources in comparison with which even the coal fields of Alaska shrink into significance."[29] The strongest statement of the conservation argument came from William Hard, who phrased his views with Rooseveltian militancy. "Every accident (and especially every unpaid-for accident) hurts the *country* as well as the *individual*," he asserted. Uncompensated industrial accidents constituted nothing less than "National Waste," "a weakening of the Human Power of the Nation in International Competition"; accident-prevention laws and automatic compensation for injury, on the contrary, represented "National Economy" and "A Saving of Physical and Financial Strength for the World Struggle."[30]

Of all the books and articles dealing with the operation of the employers' liability system, the most eloquent and the most effective in promoting reform was Crystal Eastman's contribution to the Pittsburgh survey, *Work Accidents and the Law* (1910). This study reported the findings of the author's investigation of the causes and consequences of the death or injury of about one thousand men in work accidents in Allegheny County in the period just before the survey was undertaken.[31] Miss Eastman interviewed the injured workmen, families of the deceased men, fellow employees, and witnesses of the accidents; and she consulted, to the extent that she was permitted to do so, the employers' records. Her purpose was to ascertain the circumstances of each accident, the nature of the injury, the worker's family responsibilities, his income, the extent of the financial loss suffered by the worker or his family, the share of the loss assumed by the employer, and the effect of the accident on the economic circumstances of the worker's family. Her report was a factual treatise, not a sentimental or propagandistic tract, but the sad facts themselves, skillfully marshaled and soberly stated, were enough to give the book an impressive earnestness and to make the author's conclusions seem irrefutable.

Miss Eastman's investigation indicated that roughly one third of the accidents were "nobody's fault," but seemingly unavoidable consequences of industrial production; one third resulted from "the human weaknesses of the workmen, often accentuated by their occupation and environment"; the other third stemmed from insufficient provision for the safety of workmen on the part of employers.[32] She found that employers had provided no compensation whatsoever in more than 50 per cent of the accidents, and that in the great majority of cases where it was provided the compensation was so small as to cover only an insignificant part of the income loss arising from the accident.[33] As for the law of employers' liability, Miss Eastman (who was herself an attorney) declared: "It is to be condemned from the standpoints of justice, method, and practical utility."[34]

There were two possible legal solutions to the problems described. The common law might be further amended by abrogating the fellow-servant rule, eliminating the doctrine of assumption of risk, and modifying the principle of contributory negligence; or an entirely new approach, based on European workmen's compensation laws, might be adopted. Under the former it would still be necessary for injured workmen or their families to sue for damages. Their prospects for a favorable verdict would, presumably, be brighter, but they would have no cause for action in those numerous instances in which accidents were not the result of the employer's negligent acts or omissions. Under the second, or compensation plan, negligence would be disregarded. An employer would be required to compensate all his employees injured in work accidents without regard to the cause; and the payments he made would be determined by (and limited to) a uniform scale of benefits, figured on the basis of a fixed proportion of the economic loss resulting from the injury.

The advantages and disadvantages of these alternative courses of action were examined, not only by Miss Eastman, but by the thirty state commissions appointed to investigate industrial accidents and employers' liability between 1909 and 1913. Miss Eastman, weighing the relative merits of each, unhesitatingly recommended the system of assured workmen's compensation. This was the conclusion ultimately reached by each of the state commissions.[35] The importance of the decision can hardly be underestimated; for the compensation system involved a radical departure from long-established legal principles of responsibility. Endorsement of it was another sign of a growing willingness to alter the law to meet the needs of modern conditions.

The underlying principle of workmen's compensation was that accidents, whatever their cause, were an inevitable accompaniment of the industrial process. One student sagely observed that "the human organism is imperfectly adapted to a mechanical environment."[36] Another remarked that "industrial accidents are not accidents at all, but normal results of modern industry."[37] Once this premise was accepted, the logical next step was to assert that the cost of industrial accidents, or of their prevention, was a regular part of the cost of production. Like any other cost it should be borne, in the first instance, by the producer of the goods, and ultimately by the consumer. Supporters of the plan believed that employers would desire to keep the expenses incurred by the operation of the compensation system at a minimum and that they would therefore bestir themselves to reduce the number of avoidable accidents—perhaps even find ways to eliminate supposedly unavoidable ones. When it was objected that if compensation for injuries were assured, workingmen might become more careless, Miss Eastman replied: "If the fear of death or injury does not insure caution in the workman, we cannot hope to instill it by holding over him the fear of poverty."[38]

During the decade after 1910 the movement made such rapid headway that by 1920 all but six states and the District of Columbia had enacted compensation statutes of one sort or another. "No other kind of labor legislation gained such general acceptance in so brief a period," declared one historian of the movement.[39] The rapidity with which state after state adopted the compensation principle surprised even the most sanguine reformers. Compensation laws, although not always of the same type or for the same reason, were supported by organizations as diverse in their aims and composition as the American Association for Labor Legislation and the National Association of Manufacturers.[40] Organized labor, which had at first indicated a preference for stronger employers' liability laws and had opposed some of the early compensation statutes, soon renounced its hostility; and after study of the operation of the approximately twenty workmen's compensation laws in effect at the close of 1913 the A.F.L. gave its official sanction to the movement.[41]

Workmen's compensation laws did not bring about the quick reduction in the frequency of work accidents that supporters of the movement had hoped would follow their enactment. Other factors, such as the increasing scale, speed, and complexity of industrial operations, combined to keep the rate of accidents at a high level.[42] Nevertheless, the adoption of the system did have the result of providing the nation with its first detailed and exact knowledge of the nature and extent of industrial fatalities and injuries. Heretofore estimates of the number of casualties were apt to vary according to the attitudes of statisticians toward the seriousness of the question, and it was always possible to deny the validity of those estimates that placed the annual toll of life and limb at an alarmingly high figure. With the regular collection and publication of accident statistics by state compensation agencies it became more and more difficult to doubt the gravity of the problem.[43]

The major defects of the compensation laws passed between 1910 and 1920 were that they left a substantial proportion of workers outside their coverage, usually failed to include occupational diseases among the compensable injuries, and in no instance provided an adequate scale of compensation benefits. The majority of the laws were of a voluntary type, meaning that employers, if they chose to do so, might remain outside the system. In practice few of them "elected out," but the privilege of withdrawing retained by employers acted as a brake on movements to raise the compensation scales. There was always a possibility that if benefits were increased, large numbers of employers might exercise their right of withdrawal.[44]

Most if not all of the acts specifically excluded certain occupations, typically agricultural labor and domestic service. Some statutes exempted small employers—that is, those employing fewer than ten, eleven, sixteen, or whatever number of workmen was stated in the act; a few were limited to "hazardous employments." As a consequence of such exemptions and exclusions an estimated 30 per cent of the workers in the states with compensation laws remained outside the system in 1920.[45]

At the time the original compensation laws were passed comparatively little was known about industrial medicine or hygiene. The research of Dr. Alice Hamilton, John B. Andrews, and Frederick L. Hoffman and the interest displayed by two government officials, Charles P. Neill and Royal Meeker, in promoting research and publicizing the facts about trade diseases did much to dispel the ignorance of both the public and employers. By 1920 a few of the more enlightened states had brought occupational diseases under the purview of the compensation laws, but it was not until the late 1930's that all of the important industrial states took this step.[46]

The most serious weakness of the laws was that the scale of benefits was too miserly to meet the loss suffered by victims of industrial accidents. A well-informed critic pointed out in 1924 that in most states the money benefits were insufficient to maintain a normal standard of living during the compensation period and that these payments were abruptly terminated at the end of an arbitrarily determined time limit "without regard to the needs of the injured worker or of those dependent upon him." He found that the medical benefits were inadequate either to relieve the suffering or to restore the earning capacity of severely injured workers. Consequently, and in complete violation of the assumed principle of the compensation system, the victims of industrial accidents still bore the heaviest share of the wage loss resulting from work injuries.[47]

This result may not have been entirely unforeseen or unintended by some of the more influential supporters of the compensation laws, as contrasted with the compensation principle. Writing in the midst of the campaign for the adoption of the laws, Rubinow noted that business groups commonly advocated legislation that would make compensation cheap and at the same time relieve employers of the risk and annoyance of liability suits. It was the limited compensation scale, rather than the assurance that all work injuries would be compensated, that recommended the measures to employers.[48]

Despite recognized imperfections in the compensation laws, progressives interpreted their enactment as heartening evidence of popular support for the idea of social insurance. The acceptance in theory, if not yet in fact, of collective responsibility for the wage loss resulting from industrial accidents seemed to presage similar action in other fields. Injury at work was only one of the hazards to which wage earners were exposed and with which, as individuals, they were powerless to cope. Income losses occasioned by sickness, unemployment, and old age might be dealt with in much the same way as those stemming from accident. If this were done, said the reformers, society would have protected itself against the major social causes of poverty.

"There are more accidents, more sickness, more premature old age and invalidity, and more unemployment in the United States than in most European countries," wrote one of the leading advocates of social insurance in 1913.[49] Formerly Americans had assumed that the economic condition of labor was prosperous enough to permit individuals to surmount the financial crises produced by these calamities. Wage and budget studies undertaken since the turn of the century, however, had confirmed what social workers had long suspected: that few wage earners ever rose far above the poverty line, that surpluses in their budgets were rare, and that without some sort of assistance they were economically unable to meet the drain of disaster without extreme hardship. For a century Americans had been perfecting systems of relief to meet need after its occurrence. Now the time seemed to be ripe to prevent destitution and the need for charitable relief by attacking the problem at—or nearer—its source.

Practically all the arguments for accident compensation applied with equal or greater force to sickness insurance. To the general proposition that the primary concern of the state should be the physical well-being of its citizens there was added the known fact that illness was a more important cause of poverty than industrial accident. Like most of the other tribulations of life, sickness struck the poor more frequently than the well-to-do. This was true not only because the poor were more numerous than the well-to-do, but also because their bad housing, improper diet, strenuous labor in adverse surroundings, and inability to obtain regular medical attention made the poorer classes more susceptible to the attacks of disease. Theodore Parker once reflected that rich men of old rode into battle so well covered with armor that arrows glanced from them as from stone, whereas the poor confronted war in leather jerkins, and every weapon tore their unprotected flesh. "In the modern, perennial battle with disease," said Parker, "the same thing takes place: the Poor fall and die."[50]

Even ignoring the anxiety and suffering it caused, prolonged illness brought a train of misery when it invaded the homes of the poor. Not infrequently it cut off income; in any event it diverted into other channels money sorely needed for the everyday expenses of running a household. The advent of sickness did not reduce every low-income family or even most, to destitution; usually they were able to get through the ordeal without asking for or receiving aid from sources outside their own kith and kin. They managed somehow—and often this meant by resorting to questionable economies in housing, nutrition, health, education, and recreation and by relying on the ill-compensated and unnatural labor of wives and young children. But the decay of strength, the deterioration of living standards, and the disruption of normal family life did not affect only those homes in which the unwelcome visitor stalked. Sickness had economic consequences that were scarcely less blighting to society than to the immediate families involved. Each year illness, to a greater extent than any other single factor, either directly or indirectly drafted hapless persons into the already overflowing ranks of "the army of the disheartened and ineffective."[51] It was this class of casual, unskilled, standardless—and therefore low-paid—labor that comprised the hard core of the poverty problem.

"What next in reform?" asked a group of social workers at a meeting held in 1915. Health insurance was the unanimous reply. The group contained some formidable and experienced crusaders. Jane Addams had been in the forefront of nearly every movement for social betterment for a quarter of a century; Paul Kellogg had directed the Pittsburgh survey and was editor of the influential magazine *The Survey;* Edward T. Devine was the best-known administrator and educator in the field of social work; John B. Andrews, secretary of the American Association for Labor Legislation, had played a leading role in the securing of workmen's compensation laws; and I. M. Rubinow was the nation's outstanding authority on social insurance. When these men and women promulgated the slogan "Health Insurance–the next step" all signs seemed to promise early victory. In addition to the precedent established by the recent passage of accident compensation laws there was, or seemed to be, mounting interest in the elimination of occupational diseases and in the reduction of infant mortality. Furthermore, earlier campaigns for the prevention of tuberculosis and for the control of hookworm infection had received enthusiastic public support.

Those high hopes were soon dashed by the unexpectedly bitter and widespread opposition that the very suggestion of the establishment of a system of compulsory health insurance provoked. Nearly twenty years later one of the sponsors of the movement concluded that the chief reason for its collapse was that he and other advocates of "the next step" had failed to recognize the variety and strength of the class interests that would be antagonized by the proposal.[52] These included employers' and taxpayers' associations, insurance firms, organized labor (until the 1930's), members of the medical and dental professions, druggists, producers and dispensers of patent medicines, and Christian Scientists. The success with which such groups employed ideological arguments against public health insurance revealed that, despite the adoption of accident compensation, the notion of individual responsibility for misfortune was still deeply rooted in the public mind. Eventually opponents of compulsory health insurance were able to banish consideration of need or desirability from debate on the issue and to substitute emotional appeals to patriotism for rational argumentation. When the depression era brought a revival of interest in reform, it was unemployment and old-age insurance, not health insurance, that seemed the logical next steps toward security.

CONCLUSION

The Price of Reform

> In a few years all our restless and angry hearts will be quiet in death, but those who come after us will live in the world which our sins have blighted or which our love of right has redeemed. Let us do our thinking on these great questions, not with our eyes fixed on our bank account, but with a wise outlook on the fields of the future and with consciousness that the spirit of the Eternal is seeking to distil from our lives some essence of righteousness before they pass away.
>
> WALTER RAUSCHENBUSCH, *Christianity and the Social Crisis.*

THE eclipse of reform in the 1920's did not signify any weakening of the national faith in the possibility of overcoming poverty. On the contrary, it reflected the widespread assumption that for all practical purposes the task had been accomplished. According to the prevailing view poverty, like child labor, was virtually a thing of the past; consequently there was no longer any need or justification for social reform. By inference, individual reform was likewise outdated, since the most important elements in prosperity were now held to be impersonal factors such as technology and scientific management. Conservatives boasted that under the amiable relations established between government and big business in the Harding and Coolidge administrations the American dream of material abundance was fast being realized. During the campaign of 1928 Herbert Hoover referred to the automatic solution of social problems by business processes as "our American experiment in human welfare." He cited the progress made in the preceding seven years as proof that this experiment had brought the United States "nearer to the abolition of poverty, to the abolition of the fear of want, than humanity has ever reached before."[1]

Well before the stock market crash of 1929 Hoover's critics pointed out that his optimistic view of the state of the economy was based on a rather strained reading of the evidence.[2] It was not until many months after the crash, however, that either Hoover or the nation as a whole acknowledged the full extent and seriousness of the economic debacle. By that time "the abolition of poverty, the abolition of the fear of want" had become in a very real sense the major concern of the American people. The Hoover administration then undertook such measures to promote recovery as were consistent with the President's philosophy of government. Even so, the Administration retained the outlook of the 1920's and, as Franklin D. Roosevelt observed, the program it adopted to meet the emergency delayed relief and neglected reform. Very early in the 1930's the majority of the voters made it plain that they expected their government to take more drastic action to combat the depression than Hoover believed warranted. Before the decade was over the voters had repeatedly expressed their confidence in a new administration, which was as firmly committed to reform as to recovery, and which recognized more clearly than any previous one that the basic faults in the economy were insecurity, insufficient income, and low standards of living.

If, as has recently been suggested, the advent of the New Deal marked "a drastic new departure" in the history of American reform, the reason is only partly because the Roosevelt administration took office in the midst of the worst depression in American history.[3] Equally important is the fact that the President and his major advisers, influenced in some degree by the intellectual revolution that had occurred since the 1890's, pressed experts in many lines of endeavor into government service and consciously sought to apply the new trends in social and economic thought to the issues of the day. This was especially true in the fields of welfare and social legislation, in both of which the New Deal drew heavily upon the knowledge of social workers. Without minimizing the importance of the social reforms inaugurated during the 1930's it may be said that the measures then adopted were largely implementations, amplifications, and—in some instances—but partial fulfillments of the program of preventive social work formulated before World War I.

One of the principles that the profession of social work had inherited from the scientific philanthropy of the late nineteenth century was hostility to public outdoor relief. The founders of the profession all believed that private charity should provide for the needy who did not require institutional care. This assumption regularly broke down when put to severe test in time of major disaster or depression; but, although the idea of voluntary responsibility for relief was not so vehemently asserted in the twenties as formerly, it was not seriously challenged before 1930. In the next two or three years, however, as social workers struggled with mounting case loads and diminishing revenues, they rapidly lost any lingering aversion they may have felt toward "official assistance." By 1931 some of them were taking the position that unemployment relief could no longer be regarded as a form of charity but should be recognized as a public obligation to which the jobless were entitled as a matter of right. When the resources of the local communities were exhausted —or at any rate were no longer forthcoming—social workers did not hesitate to call upon first the states and then the national government to supply additional funds for emergency relief.[4]

The question of federal participation in relief was no longer at issue when Franklin Roosevelt became president because, under a program reluctantly approved by Hoover in the summer of 1932, federal loans (which it was commonly assumed would never be repaid) were already financing 80 per cent of all state and local aid to the unemployed.[5] The problem that remained to be settled was how the federal funds should be administered, and, in particular, whether they should be used for cash or work relief. In the first year and a half of the New Deal the Administration tried both approaches but tended to rely on the former, mainly because that course seemed to arouse least controversy. Not until after the Democratic victories in the congressional elections of 1934 did President Roosevelt come out strongly in favor of work as opposed to cash relief. His message to Congress of January 4, 1935, which proposed establishment of the Works Progress Administration, denounced public assistance in the form of money and food in language reminiscent of that used by the scientific philanthropists of the 1870's and 1880's:

> The lessons of history, confirmed by the evidence immediately before me, show conclusively that continued dependence upon relief induces a spiritual and moral disintegration fundamentally destructive to the national fiber. To dole out relief in this way is to administer a narcotic, a subtle destroyer of the human spirit. It is inimical

to the dictates of sound policy. It is in violation of the traditions of America.[6]

Nineteenth-century crusaders against pauperism could scarcely have objected to the President's pronouncement "Work must be found for able-bodied but destitute workers." They would have been in complete sympathy with his assertion that not only the bodies, but the self-reliance, courage, and determination of the unemployed must be preserved from destruction. Joseph Tuckerman, Robert Hartley, Josephine Shaw Lowell, and all the earlier charity reformers would have agreed that those precious qualities deserved to be protected at any price. It is quite possible, however, that they would have been very surprised to discover how high, in monetary terms, that price would prove to be. In the case of WPA, the total cost of providing work—and with it, self-respect, hope, and patriotism—to an average of about 2,000,000 persons a month for six years amounted to $11,365,000,000.

In the same message that recommended creation of the WPA President Roosevelt declared that the time had come for action by the national government in the field of social security; two weeks later he submitted to Congress the plan for old-age and unemployment insurance prepared by his Committee on Economic Security. As already noted, support for social insurance had been building up in reform circles since 1910. Under the impact of the depression two of the major barriers that had previously impeded progress in this area—public indifference and the hostility of organized labor—rapidly broke down. By the end of 1934 the movement for public insurance, once largely confined to humanitarians and educators, and regarded mainly as a method of preventing poverty, had been broadened and made more militant by the enlistment in the cause of millions of unhappy and disgruntled people. Most of the new recruits were already in or desperately close to poverty and they looked upon old-age pensions and unemployment insurance as panaceas both for their own and the nation's ills. In these circumstances the President advised against attempts to apply social insurance on too ambitious a scale at the start, and warned that "extravagant action" might jeopardize the whole idea of social security.

During the seven months that the modest and moderate social security bill backed by President Roosevelt was before Congress, it was attacked as often from the left as from the right. Apprehension that rejection of the Administration measure might lead to increased public pressure for the passage of more sweeping proposals appears to have been an important factor in weakening conservative opposition to the bill and in bringing about its enactment.[7] As finally adopted the Social Security Act provided for a national program of old-age insurance supported by contributions from employers and employees, and for unemployment-insurance systems to be operated by the states but financed by a federal pay-roll tax. In addition, the Act authorized grants-in-aid to the states for old-age pensions, and made available further federal subsidies for a variety of public-health and welfare projects affecting mothers, dependent and neglected children, handicapped persons, and the blind. It contained no provision for insurance against sickness, for aid to the unemployed after the period of insurance coverage had expired, or for federal participation in the relief of distress caused by a multitude of other causes.

A dozen years after the passage of the Social Security Act a prominent social worker commented that in view of the items omitted from it, the measure might well have been entitled an act to furnish such means of security as provoked no serious opposition.[8] These deficiencies (which were recognized in 1935 but have not yet been corrected) in no wise lessen the significance of the Social Security Act as one of the milestones in the history of American social reform. The Act has brought about an expansion of public-welfare activities all over the country; it has raised the standards of welfare work and improved the legal status of applicants for certain kinds of assistance; it has opened the way for the development of a long-delayed and much-needed national policy on public welfare; and—not least—it has been declared constitutional.

On May 24, 1937—the very same day, as it happened, that the Supreme Court rendered its decisions upholding the constitutionality of the Social Security Act—the President charged Congress to "extend the frontiers of social progress" by adopting a minimum-wage and maximum-hour law. Until two months earlier the Supreme Court had denied even the states the right to establish minimum wages; and until April, 1937, the majority of the justices had followed such a narrow interpretation of interstate commerce that the validity of any regulation of labor conditions by the national government was extremely doubtful. The Court had reversed its position on both points, however, by the time the President sent his message to Congress. Enactment of federal legislation on wages, hours, and child labor was therefore constitutionally feasible. Nevertheless, so many other objections from conservative and labor groups still had to be overcome that it was only after a full year of debate and compromise that Congress was induced to accept a Fair Labor Standards Act providing, at the start, and in those activities not exempted from its protection, for a minimum wage of twenty-five cents an hour, a maximum work week of forty-four hours, and prohibition of the shipment in interstate commerce of goods produced by children under sixteen years of age.

Perhaps the most interesting aspect of the long debate was the tendency of President Roosevelt and other supporters of the bill to lay as much stress on its economic as on its humanitarian objectives. The latter had been the major consideration of earlier reformers, but from the start, and especially after the recession of late 1937, the President emphasized the need for raising the income and stimulating the buying power of workers in all sections of the country. Thus, somewhat ironically, the kind of legislation that had always before been attacked because of its possible adverse effects on the economy was now presented and accepted as essential to sound and lasting prosperity.

Although the New Dealers faced far more difficult problems than their immediate predecessors in reform they were no less confident than the Progressives that the economic and environmental causes of poverty could be eradicated. In the darkest days of the depression they were sustained by the same faith in American abundance that had characterized the humanitarians of the preceding generation. "I see one third of a nation ill-housed, ill-clad, ill-nourished," said President Roosevelt in his second inaugural address —but he hastened to add that the vision did not make him despair; for he also saw "a great nation, upon a great continent, blessed with a wealth of natural resources," which was fully capable of translating national wealth "into a spreading volume of human comforts hitherto unknown," and of raising the lowest standards of living high above the subsistence level.[9]

Earlier reformers and their conservative critics had sometimes suggested that the task of making fundamental improvements in the income and living conditions of the masses might be beyond the ability of capitalism. If this doubt ever assailed the New Dealers it did not appear in their actions. Confronted with the heavy responsibility of restoring the national economy to working order, President Roosevelt and his coworkers assumed, and in large measure proved, that an invigorated democracy and an enlightened capitalism could provide security and welfare for all.

For more than half a century we have known that the most valuable philanthropic work is the preventive, not the curative, and that the best way to deal with distress is to make the normal environment of life such that misfortunes, when they occur, will not find large numbers of people economically defenseless. This approach to reform is seldom challenged in principle. Nevertheless, as the preceding chapters show, attempts to put it into practice are always opposed, usually derided, and sometimes defeated. Whenever an effort is made to apply the doctrine of prevention to a specific social problem the cry goes up that the proposed remedy is socialistic, un-American, unconstitutional, untimely, a violation of economic law, and contrary to human nature. All or some of these charges may be true, but they are not the central reasons why reforms that seek to prevent distress rather than to palliate it are adopted slowly and in the face of bitter opposition. The real reasons are that prevention is expensive and that it interferes with somebody's rights or liberties.

It costs money to manufacture goods, to raise crops, to transport freight across the country, to dig minerals from the earth, and to perform all the other operations necessary to a flourishing economy. So, too, it costs to produce healthy, skilled, happy, and law-abiding citizens—more than most people realize, more than some are willing to pay. An adequate program for the prevention of distress is bound to be an expensive proposition This is true whether the distress be caused by unemployment, illness, low earning power, or some natural disaster such as flood. Relief is also expensive, and so is neglect. But there are experts who can compute the money cost of prevention; they can tell the taxpayer almost to a fraction of a cent what his share of the burden will be; and dollars and cents are the terms in which we ordinarily figure expense. Expenditures for relief and charity, although they can be estimated with fair accuracy from year to year and always amount to a very sizable sum, do not loom so large as those for prevention. The cost of neglect, including the waste, inefficiency, and disorder it creates, is so astronomical that it can scarcely be reckoned. This cost is one that we have never yet fully appreciated.

The second major objection to preventive remedies, the assertion that they will interfere with individual liberties, is no less and no more valid than the argument of expense. The chief liberties endangered by preventive social action are the supposed rights to profit or otherwise benefit from practices that may be advantageous to some individuals but are harmful to society. Depriving the strong of the power to take advantage of the weak is sure to be resisted by those who are strong and powerful. No doubt such deprivation *is* a violation of natural conditions; but it is also the essence of justice.

It is assumed by some that the chief threat to individual freedom comes from the state. In many times and places this has been and is still true. It is not true, or at least it is much less often true, in nations with free and democratic political institutions. There are a great many areas of life in which the absence of state or social controls means not freedom, but subjection to the most galling of tyrannies. Liberty, after all, is a practical matter, not an abstraction. Men can be victimized as much by the economic law of supply and demand as by the arbitrary whim of a despot.

There is still a rather widespread belief that state interference in economic matters and the assumption by the state of responsibility for activities formerly performed by individuals for their private profit are signs of decay. The broadening of the regulatory and service functions of the state may more properly be diagnosed as the mark of a healthy social life. Certainly it is not a revolutionary development, but a continuation of a long, historical process. Not in some vague state of nature, but in fairly recent times, even such matters as the gathering of taxes, the recruitment of armies, and the administration of criminal law fell within the province of private enterprise. It is not paternalism that men are establishing when, by common consent, they assign new functions to their government. On the contrary, their action is a rejection of the paternalistic authority previously exercised by private individuals; it is a substitution of democratic for dictatorial control over the material conditions of their lives.

The promise of America, both to its own and to other peoples, has always been the pledge of improved material conditions of life. Once the United States itself, by offering unique opportunities for individual advancement, seemed the world's best cure for poverty. Now we are hopeful that through the export of American capital and technical knowledge to less-favored areas of the globe we can enable depressed peoples to overcome their ancient need. The international tensions of the present give the new program the same urgency formerly held by projects to improve the lot of the "dangerous classes" at home.

As we embark on this difficult venture it is important for us to remember that American progress in the field of welfare has been obtained not so much by the encouragement of charity as by the promotion of measures that have reduced the necessity for it. We now know that the economic ills from which men suffer are not entirely of their own making, that hunger and disease cannot be exorcised by moral exhortations, and that there is no cheap remedy for poverty. We have found out that the price of reform, for society as for the individual, is not only a resolution to give up bad habits, but conscious, intelligent striving to lead a better life.

In our own country the discovery of poverty brought with it a rediscovery of the brotherhood of man. The lesson that we have learned as a result of our attempts to deal with poverty at home is the need for respect, kindness, cooperation, and justice in relations between men. Further concrete demonstrations of our belief in the dignity and supreme value of human life are as indispensable to a program of international aid as loans and technical guidance. National self-interest, hostility to communism, and sympathy for the orphaned and widowed are not sufficient foundations on which to erect a permanent program for combating want in the world. Unless and until our assistance is motivated by a genuine feeling of respect for the essential spiritual worth of all human beings, regardless of their present condition, the results will be disappointing to us and humiliating to those we try to help.

A Note on the Sources

Sources for a study of American attitudes toward poverty are abundant, varied, and accessible. There are many approaches to the topic and, out of the vast literature bearing on the subject, the individual researcher must select those works that strike him as most representative and pertinent. The particular sources I have used for specific phases of the problem are indicated in notes for each chapter, and the major works consulted in the preparation of this book are listed in the Bibliography. I have not thought it desirable to divide and subdivide the Bibliography into numerous classifications, but I should like to call the reader's attention to certain works that have proved unusually helpful.

Owing to the nature of the inquiry I have relied mainly on printed works, but Mr. J. G. Phelps Stokes of New York kindly put at my disposal his large collection of correspondence and papers dealing with charitable and reform activities since the 1890's. I have also utilized various unpublished reports in the archives of the Community Service Society of New York. I found some uncatalogued material on "Poor" in the New York Public Library Annex, and certain nineteenth-century pamphlets not readily obtainable elsewhere in the Newberry Library in Chicago.

My basic sources were the writings of humanitarian reformers such as Joseph Tuckerman, Robert M. Hartley, Charles Loring Brace, Josephine Shaw Lowell, Amos G. Warner, Jane Addams, Jacob Riis, Edward T. Devine, Robert Hunter, John A. Ryan, and Florence Kelley. In addition to the well-known books of Miss Addams and Riis the key works in this category include Brace's *Dangerous Classes of New York*, Mrs. Lowell's *Public Relief and*

Private Charity, Warner's *American Charities*, and Hunter's *Poverty*. There are worth-while studies of the life and work of Tuckerman by McColgan, of Mrs. Lowell by Stewart, and of Mrs. Kelley by Goldmark. Special aspects of nineteenth-century philanthropy are dealt with in Brackett's *Supervision and Education in Charities* and Folks's *Care of Destitute, Neglected and Delinquent Children*. Watson's *Charity Organization Movement in the United States* traces the development of scientific philanthropy and includes a very comprehensive bibliography on the subject. Devine's *When Social Work Was Young* gives a good picture of the rise of preventive social work.

The *Proceedings* of the National Conference of Social Work (formerly the National Conference of Charities and Correction) contain many articles and discussions of interest to the historian; Frank J. Bruno's *Trends in Social Work* is a handy and informative guide to the *Proceedings*. *The Survey* and its predecessors, *Charities and the Commons* and *Charities*, are among the best and most readily available sources of information on social-reform movements. The pamphlets issued by groups such as the National Child Labor Committee and the Consumers' League shed light on social conditions and also communicate the spirit of the reformers to sympathetic readers. The annual reports of philanthropic organizations frequently summarize the findings of studies conducted by charity agents. A good example is Owen's "The Story of the 'Big Flat,'" in the *Forty-third Annual Report* of the New York A.I.C.P.

Certain major investigations undertaken by both voluntary organizations and governmental agencies in the first two decades of the twentieth century are landmarks in the history of social research. Perhaps the most important of these are Kellogg's *The Pittsburgh Survey* (particularly the volumes by Crystal Eastman and John A. Fitch), De Forest's and Veiller's *The Tenement House Problem*, and the U.S. Bureau of Labor's *Report on Condition of Woman and Child Wage-Earners*. Nearly all the studies published by the Russell Sage Foundation and the Charities Publication Committee can be used with profit by the historian; and scholarly journals such as *The Annals* and the *Publications* of the American Economic Association are studded with articles on important issues.

One of the most enjoyable and rewarding phases of my task was to go through the files of magazines such as *The Arena*, *Atlantic Monthly*, *Masses*, *The Craftsman*, *The Forum*, *Harper's Weekly*,

Life, *North American Review*, *Outlook*, and *Scribner's*, all of which contain useful material in the form of articles, fiction, or illustrations. I found it illuminating to contrast the series on "The Poor in Great Cities" appearing in *Scribner's* in 1892 with the "Conquest of Poverty" articles published in the *Metropolitan Magazine* in 1910–11. Revealing insights into attitudes toward poverty can also be obtained from popular novels. Although the list could be extended almost indefinitely, works on the order of Smith's *The Newsboy*, Eggleston's *The Hoosier Schoolmaster*, Dowling's *The Wreckers*, and Rice's *Mrs. Wiggs of the Cabbage Patch* proved especially informative. *The Cry for Justice*, edited by Upton Sinclair, is an anthology that permits a rapid survey of the literature of social protest.

Frequent reference to certain general works is necessary when one undertakes a study of this kind. I found the essays and bibliographies in the *Literary History of the United States*, Egbert's and Persons' *Socialism and American Life*, and Persons' *Evolutionary Thought in America* of particular help. Larkin's *Art and Life in America*, Baur's *Revolution and Tradition in American Art*, and Davidson's *Life in America* helped me greatly in preparing the chapters on art; and Volume III of *The History of Labor in the United States* by Commons, *et al.*, was indispensable in the later stages of the investigation. The volumes by Nevins, Schlesinger, and Faulkner in *The History of American Life* series remain the best starting points for research on numerous topics in social history; and the findings of more recent scholarship are ably presented in Link's *American Epoch* and *Woodrow Wilson and the Progressive Era.*

Notes

CHAPTER 1

The Problem Emerges

[1] John H. Griscom, *The Sanitary Condition of the Laboring Population of New York with Suggestions for its Improvement* (New York, 1845), pp. 5 and 9.

[2] William Ellery Channing, "On the Elevation of the Laboring Classes" in *The Works of William E. Channing, D.D.* (Boston, 1889), p. 60.

[3] Elizabeth Oakes Smith, *The Newsboy* (New York, 1854), p. 88.

[4] Charles Dickens, *American Notes* in *The Works of Charles Dickens* (National Library Edition. 20 vols., New York, n. d.), XIV, 115–16.

[5] Robert Hartley, *Eighth Annual Report* of the New York Association for Improving the Condition of the Poor, 1851, p. 18.

[6] Matthew Hale Smith, *Sunshine and Shadow in New York* (Hartford, 1869), p. 366.

[7] Josiah Strong, *The New Era or the Coming Kingdom* (New York, 1893), p. 193.

[8] United States Commissioner of Labor, *Seventh Special Report. The Slums of Baltimore, Chicago, New York and Philadelphia* (Washington, 1894), p. 13.

[9] Charles Loring Brace, *The Dangerous Classes of New York and Twenty Years' Work Among Them* (New York, 1872), p. 31.

[10] New York Association for Improving the Condition of the Poor, *First Report of a Committee on the Sanitary Condition of the Laboring Classes in the City of New York, with Remedial Suggestions* (New York, 1853), p. 4.

[11] "Tenement Houses – Their Wrongs," *New York Daily Tribune*, Nov. 23, 1864, p. 4.

[12] New York A.I.C.P., *First Report of a Committee on the Sanitary Condition of the Laboring Classes*, p. 4.

[13] George C. Booth in *Forty-First Annual Report* of the New York A.I.C.P., 1884, pp. 50–53.

[14] *Chicago American*, June 13, 1835, quoted in James Brown, *The History of Public Assistance in Chicago, 1833 to 1893* (Chicago, 1941), p. 12.

[15] Aaron Clark, quoted in David M. Schneider, *The History of Public Welfare in New York State, 1609–1866* (Chicago, 1938), p. 299.

[16] Edith Abbott, *Historical Aspects of the Immigration Problem. Select Documents* (Chicago, 1926), pp. 559–694 contain numerous protests and complaints against the importation of alien pauperism and crime.

[17] Schneider, *The History of Public Welfare in New York State*, pp. 297–98.

[18] Ray Allen Billington, *The Protestant Crusade, 1800–1860* (New York, 1938), pp. 35 and 324.

[19] Schneider, *The History of Public Welfare in New York State*, p. 126; see also pp. 296–97. The whole problem is discussed in Oscar Handlin, *The Uprooted. The Epic Story of the Great Migrations That Made the American People* (Boston, 1952), pp. 30–93.

[20] Ferris Greenslet, *Thomas Bailey Aldrich* (Boston, 1928), pp. 168–69.

[21] Washington Gladden, "The Problem of Poverty," *The Century*, XLV (1892–93), 253; and Jacob A. Riis, "Special Needs of the Poor in New York," *The Forum*, XIV (1892–93), 492.

[22] Gladden, *op. cit.*, p. 253.

[23] John R. Commons, *Social Reform and the Church* (New York, 1894), p. 31.

[24] For an analysis of Brownson's views see Arthur M. Schlesinger, Jr., *Orestes A. Brownson, A Pilgrim's Progress* (Boston, 1939), pp. 89–111.

[25] Quoted in Foster Rhea Dulles, *Labor in America. A History* (New York, 1949), p. 75.

[26] George T. Dowling, *The Wreckers: A Social Study* (Philadelphia 1886), p. 209.

[27] Charles Dudley Warner, *Fashions in Literature and Other Social Essays and Addresses* (New York, 1902), pp. 170 and 176.

[28] James Cardinal Gibbons, "Wealth and Its Obligations," *North American Review*, CLII (1891), 393. *Cf.* General William Booth, *In Darkest England and the Way Out* (London, 1890), pp. 19–20.

[29] Lilian Brandt, *Growth and Development of AICP and COS (A Preliminary and Exploratory Review)* (New York, 1942), p. 116.

[30] W. S. Rainsford, *The Story of a Varied Life* (New York, 1922), p. 305.

[31] Samuel Rezneck, "The Depression of 1819–1822, A Social History," *The American Historical Review*, XXXIX (1933–34), 32.

[32] Harold Frances Williamson, *Edward Atkinson, The Biography of an American Liberal, 1827–1905* (Boston, 1934), pp. 269–72.

[33] This point is made by Commons in *Social Reform and the Church*, p. 7.

[34] Strong, *The New Era*, pp. 137–38 and 141.

[35] Quoted in Samuel Rezneck, "The Social History of an American Depression, 1837–1843," *The American Historical Review*, XL (1934–35), 662.

[36] William T. Stead, *If Christ Came to Chicago* (London, 1894), p. 7, quoting a Chicago newspaper.

[37] Rezneck, "Social History of an American Depression, 1837–1843," 667; Commons, *Social Reform and the Church*, p. 38; and Leah Hannah Feder, *Unemployment Relief in Periods of Depression* (New York, 1936), p. 76.

[38] Quoted in Rezneck, "Social History of an American Depression, 1837–1843," p. 666.

[39] Helen Campbell, "Prisoners of Poverty. Women Wage-Workers. Their Trades and Their Lives," *New York Daily Tribune*, October 24, 1886, p. 13.

CHAPTER 2

Shifting Attitudes

[1] Eugene Lawrence, "The New Year –The Poor," *Harper's Weekly*, XXVIII (1884), 35.

[2] The contribution of religion to the reform philosophy of the 1830's and 1840's is discussed in Merle Curti,

The Growth of American Thought (New York, 1943), pp. 380–82. On the influence of William Ellery Channing and Unitarianism on the "philanthropic renaissance" of the decade 1830–40 see Francis G. Peabody, "Unitarianism and Philanthropy," *The Charities Review*, V (1895–96), 25–26. Channing's views on the cause and cure of poverty are outlined in "On the Elevation of the Laboring Classes," *The Works of William E. Channing, D.D.* (Boston, 1889), pp. 58–60. There are interesting comments on the general problem of the relationship of religion to philanthropy in Henry Bradford Washburn, *The Religious Motive in Philanthropy* (Philadelphia, 1931), pp. 7–8 and 172.

3 On the influence of Spencer and the conservative Social Darwinists see Richard Hofstadter, *Social Darwinism in American Thought* (Philadelphia), 1944, pp. 18–37; and Stow Persons, ed., *Evolutionary Thought in America* (New Haven, 1950), particularly the essays by Robert E. L. Faris (pp. 160–80) and Edward S. Corwin (pp. 182–99).

4 "Poor Man's Pudding and Rich Man's Crumbs" in *The Complete Stories of Herman Melville*, ed. by Jay Leyda (New York, 1949), pp. 176–77. This story was originally published in *Harper's New Monthly Magazine*, June, 1854.

5 Theodore Parker, *Sermon on the Perishing Classes in Boston* (Boston, 1846), p. 10. Similar views are expressed in F. A. Walker, "The Causes of Poverty," *The Century Illustrated Monthly Magazine*, LV (1897–98), 216; and Carroll D. Wright, *Outline of Practical Sociology* (New York, 1899), p. 323. For British opinion see London Congregational Union, *The Bitter Cry of Outcast London, An Inquiry into the Condition of the Abject Poor* (Boston, 1883), p. 5; and John A. Hobson, *Problems of Poverty* (7th edition, London, 1909), p. 12. Hobson's book was first published in 1891.

6 Ira Steward, *Poverty* (Boston, 1873), p. 3.

7 Brownson's views are set forth and discussed in Arthur M. Schlesinger, Jr., *Orestes A. Brownson, A Pilgrim's Progress* (Boston, 1939), p. 91 and note 46, pp. 91–92.

8 R. C. Waterston, *An Address on Pauperism, Its Extent, Causes, and the Best Means of Prevention* (Boston, 1844), p. 10.

9 Joseph Kirkland, *Zury: The Meanest Man in Spring County. A Novel of Western Life* (Boston and New York, 1888), p. 1.

10 Rodney Welch, "Horace Greeley's Cure for Poverty," *The Forum*, VIII (1889–90), 586–93. Henry Demarest Lloyd, "The Lords of Industry," *North American Review*, CXXXVIII (1884), 552. The "Myth of the Garden" is examined in Henry Nash Smith, *Virgin Land. The American West as Symbol and Myth* (Cambridge, 1950), p. 189 *et seq.*

11 John R. Commons, *Social Reform and the Church* (New York, 1894), p. 34.

12 Josiah Strong, *The New Era or The Coming Kingdom* (New York, 1893), p. 156.

13 William Dean Howells, *Impressions and Experiences* (New York, 1896), p. 149.

14 E. B. Andrews, "The Social Plaint," *The New World*, I (1892), 206 and 212–13.

15 Josephine Shaw Lowell, "Methods of Relief for the Unemployed," *The Forum*, XVI (1893–94), 659.

16 The instructive series of legal decisions known as the Seed and Feed Cases, which reveals a gradually

broadening concept of poverty as it affected farmers, is printed in Edith Abbott, *Public Assistance* (Chicago, 1940), pp. 73–96. On this point see also Grover Cleveland's veto of a bill authorizing distribution of seeds to drought sufferers in Texas, February 16, 1887, in James D. Richardson, comp., *A Compilation of the Messages and Papers of the Presidents* (11 vols. [New York], 1910), VII, 5142–43.

17 There are interesting comments on agrarian attitudes toward political action in the late nineteenth century in Richard Hofstadter, *The Age of Reform* (New York, 1955), p. 46 *et seq.*

18 George T. Dowling, *The Wreckers: A Social Study* (Philadelphia, 1886), p. 224; and Oscar Craig, "The Prevention of Pauperism," *Scribner's Magazine,* XIV (1893), 121.

19 Richardson, comp., *A Compilation of the Messages and Papers of the Presidents,* VII, 5359 and 5361.

20 Richard T. Ely, *Problems of Today. A Discussion of Protective Tariffs, Taxation and Monopolies* (3rd edition, New York, 1890), p. 65; and Washington Gladden, "The Problems of Poverty," *The Century,* XLV (1892–93), 256.

21 Edward Eggleston, *The Hoosier Schoolmaster* (New York, 1871), p. 29.

22 The main ideas of George's *Progress and Poverty* are analyzed in Charles Albro Barker, *Henry George* (New York, 1955), pp. 265–304.

23 Thomas G. Shearman defended George's position in *The Forum,* VIII (1889–90), 40–52 and 262–73. For the contrary view of Edward Atkinson see Harold Francis Williamson, *Edward Atkinson, The Biography of an American Liberal, 1827–1905* (Boston, 1934), pp. 260–66. See also Strong, *New Era,* pp. 151–52; and Andrews, "The Social Plaint," p. 209.

24 Felix Adler, *An Ethical Philosophy of Life Presented in Its Main Outlines* (New York, 1929), p. 44.

25 Lloyd, "The Lords of Industry," p. 552. For a discussion of Theodore Parker's attitude toward competition and other economic issues see Daniel Aaron, *Men of Good Hope. A Story of American Progressives* (New York, 1951), pp. 38–50.

26 Helen Stuart Campbell, *Prisoners of Poverty* (Boston, 1887), pp. 254–55. This book is a compilation of Mrs. Campbell's articles which first appeared in the *New York Daily Tribune* on October 24, 1886, and at weekly intervals thereafter.

27 Andrews, "The Social Plaint," 215.

28 George D. Herron, *The New Redemption* (New York, 1893), p. 29.

29 Strong, *The New Era,* p. 347.

30 Washington Gladden, *Social Salvation* (Boston and New York, 1902), p. 5.

31 *Ibid.*, p. 7.

32 The development of the social gospel is treated in Aaron Ignatius Abell, *The Urban Impact on American Protestantism, 1865–1900* (Cambridge, 1943); Charles Howard Hopkins, *The Rise of the Social Gospel in American Protestantism, 1865–1915* (New Haven, 1940); and Henry F. May, *Protestant Churches and Industrial America* (New York, 1949).

33 On this point see Henry J. Browne, *The Catholic Church and the Knights of Labor* (Washington, D.C., 1949).

34 *Rerum novarum* is printed in Donald O. Wagner, *Social Reformers* (New York, 1947), pp. 617–37. For comment on the encyclical see Jacques Maritain, *Ransoming the Time* (New York, 1941), p. 208;

Arthur Mann, *Yankee Reformers in the Urban Age* (Cambridge, 1954), pp. 47–48; and Harvey Wish, *Society and Thought in Modern America* (New York, 1952), p. 171.

[35] Robert A. Woods, "The Social Awakening in London," *Scribner's Magazine*, XI (1892), 407.

[36] On the refusal of the Salvation Army to discriminate between the worthy and the unworthy, see St. John Ervine, *God's Soldier: General William Booth* (2 vols., New York, 1935), II, 709; and Walter Besant, *The Autobiography of Sir Walter Besant* (New York, 1902), pp. 256–60.

[37] Strong, *The New Era*, pp. 351–52.

[38] Charles Richmond Henderson, *The Social Spirit in America* (Chicago, 1905), p. 319. This book was first published in 1897.

[39] Richard T. Ely, "Pauperism in the United States," *North American Review*, CLII (1891), p. 395.

[40] William Booth, *In Darkest England and the Way Out* (London, 1890), p. 48.

CHAPTER 3

The Charitable Impulse

[1] Andrew Carnegie, "Wealth," *North American Review*, CXLVIII (1889), 653–64. For an earlier statement of the idea of stewardship see A. L. Stone, *The Relations of Poverty to Human Discipline* (Boston, 1851), p. 13: "God has not deserted the needy nor left them friendless. He has committed them to our keeping, making us his agents and factors, to see that they perish not...."

[2] Quoted in Samuel Rezneck, "The Depression of 1819–1822, A Social History," *The American Historical Review*, XXXIX (1933–34), 40.

[3] William Ellery Channing, *The Ministry for the Poor* (Boston, 1835), p. 15.

[4] Tuckerman's views are outlined in Joseph Tuckerman, *On the Elevation of the Poor*, ed. by Edward Everett Hale (Boston, 1874); and in his introduction to Joseph Marie de Gerando, *The Visitor of the Poor* ... (Boston, 1832). For a discussion of his work see Daniel T. McColgan, *Joseph Tuckerman; Pioneer in American Social Work* (Washington, 1940); Francis G. Peabody, "Unitarianism and Philanthropy," *The Charities Review*, V (1895–96), 26–28; Jeffrey Richardson Brackett, *Supervision and Education in Charity* (New York, 1903), pp. 6–8; and Frank D. Watson, *The Charity Organization Movement in the United States. A Study in American Philanthropy* (New York, 1922), pp. 70–76.

[5] John H. Griscom, *The Sanitary Condition of the Laboring Population of New York with Suggestions for Its Improvement* (New York, 1845), pp. 24 and 28.

[6] Elizabeth Oakes Smith, *The Newsboy* (New York, 1854), p. 88. The work of the city missionaries of the New York Mission and Tract Society is discussed in Matthew Hale Smith, *Sunshine and Shadow in New York* (Hartford, Conn., 1869), pp. 290–99. There is a wealth

of information on the subject in Charles I. Foster, "The Urban Missionary Movement, 1814–1837," *The Pennsylvania Magazine of History and Biography*, LXXV (1951), 47–65.

7 Catholic philanthropies are discussed in John O'Grady, *Catholic Charities in the United States* (Washington, D.C., 1930).

8 On Hartley's early life and career see Isaac Smithson Hartley, ed., *Memorial of Robert Milham Hartley* (Utica, New York, 1882); and William H. Allen, *Efficient Democracy* (New York, 1907), pp. 142–49. On the distillery milk problem see Robert M. Hartley, *An Historical, Scientific and Practical Essay on Milk, as an Article of Human Sustenance . . .* (New York, 1842).

9 Lilian Brandt, *Growth and Development of AICP and COS (A Preliminary and Exploratory Review)* (New York, 1942), pp. 3–47 *passim.* For the work of similar organizations in Boston see R. C. Waterston, *An Address on Pauperism, Its Extent, Causes and the Best Means of Prevention* (Boston, 1844), pp. 10–11; and Report of the Howard Benevolent Society for 1850 in Stone, *Relations of Poverty to Human Discipline*, following p. 17. The A.I.C.P. movement as a whole is discussed in Watson, *The Charity Organization Movement in the United States*, pp. 76–93.

10 New York A.I.C.P., *The Economist* (New York, 1847), p. 12.

11 New York A.I.C.P., *First Report of a Committee on the Sanitary Condition of the Laboring Classes in the City of New York, with Remedial Suggestions* (New York, 1853).

12 Robert M. Hartley, *Thirteenth Annual Report* of the New York A.I.C.P., 1856, pp. 52–54.

13 The "incidental labors" of the A.I.C.P. are described in Brandt, *Growth and Development of AICP and COS*, pp. 47–64, Allen, *Efficient Democracy*, pp. 149–52; and Community Service Society of New York, *Frontiers of Human Welfare. The Story of a Hundred Years of Service to the Community of New York, 1848–1948* (New York, 1948), pp. 13–30.

14 Robert Hartley, *Seventh Annual Report* of the New York A.I.C.P., 1850, p. 27.

15 New York A.I.C.P., *The Mistake* (New York, 1850), p. 4. See also quotations from Hartley in Robert W. Bruère, "The Good Samaritan, Incorporated," *Harper's Monthly Magazine*, CXX (1910), 385.

16 Smith, *The Newsboy*, pp. 28–29 and 33.

17 Charles Loring Brace, *The Dangerous Classes of New York and Twenty Years' Work Among Them* (New York, 1872), p. 97. On child vagrancy in Boston see Theodore Parker, *Sermon on the Perishing Classes in Boston* (Boston, 1846), pp. 5–8.

18 Brace, *The Dangerous Classes*, p. 225. This view was earlier expressed by the founders of the Boston Children's Mission, organized in 1849. In the opinion of Francis G. Peabody, the Boston Mission was the forerunner of subsequent child-saving societies in the United States —"Unitarianism and Philanthropy," pp. 28–29.

19 For the activities conducted by the Children's Aid Society a generation after its establishment see George P. Rowell, comp., *New York Charities Directory* (New York, 1888), pp. 64–65; and Jacob A. Riis, *The Children of the Poor* (New York, 1892), pp. 187–210 and 248–56.

20 Emerson David Fite, *Social and In-*

dustrial Conditions in the North During the Civil War (New York, 1910), pp. 299–301, contains material on the Children's Aid Society and similar organizations during the war period.

[21] Homer Folks, *The Care of Destitute, Neglected, and Delinquent Children* (New York, 1902), pp. 67–68. On this problem see also Riis, *Children of the Poor*, pp. 251–55; Amos G. Warner, *American Charities. A Study in Philanthropy and Economics* (New York, 1894), pp. 229–31; and Frank G. Bruno, *Trends in Social Work as Reflected in the Proceedings of the National Conference of Social Work, 1874–1946* (New York, 1948), pp. 57–60.

[22] Folks, *The Care of Destitute, Neglected, and Destitute Children*, p. 68; and Edith Abbott, *Some American Pioneers in Social Welfare. Select Documents with Editorial Notes* (Chicago, 1937), p. 131.

[23] Charles Howard Hopkins, *The History of the Y.M.C.A. in North America* (New York, 1951), pp. 189–90.

[24] This point is emphasized in Smith, *Sunshine and Shadow in New York*, p. 677.

[25] Hopkins, *History of the Y.M.C.A.*, p. 193.

[26] For a concise summary of Civil War charities see Fite, *Social and Industrial Conditions in the North*, pp. 275–311.

[27] Quoted, *ibid.*, p. 293.

[28] William Rhinelander Stewart, *The Philanthropic Work of Josephine Shaw Lowell* (New York, 1911), p. 36.

CHAPTER 4

The Rise of Social Work

[1] "The Town Poor" in *The Best Stories of Sarah Orne Jewett* selected by Willa Cather (2 vols., Boston and New York, 1925), II, 224–47.

[2] S. H. Elliot, *A Look at Home; or Life in The Poor-House of New England* (New York, 1860), p. 35.

[3] Homer Folks, *The Care of Destitute, Neglected, and Delinquent Children* (New York, 1902), pp. 3–4.

[4] *Ibid.*, pp. 8 and 39–42. T. S. Denison, *Louva the Pauper. A Drama in Five Acts* (Chicago, 1878), relates the sad story of a well-to-do girl, who, through a series of misfortunes, is bound out to service by the overseers of the poor.

[5] Amos G. Warner, *American Charities. A Study in Philanthropy and Economics* (New York, 1894), pp. 162–76. See also Daniel T. McColgan, *Joseph Tuckerman; Pioneer in American Social Work* (Washington, 1940), pp. 196–97.

[6] Josephine Shaw Lowell, *Public Relief and Private Charity* (New York, 1884), quoted in Edith Abbott, *Some American Pioneers in Social Welfare. Select Documents with Editorial Notes* (Chicago, 1937), p. 160.

[7] *Ibid.*

[8] *Ibid.*, pp. 160–61.

[9] Edward Eggleston, *The Hoosier Schoolmaster* (New York, 1871), pp. 163–64 contain a memorable de-

scription of an undifferentiated almshouse in frontier Indiana. See also Elliott, *A Look at Home*, pp. 26–32.

10 On this point see James H. and Mary Jane Rodabaugh, *Nursing in Ohio* (Columbus, Ohio, 1951), pp. 20–23.

11 On the state boards of public charity see Jeffrey Richardson Brackett, *Supervision and Education in Charity* (New York, 1903), pp. 18 *et seq.;* and Frank J. Bruno, *Trends in Social Work as Reflected in the Proceedings of the National Conference of Social Work, 1874–1946* (New York, 1948), pp. 31–43.

12 Ohio. Board of State Charities, *Third Annual Report, 1869* (Columbus, 1870), p. 28.

13 Fred. H. Wines, secretary, Board of Public Charities of the State of Illinois, *Second Biennial Report, 1872* (Springfield, Ill., 1873), p. 190.

14 William P. Letchworth, "Pauper and Destitute Children in State of New York." State Board of Charities, *Eighth Annual Report, 1875* (Albany, 1875), pp. 233–34.

15 Wines, *Second Biennial Report, 1872*, p. 189.

16 William Bristol Shaw, "Louisa Lee Schuyler," *Dictionary of American Biography*, XVI, 474–75. For an account of the work of the Visiting Committee of Bellevue Hospital see Elizabeth Christopher Hobson, "Founding of the Bellevue Training School for Nurses" in Abby Howland Woolsey, *A Century of Nursing* (New York, 1950), p. 135 *et seq.*

17 Eggleston, *The Hoosier Schoolmaster*, Chapter XXIII, "A Charitable Institution," especially pp. 163 and 168–69. For an interesting contemporary evaluation of Eggleston's work see Washington Gladden, "Edward Eggleston," *Scribner's Monthly*, VI (1873), 561–64. For a strikingly similar diagnosis of the poorhouse problem see Elliot, *A Look at Home.*

18 Folks, *The Care of Destitute, Neglected, and Delinquent Children*, pp. 72–80; see also Warner, *American Charities*, pp. 139–61.

19 For a history of the C.O.S. Movement see Charles D. Kellogg, "Charity Organization in the United States," *Proceedings* of the National Conference of Charities and Correction, 1893, pp. 52–93; and Frank Dekker Watson, *The Charity Organization Movement in the United States* (New York, 1922).

20 Community Service Society of New York, *Frontiers in Human Welfare. The Story of a Hundred Years of Service to the Community of New York, 1848–1948* (New York, 1948), p. 35.

21 Ruth Scannell, "A History of the Charity Organization Society of the City of New York from 1892 to 1935" (mimeographed report in the files of the Community Service Society of New York), p. 12.

22 Woodyard of the Charity Organization Society, Appeal for Funds, January 30, 1901 (in files of Community Service Society of New York).

23 Kellogg, "Charity Organization in the United States," Appendix F, following p. 93.

24 John Boyle O'Reilly, "In Bohemia" (1886), quoted in Jane Addams, *et al., Philanthropy and Social Progress* (New York, 1893), p. 135.

25 William T. Stead, *If Christ Came to Chicago* (London, 1894), p. 127.

26 Alice Hegan Rice, *Mrs. Wiggs of the Cabbage Patch* (New York, 1937), p. 18. First published in 1901.

27 William Dean Howells, "Tribulations of a Cheerful Giver" in *Im-*

pressions and Experiences (New York, 1896), p. 184. See also Howells' remarks on mendicancy in *A Hazard of New Fortunes* (2 vols., New York, 1890), II, 256.

[28] Frederic C. Howe, *Confessions of A Reformer* (New York, 1925), pp. 78–79; for a similar expression of opinion see Brand Whitlock, *The Turn of the Balance* (Indianapolis, 1907), p. 291.

[29] There was a 250 per cent increase in the number of paid workers employed by Charity Organization Societies between 1882 and 1892, but even in the latter year volunteers greatly outnumbered paid staff members. Kellogg, "Charity Organization in the United States," Appendix F. The difficulty encountered in enlisting volunteers during the nineties is discussed in Francis Peabody, "How Should a City Care for Its Poor," *The Forum*, XIV (1892–93), 474–91; and Jacob A. Riis, "Special Needs of the Poor in New York," *The Forum*, XIV (1892–93), 492–502.

[30] On this point see Edward T. Devine, *When Social Work Was Young* (New York, 1939), pp. 69–70; and John R. Commons, *Social Reform and the Church* (New York, 1894), pp. 46–47.

[31] On the significance of the case method see Warner, *American Charities*, p. 22 *et seq.*; and Stuart Alfred Queen, *Social Work in the Light of History* (Philadelphia, 1922), p. 114.

[32] John R. Commons, *Myself* (New York, 1934), p. 43.

[33] Lilian Brandt, *Growth and Development of AICP and COS (A Preliminary and Exploratory Review)* (New York, 1942), pp. 143 and 221; and Devine, *When Social Work Was Young*, pp. 34–35.

[34] See Warner, *American Charities*, Table IV, facing p. 34; and John Koren, *Economic Aspects of the Liquor Problem* (Boston and New York, 1899), pp. 42–44.

[35] See, for example, the bibliography of Marcus T. Reynolds, *The Housing of the Poor in American Cities* (n.p., 1893), pp. 127–32; and Devine, *When Social Work Was Young*, p. 69.

[36] The development of the concept of social work in the charity organization movement may be studied in the letters and papers of Mrs. Josephine Shaw Lowell in William Rhinelander Stewart, *The Philanthropic Work of Josephine Shaw Lowell* (New York, 1911). Mrs. Lowell's essay "Criminal Reform" in Frances A. Goodale, ed., *Literature of Philanthropy* (New York, 1893), gives a concise statement of her position. For a brief discussion of the emergence of the concept of social work see Devine, *When Social Work Was Young*, p. 149 *et seq.*

[37] Quoted in W. S. Rainsford, *The Story of a Varied Life* (Garden City, New York, 1922), p. 313.

[38] *Ibid.*; see also Rainsford's article "What Can We Do For the Poor?" *The Forum*, XI (1891), 124–25; and Alexander Irvine, *From the Bottom Up* (New York, 1910), p. 156.

[39] Aaron Ignatius Abell, *The Urban Impact on American Protestantism* (Cambridge, 1943), p. 4.

[40] For early ventures in evangelical work among the poor in Boston see Daniel T. McColgan, *Joseph Tuckerman; Pioneer in American Social Work*. In New York both the Five Points Mission and the Five Points House of Industry were founded in the 1850's, the Howard Mission in 1861, and Jerry MacAuley's Water Street Mission in 1872. For contemporary accounts

of the work of these early missions see Solon Robinson, *Hot Corn: Life Scenes in New York Illustrated* (New York, 1854), pp. 50–52; *The World* (New York), December 26, 1860, p. 6; Matthew Hale Smith, *Sunshine and Shadow in New York* (Hartford, 1869), pp. 204–6; and T. L. Cuyler, "The Five Points House of Industry," *Harper's Weekly*, XXIV (1880), 27.

[41] Paul Leicester Ford, *The Honorable Peter Sterling* (New York, 1894), p. 134.

[42] For social work conducted by various missions see Abell, *Urban Impact on American Protestantism*, p. 34 *et seq.*; and B. O. Flower, *Civilization's Inferno; or Studies in the Social Cellar* (Boston, 1893), pp. 50–51.

[43] Herbert Asbury, *The Gangs of New York, An Informal History of the Underworld* (New York and London, 1927), pp. 16–19. There is a description of Pease in Robinson, *Hot Corn*, p. 109. For the program of the Five Points House of Industry in the mid-eighties see George P. Rowell, comp., *New York Charities Directory* (New York, 1888), pp. 136–37.

[44] For Irvine's description of the environment in which his missionary work was carried on see *From the Bottom Up*, pp. 94–96. "An Experiment in Misery" is reprinted in Stephen Crane, *Twenty Stories* (New York, 1940).

[45] Irvine, *From the Bottom Up*, pp. 92 and 103.

[46] On the origins of the institutional church movement see Abell, *Urban Impact on American Protestantism*, pp. 139–42; and William Warren Sweet, *The Story of Religion in America* (New York, 1939), pp. 524–25.

[47] Josiah Strong, "Institutional Church" in W. D. P. Bliss, *Encyclopedia of Social Reforms* (New York and London, 1898), p. 629.

[48] Sweet, *Story of Religion in America*, p. 524.

[49] On Conwell, see *ibid.*, p. 525; Abell, *Urban Impact on American Protestantism*, pp. 157–58; and Ralph Henry Gabriel, *The Course of American Democratic Thought* (New York, 1940), p. 149.

[50] Rainsford, *The Story of a Varied Life*, p. 314.

[51] Charles Howard Hopkins, *The Rise of the Social Gospel in American Protestantism, 1865–1915* (New Haven, 1940), pp. 142 and 275–77.

[52] London Congregational Union, *The Bitter Cry of Outcast London. An Inquiry into the Condition of the Abject Poor* (Boston, 1883), p. 1.

[53] Gregory Weinstein, *The Ardent Eighties and After. Reminiscences of a Busy Life* (New York, 1947), pp. 89–92.

[54] Alice Hamilton, *Exploring the Dangerous Trades* (Boston, 1943), p. 27.

[55] Charles Loring Brace, *The Dangerous Classes of New York and Twenty Years' Work Among Them* (New York, 1872), p. 136.

[56] Queen, *Social Work in the Light of History*, p. 134.

[57] Graham Taylor, *Pioneering on Social Frontiers* (Chicago, 1930), pp. 8–9.

[58] O. F. Lewis, "The Conquest of Poverty. Some Things That Organized Charity Is Trying to Do," *Metropolitan Magazine*, XXXIII (1909–10), 198.

[59] Taylor, *Pioneering on Social Frontiers*, p. 292.

[60] J. G. Phelps Stokes, The Neighborhood Guild (unpublished memoir in Stokes papers), quoting Helen Moore, librarian at the Neighborhood Guild.

[61] *Ibid.*

[62] Helen Moore, "Tenement Neighborhood Idea – University Settlement," in Goodale, ed., *The Literature of Philanthropy*, pp. 35–36.

[63] Jean Fine Spahr and Fannie W. McLean, "Tenement Neighborhood Idea" in Goodale, ed., *The Literature of Philanthropy*, p. 25.

[64] Jane Addams, "Social Settlements," *Proceedings* of the National Conference of Charities and Correction, 1897, p. 345.

[65] Hamilton, *Exploring the Dangerous Trades*, pp. 65–66. The various activities sponsored by Hull House are discussed in Bruno, *Trends in Social Work*, pp. 115–16.

[66] Brander Matthews, "In Search of Local Color" in *Vignettes of Manhattan* (New York, 1894), p. 69.

[67] Mary Kingsbury Simkhovitch, *Neighborhood. My Story of Greenwich House* (New York, 1938), p. 85.

[68] Jacob A. Riis, *The Making of an American* (New York, 1903), p. 316. The role of settlements in advancing social reform is discussed in Bruno, *Trends in Social Work*, pp. 117–18.

[69] Malcolm Cowley, *Exile's Return. A Literary Odyssey of the 1920's* (New York, 1951), p. 34.

[70] Howe, *Confessions of a Reformer*, pp. 75–76.

[71] Jack London, *The People of the Abyss* (New York, 1903), p. 307. This attack was directed specifically at the settlements and settlement workers in the East End of London.

[72] *Ibid.*, p. 306.

[73] Smith, *Sunshine and Shadow in New York*, pp. 209–10.

[74] Addams, "Social Settlements," p. 344.

[75] Simkhovitch, *Neighborhood*, p. 73.

CHAPTER 5

The Condition of the Poor; Late Nineteenth-Century Social Investigations

[1] See, for example, Ned Buntline [E. Z. C. Judson], *The Mysteries and Miseries of New York* (New York, 1848); Matthew Hale Smith, *Sunshine and Shadow in New York* (Hartford, 1869); J. W. Buel, *Metropolitan Life Unveiled; or The Mysteries and Miseries of America's Great Cities* (St. Louis, 1882); and Helen Campbell, Thomas W. Knox, and Thomas Byrnes, *Darkness and Daylight: or Lights and Shadows of New York Life . . .* (Hartford, 1891).

[2] Buel, *Metropolitan Life Unveiled*, pp. 113 and 115.

[3] William A. Rogers, "Tenement Life in New York–Sketches in 'Bottle Alley,'" *Harper's Weekly*, XXIII (1879), 224.

[4] "Tenement Life in New York," *Harper's Weekly*, XXIII (1879), 267.

[5] Jacob A. Riis, *The Children of the Poor* (New York, 1892), pp. 261–62.

[6] O. B. Frothingham, "Is Poverty Increasing?" *The Arena*, I (1889–90), 115.

[7] Helen Gardener, "Thrown in with the City's Dead," *The Arena*, III (1890–91), 61–70.

[8] Robert A. Woods, *et al.*, "The Poor in Great Cities," *Scribner's Magazine*, XI (1892), 400.

[9] Washington Gladden, "The Problem of Poverty," *The Century*, XLV (1892–93), 246. *Cf.* Herbert B. Adams, "Notes on the Literature of Charities," Johns Hopkins University *Studies in Historical and Political Science*, V (1887), 283–324.

[10] Elisha Harris, Foreword to Robert L. Dugdale, *The Jukes. A Study in Crime, Pauperism, Disease and Heredity* (4th edition, New York and London, 1910), p. 4.

[11] The impact of Booth's work on American research is discussed by Gladden, "The Problem of Poverty"; Robert A. Woods, "The Social Awakening in London," *Scribner's Magazine*, XI (1892), 423; and Graham Taylor, "The Standard for a City's Survey," *Charities and the Commons*, XXI (1908–9), 508.

[12] Charles B. Spahr, *An Essay on the Present Distribution of Wealth in the United States* (New York, 1896), p. 95.

[13] *Ibid.*, p. v.

[14] Richard T. Ely, "Pauperism in the United States," *North American Review*, CLII (1891), 397.

[15] On this point see William Franklin Willoughby, "State Activities in Relation to Labor in the United States," Johns Hopkins University *Studies in Historical and Political Science*, XIX (1901), 210–12; William Franklin Willoughby, "Child Labor," *Publications* of the American Economic Association, V (1890), 147–48; and G. W. W. Hanger, "Labor Bureaus" in *The New Encyclopedia of Social Reform*, ed. by W. D. P. Bliss (New York and London, 1910), pp. 675–77.

[16] Hanger, "Labor Bureaus," p. 676, gives data on the staffing and budgets of both state and federal bureaus of labor statistics.

[17] United States. Commissioner of Labor, *Seventh Special Report. . . . The Slums of Baltimore, Chicago, New York and Philadelphia* (Washington, 1894), pp. 11–12.

[18] United States. Commissioner of Labor, *Eleventh Annual Report, 1895–96. Work and Wages of Men, Women and Children* (Washington, 1897), p. 11.

[19] Spahr, *An Essay on the Present Distribution of Wealth*, p. 52, footnote 1, and pp. 107–9.

[20] For an attack on Wright's summary in his *Fourth Annual Report* see Florence Kelley (Wischnewetsky), "A Decade of Retrogression," *The Arena*, IV (1891), 368–69.

[21] Leah Hannah Feder, *Unemployment Relief in Periods of Depression* (New York, 1936), pp. 38–39.

[22] *Ibid.*, pp. 83–87.

[23] Davis R. Dewey, "Irregularity of Employment," *Publications* of the American Economic Association, IX (1894), 532–33. Some of the factors cited by Dewey were: introduction of labor-saving machinery, elimination of certain labor processes to reduce costs, substitution of juvenile and female labor for male, migration of industry, and seasonal work.

[24] Edward W. Bemis, "Mine Labor in the Hocking Valley," *Publications* of the American Economic Association, III (1888), 185–87.

[25] Amos G. Warner, *American Charities. A Study in Philanthropy and Economics* (New York, 1894), pp. 99–100. An exception to the general rule was the New Jersey Bureau of Labor Statistics which, between 1889 and 1891, examined the effect of labor in the pottery, hat-making and glass-blowing industries on employees' health and trade life.

[26] Benjamin Harrison, First Annual Message, December 3, 1889, in James D. Richardson, comp., *A*

Compilation of the Messages and Papers of the Presidents (11 vols. [New York], 1910), VIII, 5486.

[27] *Ibid.*, and pp. 5561, 5642–43, and 5766. For the Railroad Safety Appliance Act of March 2, 1893, see 27 *Statutes at Large* 531–32.

[28] Willoughby, "Accidents to Labor as Regulated by Law in the United States," *Bulletin* of the Department of Labor, VI (1901), 1–28.

[29] On Lorenzo S. Coffin see Norman Paul, "The Coffin That Kept Railroaders Alive," *Tracks*, XXXVI (August, 1951), 2–5.

[30] Willoughby, *Workingmen's Insurance* (New York, 1898), p. 329.

[31] Clare de Graffenried, "Child Labor," *Publications* of the American Economics Association, V (1890), p. 255.

[32] Willoughby, *Workingmen's Insurance*, pp. 308–9.

[33] de Graffenried, "Child Labor," p. 255; see also Helen Campbell, *Prisoners of Poverty* (Boston, 1887), pp. 32–33.

[34] R. C. Waterston, *An Essay on Pauperism, Its Extent, Causes, and the Best Means of Prevention* (Boston, 1844), p. 19. For a discussion of Joseph Tuckerman's *Prize Essay on the Wages Paid to Females* (1830), see Daniel T. McColgan, *Joseph Tuckerman* (Washington, 1940), pp. 165–66.

[35] Louisa May Alcott, *Work* (Boston, 1873), p. 149.

[36] Campbell, *Women Wage-Earners: Their Past, Their Present and Their Future* (Boston, 1893), p. 213. For a more sensational treatment of the same theme see Louis A. Banks, *White Slaves or the Oppression of the Worthy Poor* (Boston, 1892).

[37] There is a convenient tabular summary of child-labor laws as of 1896 in F. J. Stimson, *Handbook to the Labor Law of the United States* (New York, 1896), pp. 74–75.

[38] Willoughby, "Child Labor," *Publications* of the American Economic Association, V (1890), 154. See also Bemis, "Mine Labor in the Hocking Valley," pp. 189–92.

[39] Willoughby, "Child Labor," pp. 150–51.

[40] Selection from "Honest Harry; or The Country Boy Adrift in the City" (1885), in Albert Johannsen, *The House of Beadle and Adams* . . . (2 vols., Norman, Okla., 1950), pp. 209–12.

[41] Elizabeth Oakes Smith, *The Newsboy* (New York, 1854), pp. 28–29.

[42] Bemis, "Mine Labor in the Hocking Valley," p. 189.

[43] Charles Loring Brace, *The Dangerous Classes of New York and Twenty Years' Work Among Them* (New York, 1872), p. 353 *et. seq.*

[44] Clara Sidney Potter, "Factory Conditions in New York," *The Christian Union*, XXXIX (1889), 566.

[45] de Graffenried, "Child Labor," p. 252.

[46] Willoughby, "Child Labor," pp. 182–83.

[47] *Ibid.*, p. 191; and de Graffenried, "Child Labor," pp. 270–71.

[48] "Private Life of the Gamin," *Daily Graphic* (New York), March 11, 1873, p. 3.

[49] Florence Kelley and Alzina P. Stevens, "Wage-Earning Children" in *Hull-House Maps and Papers* (New York, 1895), pp. 50 and 58. On Mrs. Kelley see Josephine Goldmark, *Impatient Crusader, Florence Kelley's Life Story* (Urbana, Ill., 1953); on Alzina P. Stevens, see Alice Hamilton, *Exploring the Dangerous Trades* (Boston, 1943), p. 62.

[50] Kelley, "The Working Child," *Proceedings* of the National Conference of Charities and Correction, 1896, pp. 161–65.

[51] Campbell, "White Child Slavery," *The Arena*, I (1889–90), 591.

52 Kelley, "The Working Child," pp. 161–63.

53 This view is well expressed in B. O. Flower, *Civilization's Inferno; or Studies in the Social Cellar* (Boston, 1893), p. 26.

54 William Ellery Channing, "On the Elevation of the Laboring Classes," in *The Works of William E. Channing, D.D.* (Boston, 1889), p. 58.

55 McColgan, *Joseph Tuckerman*, p. 176; and John Koren, *Economic Aspects of the Liquor Problem* (Boston and New York, 1899), pp. 11–12.

56 Flower, *Civilization's Inferno*, p. 36; Carroll D. Wright, *Outline of Practical Sociology* (New York, 1899), p. 323; Henderson, *The Social Spirit*, p. 28; Josiah Strong, *The New Era or the Coming Kingdom* (New York, 1893), p. 156; and John R. Commons, *Social Reform and the Church* (New York and Boston, 1894), p. 42.

57 Raymond Calkins, *Substitutes for the Saloon* (Boston and New York, 1901), p. v. The President of the Committee of Fifty was Seth Low and among its members were Washington Gladden, Carroll D. Wright, Richard Watson Gilder, Daniel Coit Gilman, Charles W. Eliot, Felix Adler, John Graham Brooks, and Richard T. Ely.

58 Koren, *Economic Aspects of the Liquor Problem*, p. 9. This volume should not be confused with a similarly titled report by Carroll D. Wright which sought to examine the place of the liquor industry in the American economy.

59 Calkins, *Substitutes for the Saloon*, p. viii. *Cf.* Paul Leicester Ford, *The Honorable Peter Stirling* (New York, 1894), p. 133; and Strong, *The New Era*, p. 244.

60 See also the essay on saloons in Chicago's Nineteenth Ward and a summary view of New York drinking places in Koren, *Economic Aspects of the Liquor Problem*, pp. 211–30.

61 Quoted in Bliss, ed. *New Encyclopedia of Social Reform*, p. 939.

62 E. R. L. Gould, *The Housing of Working People* (Washington, 1895), p. 436.

63 Julian Ralph, "A Day of the Pinochle Club" in *People We Pass, Stories of Life Among the Masses in New York City* (New York, 1896), p. 78.

64 Quoted in Joseph Lee, *Constructive and Preventive Philanthropy* (New York, 1906), p. 56.

65 For a brief account of the establishment of municipal boards of health in Eastern cities see Allan Nevins, *The Emergence of Modern America, 1865–1878* (New York, 1927), pp. 320–23.

66 "Tenement Life in New York," *Harper's Weekly*, XXIII (1879), 246.

67 Lillian W. Betts, "Tenement House Life," *The Christian Union*, XLVI (1892), 69.

68 Channing, "On the Elevation of the Laboring Classes," p. 58.

69 Riis, "Special Needs of the Poor in New York," *The Forum*, XIV (1892–93), 494.

70 Spahr, *An Essay on the Present Distribution of Wealth*, pp. 68–69 and 128–29.

71 Warner, *American Charities*, p. 26.

72 James Mavor, "The Relation of Economic Study to Public and Private Charity," *Annals* of the American Academy of Political and Social Science, IV (1893–94), pp. 39–40.

73 *Ibid.*, p. 39.

74 E. B. Andrews, "The Social Plaint," *The New World*, I (1892), 216.

CHAPTER 6

The Discovery of Poverty in Literature

[1] The social and economic attitudes of the New England writers are discussed in William Charvat, "American Romanticism and the Depression of 1837," *Science and Society*, II (1937), 67–82.

[2] Ralph Waldo Emerson, *Journals* (10 vols., Boston, 1909–14), II, 463.

[3] *Ibid.*, IV, 244–45.

[4] A. I. Cummings, *The Factory Girl: or Gardez La Coeur* [*sic*] (Lowell, 1847), pp. 48 and 151–52.

[5] The quotations are from Dickens' preface to *Oliver Twist.*

[6] William Dean Howells, *My Literary Passions* (New York, 1895), pp. 99–100.

[7] For valuable comment on Dickens' attitude toward the poor see Edgar Johnson, *Charles Dickens, His Tragedy and Triumph* (2 vols., New York, 1952), II, 793–94.

[8] Quoted in John A. Kouwenhoven, *Made in America. The Arts in Modern Civilization* (New York, 1948), p. 153. A twelve-volume edition of Lippard's works was published by T. B. Peterson and Brothers of Philadelphia in 1876.

[9] This story is told in William T. Coggeshall, "The Late George Lippard," *Genius of the West* (Cincinnati), II (1854), 85.

[10] Henry Nash Smith, *Virgin Land. The American West as Symbol and Myth* (Cambridge, 1950), p. 103.

[11] George Clinton Densmore Odell, *Annals of the New York Stage* (15 vols., New York, 1927–49), III, 684–85.

[12] *Ibid.*, V, 372–73.

[13] Dion Boucicault, *Poor of New York* (New York, 1857), p. 13. This play was acted under the title *Streets of New York.*

[14] A good example is Maria S. Cummins' extremely popular novel, *The Lamplighter* (Boston, 1854).

[15] Elizabeth Oakes Smith, *The Newsboy* (New York, 1854), p. 26.

[16] Herman Melville, *Redburn: His First Voyage: Being the Sailor-Boy Confessions and Reminiscences of the Son-of-a-Gentleman, in the Merchant Service* (New York, 1850), p. 229.

[17] "A Parable" in *The Complete Works of James Russell Lowell* (Cambridge edition, Boston and New York, 1917), p. 95.

[18] Estelle W. Stead, *My Father, Personal and Spiritual Reminiscences* (New York, 1913), p. 211; and Jack London, *The People of the Abyss* (New York, 1903), p. v.

[19] There is an appreciative essay on Lowell as a "Patrician Democrat" in Arthur Hobson Quinn, ed., *The Literature of the American People* (New York, 1951), pp. 374–83.

[20] Rebecca Harding Davis, "A Story of To-Day," *The Atlantic Monthly*, VIII (1861), 472.

[21] Davis, "Life in the Iron Mills," *The Atlantic Monthly*, VII (1861), 430.

[22] Davis, "A Story of To-Day," pp. 473 and 475.

[23] Elizabeth Stuart Phelps, "The Tenth of January," *The Atlantic Monthly*, XXI (1868), 345–46.

[24] *The Silent Partner* is discussed in Vernon Louis Parrington, *Main Currents in American Thought* (3 vols., New York, 1927–30), III, 61–62; see also Edward E. Cassady, "Muckraking in the Gilded Age," *American Literature*, XIII (1941), 137.

[25] "The Symphony" in *The Centennial Edition of the Works of Sidney*

Lanier (10 vols., Baltimore, 1945), I, 47.

[26] George T. Dowling, *The Wreckers: A Social Study* (Philadelphia, 1886), pp. 66, 394–95, and 400.

[27] Augustin Daly, Edward Harrigan, *et al.*, "American Playwrights on the American Drama," *Harper's Weekly*, XXXIII (1889), 97.

[28] *Ibid.*, p. 98.

[29] *Harrigan, Hart and Dave Braham's Immortal Songs* (n.p., n.d.), pages not numbered. This volume is in the Music Room of the New York Public Library.

[30] *Harrigan and Braham's Songs* (Henry J. Wehman, publisher, New York and Chicago, n.d. [1893?]), pages not numbered.

[31] *Ibid.*

[32] Daly, Harrigan, *et al.*, "American Playwrights on the American Drama," p. 97.

[33] Brander Matthews, *These Many Years, Recollections of a New Yorker* (New York, 1917), p. 361.

[34] Howells' comments on Harrigan are quoted in Montrose J. Moses and John Mason Brown, *The American Theater as Seen by Its Critics, 1752–1934* (New York, 1934), pp. 132–35. For Garland's view see *Crumbling Idols* (Chicago, 1894), p. 72. A recent study is E. J. Kahn, *Merry Partners; The Age and Stage of Harrigan and Hart* (New York, 1955).

[35] "Jersey and Mulberry" (1893) in *The Stories of H. C. Bunner, First Series* (New York, 1916), pp. 324–41.

[36] "The Bowery and Bohemia" (1894), *ibid.*, pp. 373–74.

[37] Garland, *Crumbling Idols*, p. 72.

[38] Brander Matthews, "Before the Break of Day" in *Vignettes of Manhattan* (New York, 1894), p. 85.

[39] Matthews, "In Search of Local Color," *ibid.*, p. 69.

[40] James L. Ford, *Forty-Odd Years in the Literary Shop* (New York, 1921), p. 118.

[41] Ford, "Low Life in Modern Fiction," *Truth*, XII (November 19, 1892), 12.

[42] Ford, *The Literary Shop and Other Tales* (New York, 1894), p. 142.

[43] Julian Ralph, "Love in the Big Barracks" in *People We Pass. Stories of Life Among the Masses of New York City* (New York, 1896), pp. 53–74.

[44] Ralph, "A Day of the Pinochle Club," *ibid.*, pp. 88–89.

[45] "The Love Letters of Smith" (1890) in *The Stories of H. C. Bunner, Short Sixes and the Suburban Sage* (New York, 1919), p. 69.

[46] Richard Harding Davis, "The Hungry Man Was Fed," in *Van Bibber and Others* (New York, 1892), pp. 47–52.

[47] Davis, "Gallegher" in *Gallegher and Other Stories* (New York, 1891), p. 2.

[48] William Dean Howells, *A Hazard of New Fortunes* (2 vols., New York, 1890), II, p. 256.

[49] Howells, *A Traveller from Altruria* (New York, 1894), p. 260.

[50] Howells, "Society," *Harper's Magazine*, XC (1895), 630.

[51] Garland, *Main-Travelled Roads* (Boston, 1891), pp. 136 and 86.

[52] Howells, "New York Streets" in *Impressions and Experiences* (New York, 1896), pp. 252–53.

[53] Garland, "Up the Coulé" in *Main-Travelled Roads*, pp. 146 and 88.

[54] Charles Dudley Warner, *The Golden House* (New York, 1894), pp. 40–42.

[55] Edward W. Townsend, *A Daughter of the Tenements* (New York, 1895), p. 61.

[56] Quoted in "Stephen Crane," *The Bookman*, I (1895), p. 229.

[57] J. Lincoln Steffens, "Extermination, Evolution in Operation on the East

Side," *Commercial Advertiser* (New York), July 24, 1897. Riis's photograph of "Bandits' Roost" (1887–88) is reproduced in Marshall B. Davidson, *Life in America* (2 vols., Boston, 1951), II, 180.

[58] Markham's explanation is quoted in Mark Sullivan, *Our Times; The United States, 1900–1925* (6 vols., New York, 1926–35), II, 236.

[59] See *ibid.*, pp. 236–49, for an account of the popular reception of "The Man with the Hoe."

[60] Garland, "The Cry of the Age," *The Outlook*, LXII (1899), 37.

CHAPTER 7

The Poverty Theme in Art and Illustration

[1] Stephen Crane, *The Third Violet* (New York, 1897), pp. 185–86.

[2] Henry B. Fuller, "Art in America," *The Bookman*, X (1899), 220.

[3] The quoted passage is from Lloyd Goodrich, *Winslow Homer* (New York, 1944), p. 23.

[4] Guy Pène Du Bois, *Artists Say the Silliest Things* (New York, 1940), pp. 163–64.

[5] John I. H. Baur, *Revolution and Tradition in Modern American Art* (Cambridge, 1951), p. 11.

[6] Frank Norris, *McTeague, A Story of San Francisco* (New York, 1903), p. 198.

[7] *Ibid.*, p. 157. *Cf.* "Making a Train" by Seymour Joseph Guy reproduced in Samuel Isham, *The History of American Painting* (New York, 1927), p. 344.

[8] Reproduced in Isham, *History of American Painting*, p. 347. For interesting comments on Brown see Virgil Barker, *American Painting, History and Interpretation* (New York, 1950), pp. 565–66.

[9] *Harper's Weekly*, III (1859), 824–25.

[10] Quoted in Goodrich, *Winslow Homer*, p. 54.

[11] *Ibid.*, pp. 51 and 54.

[12] Goodrich, *Thomas Eakins, His Life and Work* (New York, 1933), pp. 51–52.

[13] W. Mackay Laffan, "The Material of American Landscape," *The American Art Review*, I (1880), 32.

[14] Townsend, *A Daughter of the Tenements*, pp. 60–61.

[15] For reproductions of the paintings referred to in this paragraph see: Baur, *Revolution and Tradition in Modern American Art*, following p. 20 (Tiffany, "Old New York"); *Harper's Weekly*, XXVI (1882), 105 (Smith, "Under the Bridge"); Metropolitan Museum of Art, *Life in America* (New York, 1939), p. 204 (Maurer, "Forty-third Street West of Ninth Avenue").

[16] For reproductions of the works mentioned see Baur, *Revolution and Tradition in Modern American Art*, facing p. 20 (Weir, "The Gun Foundry"); Isham, *The History of American Painting*, p. 351 (Weir, "Forging the Shaft"); Davidson, *Life in America*, I, 552 (Brown, "Longshoreman's Noon"), and II, 406 (Ulrich, "The Land of Promise").

[17] Reproduced in Davidson, *Life in America*, I, 553.

[18] Larned is quoted in Baur, *Revolution and Tradition in Modern American Art*, p. 14.

[19] *Harper's Weekly*, XVII (1875), 73; XX (1876), 292; and XXVIII (1884), 461.

[20] *Ibid.*, XXVIII (1884), 1. For an appreciation of Frost's work by H. C. Bunner see *Harper's Magazine*, LXXXV (1892), 699–706.

[21] *Daily Graphic* (New York), March 11, 1873, pp. 3–4.

[22] *Ibid.*, April 2, 1873, p. 5.

[23] *Ibid.*, March 14, 1880; reproduced in Robert Taft, *Photography and the American Scene, A Social History, 1839–1889* (New York, 1938), p. 432.

[24] John T. McCutcheon, *Drawn from Memory* (Indianapolis, 1950), pp. 78–79. See also George Ade, *Stories of the Streets and of the Town from the Chicago Record, 1893–1900* (Chicago, 1941).

[25] *Harper's Weekly*, XXIX (1885), 491 and 496.

[26] *Ibid.*, XXIII (1879), 245.

[27] *Ibid.*, XXXI (1887), 529. For a similar approach see *Daily Graphic*, June 19, 1873, p. 5.

[28] W. A. Rogers, *A World Worth While* (New York, 1922), pp. 148–51; for an example of his work see *Harper's Weekly*, XXIII (1879), 224.

[29] *Forty-First Annual Report* of the New York A.I.C.P., 1884, p. 36.

[30] *Truth*, XIV (March 9, 1895), rear cover. On the Trinity tenements see below, Chapter 12.

[31] *Truth*, XI (March 4, 1893), pp. 8–9. Gibson's "An Evening with the Gentlemen's Sons' Chowder Club" is reproduced in William Murrell, *A History of American Graphic Humor* (2 vols., New York, 1935–38), II, 106.

[32] Charles Dickens, *Bleak House* (Household Edition, New York, n.d.), pp. 116 and 265.

[33] *Harper's Weekly*, XX (1876), 121; and XXIII (1879), 801.

[34] Michael Angelo Woolf, *Sketches of Lowly Life in a Great City*, ed. by Joseph Henius (New York, 1899), contains a collection of Woolf's drawings and a biographical sketch of the artist. For an example of one of Woolf's early drawings, an illustration of a Christmas dinner for newsboys and girls, see *Harper's Weekly*, XX (1876), 53.

[35] For examples of early work by Luks and Outcault see *Truth*, XII (December 3, 1892), rear cover; and XII (June 17, 1893), 6.

[36] *Harper's Weekly*, XXXV (1891), 616–17.

[37] See, for example, *Frank Leslie's Illustrated Newspaper*, LXVI (1888), 1; *Harper's Weekly*, XXIX (1885), 801; XXXI (1887), 549 and 597.

[38] *Harper's Weekly*, III (1859), 736; *Daily Graphic*, June 24, 1873, p. 4 and June 28, 1873, p. 6.

[39] Reproduced in Murrell, *A History of American Graphic Humor*, II, 82. See also Walt McDougall, *This Is the Life* (New York, 1926), pp. 96–102.

[40] *Truth*, XIV (March 30, 1895), back cover.

[41] Krausz's pictures are in the Library of Congress Collection of photographs.

[42] Stieglitz's work during the nineties, with several reproductions of photographs taken during this period, is discussed in Theodore Dreiser, "The Camera Club of New York," *Ainslee's Magazine*, IV (1899), 324–35.

[43] *Truth*, XII (December 3, 1892), 8–9.

CHAPTER 8

The New View of Poverty

[1] Robert Hunter, *Poverty* (New York, 1904), pp. 3 and 5–6.

[2] John Lewis Gillin, *Poverty and Dependency, Their Relief and Prevention* (New York, 1921), p. 23.

[3] Jacob H. Hollander, *The Abolition of Poverty* (Boston, 1914), p. 2. On Hollander see Eric F. Goldman, *Rendezvous with Destiny* (New York, 1952), p. 285, footnote 4.

[4] Hunter, *Poverty*, p. 5; Hollander, *Abolition of Poverty*, p. 6.

[5] Hollander, *Abolition of Poverty*, p. 6.

[6] New York A.I.C.P., *Shall Widows Be Pensioned?* (New York, 1914), p. 3.

[7] Andrew Carnegie, "The Advantages of Poverty," *Nineteenth Century Magazine*, XXIX (1891), 367–85.

[8] Hollander, *Abolition of Poverty*, p. 5; and New York A.I.C.P., *Shall Widows Be Pensioned?* p. 3.

[9] Lilian Brandt, "The Causes of Poverty," *The Political Science Quarterly*, XXIII (1908), 637.

[10] George Gunton, "Poverty as a Character Builder," *Gunton's Magazine*, XXIV (1903), 208.

[11] "The Struggle Against Social Despotism," *The Outlook*, LXXXII (1906), 805.

[12] Lester F. Ward, *Applied Sociology. A Treatise on the Conscious Improvement of Society by Society* (Boston, 1906), p. 228.

[13] Edward T. Devine, *Misery and Its Causes* (New York, 1909), p. 265.

[14] Walter Rauschenbusch, *Christianity and the Social Crisis* (New York, 1907), pp. 306–7.

[15] Ruth S. True, *The Neglected Girl* (New York, 1914), pp. 21–22.

[16] Russell Sage Foundation, *Boyhood and Lawlessness* (New York, 1914), p. 61.

[17] This subject is to be treated at greater length in Chapter 10.

[18] Owen Kildare, *The Wisdom of the Simple. A Tale of Lower New York* (New York, 1905), p. 250.

[19] *Ibid.*, p. 213.

[20] *Ibid.*, pp. 16–17.

[21] [William Dean Howells] "The Worst of Being Poor," *Harper's Weekly*, XLVI (1902), 261.

[22] Henry George, *Progress and Poverty* (Twenty-fifth Anniversary Edition, New York, 1911), p. 557.

[23] B. Seebohm Rowntree, *Poverty. A Study of Town Life* (London, 1901), p. 305; and Simon N. Patten, *The New Basis of Civilization* (New York, 1907), pp. 3–27, particularly pp. 9–10.

[24] Walter Lippman, *Drift and Mastery. An Attempt to Diagnose the Current Unrest* (New York, 1914), p. 253.

[25] Robert W. Bruère, "The Good Samaritan, Incorporated," *Harper's Monthly Magazine*, CXX (1910), 833.

[26] Walter Weyl, *The New Democracy. An Essay on Certain Political and Economic Tendencies in the United States* (New York, 1912), pp. 197–98.

[27] Edward T. Devine, *Social Forces* (New York, 1910), p. 90; and Hollander, *Abolition of Poverty*, p. 18.

[28] United States. Commission on Industrial Relations, *Industrial Relations. Final Report and Testimony . . .* (11 vols., Washington, 1916), I, 22.

[29] On this point see J. G. Phelps Stokes, "Report of the Committee on Preventive Social Work," *Pro-*

ceedings of the New York State Conference of Charities and Correction, 1903, p. 222.

30 See, for example, Simon N. Patten, "The Principles of Economic Interference," *The Survey*, XXII (1909), 16.

31 Robert W. Bruère, "The Conquest of Poverty. A Socialist Solution of the Problem," *Metropolitan Magazine*, XXXIII (1909–10), 655; and W. P. Capes, *The Social Doctor* (New York, 1913), p. 91.

32 J. G. Phelps Stokes, "Ye Have the Poor Always with You," *The Independent*, LVII (1904), 730.

33 See comments on this point in Hollander, *The Abolition of Poverty*, p. 16.

34 Bruère, "The Good Samaritan," p. 833.

35 John Simpson Penman, *Poverty; The Challenge to the Church* (Boston, 1915), p. 3.

36 Hunter, *Poverty*, p. 98.

37 Bailey Millard, "What Life Means to Me," *Cosmopolitan Magazine*, XLI (1906), 516.

38 Charles Edward Russell, *Bare Hands and Stone Walls, Some Recollections of a Side-Line Reformer* (New York, 1933), p. 135.

39 This point is made by Lippman in *Drift and Mastery*, p. 5.

40 Gustavus Myers, *History of the Great American Fortunes* (3 vols., Chicago, 1910); and William Allen White, *A Certain Rich Man* (New York, 1909).

41 Russell, *Bare Hands and Stone Walls*, p. 136.

42 Ernest Crosby, "Wall Street and 'Graft,'" *Cosmopolitan Magazine*, XLII (1907), 440.

43 Rauschenbusch, *Christianity and the Social Crisis*, p. 308.

44 Washington Gladden, *Recollections* (Boston, 1909), p. 404.

45 Millard, "What Life Means to Me," p. 516.

46 Alfred Henry Lewis, David Graham Phillips, *et al.*, "The Day of Discontent," *Cosmopolitan Magazine*, XL (1906), 609.

47 Harry Lee and William H. Matthews, *Little Adventures with John Barleycorn* (New York, 1916).

48 Mary E. Richmond, *Friendly Visiting Among the Poor. A Handbook for Charity Workers* (New York, 1899), p. 11.

49 Rauschenbusch, *Christianity and the Social Crisis*, p. 308.

50 Frank Julian Warne, "The Conquest of Poverty. The Program of the Labor Unions," *Metropolitan Magazine*, XXXIII (1909–10), 348.

51 C. J. Bushnell, "Causes and Conditions of Social Need" in Charles Richmond Henderson, *Modern Methods of Charity* (New York, 1904), p. 385.

52 United States. Commission on Industrial Relations, *Industrial Relations. Final Report and Testimony*, I, 22.

53 Supreme Court of the United States, October Term, 1914, Nos. 507 and 508. *Frank C. Stettler* v. *Edwin V. O'Hara et al.*, and *Elmira Simpson* v. *Edwin V. O'Hara et al. Brief for Defendants in Error*, pp. 248 and 225–52.

54 Robert Coit Chapin, *The Standard of Living Among Workingmen's Families in New York City* (New York, 1909), p. 250.

55 Scott Nearing, *Poverty and Riches. A Study of the Industrial Regime* (Philadelphia, 1916), p. 190.

56 The quotations are from *ibid.*, p. 195, and Rauschenbusch, *Christianity and the Social Crisis*, p. 217.

57 See, for example, Warne, "The Conquest of Poverty," p. 348.

58 Henry Rogers Seager, *Social Insurance. A Program of Social Reform* (New York, 1910), pp. 17–18.

59 Hunter, *Poverty*, p. 63.

60 R. H. Tawney, *Poverty as an In-*

dustrial Problem (London, 1913), pp. 11–12.

[61] Edward T. Devine, *When Social Work Was Young* (New York, 1939), p. 115. For a fuller statement of this point of view see Devine, "The Dominant Note of the Modern Philanthropy," *Proceedings* of the National Conference of Charities and Correction, 1906, pp. 1–10.

[62] Hollander, *The Abolition of Poverty*, pp. 106–7 and 113.

[63] "The Struggle against Social Despotism," *The Outlook*, LXXXII (1906), 804–5.

[64] Bessie Marsh and Charles Edward Russell, "The Cry of the Slums," *Everybody's Magazine*, XVI (1907), 35.

[65] Russell Sage Foundation, *Boyhood and Lawlessness*, p. 9.

[66] Ruth S. True, *The Neglected Girl*, p. 21.

[67] Hunter, *Poverty*, pp. 64, 328, and 338–39; and Lee K. Frankel, "Needy Families in Their Homes," *Proceedings* of the National Conference of Charities and Correction, 1906, pp. 331–32.

[68] See, for example, J. G. Phelps Stokes, "Report of the Committee on Preventive Social Work," *Proceedings* of the New York State Conference of Charities and Correction, 1903, pp. 221–30.

[69] Lee K. Frankel, "The Relation Between Standards of Living and Standards of Compensation," *Proceedings* of the New York State Conference of Charities and Correction, 1906, p. 31.

[70] Hunter, *Poverty*, pp. 328 and 340; see also True, *The Neglected Girl*, p. 16.

[71] Frankel, "The Relation Between Standards of Living and Standards of Compensation," p. 31.

[72] Tawney, *Poverty as an Industrial Problem*, p. 11.

[73] *Ibid.*, p. 10; Devine, "The Dominant Note of the Modern Philanthropy," p. 3; and Rev. John A. Ryan, "The Standard of Living and the Problem of Dependency," *Proceedings* of the National Conference of Charities and Correction, 1907, p. 347.

CHAPTER 9

A Factual Generation

[1] Ray Stannard Baker, *American Chronicle* (New York, 1945), p. 183.

[2] "The Man Who Gave Us the Word 'Graft,'" *The Literary Digest*, XXXIV (1907), 173; and Louis Filler, *Crusaders for American Liberalism* (Yellow Springs, Ohio, 1950), p. 67.

[3] Josiah Flynt, "The American Tramp," *The Contemporary Review*, LX (1891), 254.

[4] Josiah Flynt, *Tramping with Tramps. Studies and Sketches of Vagabond Life* (New York, 1901), p. 138.

[5] *Ibid.*, p. ix.

[6] Quite a different conclusion, as regards the unhealthfulness of the lodginghouses, was reached by Paul Kennaday, secretary of the Committee on Prevention of Tuberculosis of the New York C.O.S., in "New York's Hundred Lodging-Houses," *Charities*, XIII (1905), 486–92.

7 Owen Kildare, *My Old Bailiwick* (New York, 1906), p. 123.

8 *Ibid.*, p. 121.

9 *Ibid.*, p. 122.

10 Walter A. Wyckoff, *The Workers, An Experiment in Reality. The East* (New York, 1897), p. vii.

11 Lillian Pettengill, *Toilers of the Home. The Record of a College Woman's Experience as a Domestic Servant* (New York, 1903), p. viii.

12 See, for example: S. H. B. "Street Begging in New York," *Charities*, IV (1900), 2–5; Theodore Waters, "Six Weeks in Beggardom in an Attempt to Solve the Question, 'Shall We Give to Beggars?,'" *Everybody's Magazine*, XII (1905), 69–78; Alexander Irvine, *From the Bottom Up* (New York, 1910), pp. 256–71; E. A. Brown, *Broke* (Chicago, 1913); and Frances A. Kellor, *Out of Work. A Study of Employment Agencies: Their Treatment of the Unemployed and Their Influence upon Homes and Business* (New York, 1905).

13 Jack London, *The People of the Abyss* (New York, 1903), is a report of the author's exploration of the underworld of London in the disguise of a bum.

14 Mrs. John Van Vorst and Marie Van Vorst, *The Woman Who Toils. Being the Experiences of Two Gentlewomen as Factory Girls* (New York, 1903), p. 267.

15 Charles B. Spahr, *America's Working People* (New York, 1900). This work, which first appeared in *The Outlook* in 1899 and 1900, is of interest mainly because Spahr examined labor problems in communities in different stages of economic development. The most informative part of the book is the chapter on Homestead entitled "The Iron Centers."

16 Anthracite Coal Strike Commission, *Report to the President on the Anthracite Coal Strike of May–October, 1902* (Washington, 1903); for one of many magazine articles inspired by the strike see Ray Stannard Baker, "The Right to Work, The Story of the Non-striking Miners," *McClure's Magazine*, XX (1903), 323–36.

17 Peter Roberts, *Anthracite Coal Communities* (New York, 1904).

18 The Atlanta University research program, which originated in 1896, is briefly explained in W. E. Burghardt DuBois and Augustus Granville Dill, *The Negro American Artisan* (Atlanta, 1912), pp. 5–6. Mary White Ovington's research for *Half a Man, The Status of the Negro in New York* (New York, 1911), began in 1904; Miss Ovington contributed to "The Negro in the Cities of the North," *Charities*, XV (1905–6), 1–96, and to "The Industrial Condition of the Negro in the North," *The Annals*, XXVII (1906), 541–609. For an early study of the problem see "Condition of the Negro in Various Cities," *Bulletin* of the Department of Labor, II (1897), 251–309.

19 U. S. Bureau of Labor, *The Italians in Chicago. A Social and Economic Study* (Washington, 1897); "The Italians in America," *Charities*, XII (1904), 443–504; and "The Slav in America," *Charities*, XIII (1904–5), 189–266.

20 Among the more important of the early settlement studies were *Hull-House Maps and Papers* (New York, 1895); Robert A. Woods, ed. *The City Wilderness* (Boston, 1899) and *Americans in Process* (Boston, 1902); and Ernest Poole, *The Plague in Its Stronghold* (New York, 1903).

21 See, for example, Robert Hunter, *Tenement Conditions in Chicago* (Chicago, 1901).

22 On the C.O.S. Tenement House

Exhibition of 1900 see Robert W. De Forest and Lawrence Veiller, eds., *The Tenement House Problem Including the Report of the New York State Tenement House Commission of 1900* (2 vols., New York, 1903), I, 111–15; John G. Hill, Fifty Years of Social Action on the Housing Front (a mimeographed report, apparently prepared in 1948, in the archives of the Community Service Society of New York), pp. 3–7; Lillian W. Betts, "The Tenement House Exhibit," *The Outlook*, LXIV (1900), 589–92; and Jacob A. Riis, "The Tenement House Exhibition," *Harper's Weekly*, XLIV (1900), 104.

[23] On De Forest and Veiller see Edward T. Devine, *When Social Work Was Young* (New York, 1939), pp. 25–26 and 70–75.

[24] De Forest and Veiller, eds., *The Tenement House Problem*, I, 10.

[25] In 1901 the legislature passed a new tenement-house law drafted by Veiller and other members of the Commission. Meanwhile, the charter of New York City was amended to provide for the establishment of a Tenement House Department, which was given sole responsibility for regulatory functions formerly distributed among several different bureaus. In the administration of Mayor Seth Low, De Forest and Veiller served respectively as Commissioner and Deputy Commissioner of the new department. Devine, *When Social Work Was Young*, pp. 76–77.

[26] Robert Hunter, *Poverty* (New York, 1904), p. 11.

[27] *Ibid.*, p. 12.

[28] William Graham Sumner, *What Social Classes Owe to Each Other* (New York, 1883), pp. 19–20.

[29] John A. Ryan, *A Living Wage. Its Ethical and Economic Aspects* (New York, 1906), p. 136.

[30] *Ibid.*, p. 148.

[31] The following are among the more important of the prewar studies of the cost of living and wage earners' budgets: *Eighteenth Annual Report of the Commissioner of Labor, 1903. Cost of Living and Retail Prices of Food* (Washington, 1903); Louise Bolard More, *Wage Earners' Budgets* (New York, 1907); and Robert Coit Chapin, *The Standard of Living Among Workingmen's Families in New York City* (New York, 1909). See also Maurice Parmelee, *Poverty and Social Progress* (New York, 1920), pp. 87–91.

[32] Ryan, *A Living Wage*, p. 162.

[33] The findings of various prewar wage studies are summarized in Parmelee, *Poverty and Social Progress*, pp. 65–72. For later treatment of the problem see Paul H. Douglas, *Real Wages in the United States, 1890–1926* (Boston, 1930), pp. 390–95.

[34] Devine, *When Social Work Was Young*, p. 110.

[35] "The Negro in the Cities of the North," *Charities*, XV (1905–6), 1–96; and "Next Door to Congress," *Charities and the Commons*, XV (1905–6), 759–841.

[36] Devine, *When Social Work Was Young*, p. 111.

[37] On the origins and progress of the survey see *ibid.*, pp. 112–13; John M. Glenn, Lilian Brandt, and F. Emerson Andrews, *Russell Sage Foundation, 1907–1946* (2 vols., New York, 1946), I, 210–13; and Paul U. Kellogg, "The Pittsburgh Survey," *Charities and the Commons*, XXI (1908–9), 517–26.

[38] For explanation of the general coverage of the survey see Kellogg, "The Pittsburgh Survey," p. 518; and Shelby M. Harrison, *The Social Survey. The Idea Defined and Its Development Traced* (New York, 1931), pp. 15–16. Among the topics covered in the investigation were: wages, hours of work, and work

accidents; family budgets and home conditions among steel workers; typhoid fever and other problems relating to community health and sanitation; housing; taxation; public schools; city planning; playgrounds; and care of dependent children in institutions.

39 For the entire report see Paul U. Kellogg, *The Pittsburgh Survey* (6 vols., New York, 1909–14). The findings of the survey were summarized in Edward T. Devine, "The Pittsburgh Survey," *Charities and the Commons*, XXI (1908–9), 1035–36.

40 Jane Addams, *The Second Twenty Years at Hull House, September 1909 to September 1929* (New York, 1930), p. 10.

41 Robert W. De Forest, "The Initial Activities of the Russell Sage Foundation," *The Survey*, XXII (1909), 71.

42 Glenn, Brandt and Andrews, *Russell Sage Foundation*, I, 177–90; Harrison, *The Social Survey*, pp. 16–17.

43 "Birmingham. Smelting Iron Ore and Civics," *The Survey*, XXVII (1911–12), 1451–1556. John A. Fitch, "The Human Side of Large Outputs. Steel and Steel Workers in Six American States," *The Survey*, XXVII (1911–12), 929–45, 1145–60, 1285–98, 1527–40; and XXVIII (1912), 17–27. For comment on the steel survey see Edward T. Devine, "Pittsburgh in Perspective," *The Survey*, XXVII (1911–12), 917–18.

44 Orrin G. Cocks, "The Scope and Value of the Local Surveys of the Men and Religion Movement," *Proceedings* of the Academy of Political Science in the City of New York, III, 537–44.

45 See Lillian D. Wald, *The House on Henry Street* (New York, 1915), pp. 293–97, for comment on the work of the New York State Immigration Commission. On the Illinois Occupational Disease Commission see Alice Hamilton, *Exploring the Dangerous Trades* (Boston, 1943), pp. 118–21.

46 For discussion of the importance of this report see Filler, *Crusaders for American Liberalism*, p. 167; and Elting E. Morison, ed., *The Letters of Theodore Roosevelt* (8 vols., Cambridge, Mass., 1951–54), V, 176–77, and 294–96.

47 U.S. Bureau of Labor, *Report on Condition of Woman and Child Wage Earners in the United States* (19 vols., Washington, 1910–13), XVIII, 136.

48 Josephine Goldmark, *Impatient Crusader, Florence Kelley's Life Story* (Urbana, Ill., 1953), pp. 102–3.

49 "Tenement Houses–Their Wrongs," *New York Daily Tribune*, November 23, 1869, p. 4.

50 The establishment of the Children's Bureau is discussed below, Chapter 12. On the early work of the agency see Grace Abbott, "Ten Years' Work for Children," *The North American Review*, CCXVIII (1923), 189–200; and James A. Tobey, *The Children's Bureau. Its History, Activities and Organization* (Baltimore, Md., 1925), pp. 3–4.

51 Edward T. Devine, *Organized Charity and Industry* (New York, 1915), pp. 3–4.

52 United States. Commission on Industrial Relations, *Industrial Relations. Final Report and Testimony* (11 vols., Washington, 1916), I, 6.

53 *Ibid.*, I, 22. Manly referred to combined family income rather than to individual earnings.

54 *Ibid.*, I, 30.

55 See, for example, the statement of Margaret Dreier Robins, *ibid.*, I, 309–19.

56 Frances A. Kellor, *Out of Work. A Study of Unemployment* (New York, 1915), pp. 23–26.

[57] *Ibid.*, pp. 2–3.

[58] *Ibid.*, pp. 20–23. For comment on a study of unemployment made by the Bureau of Labor Statistics in 1915 see Douglas, *Real Wages in the United States, 1890–1926*, pp. 412–15.

[59] R. H. Tawney, *Poverty as an Industrial Problem* (London, 1913), p. 9.

CHAPTER 10

The Literary Record

[1] *The American Monthly Review of Reviews*, XIX (1899), 749.

[2] *Ibid.;* and see also critical comment quoted in Ernest Marchand, *Frank Norris. A Study* (Stanford University, Calif., 1942), pp. 201–4.

[3] James L. Ford, *Forty-Odd Years in the Literary Shop* (New York, 1921), p. 125.

[4] Frank Norris, *The Responsibilities of the Novelist and Other Literary Essays* (New York, 1903), p. 215.

[5] Alice Hegan Rice, *The Inky Way* (New York, 1940), p. 39.

[6] Owen Kildare, *The Good of the Wicked and the Party Sketches* (New York, 1904), unnumbered p. 4.

[7] Myra Kelly, "The Uses of Adversity" in *Little Citizens. The Humors of School Life* (New York, 1904), pp. 35–63.

[8] Vachel Lindsay, "The Knight in Disguise" in *General William Booth Enters into Heaven and Other Poems* (New York, 1924), p. 52.

[9] O. Henry, "The Cop and the Anthem," in *The Four Million* (Garden City, N. Y., 1919), p. 100.

[10] "The Furnished Room," *ibid.*, p. 240.

[11] "An Unfinished Story," *ibid.*, p. 180.

[12] Quoted in F. O. Matthiessen, *Theodore Dreiser* (New York, 1951), pp. 60 and 112.

[13] On this point see *ibid.*, pp. 159–63; Theodore Dreiser, *The "Genius"* (Garden City, N. Y., n.d.), pp. 89, 110, and 236; Joseph J. Kwiat, "Dreiser and the Graphic Artist," *American Quarterly*, III (1951), 140–41; and Cyrille Arnavon, "Theodore Dreiser and Painting," *American Literature*, XVII (1945), 113–26.

[14] Dreiser, "The City Awakes" in *The Color of a Great City* (New York, 1923), p. 5.

[15] "Six O'Clock," *ibid.*, p. 82.

[16] Quoted in Matthiessen, *Theodore Dreiser*, p. 230.

[17] Dreiser, *Sister Carrie* (Modern Library edition, New York, 1932), p. 64.

[18] Dreiser, *Jennie Gerhardt* (New York, 1911), pp. 3, 111, and 158.

[19] Dreiser, "Bums" in *The Color of a Great City*, pp. 35 and 37.

[20] Dreiser, *Sister Carrie*, pp. 545 and 554.

[21] Dreiser, *A History of Myself. Newspaper Days* (New York, 1931), p. 487.

[22] Dreiser, "Peter" in *Twelve Men* (New York, 1919), pp. 8–9.

[23] Dreiser, "W.L.S.," *ibid.*, pp. 320. See also Dreiser, "The Color of Today," *Harper's Weekly*, XLV (1901), 1273.

[24] Frank Norris, *The Octopus. A Story of California* (New York, 1924), pp. 651–52.

[25] Carl Sandburg, *Smoke and Steel* (New York, 1920), p. 5.

[26] William Vaughn Moody, "Glou-

cester Moors," *Scribner's Magazine,* XXVIII (1900), 727-28.

27 Moody, "The Brute," *The Atlantic Monthly,* LXXXVII (1901), 88.

28 Robert Herrick, *A Life for a Life* (New York, 1910), pp. 267-68.

29 Upton Sinclair, *The Jungle* (New York, 1946), p. 60.

30 "The Candle Seller" in "Poems by Morris Rosenfeld," trans. by Rose Pastor Stokes and Helena Frank, *Survey,* XXXII (1914), 268.

31 Reginald Wright Kauffman, *The House of Bondage* (New York, 1910), p. 106.

32 Morris Rosenfeld, *Songs of Labor and Other Poems,* trans. by Rose Pastor Stokes and Helena Frank (Boston, 1914), pp. 7-9.

33 Jack London, *Martin Eden* (New York, 1909), p. 158.

34 Carl Sandburg, "The Right to Grief" in *Chicago Poems* (New York, 1916), pp. 25-26.

35 Sinclair, *The Jungle,* pp. 57-58 and 60.

36 Lewis Jacobs, *The Rise of the American Film. A Critical History* (New York, 1939), pp. 46-48 and 71.

37 On early movies dealing with poverty see *ibid.*, pp. 69-72; and Lloyd Morris, *Not So Long Ago* (New York, 1949), pp. 46-47.

38 Vachel Lindsay, "The Leaden-Eyed," *Collected Poems* (New York, 1927), pp. 69-70.

39 The quotation is from Matthiessen, *Theodore Dreiser,* p. 219. For a good example of the writers' tendency to present the fruits of material success as unsatisfactory see Abraham Cahan, *The Rise of David Levinsky* (New York, 1917).

40 Jack London, "What Life Means to Me," *Cosmopolitan Magazine,* XL (1905-6), 526.

41 London, *Martin Eden,* pp. 158, 256, and 259.

42 London, "What Life Means to Me," pp. 529-30.

43 "Introduction by Jack London," in *The Cry for Justice, An Anthology of the Literature of Social Protest,* ed. by Upton Sinclair (Philadelphia, 1915), p. 4.

44 Albert Edwards (pseud. Arthur Bullard), *A Man's World* (New York, 1912), p. 105.

45 *Life,* XLVIII (1906), 609.

46 Quoted in Sinclair, ed., *The Cry for Justice,* pp. 244-46. The emergence of literary radicalism after 1910 is discussed in Lillian Symes and Travers Clement, *Rebel America. The Story of Social Revolt in the United States* (New York, 1934), pp. 265-67. For comments on the development of the proletarian novel in the United States see Donald Drew Egbert and Stow Persons, eds., *Socialism and American Life* (2 vols., Princeton, 1952), II, 473 *et seq.*

47 Ernest Poole, *The Harbor* (New York, 1915), p. 351.

48 *Ibid.*, pp. 215-16 and 321.

49 *Ibid.*, p. 15.

CHAPTER 11

Art for Life's Sake

1 The Lay Figure, "On the Cult of the Ugly," *International Studio,* XXIV (1905), 374.

2 Sadakichi Hartmann, "Plea for the Picturesqueness of New York," *Camera Notes,* IV (1900), 91-92 and 94.

3 John Corbin, "The Twentieth Cen-

tury City," *Scribner's Magazine*, XXXIII (1903), 259. This article was illustrated with reproductions of photographs by Alfred Stieglitz.

[4] Quoted in "To Revive the Art of Every-Day Life," *The Literary Digest*, XXXIV (1907), 260.

[5] "The Futility of American Art," *The Independent*, LXIV (1908), 266–68.

[6] For a convenient summary of critical comment on the work of the Henri group see J. G., "Brooklyn Revives Memories of 'The Eight,'" *The Art Digest*, XVIII (December 1, 1943), 12. See also Oliver W. Larkin, *Art and Life in America* (New York, 1949), pp. 334–36.

[7] *The Sun* (New York), February 9, 1908, p. 8.

[8] Samuel Swift, "Revolutionary Figures in American Art," *Harper's Weekly*, LI (1907), 534; and "Special Exhibition of Contemporaneous Art," *The Independent*, LXIV (1908), 200. See also Giles Edgerton, "The Younger American Painters: Are They Creating a National Art?", *The Craftsman*, XIII (1908), 512–32.

[9] B. O. Flower, "The Vital Issue in the Present Battle for a Great American Art," *The Arena*, XXXIV (1905), 480.

[10] Robert Henri, *The Art Spirit* (Philadelphia, 1923), pp. 222 and 248.

[11] John Sloan, *Gist of Art* (New York, 1939), p. 220.

[12] Guy Pène Du Bois, *Artists Say the Silliest Things* (New York, 1940), p. 82. See also Helen Appleton Read, "Introduction" to Whitney Museum of American Art, *New York Realists, 1900–1914* (New York, 1937), p. 8; Charles Wisner Barrell, "The Real Drama of the Slums as Told in John Sloan's Etchings," *The Craftsman*, XV (1909), 559–64; and Louis Baury, "The Message of Proletaire," *The Bookman*, XXXIV (1911), 399–413.

[13] Jerome Myers, *Artist in Manhattan* (New York, 1940), p. 131.

[14] John Spargo, "George Luks . . .," *The Craftsman*, XII (1907), 607. See also *The Independent*, LXIV (1908), 200–1.

[15] On the Shinn mural see "Everett Shinn's Paintings of Labor in the New City Hall at Trenton, N. J.," *The Craftsman*, XXI (1911–12), 385. For Sloan's attitude toward social criticism in art see *Gist of Art*, p. 3; and Lloyd Goodrich and Rosalind Irvine, *John Sloan, 1871–1951* (New York, 1952), pp. 22 and 44.

[16] The quoted phrase is from Charles H. Caffin, *Art for Life's Sake* (New York, 1913), p. 18.

[17] Spargo, "Eugene Higgins . . .," *The Craftsman*, XII (1907), 136. For biographical data on Higgins see Edward H. Smith, "Eugene Higgins: Painter of the Underworld," *The World Magazine* (New York), April 13, 1919, p. 9; and Dorothy M. Oldach, *Eugene Higgins* (Brooklyn, 1939).

[18] Myers, *Artist in Manhattan*, p. 48.

[19] Quoted in Baury, "The Message of Proletaire," p. 412.

[20] Quoted in Smith, "Eugene Higgins: Painter of the Underworld," p. 9.

[21] Spargo, "Charles Haag . . .," *The Craftsman*, X (1906), 433.

[22] Crystal Eastman, "Charles Haag. An Immigrant Sculptor of His Kind," *Charities and the Commons*, XVII (1906–7), 615–16.

[23] For example of Ker's *Life* style see *Life*, XLV (1905), 122, 134; and XLVI (1905), 206–7, 560–61, and 682–83.

[24] Quoted in Art Young, *Art Young. His Life and Times* (New York, 1939), p. 268.

[25] See Advertisement in *Life*, XLIX (1907), 698. Ker's picture is reproduced under the title "The Hand

of Fate" in Upton Sinclair, ed., *The Cry for Justice* (Philadelphia, 1915), facing p. 92; and under the title "From the Depths" in Harold U. Faulkner, *The Quest for Social Justice, 1898–1914* (New York, 1931), Plate I. Ker's illustrations for *The Silent War* were discussed by contemporary critics in *The Outlook*, LXXXIV (1906), 682, and *The Arena*, XXXVII (1907), 446–47.

26 Quoted in Baury, "The Message of Proletaire," p. 413. "King Canute" is reproduced in Sinclair, ed., *The Cry for Justice*, facing p. 93.

27 Young, *The Best of Art Young* (New York, 1936), p. xvi.

28 Quoted in Goodrich and Irvine, *John Sloan*, p. 47.

29 The drawings referred to were first published in *The Masses*, I (October, 1911), 12, and IV (May, 1913), 15.

30 Young, *Art Young. His Life and Times*, p. 262.

31 The drawings cited in this paragraph are reproduced *ibid.*, p. 259 ("American Mothers"); *The Best of Art Young*, p. 29 ("Poverty Develops Character"), p. 30 ("Holy Trinity"), and p. 51 ("Pigs and Children"). For other examples of Young's cartoons attacking child labor see *The Best of Art Young*, pp. 36–37.

32 Young, *Art Young. His Life and Times*, p. 244.

33 Charles F. Weller, "Neglected Neighbors," *Charities and the Commons*, XV (1905–6), 761–94. See Chapter 9.

34 Beaumont Newhall, "Lewis W. Hine," *Magazine of Art*, XXXI (1938), 636–37. Hine's photographs were used to illustrate publications of The National Child Labor Committee including E. N. Clopper, *Child Labor in West Virginia* (New York, 1908), and A. J. McKelway, *Child Labor in the Carolinas* (New York, 1909).

35 Charles Edward Russell, "Unto the Least of These," *Everybody's Magazine*, XXI (1909), 75.

36 Caffin, *Art for Life's Sake*, p. 43; and Henri, "Progress in Our National Art . . .," *The Craftsman*, XV (1909), 388.

37 Caffin, *Art for Life's Sake*, pp. 47 and 86.

CHAPTER 12

The Home and the Child

1 Robert Alston Stevenson, "The Poor in Summer," *Scribner's Magazine*, XXX (1901), 276.

2 New York C.O.S. Appeal for Funds, June 1899. Stokes Papers.

3 Ernest Poole, *The Plague in Its Stronghold* (New York, 1903), p. 26. See also Poole's Article, " 'The Lung Block,' " *Charities*, XI (1903), 193–99.

4 This story is told by Maud Nathan in *Once upon a Time and Today* (New York, 1933), pp. 135–36.

5 Bessie Marsh and Charles Edward Russell, "The Cry of the Slums," *Everybody's Magazine*, XVI (1907), 35.

6 Charles R. Henderson, *The Social Spirit in America* (Chicago, 1905), p. 62.

7 Housing surveys conducted between 1900 and 1919 are summa-

rized in Edith Elmer Wood, *The Housing of the Unskilled Wage Earner. America's Next Problem* (New York, 1919), pp. 7–8. On Albion Fellows Bacon see *ibid.*, pp. 85–86; Helen Christine Bennett, *American Women in Civic Work* (New York, 1915), pp. 117–37; and Albion Fellows Bacon, *Beauty for Ashes* (New York, 1914).

8 Wood, *Housing of the Unskilled Wage Earner*, p. 7.

9 Edith Abbott, *The Tenements of Chicago, 1908–1935* (Chicago, 1936), p. 476.

10 Wood, *Housing of the Unskilled Wage Earner*, p. 8.

11 Abbott, *The Tenements of Chicago*, p. 480.

12 James L. Ford, *The Literary Shop and Other Tales* (New York, 1899), pp. 139–41. Gilder was editor of *The Century* and, according to Ford, one of the persons most responsible for keeping realistic fiction dealing with low life out of the magazines. For Gilder's letters on the work of the Tenement House Committee see *Letters of Richard Watson Gilder* (Boston, 1916), pp. 254–93.

13 On the Big Flat, originally called the "Workingmen's Home," see Robert Hartley, *Thirteenth Annual Report of the A.I.C.P.* (New York, 1856), pp. 44–51. The terrible deterioration of this structure is described in Frederick N. Owen, "The Story of the 'Big Flat'" in *Forty-third Annual Report of the A.I.C.P.* (New York, 1886), pp. 43–73, an excellent example of muckraking. The building was the inspiration, although not the precise locale, of Julian Ralph's stories of the "Big Barracks" in *People We Pass* (New York, 1896).–Arthur Bartlett Maurice, *New York in Fiction* (New York, 1901), p. 64.

14 On the Alfred T. White Tenements see Wood, *Housing of the Unskilled Wage Earner*, pp. 96–98.

15 *Ibid.*, pp. 91–132; and Robert Hunter, *Tenement Conditions in Chicago* (Chicago, 1901), pp. 175–78.

16 Prior to joining Stanton Coit at the University Settlement Charles B. Stover managed the group of workingmen's homes built in New York City by a corporation organized in 1884 by Felix Adler and E. R. A. Seligman. Gregory Weinstein, a former resident, describes these houses in *The Ardent Eighties and After* (New York, 1947), pp. 89–90.

17 Henderson, *The Social Spirit in America*, p. 63. The work of the Octavia Hill Association of Philadelphia is described in Wood, *Housing of the Unskilled Wage Earner*, pp. 111–12.

18 Hunter, *Tenement Conditions in Chicago*, pp. 166–67.

19 Wood, *Housing of the Unskilled Wage Earner*, pp. 113–14.

20 See *ibid.*, pp. 91–92 for comments on the significance of the model-housing movement. See also Benjamin Park DeWitt, *The Progressive Movement* (New York, 1915), pp. 349–50.

21 The weaknesses of the early codes are ably summarized in John G. Hill, "Fifty Years of Social Action on the Housing Front" (New York, 1948), p. 3. (Mimeographed report in archives of Community Service Society of New York).

22 For a charity agent's report of his activity in this field see Howard Kelsey Estabrook, *Some Slums in Boston* (Boston, 1898) and a follow-up study by the same author, "Tenement Houses in Boston," *Charities*, III (August 12, 1899), 4–6. In 1892 the New York A.I.C.P. established a Department of Dwellings to make inspections of dwellings for the Metropolitan Board of Health.

23 On the New York law see Robert W. DeForest and Lawrence Veiller, eds., *The Tenement House Problem*

. . . (2 vols., New York, 1903) and Hill, "Fifty Years of Social Action on the Housing Front," pp. 7–8. The provisions of the Chicago ordinance of 1902 are outlined in Abbott, *The Tenements of Chicago*, pp. 59–61.

[24] Wood, *Housing of the Unskilled Wage Earner*, pp. 60–90; and Lawrence Veiller, *A Model Tenement House Law* (New York, 1910).

[25] Abbott, *The Tenements of Chicago*, pp. 480–82.

[26] *Ibid*., p. 480.

[27] Edith Elmer Wood, *Recent Trends in American Housing* (New York, 1931), pp. 10–12. For a defense and advocacy of "cold enforcement" of the tenement-house laws see Theodore Dreiser, *The Color of a Great City* (New York, 1923), pp. 97–98.

[28] Abbott, *The Tenements of Chicago*, pp. 477–79.

[29] Daniel Aaron, *Men of Good Hope. A Story of American Progressives* (New York, 1951), p. 45.

[30] William Dean Howells, "An East Side Ramble," in *Impressions and Experiences* (New York, 1896), p. 149.

[31] De Forest and Veiller, eds., *The Tenement House Problem*, I, 44; and Veiller, *Housing Reform* (New York, 1911), pp. 77–84.

[32] Massachusetts, General Court. House of Representatives Document 2000. *Report of the Homestead Commission* (Boston, 1913), p. 6.

[33] U. S. Bureau of Labor Statistics. Bulletin 158, *Government Aid to Home Owning and Housing of Working People in Foreign Countries* (Washington, 1914), pp. 9–10.

[34] *Report of the Proceedings* of the Thirty-Fourth Annual Convention of the American Federation of Labor (Washington, 1914), p. 355.

[35] Constitution of Massachusetts, Article of Amendment XLIII, approved November 2, 1915. See also Article of Amendment XLVII, approved November 6, 1917. In 1913 the city of Cleveland, Ohio, purchased a parcel of land to be laid out in low-cost building sites—*Cleveland Plain Dealer*, March 25, 1913; and *The Public*, XVI (1913), 346.

[36] For an example of the close relationship between tenement-house reform and the child-saving movement see Massachusetts, General Court. House Document 2000, *Report of the Homestead Commission*, p. 7.

[37] This point is emphasized by Robert Hunter in *Poverty* (New York, 1904), p. 191.

[38] *First Annual Report of the Children's Aid Society of New York*, quoted in Charles Loring Brace, *The Dangerous Classes of New York* (New York, 1872), p. 322.

[39] Edwin Markham, Ben B. Lindsey, and George Creel, *Children in Bondage* (New York, 1914), p. 151.

[40] DeWitt, *The Progressive Movement*, pp. 247–48.

[41] Material on this point is voluminous. For two of the many articles bearing on it see Jane Addams, "Child Labor and Pauperism," *Proceedings* of the National Conference of Charities and Correction, 1903, pp. 114–21; and Wilma I. Ball, "Street Trading in Ohio," *The American Child*, I (1919–20), 123–29.

[42] John Spargo, *The Bitter Cry of the Children* (New York, 1906), p. 174. This book stemmed from the controversy aroused by Hunter's *Poverty*. For interesting contemporary comment on Spargo's work see "The Struggle Against Social Despotism," *The Outlook*, LXXXII (1906), 805.

[43] S. W. Woodward, "A Business-man's View of Child Labor," *Char-*

ities and the Commons, XV (1905–6), 800–1.

44 Addams, "Child Labor and Pauperism," p. 117.

45 Ernest Poole, *The Street. Its Child Workers* (New York, 1903), p. 18. See also Poole's article "Waifs of the Street," *McClure's Magazine,* XXI (1903), 43–44.

46 Quoted in Edward N. Clopper, *Child Labor in City Streets* (New York, 1913), pp. 64–65.

47 Hunter, *Poverty,* pp. 223 and 233. See also Addams, "Child Labor and Pauperism," p. 117.

48 On this point see Homer Folks, *Changes and Trends in Child Labor and Its Control* (New York, 1938), p. 26.

49 Hunter, *Poverty,* p. 249.

50 Addams, "Child Labor and Pauperism," p. 121.

51 Spargo, *The Bitter Cry of the Children,* p. 147.

52 Felix Adler, *The Attitude of Society Toward the Child as an Index of Civilization* (New York, 1907), p. 5.

53 Addams, "Child Labor and Pauperism," p. 121.

54 The phrases quoted are from Edwin Markham, "The Hoe-Man in the Making," *Cosmopolitan Magazine,* XLI (1906), 482.

55 Edgar Gardner Murphy, *The Case Against Child Labor* (n.p., n.d.—published by Executive Committee on Child Labor in Alabama), p. 1.

56 The movement against child labor in the South is treated in Elizabeth H. Davidson, *Child Labor Legislation in the Southern Textile States* (Chapel Hill, N. C., 1939). There is a good brief discussion of the problem in C. Vann Woodward, *Origins of the New South* (Baton Rouge, La., 1951), pp. 416–20. See also Elizabeth Sands Johnson "Child Labor Legislation" in John R. Commons *et al., History of Labor in the United States* (4 vols., New York, 1918–35), III, 405–6, 414–15, and 427–28.

57 Samuel Gompers, "Organized Labor's Attitude Toward Child Labor," *The Annals,* XXVII (1906), 339. For the influence of the Knights of Labor on child-labor legislation see Johnson, "Child Labor Legislation," p. 404.

58 Johnson, "Child Labor Legislation," p. 407. On the New York Child Labor Committee see Josephine Goldmark, *Impatient Crusader, Florence Kelley's Life Story* (Urbana, Ill., 1953), pp. 81–87.

59 Edgar Gardner Murphy, "Child Labor as a National Problem; with Special Reference to the Southern States," *Proceedings* of the National Conference of Charities and Correction, 1903, p. 121.

60 On the organization of the National Child Labor Committee see Goldmark, *Impatient Crusader,* p. 92.

61 Johnson, "Child Labor Legislation," pp. 407–9.

62 *Ibid.,* pp. 413–15 and 419–21.

63 *Ibid.,* pp. 422–23; and Hunter, *Poverty,* p. 235.

64 Florence Kelley, *Obstacles to the Enforcement of Child Labor Legislation* (New York, 1907), pp. 5–6.

65 Lillian Wald. *The House on Henry Street* (New York, 1915), pp. 144–45.

66 Johnson, "Child Labor Legislation," pp. 417–18; and Folks, *Changes and Trends in Child Labor and Its Control,* p. 5.

67 Johnson, "Child Labor Legislation," p. 415.

68 Clopper, *Child Labor in City Streets,* pp. 6–7. See also "Street Trades Control in Toledo," *The American Child,* V (August, 1923), 3.

69 Goldmark, *Impatient Crusader,* pp. 94–100, traces the origins of the Children's Bureau movement. See

also James A. Tobey, *The Children's Bureau. Its History, Activities and Organization* (Baltimore, 1925), pp. 1–2.

[70] 37 United States Statutes 79 (1912).

[71] On the early work of the Children's Bureau see Grace Abbott, "Ten Years' Work for Children," *The North American Review*, CCXVIII (1923), 189–200; and Grace Abbott, *The Child and The State* (2 vols., Chicago, 1938), II, 612–15.

[72] *Proceedings* of the Conference on the Care of Dependent Children (Washington, 1909), pp. 9–10 and 41 *et seq.*

[73] DeWitt, *The Progressive Movement*, pp. 253–56.

[74] Frank J. Bruno, *Trends in Social Work as Reflected in the Proceedings of the National Conference of Social Work* (New York, 1948), pp. 178–79.

[75] See description of the cxperiments conducted by the New York A.I.C.P. after 1896 in making money allowances to distressed families in Community Service Society of New York, *Frontiers in Human Welfare . . .* (New York, 1948), p. 53.

[76] Bruno, *Trends in Social Work*, pp. 177–78.

[77] This is the point made in Karl de Schweinitz, "The Development of Governmental Responsibility for Human Welfare." Address delivered January 29, 1948, Symposium I of the 100th Anniversary Program of the Community Service Society of New York (Archives of the Community Service Society of New York).

[78] In these sentences I have attempted to state the views which seem to me to be characteristic of men and women such as Devine and Mrs. Kelley. See, for example, Devine's remarks at the White House Conference of 1909, *Proceedings* of the Conference on the Care of Dependent Children, pp. 47–48.

[79] Albert J. Beveridge, "Child Labor" in *The Meaning of the Times and Other Speeches* (Indianapolis, 1908), p. 341. The Beveridge-Parsons Bill of 1906 is printed in Abbott, *The Child and the State*, I, 472–73.

[80] U. S. Bureau of Labor, *Report on Condition of Woman and Child Wage Earners in the United States* (19 vols., Washington, 1910–13), I, 9.

[81] Folks, *Changes and Trends in Child Labor and Its Control*, p. 18; and Johnson, "Child Labor Legislation," pp. 438–39.

[82] Johnson, "Child Labor Legislation," pp. 439–41. The law of September 1, 1916 (39 United States Statutes 675), is known as the Keating-Owen Act. It went into effect September 1, 1917.

[83] *Hammer* v. *Dagenhart*, 247 U. S. 251 (1918). Lowell Mellett provides some information on the later history of Reuben and John Dagenhart in "The Sequel to the Dagenhart Case," *The American Child*, VI (January, 1924), 3. For interesting comment on the decision see Abbott, *The Child and the State*, I, 463.

[84] *Bailey* v. *Drexel Furniture Co.*, 259 U. S. 20 (1922). For comment on the decision see Elizabeth Brandeis, "Labor Legislation," in Commons *et al.*, and Brandeis, *History of Labor in the United States*, III, 694–95.

[85] The phrasing of the amendment is discussed in Abbott, *The Child and the State*, I, 536 and 544–46.

[86] Johnson, "Child Labor Legislation," pp. 448–49.

[87] Arguments against the amendment are discussed *ibid.*, pp. 446–48; Abbott, *The Child and the State*, I, 537–35; Goldmark, *Impatient Crusader*, pp. 117–18; and John A. Ryan, *Social Doctrines in Action. A Per-*

sonal History (New York, 1941), pp. 223–25.

[88] Felix Adler, *Child Labor in the United States and Its Great Attendant Evils* (New York, 1905), p. 12.

[89] Jane Addams, "Modern Devices for Minimizing Dependencies," *Proceedings* of the Conference on the Care of Dependent Children, pp. 99–101.

[90] Folks, *Changes and Trends in Child Labor and Its Control*, p. 27. Folks was at this time (1938) chairman of the National Child Labor Committee; he had for many years been secretary of the New York State Charities Aid Association.

CHAPTER 13

Women's Hours and Wages

[1] Josephine C. Goldmark, "The Necessary Sequel of Child Labor Laws," *The American Journal of Sociology*, XI (1905), 312–25.

[2] For the feminist point of view see Rheta C. Dorr, *A Woman of Fifty* (New York, 1924), pp. 163–64 and *What Eight Million Women Want* (Boston, 1910).

[3] Clara M. Beyer, *History of Labor Legislation for Women in Three States*. Bulletin of the Women's Bureau, U.S. Department of Labor, No. 66 (Washington, 1929), pp. 2–3.

[4] Elizabeth Brandeis, "Labor Legislation" in John R. Commons *et al.*, *History of Labor in the United States* (4 vols., New York, 1918–35), III, 457–66.

[5] *Ibid.*, pp. 466–67.

[6] On Mrs. Kelley's career see Josephine Goldmark, *Impatient Crusader, Florence Kelley's Life Story* (Urbana, Ill., 1953); and autobiographical sketches by Florence Kelley in *The Survey*, LVII (1926–27), 7–11+, 557–61+, and LVIII (1927), 31–35, 271–74+.

[7] Mrs. Kelley's philosophy is best expressed in her book, *Some Ethical Gains Through Legislation* (New York, 1905).

[8] On the origin of the Consumers' League see Beyer, *History of Labor Legislation for Women*, pp. 69–70. Maud Nathan, *The Story of an Epoch-Making Movement* (New York, 1926) is a history of the movement by one of its early leaders.

[9] Brandeis' remark is quoted in Alpheus Thomas Mason, *Brandeis, A Free Man's Life* (New York, 1946), pp. 248–49.

[10] Kelley, *Some Ethical Gains Through Legislation*, p. 159; and Josephine Goldmark, *Fatigue and Efficiency* (New York, 1912), pp. 247–50.

[11] See Goldmark, *Fatigue and Efficiency*, Part II, for the substances of the briefs prepared by Brandeis and Miss Goldmark for *Muller* v. *Oregon* and other cases involving the hour laws of Ohio and Illinois. Miss Goldmark tells the story of the Brandeis brief in *Impatient Crusader*, pp. 143–59; see also Mason, *Brandeis, A Free Man's Life*, pp. 248–52.

[12] State of Illinois, *Third Annual Report of the Factory Inspectors of Illinois, 1895* (Springfield, Ill., 1896), p. 7. See also Kelley, *Some Ethical Gains Through Legislation*, p. 143.

[13] Mason, *Brandeis, A Free Man's Life*, p. 245.

[14] *Ibid.*, p. 251.

[15] Elizabeth Beardsley Butler, *Women and the Trades* (New York, 1910), p. 346.

[16] *Ibid.*, pp. 347–48.

[17] *Ibid.*, p. 349.

[18] Mary Van Kleeck, "Working Hours of Women in Factories," *Charities and the Commons*, XVII (1906), 13–21.

[19] See, for example, Mary Van Kleeck, *Artificial Flower Makers* (New York, 1913) and *Women in the Bookbinding Trade* (New York, 1913). On the pin-money theory see also *The Autobiography of Mary Anderson* as told to Mary N. Winslow (Minneapolis, 1951), pp. 75 and 139.

[20] John M. Glenn, Lilian Brandt, and F. Emerson Andrews, *Russell Sage Foundation, 1907–1946* (2 vols., New York, 1947), I, 161.

[21] U.S. Bureau of Labor, *Report on Condition of Woman and Child Wage Earners in the United States* (19 vols., Washington, 1910–13), V, 62.

[22] *Ibid.*, XVIII, 35–36.

[23] Carl Sandburg, "Anna Imroth," *Chicago Poems* (New York, 1916), p. 33. *In The Nine-Tenths* (New York, 1911) James Oppenheimer attempted a fictionized treatment of the Triangle disaster. The earlier waist makers' strike figures prominently in Reginald Wright Kauffman, *The House of Bondage* (New York, 1910).

[24] Brandeis, "Labor Legislation," p. 478; and Beyer, *History of Labor Legislation for Women*, p. 7.

[25] State of New York, *Second Report of the Factory Investigating Commission* (2 vols., Albany, 1913), I, 193–212.

[26] *People* v. *Charles Schweinler Press*, 214 New York 395 (1915). See also Goldmark, *Impatient Crusader*, pp. 165–66; and Brandeis, "Labor Hour Legislation," p. 480.

[27] Mary Van Kleeck, *Artificial Flower Makers*, pp. 72–73.

[28] John A. Ryan, *A Living Wage. Its Ethical and Economic Aspects* (New York, 1906), pp. 301 *et seq.* See also Ryan's essays "The Standard of Living and the Problem of Dependency," *Proceedings* of the National Conference of Charities and Correction, 1907, p. 347, and "Programme of Social Reform by Legislation," *Catholic World*, LXXXIX (1909), 433–44, 608–14. Ryan proposed a legal minimum wage for men as well as women.

[29] Earlier experiments with minimum-wage legislation in Australia and New Zealand had not gone unnoticed in the United States, but the action of the British government aroused more widespread and serious attention. See, for example, articles by Henry R. Seager and Matthew B. Hammond in *The Annals*, XLVIII (1913), 3–12 and 22–36.

[30] Goldmark, *Impatient Crusader*, pp. 134–39; and Beyer, *History of Labor Legislation for Women*, pp. 10–11.

[31] George Kibbe Turner, "The Daughters of the Poor," *McClure's Magazine*, XXXIV (1909–10), 45–61. See also Louis Filler, *Crusaders for American Liberalism* (Yellow Springs, Ohio, 1950), pp. 285–95.

[32] Butler, *Women and the Trades*, pp. 348–49.

[33] Robert W. Bruère, "The Meaning of the Minimum Wage," *Harper's Monthly Magazine*, CXXXII (1915–16), 276 and 282.

[34] Goldmark, *Impatient Crusader*, p. 138; and Brandeis, "Labor Legislation," pp. 506–7 and 513–15.

[35] Brandeis, "Labor Legislation," pp. 508–17.

[36] *Stettler* v. *O'Hara*, 243 U.S. 629 (1917). For the minimum-wage brief see Louis D. Brandeis and Josephine Goldmark, *Brief for De-*

fendants in Error, Supreme Court of the United States, October Term, 1914, Nos. 507 and 508 *Frank C. Stettler* v. *Edwin V. O'Hara et al.*, and *Elmira Simpson* v. *Edwin V. O'Hara et al.*, pp. 66–397. For comment on the case see Goldmark, *Impatient Crusader*, pp. 167–72, and Mason, *Brandeis. A Free Man's Life*, pp. 252–53.

[37] Brandeis, "Labor Legislation," p. 521.

[38] Walter Lippmann, "The Campaign Against Sweating," *The New Republic*, II (No. 21: March 27, 1915), 8.

[39] *Adkins* v. *Children's Hospital*, 261 U. S. 525 (1923).

[40] For interesting comment on the Adkins case see Goldmark, *Impatient Crusader*, pp. 172–74. Frankfurter's approach is expressed in his article "Hours of Labor and Realism in Constitutional Law," *Harvard Law Review* XXIX (1916), 353–73.

CHAPTER 14

The Common Welfare

[1] For interesting comment on Gompers' philosophy and program see John A. Fitch, "Samuel Gompers and the Labor Movement," *The Survey*, LXXXVI (1950), 289–92.

[2] On division of opinion within the A.F.L. on hour laws see *ibid.*, p. 291; and Elizabeth Brandeis, "Labor Legislation" in John R. Commons *et al.*, *History of Labor in the United States* (4 vols., New York, 1918–35), III, 555.

[3] This was pointed out by W. Jett Lauck in "The Underlying Causes of Industrial Unrest," *Locomotive Engineers Journal*, XLIX (1915), 1179–81.

[4] See, for example, the remarks of Joseph Tuckerman cited in Daniel T. McColgan, *Joseph Tuckerman, Pioneer in American Social Work* (Washington, 1940), pp. 166–67.

[5] Baer's views are stated in a letter printed in Mark Sullivan, *Our Times. The United States, 1900–1925* (6 vols., New York, 1926–35), II, 425.

[6] Raymond Robins, "The One Main Thing," *Proceedings* of the National Conference of Charities and Correction, 1907, p. 326.

[7] *Proceedings* of the Conference on the Care of Dependent Children (Washington, 1909), p. 77.

[8] John A. Fitch, *The Steel Workers* (New York, 1910), pp. 152–65.

[9] *Ibid.*, p. 5.

[10] *Ibid.*, p. 206.

[11] *Ibid.*, p. 220.

[12] *Ibid.*, p. 214.

[13] *Ibid.*, p. vi.

[14] Frank J. Bruno, *Trends in Social Work as Reflected in the Proceedings of the National Conference of Social Work, 1874–1946* (New York, 1948), pp. 157–61.

[15] Lee K. Frankel and Miles M. Dawson, *Workingmen's Insurance in Europe* (New York, 1910); and *Twenty-Fourth Annual Report of the Commissioner of Labor, 1909. Workingmen's Insurance and Compensation Systems in Europe* (2 vols., Washington, 1911).

[16] Henry R. Seager, *Social Insurance. A Program of Social Reform* (New York, 1910).

[17] Louis D. Brandeis, "Workingmen's

Insurance–The Road to Social Efficiency," *Proceedings* of the National Conference of Charities and Correction, 1911, pp. 156–62; see also Josephine Goldmark, *Impatient Crusader, Florence Kelley's Life Story* (Urbana, Ill., 1953), pp. 133–34.

18 Owen R. Lovejoy, chairman, "Report of the Committee on Standards of Living and Labor," *Proceedings* of the National Conference of Charities and Correction, 1912, pp. 376–94.

19 Jane Addams, *The Second Twenty Years at Hull House, September 1909 to September 1929* (New York, 1930), p. 27; and Bruno, *Trends in Social Work,* pp. 163 and 221–23.

20 E. H. Downey, *Workmen's Compensation* (New York, 1924), pp. 143–44; and Harry Weiss, "Employers' Liability and Workmen's Compensation" in Commons *et al.*, *History of Labor in the United States,* III, 565–67.

21 This movement is traced in Weiss, "Employers' Liability and Workmen's Compensation," pp. 567–69.

22 Downey, *Workmen's Compensation,* p. 145.

23 For typical popular indictments of the employers' liability system see Arthur B. Reeve, "Our Industrial Juggernaut," *Everybody's Magazine,* XVI (1907), 147–52; and William Hard, *Injured in the Course of Duty* (New York, 1910).

24 Willard C. Fisher, "American Experience with Workmen's Compensation" in John R. Commons, ed., *Trade Unionism and Labor Problems* (second series, Boston, 1921), p. 33. See also Frederick L. Hoffman, *Industrial Accidents* (Washington, 1908), p. 417.

25 Frederick L. Hoffman, *Industrial Accident Statistics* (Washington, 1915), p. 6. For a somewhat higher estimate see I. M. Rubinow, *Social Insurance* (New York, 1913), pp. 54–55.

26 Hoffman, *Industrial Accidents,* p. 458.

27 Ellery Sedgwick, "The Land of Disasters," *Leslie's Magazine,* LVIII (1904), 566.

28 The quotation is from Reeve, "Our Industrial Juggernaut," p. 157.

29 Rubinow, *Social Insurance,* p. 61.

30 Hard, "Introduction" to *Injured in the Course of Duty,* pages not numbered.

31 Miss Eastman's study covered 526 fatal accidents occurring between July 1, 1906, and June 30, 1907; and 509 nonfatal accidents occurring in three months of 1907.

32 Crystal Eastman, *Work Accidents and the Law* (New York, 1910), p. 165. For other discussions of the causes of industrial accident, stressing speed and fatigue as important factors, see Fitch, *The Steel Workers,* p. 67; and Rubinow, *Social Insurance,* pp. 77–83.

33 Eastman, *Work Accidents and the Law,* p. 128.

34 *Ibid.*, p. 220.

35 *Ibid.*, pp. 207–20, particularly pp. 207–9; and Weiss, "Employers' Liability and Workmen's Compensation," pp. 572–73.

36 Downey, *Workmen's Compensation,* p. 7.

37 Rubinow, *Social Insurance,* p. 55.

38 Eastman, *Work Accidents and the Law,* p. 216.

39 Weiss, "Employers' Liability and Workmen's Compensation," p. 575.

40 Rubinow, *Social Insurance,* pp. 161–62.

41 Weiss, "Employers' Liability and Workmen's Compensation," p. 576. Fisher, "American Experience with Workmen's Compensation," p. 20, reported that as of 1920 only the railway unions continued to oppose the compensation principle, appar-

ently because they felt the awards were too low.

42 Downey, *Workmen's Compensation*, pp. 2–3.

43 Fisher, "American Experience with Workmen's Compensation," p. 33.

44 Downey, *Workmen's Compensation*, p. 148.

45 *Ibid.*, pp. 146–47; Weiss, "Employers' Liability and Workmen's Compensation," p. 594; and Fisher, "American Experience with Workmen's Compensation," p. 43.

46 The best study of the fight against occupational diseases is Alice Hamilton, *Exploring the Dangerous Trades* (Boston, 1943).

47 Downey, *Workmen's Compensation*, pp. 153–54.

48 Rubinow, *Social Insurance*, pp. 167–68.

49 *Ibid.*, p. 28.

50 Theodore Parker, *Sermon on the Perishing Classes in Boston* (Boston, 1846), p. 10.

51 Seager, *Social Insurance*, pp. 15–17.

52 I. M. Rubinow, *The Quest for Security* (New York, 1934), p. 207 *et seq.*

CONCLUSION

The Price of Reform

1 *The New York Times*, October 23, 1928.

2 See, for example, Daisy Lee Worthington Worcester, "The Standard of Living," *Proceedings* of the National Conference of Social Work, 1929, pp. 337–53.

3 Richard Hofstadter, *The Age of Reform. From Bryan to F.D.R.* (New York, 1955), pp. 301–3.

4 Joanna C. Colcord, "Social Work and the First Federal Relief Programs," *Proceedings* of the National Conference of Social Work, 1943, pp. 382–94.

5 Harry L. Hopkins, "The Developing National Program of Relief," *Proceedings* of the National Conference of Social Work, 1933, p. 67.

6 Samuel I. Rosenman, comp., *The Public Papers and Addresses of Franklin D. Roosevelt* (13 vols., New York, 1938–50), IV, 19–20.

7 Paul H. Douglas, *Social Security in the United States* (New York and London, 1936), p. 82. For an interesting defense of one of the more radical proposals for unemployment insurance that was before Congress at the same time as the Social Security bill see Mary Van Kleeck, "The Workers' Bill for Unemployment," *The New Republic*, LXXXI (1934–5), 121–24.

8 Frank J. Bruno, *Trends in Social Work* (New York, 1948), p. 309.

9 Rosenman, *The Public Papers and Addresses of Franklin D. Roosevelt*, VI, 4–5. On Roosevelt as an "apostle of abundance" see David M. Potter, *People of Plenty. Economic Abundance and the American Character* (Chicago, 1954), p. 120.

Bibliography

Aaron, Daniel. *Men of Good Hope. A Story of American Progressives*. New York: Oxford University Press, 1951.

Abbott, Edith. *Historical Aspects of the Immigration Problem. Select Documents*. Chicago: The University of Chicago Press, 1926.

——. *Public Assistance*. Chicago: The University of Chicago Press, 1940.

——. *Some American Pioneers in Social Welfare. Select Documents*. Chicago: The University of Chicago Press, 1937.

——. Sophonisba P. Breckinridge, *et al. The Tenements of Chicago, 1908–1935*. Chicago: The University of Chicago Press, 1936.

Abbott, Grace. *The Child and the State*. 2 vols. Chicago: The University of Chicago Press, 1938.

——. "Ten Years' Work for Children," *The North American Review*, CCXVIII (1923), 189–200.

Abbott, Lyman. "The Personal Problem of Charity," *The Forum*, XVI (1893–94), 663–69.

——. *Reminiscences*. Boston and New York: Houghton Mifflin Company, 1915.

Abell, Aaron Ignatius. *The Urban Impact on American Protestantism, 1865–1900*. Cambridge: Harvard University Press, 1943.

Adams, Herbert B. "Notes on the Literature of Charities," *Johns Hopkins University Studies in Historical and Political Science*, V (1887), 283–324.

Adams, Thomas Sewall, and Helen L. Sumner. *Labor Problems*. New York: The Macmillan Company, 1905.

Addams, Jane. "Child Labor and Pauperism," *Proceedings* of the National Conference of Charities and Correction, 1903, pp. 114–21.

——. *The Second Twenty Years at Hull House. September 1909 to September 1929*. New York: The Macmillan Company, 1930.

——. "Social Settlements," *Proceedings* of the National Conference of Charities and Correction, 1897, pp. 338–46.

——, *et al. Philanthropy and Social Progress*. New York: Thomas Y. Crowell and Company, 1893.

Ade, George. *Stories of the Streets and of the Town from the Chicago Record, 1893–1900.* Chicago: The Caxton Club, 1941.

Adler, Felix. *The Attitude of Society Toward the Child as an Index of Civilization.* New York: National Child Labor Committee, 1907.

———. *An Ethical Philosophy of Life Presented in Its Main Outlines.* New York: D. Appleton and Company, 1929.

Alcott, Louisa M. *Work: A Story of Experience.* Boston: Roberts Brothers, 1889.

Alger, George W., *et al.* "Industrial Accidents and Their Social Cost," *Charities and the Commons,* XVII (1906–7), 791–844.

Allen, William H. *Efficient Democracy.* New York: Dodd, Mead and Company, 1907.

Almy, Frederic. "The Problem of Charity, from Another Point of View," *Charities Review,* IV (1894–95), 169–80.

Andrews, E. Benjamin. "The Social Plaint," *The New World,* I (1892), 201–16.

Anthracite Coal Strike Commission. *Report to the President on the Anthracite Coal Strike of May–October, 1902.* Washington: Government Printing Office, 1903.

Arnavon, Cyrille. "Theodore Dreiser and Painting," *American Literature,* XVII (May, 1945), 113–26.

Asbury, Herbert. *The Gangs of New York, An Informal History of the Underworld.* New York: Alfred A. Knopf, 1927.

Atkinson, Edward. "The Problem of Poverty," *The Forum,* VII (1889), 609–22.

Bacon, Albion Fellows. *Beauty for Ashes.* New York: Dodd, Mead and Company, 1914.

Baker, Ray Stannard. *American Chronicle.* New York: Charles Scribner's Sons, 1945.

Ball, Wilma I. "Street Trading in Ohio," *The American Child,* I (1919–20), 123–29.

Barker, Charles Albro. *Henry George.* New York: Oxford University Press, 1955.

Barnard, William F. *Forty Years at the Five Points. A Sketch of the Five Points House of Industry.* New York: Five Points House of Industry, 1893.

Barrell, Charles Wisner. "The Real Drama of the Slums, as Told in John Sloan's Etchings," *The Craftsman,* XV (1909), 559–64.

———. "Robert Henri–'Revolutionary,'" *The Independent,* LXIV (1908), 1427–32.

Baur, John I. H. *Revolution and Tradition in Modern American Art.* Cambridge: Harvard University Press, 1951.

Baury, Louis. "The Message of Bohemia," *The Bookman*, XXXIV (1911), 256–66.

———. "The Message of Proletaire," *The Bookman*, XXXIV (1911), 399–413.

Bellamy, Edward. *Looking Backward, 2000–1887*. Memorial edition. Boston and New York: Houghton Mifflin Company, 1898.

Bemis, Edward W. "Mine Labor in the Hocking Valley," *Publications* of the American Economic Association, III (1888–89), 177–92.

Bennett, Helen Christine. *American Women in Civic Work*. New York: Dodd, Mead and Company, 1915.

Berryman, John. *Stephen Crane*. New York: William Sloane Associates, 1950.

Betts, Lillian W. *The Leaven in a Great City*. New York: Dodd, Mead and Company, 1903.

———. "Some Tenement-House Evils," *The Century*, XLV (1892–93), 314–16.

———. "The Tenement House Exhibit," *The Outlook*, LXIV (1900), 589–92.

———. "Tenement House Life," *The Christian Union*, XLVI (1892), 68–70.

Beveridge, Albert J. *The Meaning of the Times and Other Speeches*. Indianapolis: The Bobbs-Merrill Company, 1908.

Beyer, Clara M. *History of Labor Legislation for Women in Three States*. Washington: Government Printing Office, 1929.

"Birmingham. Smelting Iron Ore and Civics," *The Survey*, XXVII (1911–12), 1451–1556.

Bliss, William D. P., ed. *The Encyclopedia of Social Reforms*. New York and London: Funk and Wagnalls Company, 1898.

———. *The New Encyclopedia of Social Reform*. New York and London: Funk and Wagnalls Company, 1910.

Bogen, Boris D. *Jewish Philanthropy. An Exposition of Principles and Methods of Jewish Social Service in the United States*. New York: The Macmillan Company, 1917.

Bolton, Sarah K. *Lives of Poor Boys Who Became Famous*. New York: Thomas Y. Crowell and Company, 1885.

———. "Poverty and Riches," *The Chautauquan*, XXVII (1898), 256.

Booth, William. *In Darkest England and the Way Out*. London: International Headquarters of the Salvation Army, 1890.

Bosworth, Louise M. *The Living Wage of Women Workers. A Study of Incomes and Expenditures of 450 Women Workers in the City of Boston*. New York: Longmans, Green and Company, 1911.

Boucicault, Dion. *The Poor of New York.* New York: Samuel French, 1857.

Brace, Charles Loring. *The Dangerous Classes of New York and Twenty Years' Work Among Them.* New York: Wynkoop and Hallenbeck, 1872.

Brackett, Jeffrey Richardson. *Supervision and Education in Charity.* New York: The Macmillan Company, 1903.

Brandeis, Elizabeth. "Labor Legislation," in John R. Commons, *et al. History of Labor in the United States.* 4 vols. New York: The Macmillan Company, 1918–35, III, 399–697.

Brandeis, Louis D. "Workingmen's Insurance—The Road to Social Efficiency," *Proceedings* of the National Conference of Charities and Correction, 1911, pp. 156–62.

———, and Josephine Goldmark. *Brief for Defendants in Error: Stetler* v. *O'Hara et al.* and *Simpson* v. *O'Hara et al.* Washington: Supreme Court of the United States, 1914.

Brandt, Lilian. "The Causes of Poverty," *The Political Science Quarterly,* XXIII (1908), 637–51.

———. *Growth and Development of AICP and COS (A Preliminary and Exploratory Review).* New York: Community Service Society of New York, 1942.

Breckinridge, Sophonisba P., ed. *Public Welfare Administration in the United States. Select Documents.* Chicago: The University of Chicago Press, 1938.

Brooks, John Graham. *The Social Unrest: Studies in Labor and Socialist Movements.* New York: The Macmillan Company, 1903.

Brooks, Van Wyck. *The Confident Years: 1885–1915.* New York: E. P. Dutton and Company, 1952.

———. *John Sloan: A Painter's Life.* New York: E. P. Dutton and Company, 1955.

———. *The Times of Melville and Whitman.* New York: E. P. Dutton and Company, 1947.

Brown, Edwin A. *Broke.* Chicago: Browne and Howell Company, 1913.

Brown, James. *The History of Public Assistance in Chicago, 1833 to 1893.* Chicago: The University of Chicago Press, 1941.

Brown, Josephine C. *Public Relief, 1929–1939.* New York: Henry Holt and Company, 1940.

Browne, Henry J. *The Catholic Church and the Knights of Labor.* Washington: The Catholic University of America Press, 1949.

Bruère, Robert W. "The Conquest of Poverty. A Socialist Solution of the Problem," *Metropolitan Magazine*, XXXIII (1909–10), 651–60.

——. "The Good Samaritan, Incorporated," *Harper's Monthly Magazine*, CXX (1909–10), 833–38.

——. "The Meaning of the Minimum Wage," *Harper's Monthly Magazine*, CXXXII (1915–16), 276–82.

Bruno, Frank J. *Trends in Social Work as Reflected in the Proceedings of the National Conference of Social Work, 1874–1946*. New York: Columbia University Press, 1948.

Bryant, William Cullen. *The Song of the Sower*. New York: D. Appleton and Company, 1871.

Bryce, James. *The American Commonwealth*. 2 vols. London and New York: Macmillan and Co., 1888.

Buel, J. W. *Metropolitan Life Unveiled; or the Mysteries and Miseries of America's Great Cities*. St. Louis: Historical Publishing Company, 1882.

Bunner, H. C. "A. B. Frost," *Harper's Magazine*, LXXXV (1892), 699–706.

——. *Airs from Arcady and Elsewhere*. New York: Charles Scribner's Sons, 1884.

——. *The Stories of H. C. Bunner, First Series*. New York: Charles Scribner's Sons, 1916.

——. *The Stories of H. C. Bunner. Short Sixes and the Suburban Sage*. New York: Charles Scribner's Sons, 1919.

Buntline, Ned [E.Z.C. Judson]. *The Mysteries and Miseries of New York*. New York: Berford and Company, 1848.

Butler, Elizabeth Beardsley. *Saleswomen in Mercantile Stores*. New York: Russell Sage Foundation, 1912.

——. *Women and the Trades*. New York: Charities Publication Committee, 1910.

Byington, Margaret F. *Homestead. The Households of a Mill Town*. New York: Charities Publication Committee, 1910.

Caffin, Charles H. *Art for Life's Sake*. New York: The Prang Company, 1913.

——. "Rumpus in a Hen-House," *Camera Work*, No. 22 (April, 1908), pp. 42–43.

Cahan, Abraham. "A Ghetto Wedding," *The Atlantic Monthly*, LXXXI (1898), 265–73.

——. *The Rise of David Levinsky*. New York and London: Harper and Brothers, 1917.

Calkins, Raymond. *Substitutes for the Saloon.* Boston and New York: Houghton Mifflin Company, 1901.

Campbell, Helen. "Certain Convictions as to Poverty," *The Arena,* I (1889–90), 101–13.

———. *Prisoners of Poverty. Women Wage-Earners, Their Trades and Their Lives.* Boston: Roberts Brothers, 1887.

———. "White Child Slavery," *The Arena,* I (1889–90), 589–91.

———. *Women Wage-Earners. Their Past, Their Present, and Their Future.* Boston: Roberts Brothers, 1893.

———. "The Working-Women of To-day," *The Arena,* IV (1891), 329–39.

———, *et al. Darkness and Daylight: or Lights and Shadows of New York Life. A Woman's Narrative.* Hartford: A. D. Worthington and Company, 1891.

Capes, W. P. *The Social Doctor.* New York: New York A.I.C.P., 1913.

Carey, Alice. "The Poor," *The Herald of Truth,* I (1847), 213–14.

Cargill, Oscar. *Intellectual America. Ideas on the March.* New York: The Macmillan Company, 1941.

Carnegie, Andrew. "The Advantages of Poverty," *Nineteenth Century Magazine,* XXIX (1891), 370–71.

———. "Wealth," *The North American Review,* CXLVIII (1889), 653–64.

Cassady, Edward E. "Muckraking in the Gilded Age," *American Literature,* XIII (1941), 134–41.

Channing, William E. *The Ministry for the Poor.* Boston: Russell, Odiorne, and Metcalf, 1835.

———. *The Works of William E. Channing, D.D.* Boston: American Unitarian Association, 1889.

Chapin, Robert Coit. *The Standard of Living Among Workingmen's Families in New York City.* New York: Charities Publication Committee, 1909.

Charvat, William. "American Romanticism and the Depression of 1837," *Science and Society,* II (1937), 67–82.

"The City in Modern Life," *The Atlantic Monthly,* LXXXV (1895), 552–56.

Clopper, Edward N. *Child Labor in City Streets.* New York: The Macmillan Company, 1913.

———. *Child Labor in Indiana.* New York: National Child Labor Committee, 1909.

——. *Child Labor in West Virginia.* New York: National Child Labor Committee, 1908.

Cocks, Orrin G. "The Scope and Value of the Local Surveys of the Men and Religion Movement," *Proceedings* of the Academy of Political Science in the City of New York, 1911–12, pp. 537–44.

Coggeshall, William T. "The Late George Lippard," *Genius of the West,* II (1854), 83–86.

Cohen, Mary M. "Hebrew Charities," *Journal of Social Science,* XIX (1884), 168–76.

Colcord, Joanna C. "Social Work and the First Federal Relief Programs," *Proceedings* of the National Conference of Social Work, 1943, pp. 382–94.

Commager, Henry Steele. *The American Mind.* New Haven: Yale University Press, 1950.

Commons, John R., *et al. History of Labor in the United States.* 4 vols. New York: The Macmillan Company, 1918–35.

——. *Myself.* New York: The Macmillan Company, 1934.

——. *Social Reform and the Church.* New York: Thomas Y. Crowell and Company, 1894.

——, ed. *Trade Unionism and Labor Problems.* Second series. Boston: Ginn and Company, 1921.

Community Service Society of New York. *Frontiers in Human Welfare. The Story of a Hundred Years of Service to the Community of New York, 1848–1948.* New York: Community Service Society of New York, 1948.

"Condition of the Negro in Various Cities," *Bulletin* of the Department of Labor, II (1897), 257–369.

Corbin, John. "The Twentieth Century City," *Scribner's Magazine,* XXXIII (1903), 259–72.

Cournos, John. "Three Painters of the New York School," *International Studio,* LVI (1915), 239–46.

Cowley, Malcolm. *Exile's Return. A Literary Odyssey of the 1920's.* New York: The Viking Press, 1951.

Crafts, Wilbur F. "The New Charity and the Newest," *The Charities Review,* V (1895–96), 19–24.

Craig, Oscar. "The Prevention of Pauperism," *Scribner's Magazine,* XIV (1893), 121–28.

Crane, Stephen. *Maggie, a Girl of the Streets.* New York: Newland Press, n.d.

——. *The Third Violet.* New York: D. Appleton and Company, 1897.

"Stephen Crane," *The Bookman*, I (1895), 229–30.

Crooker, Joseph Henry. *Problems in American Society*. Boston: George H. Ellis, 1889.

Crosby, Ernest. "Wall Street and 'Graft,'" *Cosmopolitan Magazine*, XLII (1907), 439–40.

Cummings, A. I. *The Factory Girl or Gardez la Coeur* [*sic.*], Lowell, Mass.: J. E. Short and Company, 1847.

Cummins, Maria S. *The Lamplighter*. Boston and New York: Houghton Mifflin Company, 1888.

Curti, Merle. *The Growth of American Thought*. New York: Harper and Brothers, 1943.

Cuyler, T. L. "The Five Points House of Industry," *Harper's Weekly*, XXIV (1880), 27.

Daly, Augustin, Edward Harrigan, *et al.* "American Playwrights on the American Drama," *Harper's Weekly*, XXXIII (1889), 97–100.

Davidson, Elizabeth H. *Child Labor Legislation in the Southern Textile States*. Chapel Hill: The University of North Carolina Press, 1939.

Davidson, Marshall B. *Life in America*. 2 vols. Boston: Houghton Mifflin Company, 1951.

Davis, Rebecca Harding. "Life in the Iron-Mills," *The Atlantic Monthly*, VII (1861), 430–51.

———. "A Story of To-Day," *The Atlantic Monthly*, VIII (1861), 471 *et seq.*

Davis, Richard Harding. *From "Gallegher" to "the Deserter," The Best Stories of Richard Harding Davis*. Selected with an Introduction by Roger Burlingame. New York: Charles Scribner's Sons, 1927.

———. *Gallegher and Other Stories*. New York: Charles Scribner's Sons, 1904.

———. *Van Bibber and Others*. New York: Harper and Brothers, 1892.

Davis, R. T. "Pauperism in the City of New York," *Proceedings* of the Conference of Charities and Correction, 1874, pp. 18–28.

"The Day of Discontent," *Cosmopolitan Magazine*, XL (1906), 603–10.

De Forest, Robert W. "The Initial Activities of the Russell Sage Foundation," *The Survey*, XXII (1909), 68–75.

———., and Lawrence Veiller, eds. *The Tenement House Problem Including the Report of the New York State Tenement House Commission of 1900*. 2 vols. New York: The Macmillan Company, 1903.

Denison, T. S. *Louva, the Pauper*. A Drama in Five Acts. Sixth edition. Chicago: T. S. Denison, 1878.

Devine, Edward T. "The Dominant Note of the Modern Philanthropy," *Proceedings* of the National Conference of Charities and Correction, 1906, pp. 1–10.

——. *Misery and Its Causes.* New York: The Macmillan Company, 1909.

——. *Organized Charity and Industry.* New York: New York School of Philanthropy, 1915.

——. "Pittsburgh in Perspective," *The Survey*, XXVII (1911–12), 917–18.

——. "The Pittsburgh Survey," *Charities and the Commons*, XXI (1908–9), 1035–36.

——. *Social Forces.* New York: Survey Associates, Incorporated, 1914.

——. *When Social Work Was Young.* New York: The Macmillan Company, 1939.

Dewey, Davis R. "Irregularity of Employment," *Publications* of the American Economic Association, IX (1894), 525–39.

DeWitt, Benjamin Parke. *The Progressive Movement. A Nonpartisan, Comprehensive Discussion of Current Tendencies in American Politics.* New York: The Macmillan Company, 1915.

Dickens, Charles. *The Works of Charles Dickens.* National Library edition. 20 vols. New York: Bigelow Brown and Company, Inc., n.d.

Dorr, Rheta Childe. *A Woman of Fifty.* New York and London: Funk and Wagnalls Company, 1924.

——. *What Eight Million Women Want.* Boston: Small, Maynard and Company, 1910.

Douglas, Dorothy W. "American Minimum-Wage Laws at Work," *The American Economic Review*, IX (1919), 701–38.

Douglas, Paul H. *Real Wages in the United States, 1890–1926.* Boston and New York: Houghton Mifflin Company, 1930.

——. *Social Security in the United States. An Analysis and Appraisal of the Federal Social Security Act.* New York and London: Whittlesey House, 1936.

Dowling, George. *The Wreckers: A Social Study.* Philadelphia: J. B. Lippincott Company, 1886.

Downey, E. H. *Workmen's Compensation.* New York: The Macmillan Company, 1924.

Dreiser, Theodore. "The Camera Club of New York," *Ainslee's Magazine*, IV (1899), 324–35.

——. *The Color of a Great City.* New York: Boni and Liveright, 1923.

Dreiser, Theodore. "The Color of To-Day," *Harper's Weekly*, XLV (1901), 1272–73.

——. *The "Genius."* Garden City, New York: Garden City Publishing Company, n.d.

——. *A History of Myself. Newspaper Days.* New York: Horace Liveright, Incorporated, 1931.

——. *Jennie Gerhardt.* New York: Boni and Liveright, n.d.

——. *Sister Carrie.* New York: B. W. Dodge and Company, 1907.

——. *A Traveler at Forty.* New York: The Century Company, 1923.

——. *Twelve Men.* New York: Boni and Liveright, 1927.

Du Bois, Guy Pène. *Artists Say the Silliest Things.* New York: American Artists Group, Inc., and Duell, Sloan and Pearce, Inc., 1940.

——. "The Eight at the Brooklyn Museum," *Magazine of Art*, XXVI (1943), 293–97.

Du Bois, W. E. Burghardt. "The Negroes of Farmville, Virginia: A Social Study," *Bulletin* of the Department of Labor, III (1898), 1–38.

——, and Augustus Granville Dill. *The Negro American Artisan.* Atlanta: The Atlanta University Press, 1912.

Dugdale, Robert L. *The Jukes. A Study in Crime, Pauperism, Disease, and Heredity.* Fourth edition. New York and London: G. P. Putnam's Sons, 1910.

Dulles, Foster Rhea. *Labor in America, a History.* New York: Thomas Y. Crowell Company, 1949.

Eastman, Crystal. "Charles Haag. An Immigrant Sculptor of His Kind," *Charities and the Commons*, XVII (1906–7), 607–17.

——. *Work-Accidents and the Law.* New York: Charities Publication Committee, 1910.

Edgerton, Giles. "The Younger American Painters: Are They Creating a National Art?" *The Craftsman*, XIII (1908), 512–32.

Edwards, Albert [Arthur Bullard]. *A Man's World.* New York: The Macmillan Company, 1912.

Egbert, Donald Drew, and Stow Persons, eds. *Socialism and American Life.* 2 vols. Princeton: Princeton University Press, 1952.

Eggleston, Edward. *The Hoosier School-Master.* New York: Orange Judd and Company, 1871.

Elliot, S. H. *A Look at Home; or Life in the Poor-House of New England.* New York: H. Dexter and Company, 1860.

Elsing, William T. "Life in New York Tenement-Houses," *Scribner's Magazine*, XI (1892), 697–721.

Ely, Richard T. "Pauperism in the United States," *The North American Review*, CLII (1891), 395–409.

———. *Problems of To-day. A Discussion of Protective Tariffs, Taxation and Monopolies.* Third edition. New York: Thomas Y. Crowell and Company, 1890.

Emerson, Ralph Waldo. *Journals.* 10 vols. Boston: Houghton Mifflin Company, 1909–14.

Ervine, St. John. *God's Soldier: General William Booth.* 2 vols. New York: The Macmillan Company, 1935.

"Everett Shinn's Paintings of Labor in the New City Hall of Trenton, N. J.," *The Craftsman*, XXI (1911–12), 378–85.

Faulkner, Harold U. *The Decline of Laissez Faire, 1897–1917.* New York: Rinehart and Company, Inc., 1951.

———. *The Quest for Social Justice, 1898–1914.* New York: The Macmillan Company, 1931.

Feder, Leah Hannah. *Unemployment Relief in Periods of Depression.* New York: Russell Sage Foundation, 1936.

Filler, Louis. *Crusaders for American Liberalism.* Yellow Springs, Ohio: The Antioch Press, 1950.

Fitch, John A. "The Human Side of Large Outputs. Steel and Steel Workers in Six American States," *The Survey*, XXVII (1911–12), 929–45, 1145–60, 1285–98, 1527–40, 1706–20; and XXVIII (1912), 17–27.

———. "Samuel Gompers and the Labor Movement," *The Survey*, LXXXVI (1950), 289–92.

———. *The Steel Workers.* New York: Charities Publication Committee, 1910.

Fite, Emerson David. *Social and Industrial Conditions in the North During the Civil War.* New York: The Macmillan Company, 1910.

Flower, B. O. *Civilization's Inferno; or, Studies in the Social Cellar.* Boston: Arena Publishing Company, 1893.

———. "The Vital Issue in the Present Battle for a Great American Art," *The Arena*, XXXIV (1905), 479–84.

Flynt, Josiah. "The American Tramp," *The Contemporary Review*, LX (1891), 253–61.

———. *My Life.* New York: The Outing Publishing Company, 1908.

———. *Tramping with Tramps. Studies and Sketches of Vagabond Life.* New York: The Century Company, 1901.

Folks, Homer. *The Care of Destitute, Neglected, and Delinquent Children.* New York: The Macmillan Company, 1902.

———. *Changes and Trends in Child Labor and Its Control.* New York: National Child Labor Committee, 1938.

Ford, James, *et al. Slums and Housing. With Special Reference to New York City. History. Conditions. Policy.* 2 vols. Cambridge: Harvard University Press, 1936.

Ford, James L. *Forty-odd Years in the Literary Shop.* New York: E. P. Dutton and Company, 1921.

——. *The Literary Shop and Other Tales.* New York: The Chelsea Company, 1894.

——. "Low Life in Modern Fiction," *Truth*, XII (1892), 12.

Ford, Paul Leicester. *The Honorable Peter Stirling and What People Thought of Him.* Seventh edition. New York: Henry Holt and Company, 1897.

"Foremost American Illustrators: Vital Significance of Their Work," *The Craftsman*, XVII (1909), 266–80.

Forman, S. E. "Standards of Living," *Proceedings* of the National Conference of Charities and Correction, 1906, pp. 342–49.

Foster, Charles I. "The Urban Missionary Movement, 1814–1837," *The Pennsylvania Magazine of History and Biography*, LXXV (1951), 47–65.

Frankel, Lee K. "Needy Families in Their Homes," *Proceedings* of the National Conference of Charities and Correction, 1906, pp. 325–34.

——. "The Relation Between Standards of Living and Standards of Compensation," *Proceedings* of the New York State Conference of Charities and Correction, 1906, pp. 22–31.

——, and Miles M. Dawson. *Workingmen's Insurance in Europe.* New York: Charities Publication Committee, 1910.

Franklin, Benjamin. "On the Price of Corn, and Management of the Poor," in Albert Henry Smyth, ed. *The Writings of Benjamin Franklin.* 10 vols. New York: The Macmillan Company, 1907.

Freeman, Joseph. *An American Testament. A Narrative of Rebels and Romantics.* New York: Farrar and Rinehart, Inc., 1936.

Freidel, Frank. *Franklin D. Roosevelt. The Apprenticeship.* Boston: Little, Brown and Company, 1952.

Friedman, Isaac Kahn. *The Autobiography of a Beggar.* Boston: Small, Maynard and Company, 1903.

——. *By Bread Alone.* New York: McClure, Phillips and Company, 1901.

——. *Poor People.* Boston and New York: Houghton Mifflin and Company, 1900.

Frohman, Louis H. "Everett Shinn, The Versatile," *International Studio*, LXXVIII (1923), 85–89.

Frothingham, Octavius B. "Is Poverty Increasing?," *The Arena*, I (1889–90), 115.

Fuller, Henry B. "Art in America," *The Bookman*, X (1899), 218–24.

"The Futility of American Art," *The Independent*, LXIV (1908), 266–68.

G., J. "Brooklyn Revives Memories of 'The Eight,'" *The Art Digest*, XVIII (December 1, 1943), 12.

Gabriel, Ralph Henry. *The Course of American Democratic Thought. An Intellectual History Since 1815*. New York: The Ronald Press Company, 1940.

Gardener, Helen H. "Thrown in with the City's Dead," *The Arena*, III (1890–91), 61–70.

Garland, Hamlin. *Crumbling Idols*. Chicago and Cambridge: Stone and Kimball, 1894.

——. "The Cry of the Age," *The Outlook*, LXII (1899), 37.

——. *Main-Travelled Roads*. Boston: Arena Publishing Company, 1891.

Geismar, Maxwell. *Rebels and Ancestors, The American Novel, 1890–1915*. Boston: Houghton Mifflin Company, 1953.

George, Henry. *Progress and Poverty*. Twenty-fifth anniversary edition. Garden City, New York: Doubleday, Page and Company, 1911.

Gibbons, James, Cardinal. *Our Christian Heritage*. Baltimore and New York: John Murphy Company, 1889.

——. "The Conquest of Poverty. What the Catholic Church Is Doing to Solve the Problem," *Metropolitan Magazine*, XXXIII (1909–10), 479–88.

——. "Wealth and Its Obligations," *North American Review*, CLII (1891), 385–94.

Gilder, Rosamond, ed. *Letters of Richard Watson Gilder*. Boston and New York: Houghton Mifflin Company, 1916.

Gillin, John Lewis. *Poverty and Dependency. Their Relief and Prevention*. New York: The Century Company, 1921.

Gladden, Washington. "Edward Eggleston," *Scribner's Monthly*, VI (1873), 561–64.

——. "The Problem of Poverty," *The Century*, XLV (1892–93), 245–56.

——. *Social Salvation*. Boston and New York: Houghton Mifflin Company, 1902.

Glenn, John M., Lilian Brandt and F. Emerson Andrews. *Russell Sage Foundation, 1907–1946*. 2 vols. New York: Russell Sage Foundation, 1947.

Goldman, Eric F. *Rendezvous with Destiny*. New York: Alfred A. Knopf, 1953.

Goldmark, Josephine. *Fatigue and Efficiency*. New York: Russell Sage Foundation, 1912.

——. *Impatient Crusader, Florence Kelley's Life Story*. Urbana, Illinois: University of Illinois Press, 1953.

——. "The Necessary Sequel of Child-Labor Laws," *The American Journal of Sociology*, XI (1906), 312–25.

Gompers, Samuel. "Organized Labor's Attitude Toward Child Labor," *The Annals*, XXVII (1906), 337–41.

Goodale, Frances A. *The Literature of Philanthropy*. New York: Harper and Brothers, 1893.

Goodrich, Lloyd. *Thomas Eakins. His Life and Work*. New York: Whitney Museum of American Art, 1933.

——. *Winslow Homer*. New York: The Macmillan Company, 1944.

—— and Rosalind Irvine. *John Sloan*. New York: Whitney Museum of American Art, 1952.

Gould, E. R. L. *The Housing of the Working People*. Washington: Government Printing Office, 1895.

Graffenried, Clare de. "Child Labor," *Publications* of the American Economic Association, V (1890), 195–271.

Greeley, Horace. *Recollections of a Busy Life*. New York: J. B. Ford and Company, 1868.

Greenslet, Ferris. *Thomas Bailey Aldrich*. Boston and New York: Houghton Mifflin Company, 1928.

Griscom, John H. *The Sanitary Condition of the Laboring Population of New York with Suggestions for Its Improvement*. New York: Harper and Brothers, 1845.

Gunton, George. "Poverty as a Character Builder," *Gunton's Magazine*, XXIV (1903), 206–9.

—— and Frank M. Life. "Is Poverty an Obstacle or an Opportunity?" *Gunton's Magazine*, XXIV (1903), 397–401.

Gurteen, S. Humphrey. "Beginning of Charity Organization in America," *Lend a Hand*, XIII (1894), 352–67.

Hamilton, Alice. *Exploring the Dangerous Trades. The Autobiography of Alice Hamilton, M.D.* Boston: Little Brown and Company, 1943.

Hammond, Matthew B. "The Minimum Wage in Great Britain and Australia," *The Annals*, XLVIII (1913), 22–36.

Hampton, Benjamin B. *A History of the Movies*. New York: Covici-Friede, 1931.

Handlin, Oscar. *The Uprooted. The Epic Story of the Great Migra-*

tions That Made the American People. Boston: Little Brown and Company, 1952.

Hapgood, Hutchins. *The Autobiography of a Thief*. New York: Fox, Duffield and Company, 1903.

——. "Four Poets of the Ghetto," *The Critic*, XXXVI (1900), 250–61.

——. *The Spirit of the Ghetto. Studies of the Jewish Quarter in New York*. New York and London: Funk and Wagnalls Company, 1902.

——. *Types from City Streets*. New York and London: Funk and Wagnalls Company, 1910.

Hard, William. "De Kid Wot Works at Night," *Everybody's Magazine*, XVIII (1908), 25–37.

——. *Injured in the Course of Duty*. New York: The Ridgway Company, 1910.

Harrigan, Edward, *et al. Harrigan, Hart and Dave Braham's Immortal Songs*. n.p., n.d.

Harrigan and Braham's Songs. New York and Chicago: Henry J. Wehman, n.d. [1893].

Harrison, Shelby M. *The Social Survey. The Idea Defined and Its Development Traced*. New York: Russell Sage Foundation, 1931.

Hartley, Isaac Smithson, ed. *Memorial of Robert Milham Hartley*. Utica, New York: 1882.

Hartley, Robert M. *An Historical, Scientific and Practical Essay on Milk, as an Article of Human Sustenance; with a Consideration of the Effects Consequent upon the Present Unnatural Methods of Producing It for the Supply of Large Cities*. New York: Jonathan Leavitt, 1842.

——. *Ninth Annual Report* of the New York A.I.C.P. New York, 1852.

——. *Seventh Annual Report* of the New York A.I.C.P. New York, 1850.

——. *Thirteenth Annual Report* of the New York A.I.C.P. New York, 1856.

Hartmann, Sadakichi. *A History of American Art*. Revised edition. 2 vols. New York: Tudor Publishing Company, 1934.

——. "Plea for the Picturesqueness of New York," *Camera Notes*, IV (1900), 91–97.

Henderson, Charles Richmond. *Modern Methods of Charity*. New York: The Macmillan Company, 1904.

——. *The Social Spirit in America*. Chicago: Scott, Foresman and Company, 1905.

Henri, Robert. *The Art Spirit.* Compiled by Margery Ryerson. Philadelphia and London: J. B. Lippincott Company, 1923.

———. "Progress in Our National Art Must Spring from the Development of Individuality of Ideas and Freedom of Expression," *The Craftsman,* XV (1908–9), 387–401.

Henry, O. [William Sydney Porter]. *The Four Million.* Garden City, New York: Doubleday, Page and Company, 1919.

———. *Waifs and Strays, Twelve Stories Together with a Representative Selection of Critical and Biographical Comment.* Garden City, New York: Doubleday, Page and Company, 1919.

Herne, James A. "Art for Truth's Sake in the Drama," *The Arena,* XVII (1896–97), 361–70.

Herron, George D. *The New Redemption.* New York: Thomas Y. Crowell Company, 1893.

Hill, John G. Fifty Years of Social Action on the Housing Front. (1948). Unpublished report in files of the Community Service Society of New York.

Hine, L. A. "The Rich, the Poor," *The Herald of Truth,* I (1847), 109–21.

Hine, Lewis W. "Charity on a Business Basis," *The World Today,* XIII (1907), 1254–60.

——— and Charles Edward Russell. "Unto the Least of These," *Everybody's Magazine,* XXI (1909), 75–87.

"Lewis W. Hine," *Survey Graphic,* XXIX (1940), 622.

Hobson, John A. *Problems of Poverty.* Seventh edition. London: Methuen and Company, 1909.

Hoffman, Frederick L. *Industrial Accidents.* Washington: Government Printing Office, 1908.

———. *Industrial Accident Statistics.* Washington: Government Printing Office, 1915.

Hofstadter, Richard. *The Age of Reform. From Bryan to F.D.R.* New York: Alfred A. Knopf, 1955.

———. *Social Darwinism in American Thought.* Philadelphia: University of Pennsylvania Press, 1944.

Hollander, Jacob H. *The Abolition of Poverty.* Boston: Houghton Mifflin Company, 1914.

Hopkins, Charles Howard. *History of the Y.M.C.A. in North America.* New York: Association Press, 1951.

———. *The Rise of the Social Gospel in American Protestantism, 1865–1915.* New Haven: Yale University Press, 1940.

Hopkins, Harry L. "The Developing National Program of Relief," *Proceedings* of the National Conference of Social Work, 1933, pp. 65–71.

Howells, William Dean. *A Hazard of New Fortunes*. 2 vols. New York: Harper and Brothers, 1890.

——. *Impressions and Experiences*. New York: Harper and Brothers, 1896.

——. *My Literary Passions*. New York: Harper and Brothers, 1895.

——. *The Rise of Silas Lapham*. Boston and New York: Houghton Mifflin Company, 1884.

——. "Society," *Harper's Monthly Magazine*, XC (1895), 630.

——. *A Traveller from Altruria*. New York: Harper and Brothers, 1894.

——. "The Worst of Being Poor," *Harper's Weekly*, XLVI (1902), 261.

Hull-House Maps and Papers. A Presentation of Nationalities and Wages in a Congested District of Chicago. New York: Thomas Y. Crowell and Company, 1895.

Hunter, Robert. "A Plea for the Investigation of the Conditions Affecting the Length of Trade Life," *The Annals*, XXVII (1906), 500–3.

——. *Poverty*. New York: The Macmillan Company, 1904.

——. "The Relation between Social Settlements and Charity Organization," *Journal of Political Economy*, XI (1902–3), 75–88.

——. *Tenement Conditions in Chicago. Report by the Investigating Committee of the City Homes Association*. Chicago: City Homes Association, 1901.

Illinois. Board of Public Charities. *Second Biennial Report*, 1872. Springfield: State Journal Steam Print., 1873.

"The Industrial Condition of the Negro in the North," *The Annals*, XXVII (1906), 541–609.

Irvine, Alexander. *From the Bottom Up*. New York: Doubleday, Page and Company, 1910.

Isham, Samuel. *The History of American Painting*. New edition with supplementary chapters by Royal Cortissoz. New York: The Macmillan Company, 1927.

Jacobs, Lewis. *The Rise of the American Film. A Critical History*. New York: Harcourt, Brace and Company, 1939.

Jewett, Sarah Orne. *The Best Stories of Sarah Orne Jewett*. Selected and arranged by Willa Cather. 2 vols. Boston and New York: Houghton Mifflin Company, 1925.

Johannsen, Albert. *The House of Beadle and Adams and Its Dime and Nickel Novels. The Story of a Vanished Literature*. 2 vols. Norman, Oklahoma: University of Oklahoma Press, 1950.

Johnson, Edgar. *Charles Dickens. His Tragedy and Triumph.* 2 vols. New York: Simon and Schuster, 1952.

Johnson, Elizabeth Sands. "Child Labor Legislation," in John R. Commons, *et al. History of Labor in the United States.* (4 vols. New York: The Macmillan Company, 1918–35), III, 403–56.

Jones, Mother. *Autobiography of Mother Jones.* Edited by Mary Field Parton. Chicago: Charles H. Kerr and Company, 1925.

Kahn, E. J., Jr. *Merry Partners; The Age and Stage of Harrigan and Hart.* New York: Random House, 1955.

Kauffman, Reginald Wright. *The House of Bondage.* New York: Grosset and Dunlap, 1910.

Keith-Lucas, Alan. "The Political Theory Implicit in Social Casework Theory," *The American Political Science Review,* XLVII (1953), 1076–91.

Keller, Helen. *Out of the Dark.* Garden City, New York: Doubleday, Page and Company, 1914.

Kelley, Florence. "Autobiographical Essays," *The Survey,* LVII (1926–27), 7–11, 557–61; LVIII (1927), 31–35, 271–74.

———. "A Boy Destroying Trade," *Charities,* XI (1903), 15–19.

———. "A Decade of Retrogression," *The Arena,* IV (1891), 365–72.

———. *The Federal Government and the Working Children.* New York: National Child Labor Committee, 1906.

———. "Labor Legislation and Philanthropy in Illinois," *The Charities Review,* X (1900–1), 285–91.

———. "Need of Uniformity in Labor Legislation," *Proceedings* of the Eighth Annual Convention of the International Association of Factory Inspectors of North America, 1894, pp. 21–27.

———. *Obstacles to the Enforcement of Child Labor Legislation.* New York: National Child Labor Committee, 1907.

———. *The Present Status of Minimum Wage Legislation.* New York: National Consumers' League, 1913.

———. *Some Ethical Gains Through Legislation.* New York: The Macmillan Company, 1905.

———. *Third Annual Report of the Factory Inspectors of Illinois.* Springfield, Illinois: Ed. F. Hartman, State Printer, 1896.

———. *Women in Industry. The Eight Hours Day and Rest at Night.* New York: National Consumers' League, 1916.

———. "The Working Child," *Proceedings* of the National Conference of Charities and Correction, 1896, pp. 161–65.

Kellogg, Charles D. "Charity Organization in the United States," *Proceedings* of the National Conference of Charities and Correction, 1893, pp. 52–93.

Kellogg, Paul Underwood. *The Pittsburgh Survey.* 6 vols. New York: Charities Publication Committee, 1909–14.

——. "The Pittsburgh Survey," *Charities and the Commons,* XXI (1908–9), 517–26.

——. "The Spread of the Survey Idea," *Proceedings* of the Academy of Political Science in the City of New York, 1911–12, pp. 475–91.

Kellor, Frances A. *Out of Work. A Study of Employment Agencies: Their Treatment of the Unemployed, and Their Influence upon Homes and Business.* New York and London: G. P. Putnam's Sons, 1905.

——. *Out of Work. A Study of Unemployment.* New York and London: G. P. Putnam's Sons, 1915.

Kelly, Myra. *Little Citizens. The Humors of School Life.* New York: McClure, Phillips and Company, 1905.

——. "A Soul Above Buttons," *McClure's Magazine,* XXVII (1906), 337–45.

Kendall, Edith. "The Conquest of Poverty. How the Protestant Churches Are Awakening to the Problem," *Metropolitan Magazine,* XXXIV (1910), 105–12.

Kennaday, Paul. "New York's Hundred Lodging-Houses," *Charities,* XIII (1905), 486–92.

Kenyon, Charles. *Kindling.* New York: Doubleday, Page and Company, 1914.

Kildare, Owen. *The Good of the Wicked, and the Party Sketches.* New York: The Baker and Taylor Company, 1904.

——. *My Mamie Rose. The Story of My Regeneration. An Autobiography.* New York: The Baker and Taylor Company, 1903.

——. *My Old Bailiwick.* New York: Grosset and Dunlap, 1906.

——. *The Wisdom of the Simple. A Tale of Lower New York.* New York: Fleming H. Revell Company, 1905.

King, Willford Isbell. *The Wealth and Income of the People of the United States.* New York: The Macmillan Company, 1917.

Kirkland, Joseph. "Among the Poor of Chicago," *Scribner's Magazine,* XII (1892), 3–27.

——. *Zury: the Meanest Man in Spring County. A Novel of Western Life.* Boston and New York: Houghton Mifflin Company, 1888.

Koren, John. *Economic Aspects of the Liquor Problem.* Boston and New York: Houghton Mifflin Company, 1899.

Kouwenhoven, John A. *Made in America. The Arts in Modern Civilization.* Garden City, New York: Doubleday and Company, 1948.

Kwiat, Joseph J. "Dreiser and the Graphic Artist," *American Quarterly,* III (1951), 127–41.

——. "Dreiser's The 'Genius' and Everett Shinn, The 'Ash Can'

Painter," *Publications* of the Modern Language Association of America, LXVII (1952), 15–31.

Laffan, W. Mackay. "The Material of American Landscape," *The American Art Review*, I (1880), 29–32.

Lanier, Sidney. *The Centennial Edition of the Works of Sidney Lanier.* 10 vols. Baltimore: The Johns Hopkins Press, 1945.

Larkin, Oliver W. *Art and Life in America.* New York: Rinehart and Company, 1949.

Lauck, W. Jett. "The Underlying Economic Causes of Industrial Unrest," *Locomotive Engineers Journal*, XLIX (1915), 1179–87.

Lawrence, Eugene. "The New Year–The Poor," *Harper's Weekly*, XXVIII (1884), 34–35.

The Lay Figure. "On the Cult of the Ugly," *The International Studio*, XXIV (1905), 374.

Lee, Harry, and William H. Matthews. *Little Adventures with John Barleycorn.* New York: New York A.I.C.P. [1916].

Lee, Joseph. *Constructive and Preventive Philanthropy.* New York: The Macmillan Company, 1906.

Lenroot, Katharine F. "The Opportunity before Us," *The Survey*, LXXXVII (1951), 521–24.

Lescohier, Don D. "Working Conditions," in John R. Commons, *et al. History of Labor in the United States.* (4 vols. New York: The Macmillan Company, 1918–35), III, 3–396.

Lewis, O. F. "The Conquest of Poverty. Some Things That Organized Philanthropy Is Trying to Do," *Metropolitan Magazine*, XXXIII (1909–10), 193–204.

Lindsay, Samuel McCune. "The Causes of Poverty," *Proceedings* of the National Conference of Charities and Correction, 1899, pp. 369–73.

Lindsay, Vachel. *Collected Poems.* New York: The Macmillan Company, 1927.

———. *General William Booth Enters into Heaven and Other Poems.* New York: The Macmillan Company, 1924.

Link, Arthur S. *American Epoch. A History of the United States Since the 1890's.* New York: Alfred A. Knopf, 1955.

———. *Woodrow Wilson and the Progressive Era, 1910–1917.* New York: Harper and Brothers, 1954.

Lippmann, Walter. "The Campaign Against Sweating," *The New Republic*, II (March 27, 1915), 1–8.

———. *Drift and Mastery. An Attempt to Diagnose the Current Unrest.* New York: Mitchell Kennerley, 1914.

———. *A Preface to Politics.* New York: Mitchell Kennerley, 1914.

Lloyd, Henry Demarest. "The Lords of Industry," *The North American Review*, CXXXVIII (1884), 535–52.

London Congregational Union. *The Bitter Cry of Outcast London. An Inquiry into the Condition of the Abject Poor.* Boston: Cupples, Upham and Company, 1883.

London, Jack. *The Iron Heel.* New York: The Macmillan Company, 1908.

———. *Martin Eden.* New York: The Macmillan Company, 1909.

———. *The People of the Abyss.* New York: Grosset and Dunlap, 1903.

———. *Revolution and Other Essays.* New York: The Macmillan Company, 1910.

Longfellow, Henry Wadsworth. *The Complete Poetical Works of Henry Wadsworth Longfellow.* Cambridge edition. Boston and New York: Houghton Mifflin Company, 1893.

Lovejoy, Owen R. "Report of the Committee on Standards of Living and Labor," *Proceedings* of the National Conference of Charities and Correction, 1912, pp. 376–94.

Lowell, James Russell. *The Complete Works of James Russell Lowell.* Cambridge edition. Boston and New York: Houghton Mifflin Company, 1917.

Lowell, Josephine Shaw. "Methods of Relief for the Unemployed," *The Forum*, XVI (1893–94), 655–62.

———. *Public Relief and Private Charity.* New York: G. P. Putnam's Sons, 1884.

———. "The True Aim of Charity Organization Societies," *The Forum*, XXI (1896), 494–500.

McColgan, Daniel T. *Joseph Tuckerman; Pioneer in American Social Work.* Washington: The Catholic University of America Press, 1940.

McCutcheon, John T. *Drawn from Memory.* Indianapolis: The Bobbs-Merrill Company, 1950.

McDougall, Walt. *This Is the Life!* New York: Alfred A. Knopf, 1926.

Mackaye, James. "Poverty: Its Causes and Cure," *The Independent*, LXII (1907), 123–33.

McIlwaine, Shields. *The Southern Poor-White from Lubberland to Tobacco Road.* Norman, Oklahoma: University of Oklahoma Press, 1939.

McKelway, A. J. *Child Labor in the Carolinas.* New York: National Child Labor Committee, 1909.

"The Man Who Gave Us the Word 'Graft,'" *The Literary Digest*, XXXIV (1907), 173.

Mann, Arthur. *Yankee Reformers in the Urban Age.* Cambridge: Harvard University Press, 1954.

Marchand, Ernest. *Frank Norris. A Study.* Stanford University, California: Stanford University Press, 1942.

Markham, Edwin. "The Hoe-Man in the Making," *Cosmopolitan Magazine,* XLI (1906), 480–87, 567–74.

———, Lindsey, Benjamin B., and Creel, George. *Children in Bondage.* New York: Hearst's International Library Company, 1914.

Marsh, Bessie, and Charles Edward Russell. "The Cry of the Slums," *Everybody's Magazine,* XVI (1907), 34–40.

Mason, Alpheus Thomas. *Brandeis, A Free Man's Life.* New York: The Viking Press, 1946.

Massachusetts. General Court. House of Representatives. *Report of the Homestead Commission.* Boston: 1913.

Massachusetts. General Court. House of Representatives. *Report of the Massachusetts Commission on Minimum Wage Boards.* Boston: 1912.

Matthews, James Brander. *These Many Years. Recollections of a New Yorker.* New York: Charles Scribner's Sons, 1917.

———. *Vignettes of Manhattan.* New York: Harper and Brothers, 1894.

Matthiessen, F. O. *Theodore Dreiser.* New York: William Sloane Associates, 1951.

Maurice, Arthur Bartlett. *New York in Fiction.* New York: Dodd, Mead and Company, 1901.

Mavor, James. "The Relation of Economic Study to Public and Private Charity," *The Annals,* IV (1893–94), 34–60.

May, Henry F. *Protestant Churches and Industrial America.* New York: Harper and Brothers, 1949.

Mellett, Lowell. "The Sequel to the Dagenhart Case," *The American Child,* VI (January, 1924), 3.

Mellquist, Jerome. *The Emergence of an American Art.* New York: Charles Scribner's Sons, 1942.

Melville, Herman. *The Complete Stories of Herman Melville.* Edited with an Introduction and Notes by Jay Leyda. New York: Random House, 1949.

———. *Redburn: His First Voyage. Being the Sailor-Boy Confessions and Reminiscences of the Son-of-a-Gentleman, in the Merchant Service.* New York: Harper and Brothers, 1850.

Metropolitan Museum of Art. *Life in America.* New York: Metropolitan Museum of Art, 1939.

Miles, Arthur Parker. *Federal Aid and Public Assistance in Illinois.* Chicago: The University of Chicago Press, 1941.

Millard, Bailey. "What Life Means to Me," *Cosmopolitan Magazine*, XLI (1906), 512–16.

Mitchell, John Ames. *The Silent War*. New York: Life Publishing Company, 1906.

Montgomery, Louise. *The American Girl in the Stockyards District*. Chicago: The University of Chicago Press, 1913.

Moody, William Vaughn. "The Brute," *The Atlantic Monthly*, LXXXVII (1901), 88–90.

———. "Gloucester Moors," *Scribner's Magazine*, XXVIII (1900), 727–28.

More, Louise Bolard. *Wage-Earners' Budgets. A Study of Standards and Cost of Living in New York City*. New York: Henry Holt and Company, 1907.

Morison, Elting E., ed. *The Letters of Theodore Roosevelt*. 8 vols. Cambridge: Harvard University Press, 1951–54.

Morris, Lloyd. *Not So Long Ago*. New York: Random House, 1949.

Moses, Montrose J., and John Mason Brown. *The American Theatre as Seen by Its Critics, 1752–1934*. New York: W. W. Norton and Company, 1934.

Mumford, Lewis. *The Culture of Cities*. New York: Harcourt Brace and Company, 1938.

Murphy, Edgar Gardner. *The Case Against Child Labor*. Montgomery: Executive Committee on Child Labor in Alabama (1902).

———. "Child Labor as a National Problem; with Special Reference to the Southern States," *Proceedings* of the National Conference of Charities and Correction, 1903, pp. 121–34.

Murrell, William. *A History of American Graphic Humor*. 2 vols. New York: The Whitney Museum of Modern Art (Vol. I), 1935; The Macmillan Company (Vol. II), 1938.

Myers, Jerome. *Artist in Manhattan*. New York: American Artists Group, Inc., 1940.

Nathan, Maud. *Once upon a Time and Today*. New York: G. P. Putnam's Sons, 1933.

———. *The Story of an Epoch-Making Movement*. Garden City, New York: Doubleday, Page and Company, 1926.

———. "Women Who Work and Women Who Spend," *The Annals*, XXVII (1906), 646–50.

Nearing, Scott. *Poverty and Riches, a Study of the Industrial Regime*. Philadelphia: The John C. Winston Company, 1916.

"The Negro in the Cities of the North," *Charities*, XV (1905–6), 1–96.

Nevins, Allan. *The Emergence of Modern America, 1865–1878.* New York: The Macmillan Company, 1927.

Newhall, Beaumont. "Lewis W. Hine," *Magazine of Art,* XXXI (1938), 636–37.

"New-Year's with the Poor," *Harper's Weekly,* XV (1871), 1–2.

New York. State Board of Charities. *Eighth Annual Report,* 1875. Albany: Weed, Parsons and Company, 1875.

New York. State Factory Investigating Commission. *Preliminary Report of the Factory Investigating Commission, 1912.* 3 vols. Albany: Argus Company, 1912.

——. *Second Report of the Factory Investigating Commission, 1913.* 2 vols. Albany: J. B. Lyon Company, 1913.

New York. State Tenement House Committee, 1894. *Report of the Tenement House Committee as Authorized by Chapter 479 of the Laws of 1894.* Albany: 1895.

New York Association for Improving the Condition of the Poor. *The Economist.* New York: 1847.

——. *Fighting Poverty. What the A.I.C.P. Does to Eliminate the Causes of Distress and to Prevent Their Recurrence.* New York: New York A.I.C.P., 1912.

——. *First Report of a Committee on the Sanitary Condition of the Laboring Classes in the City of New York, with Remedial Suggestions.* New York: John F. Trow, Printer, 1853.

——. *The Mistake.* New York: 1850.

——. *Shall Widows Be Pensioned?* New York: New York A.I.C.P., 1914.

"Next Door to Congress," *Charities and the Commons,* XV (1905–6), 739–41, 759–831.

Nichols, Francis H. "Children of the Coal Shadow," *McClure's Magazine,* XX (1902–3), 435–44.

Norris, Frank. *McTeague. A Story of San Francisco.* New York: Doubleday, Page and Company, 1903.

——. *The Octopus. A Story of California.* Garden City, New York: Doubleday, Page and Company, 1924.

——. *The Responsibilities of the Novelist and Other Literary Essays.* New York: Doubleday, Page and Company, 1903.

Odell, George Clinton Densmore. *Annals of the New York Stage.* 15 vols. New York: Columbia University Press, 1927–49.

O'Grady, John. *Catholic Charities in the United States. History and Problems.* Washington: National Conference of Catholic Charities, 1930.

Ohio. Board of State Charities. *Third Annual Report,* 1869. Columbus: Columbus Printing Company, 1870.

"The Old Rookeries of New York," *The Daily Graphic* (New York), June 19, 1873, p. 5.

Oldach, Dorothy M. *Eugene Higgins*. Brooklyn, New York: Globe Crayon Company, 1939.

Ovington, Mary White. *Half a Man, The Status of the Negro in New York*. New York: Longmans Green and Company, 1911.

——. "The Negro Home in New York," *Charities*, XV (1905–6), 25–30.

——. *The Walls Came Tumbling Down*. New York: Harcourt Brace and Company, 1947.

Owen, Frederick N. "The Story of the 'Big Flat,'" *Forty-third Annual Report* of the New York A.I.C.P., 1886, pp. 43–73.

Paine, Robert Treat. "Pauperism in Great Cities: Its Four Chief Causes," *Proceedings* of the International Congress of Charities, Corrections, and Philanthropy, 1893, I, 23–58.

Parker, Theodore. *Sermon on the Perishing Classes in Boston*. Boston: I. R. Butts, 1846.

Parmelee, Maurice. *Poverty and Social Progress*. New York: The Macmillan Company, 1920.

Parrington, Vernon Louis. *Main Currents in American Thought*. 3 vols. New York: Harcourt, Brace and Company, 1927–30.

Patten, Simon N. *The New Basis of Civilization*. New York: The Macmillan Company, 1907.

——. "The Principles of Economic Interference," *The Survey*, XXII (1909), 14–16.

Paul, Norman. "The Coffin That Kept Railroaders Alive," *Tracks*, XXXVI (August, 1951), 2–5.

Paulding, J. K. *Charles B. Stover. July 14, 1861–April 24, 1929. His Life and Personality*. New York: The International Press, 1938.

Peabody, Francis G. "How Should a City Care for Its Poor?," *The Forum*, XIV (1892–93), 474–91.

——. *Jesus Christ and the Social Question*. New York: The Macmillan Company, 1912.

——. "Unitarianism and Philanthropy," *The Charities Review*, V (1895–96), 25–32.

Penman, John Simpson. *Poverty: the Challenge to the Church*. Boston: The Pilgrim Press, 1915.

Perkins, Frances. *People at Work*. New York: The John Day Company, 1934.

——. *The Roosevelt I Knew*. New York: The Viking Press, 1946.

Persons, Stow, ed. *Evolutionary Thought in America*. New Haven: Yale University Press, 1950.

Pettengill, Lillian. *Toilers of the Home. The Record of a College Woman's Experience as a Domestic Servant.* New York: Doubleday, Page and Company, 1903.

Phelps, Elizabeth Stuart. *Chapters from a Life.* Boston and New York: Houghton Mifflin Company, 1897.

——. *The Silent Partner.* Boston: James R. Osgood and Company, 1871.

——. "The Tenth of January," *The Atlantic Monthly,* XXI (1868), 345–62.

Philadelphia Museum of Art. "Artists of the Philadelphia Press," *Philadelphia Museum Bulletin,* XLI (November, 1945), 1–32.

"A Photographer East of the Bowery," *Charities,* X (1903), 344–49.

Poole, Ernest. "The Book of Life," *Everybody's Magazine,* XXI (1909), 656–64.

——. *The Bridge. My Own Story.* New York: The Macmillan Company, 1940.

——. *The Harbor.* New York: The Macmillan Company, 1917.

——. "'The Lung Block,'" *Charities,* XI (1903), 193–99.

——. *The Plague in Its Stronghold.* New York: Charity Organization Society of the City of New York, 1903.

——. "The Song That Failed," *Charities,* XII (1904), 408.

——. *The Street. Its Child Workers.* New York: University Settlement Society [1903].

——. *Voice of the Street; a Story of Temptation.* New York: Barnes, 1906.

——. "Waifs of the Street," *McClure's Magazine,* XXI (1903), 40–48.

Potter, Clara Sidney. "Factory Conditions in New York," *The Christian Union,* XXXIX (1889), 566.

Potter, David M. *People of Plenty. Economic Abundance and the American Character.* Chicago: The University of Chicago Press, 1954.

"Poverty and Fiction," *Scribner's Magazine,* XXXIX (1906), 379–80.

"Private Life of the Gamin," *The Daily Graphic* (New York), March 11, 1873, p. 3.

"The Problem of Poverty," *The Outlook,* LXXIX (1905), 902–5.

Proceedings of the Conference on the Care of Dependent Children Held at Washington, D.C., January 25, 26, 1909. Washington: Government Printing Office, 1909.

Queen, Stuart Alfred. *Social Work in the Light of History.* Philadelphia: J. B. Lippincott Company, 1922.

Quinn, Arthur Hobson. *A History of the American Drama from the Beginning to the Civil War*. New York and London: Harper and Brothers, 1923.

———. *A History of the American Drama from the Civil War to the Present Day*. 2 vols. New York and London: Harper and Brothers, 1927.

———. *The Literature of the American People*. New York: Appleton-Century-Crofts, 1951.

"The Rag Pickers of New York," *The Daily Graphic* (New York), March 11, 1873, pp. 3–4.

Rainsford, W. S. *The Story of a Varied Life*. Garden City, New York: Doubleday, Page and Company, 1922.

———. "What Can We Do for the Poor?," *The Forum*, XI (1891), 115–26.

Ralph, Julian. *People We Pass. Stories of Life Among the Masses of New York City*. New York: Harper and Brothers, 1896.

Ramsaye, Terry. *A Million and One Nights. A History of the Motion Picture*. 2 vols. New York: Simon and Schuster, 1926.

Rauschenbusch, Walter. *Christianity and the Social Crisis*. New York: The Macmillan Company, 1907.

———. *Christianizing the Social Order*. New York: The Macmillan Company, 1912.

Read, Helen Appleton. *Robert Henri*. New York: Whitney Museum of American Art, 1931.

Reeve, Arthur B. "Our Industrial Juggernaut," *Everybody's Magazine*, XVI (1907), 147–52.

Report of Proceedings of the Thirty-fourth Annual Convention of the American Federation of Labor. Washington: The Law Reporter Printing Company, 1914.

Reynolds, Marcus T. "The Housing of the Poor in American Cities," *Publications* of the American Economic Association, VIII (1893), 131–262.

Rezneck, Samuel. "The Depression of 1819–1822, A Social History," *The American Historical Review*, XXXIX (1933–34), 28–47.

———. "The Social History of an American Depression, 1837–1843," *The American Historical Review*, XL (1934–35), 662–87.

Rice, Alice Hegan. "Cupid Goes Slumming," *The American Magazine*, LXIV (1907), 372–80.

———. *The Inky Way*. New York: D. Appleton-Century Company, 1940.

———. *Mrs. Wiggs of the Cabbage Patch*. New York: D. Appleton-Century Company, 1937.

Richardson, Dorothy. "The Difficulties and Dangers Confronting the Working Woman," *The Annals*, XXVII (1906), 624–26.

——. *The Long Day. The Story of a New York Working Girl as Told by Herself*. New York: The Century Company, 1906.

Richardson, James D., comp. *A Compilation of the Messages and Papers of the Presidents*. 11 vols. Bureau of National Literature and Art, 1910.

Richmond, Mary Ellen. *Friendly Visiting Among the Poor. A Handbook for Charity Workers*. New York: The Macmillan Company, 1899.

——. *Social Diagnosis*. New York: Russell Sage Foundation, 1917.

——. "What Is Charity Organization?," *The Charities Review*, IX (1899–1900), 490–500.

Riegel, Robert E. *America Moves West*. Revised edition. New York: Henry Holt and Company, 1947.

Riis, Jacob A. *The Children of the Poor*. New York: Charles Scribner's Sons, 1892.

——. "The Children of the Poor," *Scribner's Magazine*, XI (1892), 531–56.

——. *How the Other Half Lives*. New York: Charles Scribner's Sons, 1890.

——. *The Making of an American*. New York: The Macmillan Company, 1903.

——. "Special Needs of the Poor in New York," *The Forum*, XIV (1892–93), 492–502.

——. "The Tenement House Exhibition," *Harper's Weekly*, XLIV (1900), 104.

——. *A Ten Years' War. An Account of the Battle with the Slum in New York*. Boston and New York: Houghton Mifflin Company, 1900.

Roberts, Peter. *Anthracite Coal Communities*. New York: The Macmillan Company, 1904.

Robins, Raymond. "The One Main Thing," *Proceedings* of the National Conference of Charities and Correction, 1907, pp. 326–34.

Robinson, Solon. *Hot Corn: Life Scenes in New York Illustrated*. New York: DeWitt and Davenport, 1854.

Rodabaugh, James H., and Mary Jane Rodabaugh. *Nursing in Ohio. A History*. Columbus: The Ohio State Nurses' Association, 1951.

Rogers, W. A. *A World Worth While*. New York: Harper and Brothers, 1922.

Rollins, Alice W. "The New Uncle Tom's Cabin," *The Forum*, IV (1887–88), 220–27.

Roosevelt, Theodore. "Reform Through Social Work," *McClure's Magazine*, XVI (1900–1), 448–54.

Rosenfeld, Morris. "Poems by Morris Rosenfeld," translated by Rose Pastor Stokes and Helena Frank, *The Survey*, XXXII (1914), 266–68.

——. *Songs from the Ghetto*. Prose translation by Leo Wiener. Boston: Copeland and Day, 1898.

——. *Songs of Labor and Other Poems*. Translated from the Yiddish by Rose Pastor Stokes and Helena Frank. Boston: Richard G. Badger, 1914.

Rosenman, Samuel I., comp. *The Public Papers and Addresses of Franklin D. Roosevelt*. 13 vols. New York: Random House (Vols. I–V), 1938; The Macmillan Company (Vols. VI–IX), 1941; Harper and Brothers (Vols. X–XIII), 1950.

Rowell, George P., comp. *New York Charities Directory. A Descriptive Catalogue and Alphabetical Analysis of the Charitable and Beneficent Societies and Institutions of the City*. New York: Charity Organization Society of the City of New York, 1888.

Rowntree, B. Seebohm. *Poverty. A Study of Town Life*. London and New York: Macmillan and Company, Limited, 1901.

Rubinow, I. M. *The Quest for Security*. New York: Henry Holt and Company, 1934.

——. *Social Insurance. With Special Reference to American Conditions*. New York: Henry Holt and Company, 1913.

Russell, Charles Edward. *Bare Hands and Stone Walls. Some Recollections of a Side-line Reformer*. New York: Charles Scribner's Sons, 1933.

—— and Lewis W. Hine. "Unto the Least of These," *Everybody's Magazine*, XXI (1909), 75–87.

Russell Sage Foundation. *Boyhood and Lawlessness*. New York: Survey Associates, Inc., 1914.

Ryan, John A. *A Living Wage. Its Ethical and Economic Aspects*. New York: The Macmillan Company, 1906.

——. "Programme of Social Reform by Legislation," *Catholic World*, LXXXIX (1909), 433–44, 608–14.

——. *Social Doctrine in Action. A Personal History*. New York: Harper and Brothers, 1941.

——. "The Standard of Living and the Problem of Dependency," *Proceedings* of the National Conference of Charities and Correction, 1907, pp. 342–47.

Saint-Gaudens, Homer. *The American Artist and His Times*. New York: Dodd, Mead and Company, 1941.

Sandburg, Carl. *Chicago Poems*. New York: Henry Holt and Company, 1916.

———. *Smoke and Steel*. New York: Harcourt Brace and Company, 1920.

Scannell, Ruth. A History of the Charity Organization Society of the City of New York from 1892 to 1935 (1948). Unpublished report in files of the Community Service Society of New York.

Schlesinger, Arthur M. *The Rise of the City, 1878–1898*. New York: The Macmillan Company, 1933.

Schlesinger, Arthur M., Jr. *Orestes A. Brownson. A Pilgrim's Progress*. Boston: Little, Brown and Company, 1939.

Schneider, David M. *The History of Public Welfare in New York State, 1609–1866*. Chicago: The University of Chicago Press, 1938.

Schweinitz, Karl de. *England's Road to Social Security. From the Statute of Laborers in 1349 to the Beveridge Report of 1942*. Philadelphia: University of Pennsylvania Press, 1943.

———. The Development of Governmental Responsibility for Human Welfare. Address delivered January 29, 1948, Symposium I of the 100th Anniversary Program of the Community Service Society of New York. New York: 1948.

Seager, Henry R. "The Minimum Wage as Part of a Program for Social Reform," *The Annals*, XLVIII (1913), 3–12.

———. *Social Insurance. A Program of Social Reform*. New York: The Macmillan Company, 1921.

Sedgwick, Ellery. "The Land of Disasters," *Leslie's Monthly Magazine*, LVIII (1904), 566–67.

Shearman, Thomas G. "The Coming Billionaire," *The Forum*, X (1890–91), 546–57.

———. "Henry George's Mistakes," *The Forum*, VIII (1889–90), 40–52.

———. "The Owners of the United States," *The Forum*, VIII (1889–90), 262–73.

Sherwood, Robert E. *Roosevelt and Hopkins, an Intimate History*. New York: Harper and Brothers, 1948.

Simkhovitch, Mary Kingsbury. *Neighborhood, My Story of Greenwich House*. New York: W. W. Norton and Company, 1938.

——— and Elizabeth Ogg. *Quicksand, the Way of Life in the Slums*. Evanston, Illinois: Row, Peterson and Company, 1946.

Simons, A. M. *Packingtown*. Chicago: Charles H. Kerr and Company, 1899.

Sinclair, Upton. *The Jungle.* New York: The Viking Press, 1946.

——, ed. *The Cry for Justice. An Anthology of the Literature of Social Protest.* Philadelphia: The John C. Winston Company, 1915.

"The Slav in America," *Charities*, XIII (1904–5), 189–266.

Sloan, John. *Gist of Art.* New York: American Artists Group, Inc., 1939.

Smith, Edward H. "Eugene Higgins: Painter of the Underworld," *The World Magazine*, April 13, 1919, p. 9.

Smith, Elizabeth Oakes. *The Newsboy.* New York: J. C. Derby, 1854.

Smith, Henry Nash. *Virgin Land. The American West as Symbol and Myth.* Cambridge: Harvard University Press, 1950.

Smith, Matthew Hale. *Sunshine and Shadow in New York.* Hartford: J. B. Burr and Company, 1869.

Solenberger, Alice Willard. *One Thousand Homeless Men.* New York: Survey Associates, 1914.

Solenberger, Edwin D. "Relief Work of the Salvation Army," *Proceedings* of the National Conference of Charities and Correction, 1906, pp. 349–66.

"The South End Industrial School," *Frank Leslie's Illustrated Newspaper*, LXVI (1888), 139 and 141.

Spahr, Charles B. *America's Working People.* New York: Longmans, Green and Company, 1900.

——. *An Essay on the Present Distribution of Wealth in the United States.* New York: Thomas Y. Crowell and Company, 1896.

Spargo, John. *The Bitter Cry of the Children.* New York: The Macmillan Company, 1907.

——. "Charles Haag," *The Craftsman*, X (1906), 433–42.

——. "Eugene Higgins," *The Craftsman*, XII (1907), 135–46.

——. "George Luks," *The Craftsman*, XII (1907), 599–607.

Spiller, Robert E., Willard Thorp, Thomas H. Johnson, Henry Seidel Canby, eds. *Literary History of the United States.* 3 vols. New York: The Macmillan Company, 1949.

Spooner, Lysander. *Poverty: Its Illegal Causes and Legal Cure.* Boston: Bela Marsh, 1846.

Stead, Estelle W. *My Father, Personal and Spiritual Reminiscences.* New York: George H. Doran Company, 1913.

Stead, William T. *If Christ Came to Chicago.* London: *The Review of Reviews*, 1894.

Steffens, J. Lincoln. "Extermination. Evolution in Operation on the East Side," *Commercial Advertiser* (New York), July 24, 1897.

Stevenson, Robert Alston. "The Poor in Summer," *Scribner's Magazine*, XXX (1901), 259–77.

Steward, Ira. *Poverty*. Boston: The Boston Eight Hour League, 1873.

Stewart, William Rhinelander. *The Philanthropic Work of Josephine Shaw Lowell*. New York: The Macmillan Company, 1911.

Stimson, F. J. *Handbook to the Labor Law of the United States*. New York: Charles Scribner's Sons, 1896.

Stokes, I. N. Phelps. *Iconography of Manhattan Island, 1498–1909*. 6 vols. New York: R. H. Dodd, 1915–28.

Stokes, J. G. Phelps. "Report of the Committee on Preventive Social Work," *Proceedings* of the New York State Conference of Charities and Correction, 1903, pp. 221–30.

——. "Ye Have the Poor Always with You," *The Independent*, LVII (1904), 730–34.

Stone, A. L. *The Relations of Poverty to Human Discipline . . . A Discourse before the Howard Benevolent Society*. Boston: Ticknor, Reed, and Fields, 1851.

"Street Trades Control in Toledo," *The American Child*, V (August, 1923), 3.

Streightoff, Frank Hatch. *The Standard of Living Among the Industrial People of America*. Boston and New York: Houghton Mifflin Company, 1911.

Strong, Josiah. *The New Era or the Coming Kingdom*. New York: The Baker and Taylor Company, 1893.

"The Struggle Against Social Despotism," *The Outlook*, LXXXII (1906), 804–6.

Sullivan, Louis H. "Is Our Art a Betrayal Rather Than an Expression of American Life?" *The Craftsman*, XV (1908–9), 402–4.

Sullivan, Mark. *Our Times: the United States, 1900–1925*. 6 vols. New York: Charles Scribner's Sons, 1926–35.

Sumner, William Graham. *What Social Classes Owe to Each Other*. New York: Harper and Brothers, 1883.

Swift, Samuel. "Revolutionary Figures in American Art," *Harper's Weekly*, LI (1907), 534–36.

Symes, Lillian, and Travers Clement. *Rebel America. The Story of Social Revolt in the United States*. New York: Harper and Brothers, 1934.

Taft, Robert. *Photography and the American Scene, a Social History, 1839–1889*. New York: The Macmillan Company, 1938.

Tawney, R. H. *Poverty as an Industrial Problem*. London: Ratan Tata Foundation. London School of Economics, 1913.

Taylor, Graham. *Pioneering on Social Frontiers.* Chicago: The University of Chicago Press, 1930.

"Tenement Life in New York," *Harper's Weekly*, XXIII (1879), 246 and 266–67.

"Tenement Houses–Their Wrongs," *New York Daily Tribune*, November 23, 1864, p. 4.

Tobey, James A. *The Children's Bureau. Its History, Activities and Organization.* Baltimore: The Johns Hopkins University Press, 1925.

Tolman, W. H. "Half a Century of Improved Housing Effort by the New York Association for Improving the Condition of the Poor," *Yale Review*, V (1896–97), 288–302, 389–402.

Townsend, Edward W. *A Daughter of the Tenements.* New York: Lovell, Coryell and Company, 1895.

True, Ruth S. *The Neglected Girl.* New York: Survey Associates, Inc., 1914.

Tuckerman, Joseph. "Introduction" to Joseph Marie de Gerando. *The Visitor of the Poor.* Boston: Gray, Little and Wilkins, 1832.

——. *On the Elevation of the Poor. A Selection from His Reports as Minister at Large in Boston.* Introduction by E. E. Hale. Boston: Roberts Brothers, 1874.

Turner, George Kibbe. "The Daughters of the Poor," *McClure's Magazine*, XXXIV (1909–10), 45–61.

Tyler, Alice Felt. *Freedom's Ferment. Phases of American Social History to 1860.* Minneapolis: The University of Minnesota Press, 1944.

"Undercurrents of New York Life, Sympathetically Depicted in the Drawings of Glenn Coleman," *The Craftsman*, XVII (1909), 142–49.

United States. Bureau of Labor. *The Italians in Chicago. A Social and Economic Study.* Washington: Government Printing Office, 1897.

——. *Report on Condition of Woman and Child Wage Earners in the United States.* 19 vols. Washington: Government Printing Office, 1910–13.

United States. Bureau of Labor Statistics. *Bulletin 158. Government Aid to Home Owning and Housing of Working People in Foreign Countries.* Washington: Government Printing Office, 1915.

United States. Commissioner of Labor. *Eighteenth Annual Report. The Cost of Living and Retail Prices of Food, 1903.* Washington: Government Printing Office, 1903.

——. *Eleventh Annual Report, 1895–96. Work and Wages of Men, Women and Children.* Washington: Government Printing Office, 1897.

——. *First Annual Report, 1886. Industrial Depressions.* Washington: Government Printing Office, 1886.

United States. Commissioner of Labor. *Seventh Special Report. . . . The Slums of Baltimore, Chicago, New York and Philadelphia.* Washington: Government Printing Office, 1894.

——. *Twenty-fourth Annual Report, 1909. Workingmen's Insurance and Compensation Systems in Europe.* 2 vols. Washington: Government Printing Office, 1911.

United States. Commission on Industrial Relations. *Industrial Relations. Final Report and Testimony.* 11 vols. Washington: Government Printing Office, 1916.

United States Industrial Commission. *Reports.* 19 vols. Washington: Government Printing Office, 1900–2.

Van Kleeck, Mary. *Artificial Flower Makers.* New York: Russell Sage Foundation, 1913.

——. *A Seasonal Industry. A Study of the Millinery Trade in New York.* New York: Russell Sage Foundation, 1917.

——. *Women in the Bookbinding Trade.* New York: Russell Sage Foundation, 1913.

——. "The Workers' Bill for Unemployment," *The New Republic,* LXXXI (1934–5), 121–24.

——. "Working Hours of Women in Factories," *Charities and the Commons,* XVII (1906), 13–21.

Van Vorst, Mrs. John, and Marie Van Vorst. *The Woman Who Toils, Being the Experiences of Two Gentlewomen as Factory Girls.* New York: Doubleday, Page and Company, 1903.

Veiller, Lawrence. *Housing Reform. A Handbook for Practical Use in American Cities.* New York: Charities Publication Committee, 1911.

——. *A Model Tenement House Law.* New York: Charities Publication Committee, 1910.

Wagner, Donald O. *Social Reformers, Adam Smith to John Dewey.* New York: The Macmillan Company, 1947.

Wald, Lillian D. *The House on Henry Street.* New York: Henry Holt and Company, 1915.

Walker, Francis A. "The Causes of Poverty," *The Century Illustrated Monthly Magazine,* LV (1897–98), 210–16.

Ward, Lester F. *Applied Sociology. A Treatise on the Conscious Improvement of Society by Society.* Boston: Ginn and Company, 1906.

Warne, Frank Julian. "The Conquest of Poverty. The Program of the Labor Unions," *Metropolitan Magazine,* XXXIII (1909–10), 346–56.

Warner, Amos G. *American Charities. A Study in Philanthropy and Economics.* New York: Thomas Y. Crowell and Company, 1894.

——. "Notes on the Statistical Determination of the Causes of Poverty," *Publications* of the American Statistical Association, I (1888–89), 183–201.

Warner, Charles Dudley. *Fashions in Literature and Other Literary and Social Essays and Addresses.* New York: Dodd, Mead and Company, 1902.

——. *The Golden House.* New York: Harper and Brothers, 1894.

Washburn, Henry Bradford. *The Religious Motive in Philanthropy.* Philadelphia: University of Pennsylvania Press, 1931.

Waters, Theodore. "Six Weeks in Beggardom in an Attempt to Solve the Question, 'Shall We Give to Beggars?,'" *Everybody's Magazine,* XII (1905), 69–78.

Waterston, R. C. *An Address on Pauperism, Its Extent, Causes, and the Best Means of Prevention.* Boston: Charles C. Little and James Brown, 1844.

Watson, Frank Dekker. *The Charity Organization Movement in the United States. A Study in American Philanthropy.* New York: The Macmillan Company, 1922.

Wayland, H. L. "A Scientific Basis of Charity," *The Charities Review,* III (1893–94), 263–74.

Weiss, Harry. "Employers' Liability and Workmen's Compensation," in John R. Commons, *et al. History of Labor in the United States.* (4 vols. New York: The Macmillan Company, 1918–35), III, 564–610.

Welch, Rodney. "Horace Greeley's Cure for Poverty," *The Forum,* VIII (1889–90), 586–93.

Weller, Charles Frederick. *Neglected Neighbors. Stories of Life in the Alleys, Tenements and Shanties of the National Capital.* Philadelphia: The John C. Winston Company, 1908.

Weyl, Walter E. *The New Democracy. An Essay on Certain Political and Economic Tendencies in the United States.* New York: The Macmillan Company, 1912.

White, William Allen. *A Certain Rich Man.* New York: The Macmillan Company, 1941.

Whitlock, Brand. *The Turn of the Balance.* Indianapolis: The Bobbs-Merrill Company, 1907.

Whitney Museum of American Art. *American Genre. The Social Scene in Painting and Prints.* New York: Whitney Museum of American Art, 1935.

Wiener, Leo. "A Yiddish Poet," *The Century Illustrated Monthly Magazine,* LIX (1899–1900), 156–57.

Williamson, Harold Francis. *Edward Atkinson, The Biography of an American Liberal, 1827–1905*. Boston: Old Corner Book Store, Inc., 1934.

Willoughby, William Franklin. "Accidents to Labor as Regulated by Law in the United States," *Bulletin* of the Department of Labor, VI (1901), 1–28.

———. "Child Labor," *Publications* of the American Economic Association, V (1890), 129–92.

———. "Industrial Communities," *Bulletin* of the Department of Labor, I (1895–96), 223–64, 479–517, 567–609, and 693–720.

———. "State Activities in Relation to Labor in the United States," Johns Hopkins University *Studies in Historical and Political Science*, XIX (1901), 181–269.

———. *Workingmen's Insurance*. New York: Thomas Y. Crowell and Company, 1898.

Wilson, Woodrow. *The New Freedom. A Call for the Emancipation of the Generous Energies of a People*. New York: Doubleday, Page and Company, 1913.

Wines, Fred H. "Causes of Pauperism and Crime," *Proceedings* of the National Conference of Charities and Correction, 1886, pp. 207–14.

Winter, William. *Old Friends, Being Literary Recollections of Other Days*. New York: Moffat, Yard and Company, 1909.

Wish, Harvey. *Society and Thought in America*. 2 vols. New York: Longmans, Green and Company, 1950–52.

Wood, Edith Elmer. *The Housing of the Unskilled Wage Earner. America's Next Problem*. New York: The Macmillan Company, 1919.

———. *Recent Trends in American Housing*. New York: The Macmillan Company, 1931.

Woods, Robert A. "The Social Awakening in London," *Scribner's Magazine*, XI (1892), 401–24.

———, ed. *Americans in Process*. Boston and New York: Houghton Mifflin Company, 1902.

———, ed. *The City Wilderness*. Boston and New York: Houghton Mifflin Company, 1899.

———, *et al. The Poor in Great Cities*. New York: Charles Scribner's Sons, 1895.

Woodward, C. Vann. *Origins of the New South, 1877–1913*. Baton Rouge: Louisiana State University Press, 1951.

Woodward, S. W. "A Businessman's View of Child Labor," *Charities and the Commons*, XV (1905–6), 800–1.

Woolf, Michael Angelo. *Sketches of Lowly Life in a Great City*. New York: G. P. Putnam's Sons, 1899.

Woolsey, Abbey Howland. *A Century of Nursing* . . . . New York: G. P. Putnam's Sons, 1950.

Worcester, Daisy Lee Worthington. "The Standard of Living," *Proceedings* of the National Conference of Social Work, 1929, pp. 337–53.

Wright, Carroll D. *Outline of Practical Sociology*. New York: Longmans, Green and Company, 1899.

Wyckoff, Walter A. *The Workers. An Experiment in Reality. The East.* New York: Charles Scribner's Sons, 1897.

——. The Workers. *An Experiment in Reality. The West.* New York: Charles Scribner's Sons, 1899.

Wyman, Mary Alice, ed. *Selections from the Autobiography of Elizabeth Oakes Smith.* New York: Columbia University Press, 1924.

——. *Two American Pioneers, Seba Smith and Elizabeth Oakes Smith.* New York: Columbia University Press, 1927.

Young, Art. *Art Young, His Life and Times.* Edited by John Nicholas Beffel. New York: Sheridan House, 1939.

——. *The Best of Art Young*. New York: The Vanguard Press, 1936.

Index